LANDMARKS
OF
ENGLISH LITERATURE

LANDMARKS
OF
ENGLISH LITERATURE

By
HENRY J. NICOLL,
AUTHOR OF "GREAT MOVEMENTS," ETC.

GYAN

Published by

GYAN

Gyan Publishing House
5, Ansari Road
Daryaganj, New Delhi-110002
Phone: 011-47034999, 9811692060
E-mail: books@gyanbooks.com

Distribution Network
gyanbooks.com
India, USA, Canada, UK, Australia, France

ISBN : 978-81-212-6575-1 (PB)
First Published, 1886

2nd Impression 2022

Printed at: Gyan Press, Delhi.

LANDMARKS OF ENGLISH LITERATURE
Author: HENRY J. NICOLL

LANDMARKS

OF

ENGLISH LITERATURE.

BY

HENRY J. NICOLL,

AUTHOR OF "GREAT MOVEMENTS," ETC.

1886.

CONTENTS AND CHRONOLOGY.

INTRODUCTION.

CHAPTER I.—THE DAWN OF ENGLISH LITERATURE.

1300. Mandeville born.
1324. Wicklif born.
1340. Chaucer born.
1356. Mandeville's "Travels."
1371. Mandeville died.
1380. Wicklif's translation of the Bible.
1380–1400. Chaucer's "Canterbury Tales."
1384. Wicklif died.
1394. James I. born.
1400. Chaucer died.
1437. James I. died.
1460. Dunbar born.
1470. Sir Thomas Malory, *fl.*
1475. Gawain Douglas born.
1476. Caxton settled in England.
1480. More born.
1484. Tyndale born.
1490. Sir David Lyndsay born.
1491. Latimer born.
1508. Dunbar's "Golden Targe."
1513. Douglas's translation of the "Æneid."
1513. More's "History of Edward the Fifth." (?)
1516. More's "Utopia."
1517. Foxe born.
1520. Dunbar died.
1522. Gawain Douglas died.
1526. Tyndale's translation of the New Testament.
1535. Coverdale's Bible.
1535. More died.
1536. Tyndale died.
1537. "Matthew's Bible."
1539. Cranmer's Bible.
1539. Lyndsay's "Satire of the Three Estates."
1549. Latimer's "Sermon on the Ploughers."
1553. Lyndsay's "Monarchy."
1555. Latimer died.
1557. Lyndsay died.
1587. Foxe died.

Chapter II.—The Elizabethan Era.

1503. Wyatt born.
1515. Ascham born.
1516. Surrey born.
1541. Wyatt died.
1545. Ascham's "Toxophilus."
1547. Surrey died.
1552 (?). Spenser born.
1552. Raleigh born.
1553. Hooker born.
1554. Sidney born.
1554. Lyly born.
1557. Tottel's "Miscellany."
1568. Ascham died.
1570. Ascham's "Schoolmaster."
1579. Spenser's "Shepherd's Calendar."
1579. Lyly's "Euphues, the Anatomy of Wit."
1580. Sidney's "Arcadia."
1580. Lyly's "Euphues and his England."
1581. Sidney's "Apologie for Poetry."
1586. Sidney died.
1590. Spenser's "Faerie Queen" (first three books).
1594. Hooker's "Ecclesiastical Polity" (first four books).
1595. Spenser's "Epithalamion."
1596. Spenser's "Faerie Queen" (last three books).
1597. Hooker's "Ecclesiastical Polity" (fifth book)
1599. Spenser died.
1600. Hooker died.
1606. Lyly died.
1611. Authorised Version of the Bible.
1618. Raleigh died.

The Elizabethan Dramatists.

1551. Udall's "Ralph Roister Doister" (first English comedy) acted.
1558. Peele born.
1559. Chapman born.
1560 (?). Greene born.
1562. Sackville and Norton's "Gorboduc" (first English tragedy) acted.
1564. Marlowe born.
1564. Shakespeare born.
1573. Ben Jonson born.
1576. First theatre erected in London.
1579. Fletcher born.
1582. Shakespeare's marriage.
1584. Massinger born.
1586 (?). Shakespeare goes to London.
1586. Ford born.
1586. Beaumont born.
1587. Marlowe's "Tamburlaine."
1588–94. Shakespeare's "First Period."
1592. Greene died.
1592. Greene's reference to Shakespeare.
1592. Peele died.
1593. Marlowe died.
1593. Shakespeare's "Venus and Adonis."
1594. Shakespeare's "Rape of Lucrece."
1595–1601. Shakespeare's "Second Period."
1596. Shirley born.
1596. Ben Jonson's "Every Man in his Humour."

1601–8. Shakespeare's "Third Period."
1603. Ben Jonson's "Sejanus."
1605. Ben Jonson's "Volpone."
1609. Shakespeare's Sonnets.
1609–13 (?). Shakespeare's "Fourth Period."
1610. Ben Jonson's "Alchemist."
1612. Webster's "Vittoria Corombona."
1612 (?). Shakespeare returns to Stratford.
1616. Shakespeare died.
1616. Beaumont died.
1623. Webster's "Duchess of Malfi."
1625. Fletcher died.
1634. Chapman died.
1637. Ben Jonson died.
1640. Ford died.
1640. Massinger died.
1642 Theatres closed.
1667. Shirley died.

Chapter III.—The Successors of the Elizabethans.

1561. Bacon born.
1573. Donne born.
1588. Hobbes born.
1593. Isaak Walton born.
1597. First edition of Bacon's "Essays."
1605. Bacon's "Advancement of Learning."
1605. Waller born.
1605. Browne born.
1608. Fuller born.
1608. Suckling born.
1608. Clarendon born.
1608. Milton born.
1612. Second edition of Bacon's "Essays."
1613. Jeremy Taylor born.
1615. Baxter born.
1615. Denham born.
1618. Bacon made Lord Chancellor.
1618. Lovelace born.
1618. Cowley born.
1620. Bacon's "Novum Organum."
1621. Bacon's fall from power.
1625. Third edition of Bacon's "Essays."
1626. Bacon died.
1628. Bunyan born.
1629. Milton B.A. at Cambridge.
1631. Donne died.
1633. Herbert's "Temple."
1633. Milton's "Arcades," "L'Allegro," "Il Penseroso."
1634. Milton's "Comus" acted.
1637. Milton's "Lycidas."
1640–78. Walton's "Lives."
1641. Suckling died.
1641–42. Milton's Pamphlets on Church Government.
1642. Fuller's "Holy State."
1643. Browne's "Religio Medici."
1644. Milton's "Areopagitica."
1644–45. Milton's Divorce Tracts.
1645. Fuller's "Good Thoughts in Bad Times."
1646. Browne's "Vulgar Errors."
1646. Collected edition of Milton's Poems.
1647. Cowley's "Mistress."
1648. Fuller's "Profane State."
1648. Herrick's "Hesperides."
1649. Milton's "Eikonoclastes."
1653. Walton's "Complete Angler."
1656. Fuller's "Church History."
1658. Lovelace died.
1659–60. Milton's Restoration Pamphlets.

1661. Fuller died.
1662. Fuller's "Worthies of England."
1667. Milton's "Paradise Lost."
1667. Cowley died.
1667. Jeremy Taylor died.
1668. Denham died.
1671. Milton's "Paradise Regained" and "Samson Agonistes."
1674. Clarendon died.
1674. Milton died.
1678. Bunyan's "Pilgrim's Progress."
1679. Hobbes died.
1682. Browne died.
1683. Walton died.
1687. Waller died.
1688. Bunyan died.
1691. Baxter died.

Chapter IV.—The Restoration.

1612. Butler born.
1630. John Tillotson born.
1630. Dr. Isaac Barrow born.
1631. John Dryden born.
1632. John Locke born.
1633. Robert South born.
1635. Edward Stillingfleet born.
1640. William Wycherley born.
1641. William Sherlock born.
1642. Sir Isaac Newton born.
1643. Gilbert Burnet born.
1651. Thomas Otway born.
1658. Dryden's first poem published.
1660. Dryden's "Astræa Redux."
1661. Dryden's "Panegyric on the Coronation."
1662. Royal Society incorporated.
1662. First part of Butler's "Hudibras."
1662. Dryden's "Epistle on the Lord Chancellor."
1663. Second part of "Hudibras."
1663. Dryden's "Epistle to Dr. Charlton" and "Wild Gallant."
1663. Dryden married.
1666. Sir John Vanbrugh born.
1667. Dryden's "Annus Mirabilis."
1668. Dryden's "Essay of Dramatic Poesy."
1670. Dryden's "Conquest of Granada."
1670. Dryden appointed Historiographer Royal and Poet Laureate.
1670. Congreve born.
1671. The "Rehearsal."
1672. Wycherley's "Love in a Wood."
1673. Nicholas Rowe born.
1675. Wycherley's "Country Wife."
1677. Dryden's "All for Love."
1677. Wycherley's "Plain Dealer."
1677. Dr. Isaac Barrow died.
1678. Third part of "Hudibras."
1678. George Farquhar born.
1680. Gilbert Burnet's "Account of the Life and Death of the Earl of Rochester."
1680. Butler died.
1680. Sir Robert Filmer's "Patriarcha."
1681. Dryden's "Absalom and Achitophel."
1682. Dryden's "The Medal," "MacFlecknoe," and "Religio Laici."
1685. Thomas Otway died.
1686. Dryden joined the Church of Rome.

1686. Dryden's poem "To the Memory of Miss Anne Killegrew."
1687. Dryden's "Hind and Panther."
1687. Sir Isaac Newton's "Principia."
1689. Dryden's "Don Sebastian."
1689. Burnet appointed Bishop of Salisbury.
1689. Locke's "Letter on Toleration" and "Two Treatises on Government."
1690. Locke's "Essay on the Human Understanding."
1691. Tillotson appointed Archbishop of Canterbury.
1692. Locke made Secretary of Prosecutions.
1692. Nathaniel Lee died.
1693. Congreve's "Old Bachelor."
1694. Dryden's "Love Triumphant."
1694. Congreve's "Double Dealer."
1694. Tillotson died.
1695. Congreve's "Love for Love."
1697. Dryden's translation of "Virgil."
1697. Congreve's "Mourning Bride."
1697. Vanbrugh's "Relapse" and "Provoked Wife."
1698. Jeremy Collier's "Short View."
1699. Edward Stillingfleet died.
1699. Dryden's "Fables."
1700. Dryden died.
1700. Congreve's "Way of the World."
1704. John Locke died.
1706. Farquhar's "Recruiting Officer."
1707. Farquhar's "Beaux Stratagem."
1707. William Sherlock died.
1707. Sir Isaac Newton died.
1715. Gilbert Burnet died.
1715. Wycherley died.
1716. Robert South died.
1718. Nicholas Rowe died.
1726. Sir John Vanbrugh died.
1728. Congreve died.
1751. Richard B. Sheridan born.
1759. Butler's "Genuine Prose Remains" published.
1775. Sheridan's "The Rivals," "St. Patrick's Day," and "The Duenna."
1777. Sheridan's "School for Scandal."
1779. Sheridan's "The Critic."
1780. Sheridan became a Member of Parliament.
1816. Sheridan died.

1664. Prior born.
1667. Arbuthnott born.
1667. Swift born.
1671. Steele born.
1672. Addison born.
1678. Bolingbroke born.
1681. Young born.
1684. Berkeley born.
1688. Pope born.
1692. Butler born.
1698. Warburton born.
1699. Thomson born.
1701. Swift's "Discourse."
1701. Steele's "The Christian Hero."
1702. Steele's "The Funeral"
1703. Steele's "The Tender Husband" and "The Dying Lover."
1704. Swift's "Tale of a Tub."

1704. Addison's "The Campaign."
1707. Addison's "Present State of the War."
1708-9. Swift's "Argument against the Abolishing of Christianity" and "Predictions of Isaac Bickerstaff."
1709. Steele's "Tatler" begun.
1709. Pope's "Pastorals."
1711. Pope's "Essay on Criticism."
1711. The "Tatler" closed.
1711. The "Spectator" begun.
1712. Pope's first edition of the "Rape of the Lock."
1713. Gay's "Rural Sports."
1713. Addison's "Cato."
1713. Steele's "Guardian."
1714. Steele's "Englishman" and "The Crisis."
1714. Pope's second edition of the "Rape of the Lock."
1715-16. Addison's "Freeholder."
1716. Gray born.
1719. Addison died.
1720. Swift's "Universal Use of Irish Manufactures."
1720. Collins born.
1720. Pope's "Iliad."
1721. Prior dead.
1722. Steele's "The Conscious Lovers."
1723. Swift's "Drapier's Letters."
1725. Pope's "Odyssey."
1726-27. Swift's "Gulliver's Travels."
1726-30. Thomson's "Seasons."
1728. Gay's "Beggar's Opera."
1728. Pope's "Dunciad."
1729. Steele died.
1731. Churchill born.
1732. Pope's "Essay on Man."
1732. Gay died.
1733-38. Pope's "Satires and Epistles of Horace Imitated."
1735. Arbuthnott died.
1736. Butler's "Analogy of Religion."
1741. Pope's revised edition of the "Dunciad."
1744. Young's "Night Thoughts."
1744. Pope died.
1744. Akenside's "Pleasures of the Imagination."
1745. Swift died.
1748. Thomson's "Castle of Indolence."
1748. Thomson died.
1750. Gray's "Elegy in a Country Churchyard."
1751. Bolingbroke died.
1752. Butler died.
1753. Berkeley died.
1756. Collins died.
1764. Churchill died.
1765. Young died.
1771. Gray died.
1779. Warburton died.

CHAPTER VI.—OUR FIRST GREAT NOVELISTS.

1661. Defoe born.
1689. Richardson born.
1704. Defoe's "Review" started.
1707. Fielding born.
1713. Sterne born.
1719. Defoe's "Robinson Crusoe."
1721. Smollett born.
1722. Defoe's "Journal of the Plague."
1731. Defoe died.
1740. Richardson's "Pamela."
1742. Fielding's "Joseph Andrews."
1743. Fielding's "Jonathan Wild."
1748. Richardson's "Clarissa."
1748. Smollett's "Roderick Random."
1749. Fielding's "Tom Jones."

1751. Fielding's "Amelia."
1751. Smollett's "Peregrine Pickle."
1753. Smollett's "Count Fathom."
1754. Richardson's "Sir Charles Grandison."
1754. Fielding died.
1759–67. Sterne's "Tristram Shandy."
1761. Richardson died.
1764. Walpole's "Castle of Otranto."
1768. Sterne's "Sentimental Journey."
1768. Sterne died.
1771. Smollett's "Humphrey Clinker."
1771. Smollett died.
1771. Mackenzie's "Man of Feeling."
1778. Fanny Burney's "Evelina."
1784. Beckford's "Vathek."
1794. Mrs. Radcliffe's "Mysteries of Udolpho."
1794. Godwin's "Caleb Williams."
1811. Miss Austen's "Sense and Sensibility."
1812. Miss Edgeworth's "Absentee."
1812. Miss Austen's "Pride and Prejudice."
1814. Miss Austen's "Mansfield Park."
1816. Miss Austen's "Emma."
1818. Miss Austen's "Northanger Abbey."
1818. Miss Austen's "Persuasion."

CHAPTER VII.—DR. JOHNSON AND HIS CONTEMPORARIES.

1709. Johnson born.
1711. Hume born.
1721. Robertson born.
1728. Goldsmith born.
1729. Burke born.
1735. Johnson's translation of Lobo's "Voyage to Abyssinia."
1737. Gibbon born.
1738. Hume's "Treatise of Human Nature."
1738. Johnson's "London."
1740. Boswell born
1742. Hume's "Essays."
1744. Johnson's "Life of Savage."
1749. Johnson's "Vanity of Human Wishes."
1749. Johnson's "Irene."
1750–52. Johnson's "Rambler."
1752. Hume's "Political Discourses."
1754–61. Hume's "History of England."
1755. Johnson's Dictionary.
1756. Burke on the "Sublime and Beautiful."
1758–60. Johnson's "Idler."
1758. Robertson's "History of Scotland."
1759. Johnson's "Rasselas."
1759. Goldsmith's "Enquiry into the State of Literature."
1764. Goldsmith's "Traveller."
1766. Goldsmith's "Vicar of Wakefield."
1768. Goldsmith's "Good-Natured Man."
1769. Robertson's "Charles V."
1769–72. "Letters of Junius."
1770. Goldsmith's "Deserted Village."
1770. Burke's "Thoughts on Present Discontents."
1773. Goldsmith's "She Stoops to Conquer."
1774. Goldsmith died.

1775. Johnson's "Tour to the Western Isles."
1776. Hume died.
1776. Adam Smith's "Wealth of Nations."
1776. Campbell's "Philosophy of Rhetoric."
1776–88. Gibbon's "Decline and Fall of the Roman Empire."
1777. Robertson's "History of America."
1779–81. Johnson's "Lives of the Poets."
1784. Johnson died.
1785. Burke's speech on the "Nabob of Arcot's Debts."
1786. Burke's speech on the Impeachment of Warren Hastings.
1790. Burke's "Reflections on the French Revolution."
1791. Robertson's "Disquisition on Ancient India."
1791. Boswell's "Life of Johnson."
1793. Robertson died.
1794. Gibbon died.
1795. Boswell died.
1797. Burke died.

Chapter VIII.—The New Era in Poetry.

1725. Ramsay's "Gentle Shepherd."
1731. Cowper born.
1742. Shenstone's "Schoolmistress."
1754. Crabbe born.
1757. Blake born.
1759. Burns born.
1762. "Ossian."
1765. Percy's "Reliques."
1768. Chatterton's "Mediæval Romances."
1770. Wordsworth born.
1772. Coleridge born.
1774. Beattie's "Minstrel."
1774. Southey born.
1774–78. Warton's "History of English Poetry."
1777. Blake's "Poetical Sketches."
1779. "Olney Hymns."
1782. Cowper's "Table-Talk," &c.
1783. Crabbe's "Village."
1785. Cowper's "Task."
1786. Burns's Poems.
1788. Byron born.
1791. Cowper's translation of "Homer."
1792. Shelley born.
1792. Rogers's "Pleasures of Memory."
1795. Keats born.
1796. Burns died.
1796. Southey's "Joan of Arc."
1798. Wordsworth's "Lyrical Ballads."
1799. Campbell's "Pleasures of Hope."
1800. Cowper died.
1801. Southey's "Thalaba."
1805. Southey's "Madoc."
1807. Wordsworth's Poems.
1807. Byron's "Hours of Idleness."
1809. Byron's "English Bards and Scotch Reviewers."
1809. Campbell's "Gertrude of Wyoming."
1810. Southey's "Kehama."
1812. Crabbe's "Tales in Verse."
1812–18. Byron's "Childe Harold."
1813. Southey's "Life of Nelson."

1813. Hogg's "Queen's Wake."
1814. Southey's "Roderick."
1814. Wordsworth's "Excursion."
1815. Wordsworth's "White Doe of Rylstone."
1816. Coleridge's "Christabel."
1817. Coleridge's "Biographia Literaria."
1817. Shelley's "Revolt of Islam."
1817. Moore's "Lalla Rookh."
1818. Coleridge's "Friend."
1818. Keats's "Endymion."
1819. Crabbe's "Tales of the Hall."
1819. Shelley's "Prometheus Unbound" and "The Cenci."
1819–24. Byron's "Childe Harold."
1820. Keats's "Lamia," &c.
1821. Keats died.
1822. Shelley died.
1824. Byron died.
1825. Coleridge's "Aids to Reflection."
1828. Blake died.
1832. Crabbe died.
1834. Coleridge died.
1843. Southey died.
1850. Wordsworth died.
1850. Wordsworth's "Recluse."

1765. Sir James Mackintosh born.
1771. Scott born.
1771. Sydney Smith born.
1773. Jeffrey born.
1775. Lamb born.
1775. Landor born.
1777. Hallam born.
1778. Hazlitt born.
1780. Chalmers born.
1784. Leigh Hunt born.
1785. John Wilson born.
1785. De Quincey born.
1792. Alison born.
1794. Lockhart born.
1802–3. Scott's "Minstrelsy of the Border."
1802–28. Sydney Smith's Contributions to "The Edinburgh Review."
1802–40. Jeffrey's Contributions to "The Edinburgh Review."
1805. Scott's "Lay of the Last Minstrel."
1808. Scott's "Marmion."
1810. Scott's "Lady of the Lake."
1811. Scott's "Vision of Don Roderick."
1812. Scott's "Rokeby."
1812. Wilson's "Isle of Palms."
1813. Scott's "Bridal of Triermain."

The Waverley Novels.

1814. "Waverley."
1815. "Guy Mannering."
1816. "The Antiquary;" "Black Dwarf;" "Old Mortality."
1817. "Rob Roy."
1818. "The Heart of Midlothian."
1819. "Bride of Lammermoor;" "Legend of Montrose;" "Ivanhoe."

1820. "The Monastery;" "The Abbot."
1821. "Kenilworth;" "The Pirate."
1822. "The Fortunes of Nigel."
1823. "Peveril of the Peak;" "Quentin Durward;" "St. Ronan's Well."
1824. "Redgauntlet."
1825. "The Betrothed;" "The Talisman."
1826. "Woodstock."
1827. "The Two Drovers;" "The Highland Widow;" "The Surgeon's Daughter."
1828. "The Fair Maid of Perth."
1829. "Anne of Geierstein."
1831. "Count Robert of Paris;" "Castle Dangerous."

1816. Wilson's "City of the Plague."
1816. Leigh Hunt's "Story of Rimini."
1818. Hallam's "State of Europe during the Middle Ages."
1819. Lockhart's "Peter's Letters to his Kinsfolk."
1821. Lockhart's "Spanish Ballads."
1821. De Quincey's "Confessions of an Opium-Eater."
1823. Lamb's "Essays of Elia."
1824–29. Landor's "Imaginary Conversations."
1825. Hazlitt's "Spirit of the Age."
1827. Lockhart's "Life of Burns."
1827. Scott's "Life of Napoleon."
1827. Hallam's "Constitutional History of England."
1828–30. Hazlitt's "Life of Napoleon."
1830. Hazlitt died.
1830. Mackintosh's "Dissertation on Ethical Philosophy."
1830-32. Mackintosh's "History of England."
1832. Sir James Mackintosh died.
1832. Scott died.
1834. Mackintosh's "History of the Revolution, 1688."
1834. Lamb died.
1836–38. Lockhart's "Life of Scott."
1838–39. Hallam's "Literature of Europe."
1839–42. Alison's "History of Europe."
1842. Wilson's "Recreations of Christopher North."
1845. Sydney Smith died.
1847. Chalmers died.
1850. Jeffrey died.
1850. Leigh Hunt's "Autobiography."
1854. John Wilson died.
1854. Lockhart died.
1859. Hallam died.
1859. De Quincey died.
1859. Leigh Hunt died.
1867. Alison died.

CHAPTER X.—OUR OWN TIMES.

Dickens, Thackeray, Lytton, Charlotte Brontë, George Eliot, Lever, Charles Kingsley, Beaconsfield, Charles Reade, Anthony Trollope, Blackmore, Hardy, Black; Tennyson, Browning, Mrs. Browning, Rossetti, Morris, Swinburne; Macaulay, Carlyle,

1795. Carlyle born.
1800. Macaulay born.
1805. Lytton born.
1809. Tennyson born.
1809. Mrs. Browning born.
1811. Thackeray born.
1812. Dickens born.
1819. Ruskin born.
1820. George Eliot born.
1825. Macaulay's *Edinburgh Review* article on Milton.
1826. B. Disraeli's "Vivian Grey."
1828. Lytton's "Pelham."
1831. Lytton's "Paul Clifford."
1833–34. Carlyle's "Sartor Resartus" published in *Fraser's Magazine.*
1834. Lytton's "Last Days of Pompeii."
1836. Dickens's "Sketches by Boz."
1837. Dickens's "Pickwick Papers."
1837. Carlyle's "French Revolution."
1839. Lever's "Harry Lorrequer."
1839. Carlyle's "Chartism."
1841. Carlyle's "Heroes and Hero-Worship."
1841–46. Browning's "Bells and Pomegranates."
1842. Macaulay's "Lays of Ancient Rome."
1842. Tennyson's Poems.
1843. Macaulay's *Edinburgh Review* Articles republished.
1843. Carlyle's "Past and Present."
1843–60. Ruskin's "Modern Painters."
1844. Dickens's "Martin Chuzzlewit."
1845. Carlyle's "Cromwell."
1846–48. Thackeray's "Vanity Fair."
1846–56. Grote's "History of Greece."
1847. Charlotte Brontë's "Jane Eyre."
1847. Tennyson's "Princess."
1847–49. Helps's "Friends in Council."
1848–55. Macaulay's "History of England."
1849. Lytton's "Caxtons."
1849. Charlotte Brontë's "Shirley."
1849. Ruskin's "Seven Lamps of Architecture."
1850. Thackeray's "Pendennis."
1850. Kingsley's "Alton Locke."
1850. Tennyson's "In Memoriam."
1850. Carlyle's "Latter-Day Pamphlets."
1851. Carlyle's "Life of Sterling."
1851. Mrs. Browning's "Casa Guidi Windows."
1851–53. Ruskin's "Stones of Venice."
1852. Charlotte Brontë's "Villette."
1852. Thackeray's "Esmond."
1853. Dickens's "Bleak House."
1853. Matthew Arnold's "Poems."
1855. Tennyson's "Maud."
1855. Thackeray's "Newcomes."
1855. Charlotte Brontë died.
1856–70. Froude's "History of England."
1856. Mrs. Browning's "Aurora Leigh."
1857. George Eliot's "Scenes from Clerical Life."
1857. Dickens's "Little Dorrit."
1858–65. Carlyle's "Frederick the Great."
1859. George Eliot's "Adam Bede."
1859. Tennyson's "Idylls of the King."
1859. Macaulay died.
1859. Darwin's "Origin of Species."
1861. Mrs. Browning died.
1862. Thackeray's "Adventures of Philip."
1863. George Eliot's "Romola."
1863. Thackeray died.

1864. Tennyson's "Enoch Arden."
1865. Matthew Arnold's "Essays in Criticism."
1867–79. Freeman's "Norman Conquest."
1868. George Eliot's "Spanish Gipsy."
1870. Dickens's "Mystery of Edwin Drood."
1870. Dickens died.
1872. George Eliot's "Middlemarch."
1873. Lytton's "Kenelm Chillingly."
1873. Lytton died.
1875. Tennyson's "Queen Mary."
1877. George Eliot's "Daniel Deronda."
1877. Tennyson's "Harold."
1880. Lord Beaconsfield's "Endymion."
1880. George Eliot died.
1881. Tennyson's "Poems and Ballads."

CHAP. XI.—PERIODICALS, REVIEWS, AND ENCYCLOPÆDIAS.

The Eighteenth-Century Periodical Essayists; New Departures in Periodical Literature in the Nineteenth Century; the great English Encyclopædias, . . . Pp. 443–458

INTRODUCTION.

PLAN OF THE WORK—SOME HINTS ON THE STUDY OF ENGLISH LITERATURE.

THE present volume does not pretend to be a full record of the literary activity of our country. Not only are many writers omitted whose works are dear to those laborious pedants who speak contemptuously of the literature of our own time, but regard with admiring reverence the rubbish bequeathed to us by wretched playwrights and dreary prose writers of three or four centuries ago; not only are the names of these forgotten worthies, whose proper place is in bibliographies and biographical dictionaries, passed over, but a great number of authors whose writings are of real and permanent value, and should in nowise be neglected by those who can find time and opportunity for the thoroughgoing study of our noble literature, are either not mentioned at all, or only very slightly alluded to. The plan adopted in this book has been to deal solely with the very greatest names in the several departments of English literature—with those writers whose works are among the most imperishable glories of Britain, and with whom it is a disgrace for even the busiest to remain unacquainted. The time which most people are able to devote to literature proper is very limited; and if second or third rate authors are read by them, the result must inevitably be that first-rate authors will be neglected. "Always in books keep the best company," wrote Sydney Smith to his son with his usual good sense. "Don't read a line of Ovid till you have mastered Virgil, nor a line of Thomson till you have exhausted Pope, nor of Massinger till you are familiar with Shakespeare." It is very obvious that those who read Pollok's "Course of Time" while remaining ignorant of Milton's "Paradise Lost," or the writings of "A. K. H. B." while neglecting Bacon's "Essays" and Addison's *Spectator*, are guilty of a lamentable waste of time and misexpenditure of energy. "If you should transfer the amount of your reading day by day," says Emerson,[1] "from the newspapers to the standard authors—but who dare speak of such a thing?" To expect people to give up newspaper-reading is certainly a very Utopian speculation, nor, indeed, is it desirable in many respects that they should give it up. But it is a very easy and practicable thing to obey the rule to study the best authors first, for it may be safely laid down as a general principle that the greatest works of our literature are also the most attractive. No dramatist is so readable as Shakespeare; to no works of fiction can we return again and again with greater pleasure than to the masterpieces of Fielding and Scott; nowhere can the blood-stained story of the French Revolution be followed with keener interest than in the pages of Carlyle.

Literature is a word often so loosely applied, that it may be well at the outset to define exactly what we mean by it. By people in general it is used with a very wide range of meaning. Milton's "Paradise Lost" and Buchan's "Domestic Medicine;" Rhymer's "Foedera" and Macaulay's "History of England," are ranked under the same all-embracing name. But literature rightly so termed is a word of much narrower signification. To entitle anything to be classed as literature, it must be so written that, apart from the meaning conveyed, its mere style shall be such as to give pleasure. Neither wealth of information nor depth of thought gives a work a right to be called literature unless the information and the thought be attractively expressed. From this it is clear that many books, otherwise of great merit, have no claim to consideration in a literary history. A plan of a country may have more practical utility than the most beautiful landscape ever painted, but as it lacks the essential element of beauty, it will not be placed in the same category. In like manner many

[1] "Society and Solitude," p. 164 (English edition).

books which we could very ill afford to dispense with, being destitute of attractiveness and distinction of style, have no value viewed merely as literature. The true literary man is an artist, using his words and phrases with the same felicity and care as a painter uses his colours; and whoever aspires to win literary fame must pay the closest attention not only to *what* he says, but to *how* he says it.

De Quincey, whose speculations on such subjects are always ingenious and worth attending to, if sometimes over-refined and far-fetched, in one of his essays[1] lays down a distinction, first suggested by Wordsworth, which bears upon what we have been saying. As De Quincey's critical writings are not so generally read as they should be, we may quote part of his remarks. "In that great social organ, which collectively we call literature, there may be distinguished two separate offices, that may blend, and often do so, but capable severally of a severe insulation, and naturally fitted for reciprocal repulsion. There is first the literature of *knowledge*, and secondly the literature of *power*. The function of the first is to *teach*; the function of the second is to *move*. The first is a rudder, the second an oar or a sail. The first speaks to the *mere* discursive understanding; the second speaks ultimately, it may happen, to the higher understanding or reason, but always *through* affections of pleasure or sympathy. . . . What do you learn from 'Paradise Lost?' Nothing at all. What do you learn from a cookery-book? Something new, something that you did not know before, in every paragraph. But would you therefore put the wretched cookery-book on a higher level of estimation than the divine poem? What you owe to Milton is not any knowledge, of which a million separate items are still but a million of advancing steps on the same earthly level; what you owe is *power*, that is, exercise and expansion to your own latent capacity of sympathy with the infinite, when every pulse and each separate influx is a step upwards—a step ascending as from a Jacob's ladder from

[1] Originally published in *North British Review* for August 1848, article on Pope.

earth to mysterious altitudes above the earth. . . . All the literature of knowledge builds only ground nests, that are swept away by floods, or confounded by the plough; but the literature of power builds nests in aërial altitudes of temples sacred from violation, or of forests inaccessible to fraud. *This* is a great prerogative of the *power* literature; and it is a greater which lies in the mode of its influence. The knowledge literature, like the fashion of this world, passeth away. An Encyclopædia is its abstract; and, in this respect, it may be taken for its speaking symbol, that, before one generation has passed, an Encyclopædia is superannuated, for it speaks through the dead memory and unimpassioned understanding, which have not the *rest* of higher faculties, but are continually enlarging and varying their phylacteries."

In the preceding extracts, as will be seen, De Quincey uses the phrase "literature of knowledge" to express that class of writings to which the term literature cannot, as he himself afterwards says, be with propriety applied—writings the sole aim of which is to convey information without any effort after beauty of style; and the phrase "literature of power" to express that class of writings—fiction and poetry—of which the object is, not to instruct, but to move the feelings and to give pleasure, and of which, therefore, attractiveness of style is an essential characteristic. But, as he himself says in a note, a great proportion of books—history, biography, travels, miscellaneous essays, &c.—belong strictly to neither of these two classes. Macaulay's "History of England" contains a vast amount of information, but it is not its stores of information which have attracted to it millions of readers; it is the fascinating style in which the information is conveyed, making the narrative as pleasing as a novel, and giving some passages a power of exciting the emotions which not many poems possess. And though to instruct be not the prime function of the novel or the poem, a great fund of instruction as to morals and manners is embodied in almost all good poems and novels. Shakespeare abounds in pithy aphorisms as to the conduct of life, which have become part of the moralist's stock-in-trade;

Scott, in the "Heart of Midlothian" (to give only one example out of many), preaches a very effective homily on the evil consequences of giving up inward peace of mind for the sake of outward grandeur; and such writers as Thackeray and Miss Austen have done much to make people ashamed of angularities and affectations of manner. So that De Quincey's distinction, though true in a wide sense, and very suggestive in many ways, is not to be accepted as absolutely correct. All literature worthy of the name is "literature of power," but it may be, and very often is, "literature of knowledge" also.

Having defined what literature is, we now proceed to consider the way in which its study may be most profitably pursued. In order fully to comprehend any author's work, and to place him in his true position among his fellows, not only must his writings be studied with due care, but we must pay regard to his outward "environment" and to the circumstances of the times in which he lived. Sainte Beuve, the prince of French critics, in all his inquiries made it a rule before studying the *author* to study the *man*, thinking that "as the tree is so will be the fruit." He was of opinion "that so long as you have not asked yourself a certain number of questions and answered them satisfactorily—if only for your own private benefit and *sotto voce*—you cannot be sure of thoroughly understanding your model, and that even though these questions may seem to be quite foreign to the nature of his writings. For instance, what were his religious views? how did the sight of nature affect him? what was he in his dealings with women and in his feelings respecting money? was he rich, was he poor? what was his regimen? what his daily manner of life? &c. Finally, to what vice was he addicted or to what weakness subject? for no man is entirely free from such. There is not one of the answers to these questions that is without its value in judging the author of a book, or even the book itself, if it be not a treatise on pure mathematics, but a literary work into the composition of which some of the writer's whole nature has perforce entered." The practice which now prevails of publishing full and authentic memoirs of celebrities, if perhaps not unobjectionable in some respects, is certainly an incalculable gain to the fruitful and intelligent study of literature. If we were so fortunate as to find a Life of Shakespeare similar to that which Boswell wrote of Dr. Johnson, can any one doubt that it would throw an immense light upon the many literary puzzles which are to be found in his writings, and which have perplexed generations of commentators and evoked hundreds of volumes? How many ingenious and elaborate studies on "Hamlet" would be shown to be as the baseless fabric of a vision? how many passages which verbal critics have (as they thought) proved to demonstration not to have come from Shakespeare's pen would be claimed as his? how, perchance, every one of the theories about the Sonnets would crumble into dust, never again to be mentioned but with laughter after their mystery had been unveiled by unimpeachable evidence? Again, to take a case from our own time, how would we explain the gloomy pessimism of the latter writings of Carlyle as contrasted with the sanguine optimism of Macaulay if no records of his life were to be found, and we were compelled to judge of him by his works alone? Carlyle's temperament, no doubt, was naturally gloomy, but that fact alone would not be a sufficient solution of the enigma. But when we study the story of his life, and learn how he was constantly tormented by ill-health; how, eagerly ambitious of literary fame, he had to toil on for many a long year unnoticed and unknown, with bitter experience of that deferred hope which makes the heart sick; how, when the day of triumph came, it came so late that the flower of success had well-nigh lost its fragrance—then we have no difficulty in understanding the cause of his frequently dark and harsh views of human character and destiny. We need hardly dwell on the additional interest given to a book by a knowledge of the circumstances under which it was composed. Byron's poetry owes half its attractiveness to the fascination exercised by his singular and strongly marked personality. Johnson's works, excellent though some of them are, would now, we imagine, be very little read if Boswell's Life of him had not made him one of the best known, and (with all his eccentricities) one of the best-loved characters in our literary history. One's interest even in such a book as Gibbon's "Decline and Fall" is perceptibly quickened by the full and curious portrait of himself which he has drawn in his Autobiography.

But for the thorough and profitable study of an author, it is not enough that we know the circumstances of his private history: we must also make ourselves acquainted with the period in which his lot was cast. No writer, however great and original his genius, can escape the influence of the spirit of the age in which he lives; whether with or without his consent, his way of looking at things will be modified by the intellectual atmosphere by which he is surrounded. Literary men alike influence and are influenced by their time; and as no history of a country can be considered complete which ignores the influence exerted by its literature, so any literary history which ignores the currents of thought and opinion set afloat by political movements must necessarily be partial and inadequate. There is no greater desideratum in our literature at present than a complete and able account of the history of English literature, in which the connection between the literary and political history of our country shall be fully dealt with; and it is very much to be desired that some one of sufficient talents and acquirements may be induced to undertake the task. He will have comparatively unbeaten ground to deal with. M. Taine, indeed, in his "History of English Literature," has done something in this direction; but his erratic brilliancy is not to be implicitly relied upon.[1] In periods of great national emotion, the influence exerted on literature by the powerful currents of thought and action

[1] It is not to the credit of England that the only full survey of its literature possessing any high merit from a purely literary point of view should be the work of a Frenchman. We have among us not a few writers, any one of whom, if they would abandon for a few years the practice, now unhappily too prevalent, of writing merely Review articles and brief monographs, could produce a work on the subject worthy of so great a theme.

sweeping on around it is so strong and so manifest that it cannot escape the notice of the most careless observer. The mighty burst of song in England during the reign of Elizabeth, a time of great men and great deeds, when new ideas and new influences were powerfully at work among all sections of society, has often been commented on. The impurity and heartlessness of the drama of the Restoration was a true type of the nation's wild outburst of revelry after its escape from the austere chains of Puritanism. Not so strikingly apparent, yet very noticeable, is the connection between the tortuous and shifty politics of the early years of the eighteenth century and the absence from the literature of that period of any high ideal or elevating principle. Coming nearer our own time, all are aware that the revolutionary movement of the close of the last century was active not only in politics but in letters; that as old laws and old principles were found inadequate to the needs of the time, so the literary forms and rules of the preceding generation were cast to the winds as quite incapable of expressing the novel ideas and imaginations of a race of writers who possessed little or nothing in common with their predecessors. But even in quieter times, when the broad river of national life is unruffled by violent storms, careful inquiry will make it apparent that its influence upon literature is very close and very real.

The most useful commentary on a great writer is to be found in the works of his contemporaries. It is mainly the service which they render in this direction that prevents one from agreeing with Emerson when he says that perhaps the human mind would be a gainer if all secondary writers were lost. From an author's contemporaries we may learn what ideas in his time were, to use Dr. Newman's phrase, "in the air," and thus be able to gauge with some degree of accuracy the extent of his originality. We have all been taught that Shakespeare far outshone any of the brilliant constellations of dramatic stars which adorned the reign of Elizabeth; but this is only a barren phrase to us till we have studied the other dramatists of his time, and are thus in a position to realise what it really means. The writings of contemporaries, moreover, often help us to account for the flaws and deficiencies which not unfrequently occur even in authors of the highest class, by giving us a clue to the literary fashions which prevailed in their time. Shakespeare's tendency to indulge in puns and verbal quibbles, which mars some of his finest passages, was, no doubt, due not so much to any natural inclination as because he lived in an age extravagantly fond of such ingenuities; and even he, immeasurably great man as he was, proved unable to resist the contagion which spread everywhere around him. In this connection we should not omit to notice the valuable aid which writers destitute of original power, but with a faculty for assimilating the ideas and imitating the style of others, often afford to the study of those whose voices they echo. Every great writer, while his popularity is at its height, is surrounded by a crowd of imitators, who copy in an exaggerated fashion his peculiar mannerism, and thus afford a very ready means of observing the minute traits of its style, and its little weaknesses and affectations, which might otherwise escape our notice. If imitation be the sincerest form of flattery, it is often also the bitterest satire. The severest critics of Mr. Tennyson and Mr. Swinburne have not so accurately shown the imperfections in the work of these writers, nor have they, it is probable, caused them so much pain as the verses of certain minor singers of our day have done. No parody is at once so scathing and so ridiculous as an attempt made by a writer of feeble powers to emulate the production of a man of genius.

If ten men of literary culture were asked to write down the names of the thirty English writers (exclusive of authors of our own time) who are their greatest favourites, of whom they make as it were companions and friends, the lists, we may be sure, would differ widely. But if these ten men were asked to write down the names of the thirty English writers who occupy the highest rank, who are accepted as the best representatives of our literature, the lists would probably resemble each other very closely. In the former case, single lists would contain names which were found in none of the others; in the latter case, it is very unlikely that any list would contain a name which was not also mentioned in several. "If I were confined to a score of English books," said Southey, "Sir Thomas Browne would, I think, be one of them; nay, probably it would be one if the selection were cut down to twelve. My library, if reduced to these bounds, would consist of Shakespeare, Chaucer, Spenser, and Milton; Jackson, Jeremy Taylor, and South; Isaac Walton, Sydney's "Arcadia," Fuller's "Church History," and Sir Thomas Browne;[1] and what a wealthy and well-stored mind would that man have, what an inexhaustible reservoir, what a Bank of England to draw upon for profitable thoughts and delightful associations, who should have fed upon them." Some of the names in the above list will strike the reader as curious. Jackson, South, and even Fuller's "Church History" and Sydney's "Arcadia" are not books which can be ranked among general favourites. But Southey found in them the mental food best adapted to his constitution, and therefore preferred them to others of greater intrinsic merit and much wider popularity. In books, as in other things, tastes differ very much. Not a few, whether they are honest enough to confess it or not, agree with worthy George III. in thinking that Shakespeare often wrote "sad stuff;" some people, by no means deficient in abilities, can read "Pickwick" without a laugh or even a smile; Macaulay, Mr. Trevelyan tells us, was so disgusted with the unconventional style of Ruskin and Carlyle that he refused even to look at their works.

It is, therefore, not at all surprising that when a young reader takes up a book which, he has heard, is enrolled in the list of English classics, he should not unfrequently find little in it to please him, and thus be tempted to think that it has been overrated. But if, as in the case we suppose, the book is one which has stood the test of time, he may be sure he is wrong. "Nature," writes Emerson, "is much our friend in

[1] Doubtless from inadvertence, Southey mentions only eleven writers. Who the twelfth was affords matter for curious speculation.

this matter. Nature is always clarifying her water and her wine; no filtration can be so perfect. She does the same thing by books as by her gases and plants. There is always a selection in writers, and then a selection from the selection. In the first place, all books that get fairly into the open air of the world were written by the successful class, by the affirming and advancing class, who utter what tens of thousands feel though they cannot say. There has already been a scrutiny and choice from many hundreds of young pens before the pamphlet or political chapter which you read in a fugitive journal comes to your eye. All these are young adventurers, who produce their performances to the wise ear of Time, who sits and weighs, and ten years hence out of a million of pages reprints one. Again, it is judged, it is winnowed by all the winds of opinion—and what terrific selection has not passed on it before it can be reprinted after twenty years—and reprinted after a century! It is as if Minos and Rhadamanthus had indorsed the writing. 'Tis therefore an economy of time to read old and famed books. Nothing can be preserved which is not good." We might almost add that whatever has not been preserved is not good. Those whose duty or inclination leads them to wander in literary bypaths sometimes come across forgotten writers in whom they find a certain tone of manner or feeling which gives them, in their eyes, more attractiveness than is possessed by writers whose praises are echoed by thousands. But all attempts to resuscitate such books fail as utterly as attempts to lower the position of books which have been accepted as classical. The opinion of the majority of readers during many years is better than that of any individual reader, or any small coterie of readers, however high their gifts or attainments may be.

It often happens that wider knowledge and culture lead one who at first was unable to recognise the merits of a classical author to see his error and acquiesce in the general verdict. In the case of our older authors, there are preliminary difficulties of style and language, which must, at the cost of some trouble, be vanquished before they can be read with pleasure.

The practice of "dipping into" an author and reading bits here and there is productive of a great deal of literary heterodoxy. It is, for example, a not uncommon remark that articles, of which the writers are never heard of, but which are as good as any in the *Spectator* or *Tatler*, appear in our newspapers every day. No doubt there is a very large amount of talent now employed in newspaper-writing; nevertheless our average journalists are not Steeles or Addisons. The reason, in most cases, why newspaper articles are thought equal to the *Spectator* is because the former deal with *living* subjects, subjects which are interesting people at the moment, while the latter, having been written more than a century and a half ago, has an antique flavour about it. The *Spectator* cannot be appreciated but by those who, not content with dipping into it here and there, have read at least a considerable portion of it, and thus gained such a knowledge of the manners and opinions which prevailed when it was written as to be able to enter into the spirit of the work. A newspaper article, referring to matters occupying the minds of all, may be perused with pleasure without any preparation.

But though increased knowledge and wider culture generally lead one to acquiesce in received opinions regarding the value of authors, they do not always do so. Every critic, however large his range and however keen his discernment, occasionally meets in with works of great fame of which he cannot appreciate the merit. He may, indeed, be able to perceive the qualities which cause others to admire them, but they are written in a vein which he cannot bring himself to like: the tone of sentiment running through them, or the style in which they are written, is repugnant to his nature. The fact that this is so, generally leads to a plentiful indulgence in what Mr. James Payn has so happily christened "sham admiration in literature." People praise books which they have never been able to read, or which they have only read at the cost of much labour and weariness, not because they like them themselves, but simply because they have heard others praise them. It is melancholy to reflect how much of our current criticism upon classical authors is of this nature, consisting of mere windy rhetoric, not of the unbiassed and honest expression of the critic's real opinions. The practice is both an unprofitable and a dishonest one. Much more is to be learned from the genuine opinions of an able man, even though these opinions be erroneous, than from the repetition of conventional critical *dicta*. Johnson's "Lives of the Poets" contain many incorrect critical judgments; but does any one suppose that the work would have been of more value if, instead of relating in manly and straightforward fashion the opinions of his own powerful, if somewhat narrow, understanding, he had merely repeated the "orthodox" criticisms on such writers as Milton and Gray? Even Jeffrey's articles on Wordsworth—those standing examples of blundering criticism—are much more useful and interesting to the intelligent reader than the thrice-repeated laudatory criticisms which are now so often uttered by countless insincere devotees of the poet of the Lakes. Every student of literature should make an honest effort to form opinions for himself, and not take up too much with borrowed criticism. Critical essays, books of literary history, books of select extracts, are all very useful as aids to the study of great writers, but they ought not, as is too often the case, to be made a substitute for the study of the writers themselves. Infinitely more is to be learned from the reading of "Hamlet" than from the reading of a hundred studies on that drama. If, after having made a fair attempt to peruse some author whose works are in high repute, the reader finds that he is engaged in a field of literature which presents no attractions to him; that he is studying a writer with whom he has no sympathy, who strikes no respondent chord in his own nature; the best course for him is to abandon the vain attempt to like what he does not like, to admire what he really does not admire. Shakespeare's famous lines—

> "No profit goes where is no pleasure ta'en,
> In brief, sir, study what you most affect,"—

convey thoroughly sound advice, provided, of course, that

proper pains be taken to extend one's culture as widely as possible, and that opinions regarding the profitableness or unprofitableness of studying certain authors be not formed without due deliberation. In the study of literature, as in other studies, interest advances as knowledge increases; very frequently books which to the tyro seem "weary, stale, flat, and unprofitable," are those which he afterwards comes to regard as among his most cherished intellectual possessions.

A very attractive and instructive way of studying literature is to select some great book or some great author as a nucleus round which to group one's knowledge of the writers of a period. If, for example, one studies that universally delightful book, Boswell's "Life of Johnson," and follows up the clues which its perusal suggests, a very competent knowledge of a large part of the literature of the eighteenth century may be acquired. Boswell's frequent cutting allusions to his rival, Sir John Hawkins, naturally induce us to read that worthy's Life of the "great lexicographer," in which, amid much trash and tedious moralising, many curious and suggestive details are to be found. In a similar way, his obvious dislike of Mrs. Piozzi draws attention to that lively lady's entertaining gossip; while the glimpses he gives of the life and conversation of most of the celebrated writers of the period, such as Burke, Goldsmith, Robertson, Hume, inspire us with a desire to become acquainted with their writings and with the particulars of their lives. Or if Pope be taken as the vantage-ground from which to survey the literary landscape around, how easily and pleasantly are we introduced to the acquaintance, not only of the greater figures of the time,—Addison, Swift, Bolingbroke, Arbuthnot, and others,—but of the smaller fry, the ragged denizens of Grub Street, so mercilessly satirised in the "Dunciad." No one can know Dryden thoroughly without picking up, almost imperceptibly it may be, an immense fund of information about the many curious literary products of the Restoration; and few more interesting literary studies could be suggested than, taking Shakespeare as a centre, to mark wherein he differed from his predecessors and contemporaries, how far he availed himself of what they had done, how far he influenced them, and how far he was influenced by them, and to trace the whole course of the Elizabethan drama from its first dim dawnings to its melancholy but not inglorious close. When one has made oneself at home in the literature of any period, so as to be able to conjure up before the mind's eye its more important writers, even its minutest details, which in themselves seem trifling and tedious, acquire an interest and importance, every fresh particular adding a new shade of colour to the mental picture we form of the epoch.

In the pages which follow, considerable space has been devoted to the literature of the last hundred years, while our earlier writers have been dealt with briefly, many of considerable importance having been altogether omitted. To this arrangement not a few may possibly be inclined to object; nevertheless, I believe that, for a work like the present, intended mainly for young readers and others whose time is limited, it is the best arrangement. Literary history becomes much more interesting to most people the nearer it approaches to our own time; and very few are likely to acquire a taste for reading by having their attention directed mainly to our older authors. Now, what every writer of a book like the present and every teacher of English literature ought to aim at is, to give his readers or his pupils a taste for literature. If the teacher of English literature fails in this, his labours are almost in vain. The amount of knowledge which he is able to communicate is comparatively small; but if he manages to impress on his pupils a sense of the greatness and importance of literature, and of the countless benefits and pleasures which may be derived from its study, he has sown the seeds of what will yet produce a very abundant harvest. The remark is very often made that young people are of their own accord likely to peruse writers of the day, while leaving the classical writers of former generations neglected. No doubt there is a good deal of truth in this; but I am disposed to question very much whether the practice of using mainly our older writers for educational purposes has any appreciable effect whatever in extending their general perusal; and when one considers how literature—even literature of the day—is neglected by numbers of educated people, one is inclined to have some doubt as to the wisdom of leaving recent writers out of the educational curriculum. Few will be disposed to deny that the most important section of political history is that which relates to recent times. To a large extent, the same is true of literature. Nothing is more likely to quicken one's interest in books, and to serve as an incentive to further research, than an acquaintance with the various literary modes that have been prevalent in recent times or which are still in vogue. Moreover, if the study of English literature is pursued partly as a means of acquiring a correct style, there can be no doubt whatever that the prose writers of the last two centuries will prove much more useful guides than their predecessors. The following interesting remarks on this subject, quoted from a lecture "On Teaching English," recently delivered by Dr. Alexander Bain before the Birmingham Teachers' Association, appear to me to have much force, though the views expressed are perhaps rather extreme. "Irrespective of any question as to the superiority of Shakespeare and Milton, it must from necessity be the case that the recent classics possess the greatest amount of unexhausted interest. Their authors have studied and been guided by the greatest works of the past, have reproduced many of their effects, as well as added new strokes of genius; and thus our reading is naturally directed to them by preference. A canto of 'Childe Harold' has not the genius of 'Macbeth' or of the second book of 'Paradise Lost,' but it has more freshness of interest. This is as regards the reader of mature years, but it must be taken into account in the case of the youthful reader also.

"So with regard to the older prose. The 'Essays' of Bacon cannot interest this generation in any proportion to the author's transcendent genius. They have passed into subsequent literature until their interest is exhausted, except from the occasional quaint felicity of the phrases. Bacon's maxims on the conduct of business are completely superseded by Sir Arthur Helps's essay on that subject, simply because Sir Arthur absorbed all that was in Bacon, and augmented it by subsequent wisdom and experience. To make Bacon's original a text-book of the present day, whether for thought or for style, is to abolish the three intervening centuries.

"Of Richard Hooker's 'Ecclesiastical Polity,' another literary monument of the Elizabethan age, while I give it every credit as a work suited to its own time, I am obliged to concur in the judgment of an authority great both in jurisprudence and in English style—the late John Austin—who denounced its language as 'fustian.'

"So much as regards the decay of interest in the old classics. Next as to their use in teaching style or in exercising pupils in the practice of good composition. Here, too, I think, they labour under incurable defects. Their language is not our language; their best expressions are valuable as having the stamp of genius, and are quotable to all time, but we cannot work them into the tissue of our own familiar discourse."

The concluding chapter of this book, dealing with Periodicals, Reviews, and Encyclopædias, gives a brief account of the more remarkable papers of the *Spectator* class, which form a noticeable feature of the literature of the eighteenth century; of the origin of the two great Quarterlies, which exercised an almost fabulous influence over criticism in the beginning of their career; of some of the more prominent new departures in periodical literature made during the present century; and of the various great English Encyclopædias. A good deal of our best literature, especially of a critical kind, has appeared in serial publications; and Encyclopædias, besides having been in recent times adorned by contributions from the ablest pens of the day, have, as digests of knowledge, afforded immense aid to all sorts of literary workers. No apology accordingly is required for devoting a chapter to the origin and history of publications belonging to the classes mentioned.

Much difference of opinion will naturally prevail as to the

writers selected for notice in this work. Some will think that names are included which would have been better omitted; others, that names are omitted which ought to have been included. I can only say that I have endeavoured to make as representative and catholic a selection as possible; and that, in choosing writers for brief notice, I have tried to fix on such as are especially remarkable, not only on account of their intrinsic merit, but as showing the literary tendencies of their time. It is with great regret that many authors of high merit and interest have been altogether left unnoticed; but more names could not have been inserted without destroying the distinctive character of the work.

As strict chronological order has not been adopted in dealing with the various authors mentioned, chronological tables giving the leading dates belonging to each chapter have been given in the Contents. These will, it is hoped, be useful for reference.

LANDMARKS OF ENGLISH LITERATURE.

I.

THE DAWN OF ENGLISH LITERATURE.

Chaucer; James I. of Scotland, Dunbar, Gawain Douglas, Sir David Lyndsay; Mandeville; Wiclif, Tyndale, Coverdale, Rogers (translations of the Bible); Sir Thomas Malory, More, Latimer, Foxe.

> "Dan Chaucer, the first warbler, whose sweet breath
> Preluded those melodious bursts, that fill
> The spacious times of great Elizabeth
> With sounds that echo still."—TENNYSON.

IF this book were a history of the English language, or if it dealt with such writers as have an interest only to those who have made them the subjects of special study, not a few names would have to be mentioned ere we came to deal with our first really great poet. Literature is a plant of slow and gradual growth: its beginnings, like the source of some great river, are obscure and difficult to trace: it is not till many influences have been at work, and many busy pens employed in moulding and forming the language, that the appearance of a writer who deserves to be ranked as a classic is possible. The authors before Chaucer (be it said with reverence to those zealous antiquaries whose enthusiasm has done so much to make the study of our old literature attractive and profitable) are interesting only for historical reasons: Chaucer is interesting for himself alone, apart from all considerations regarding his influence upon the language, or the admirable representations which his works afford of the social life of his time. His was a genial, sunny nature, Shakespearean in its breadth and sweet placidity; and hence he was able to look human life straight in the face and to hold the mirror up to nature without flinching. "All sorts and conditions of men" are described by him with sly humour, and, in general, a strong undercurrent of sympathy: like the character in Terence, he might have said, "I am a man, and think nothing human alien from me." Had he lived in our day, we cannot doubt that he would have made an admirable novelist had he chosen to employ his pen in that direction. But in addition to his gifts as a story-teller, he was a genuine poet: our first, and still, after the lapse of more than six centuries, one of our greatest. He had the poet's command of language, the poet's ear for rhythm, the poet's love of the beautiful, the poet's love of nature. So great was he, that we have to leap over nearly two centuries ere we come to a poet fit to be mentioned in the same breath with him.

Of the story of Chaucer's life we do not know so much as could be wished, but within the past few years a good deal has been done by earnest students both in the way of finding out new facts and in demolishing traditional fictions. He was the son of a London vintner, and was born about 1340, the date given in all the older biographies, 1328, being now almost universally abandoned as inconsistent with certain other facts in his life. Of his early years almost nothing is known. It has been supposed that he studied at Oxford or Cambridge; but this is mere baseless conjecture. At all events, we are safe to imagine that from his childhood he was fond of reading, and improved his opportunities in that direction to the best of his ability. Few, indeed, are the men who neglect books in their youth, and find pleasure in them when they are grown up; and Chaucer's works conclusively prove that he was, for his time, a man of great learning. "The acquaintance," writes Sir Harris Nicolas, "he possessed with the classics, with divinity, with astronomy, with so much as was then known of chemistry, and indeed with every other branch of the scholastic learning of the age, proves that his education had been particularly attended to; and his attainments render it impossible to believe that he quitted college at the early period at which persons destined for a military life usually began their career. It was not then the custom for men to pursue learning for its own sake; and the most natural manner of accounting for the extent of Chaucer's acquirements is to suppose that he was educated for a learned profession. The knowledge he displays of divinity would make it more likely that he was intended for the Church than for the Bar, were it not that the writings of the Fathers were generally read by all classes of students."

Whether educated at a university, whether intended for the Church or the Bar (all which conjectures rest on no real basis of fact), it is certain that in 1359 Chaucer accompanied the expedition of Edward III. into France. He was taken prisoner during the campaign, but was promptly released—the king paying £16 for his ransom early in 1360. Seven years later we find him one of the king's valets, at the same time receiving a yearly pension of twenty marks in consideration of former and future services. For some time after this his career seems to have been one of unbroken prosperity. From 1370 to 1380 he was employed in no fewer than seven diplomatic services, in which he appears to have acquitted himself well, as indeed the tact and knowledge of human nature shown in his writings would lead us to expect. Of these diplomatic missions, three were to Italy, where Chaucer is supposed by some to have met Petrarch, the most consummate master of poetical form then living, and Boccaccio, that prince of story-tellers, whose gay raillery and cheerful spirit must have been eminently congenial to Chaucer. Whether he became personally acquainted with these great writers is not certain: it is certain that he knew and loved their works, and that they exerted a great influence over his genius. During the same ten years honours and offices were freely showered on him. In 1374 he was appointed comptroller of the customs and subsidy of wools, skins, and tanned hides in the port of London, and about the same time he received other remunerative appointments which gave him an income equivalent to about £1000 a year of our money. In 1382 he was made comptroller of the petty customs, and in 1386 member of Parliament for the shire of Kent. This was the culminating point of his fortunes. His patron, John of Gaunt, was abroad, and his brother, the Duke of Gloucester, showed little favour to the poet, who was deprived of his two comptrollerships. Chaucer seems to have possessed in abundance that "perfect readiness to spend whatever could be honestly got," which is said to be characteristic of men of letters, and of the ample revenues which he had enjoyed during the preceding years he had probably saved little. In 1388 we find him raising money by transferring the two pensions he enjoyed to another man. In 1389 a gleam of returning prosperity shone on him. He was appointed clerk of the king's works, receiving two shillings a day, equal to £1 of our money. This office, however, he did not hold long. By the end of 1391 he had lost it, "and for the next three years his only income was his annuity of £10 from the Duke of Lancaster, and an allowance of 40s., payable half-yearly, for robes as the king's esquire." In 1394 he obtained an annuity of £20 from the king for life, but his pecuniary embarrassments still continued. To them he pathetically alludes in the verses "To his Empty Purse:"—

> "To yow, my Purse, and to noon other wight,
> Complayn I, for ye be my lady dere;
> I am so sory now that ye been lyght,
> For, certes, but yf ye make me hevy chere,
> Me were as leef be layd upon my bere."

By and by, it is satisfactory to be able to say, his purse was made heavier. In 1398 the king made him a grant of a tun of wine a year for life—a suitable donation to a poet who, it should seem, was by no means destitute of convivial qualities.

In 1399 Henry Bolingbroke doubled his annual pension of twenty marks. Chaucer did not live long to enjoy his newly recovered prosperity. He died in a house in the garden of St. Mary at Westminster, on October 25, 1400.

Chaucer's personal appearance is well known from the portrait of him by Occleve, which, in a greater degree than most portraits, confirms the ideas regarding him which one might gather from reading his works. There we see the meditative, downcast, yet slyly observant eyes, the broad brow, the sensuous mouth, the general expression of good-humour which are all so characteristic of the describer of the Canterbury pilgrims. In the "Prologue to the Rime of Sir Thopas," Chaucer has put into the mouth of the host a half-bantering description of his personal appearance :—

> "And then at first he lookèd upon me
> And saydë thus, 'What man art thou?' quoth he ;
> 'Thou lookest as thou wouldest find a hare,
> And ever upon the ground I see thee stare ;
> Approchë near, and lookë merrily !
> Now ware you, sirs, and let this man have space,
> He in the waist is shaped as well as I ;
> This were a puppet in an arm to embrace
> For any woman, small and fair of face.
> He seemeth elvish by his countenance,
> For unto no wight doth he daliaunnce."

Two great traits of character prominently distinguished him—traits not very often found united in the same individual. He was an insatiable reader, and he was also an enthusiastic admirer of the beauties of nature. When the two tastes came in conflict, it was the latter that had to give way, as he tells us in a charming passage :—

> "And as for me, though I have knowledge slight,
> In bookës for to read I me delight,
> And to them give I faith and full credénce,
> And in my heart have them in reverence
> So heartily, that there is gamë none
> That from my bookës maketh me begone,

> But it be seldom on the holiday,—
> Save, certainly, when that the month of May
> Is come, and that I hear the fowlës sing
> And see the flowers as they begin to spring,
> Farewell my book, and my devotion."

Other features in Chaucer we shall have occasion to indicate when dealing with the "Canterbury Tales."

By the most recent critics of Chaucer his work has been divided into three periods—the French period, the Italian period, and the English period. To the first is assigned his "A. B. C.," a prayer to the Virgin, translated from the French; a translation of the "Romance of the Rose;"[1] the "Compleynte of Pity" (1368?), and the "Book of the Duchess," a poem commemorating the death in 1369 of the Duchess Blanche. To the second period, extending from 1372 to 1384, during which, as we have seen, Chaucer three times visited Italy, and is supposed to have fallen under Italian literary influence, are assigned his "Parliament of Fowls," "Troilus and Cresside," certain of the "Canterbury Tales," the "House of Fame," and some minor poems. To the third period belong the rest of the "Canterbury Tales." This division rests on no solid basis of fact, and must be taken for what it is worth. Though, of course, every deference is to be paid to the opinion of those who have devoted great attention to Chaucerian study, it must be confessed that there is something arbitrary and artificial in thus parcelling a man's work out into periods divided by a distinct line of demarcation. Professor Minto, whose soundness of judgment gives his opinion great weight, is inclined to reject the division as throwing a factitious, and, upon the whole, misleading light on the natural development of Chaucer's genius.[2] Of certain other works, the "Court of Love," the "Flower and the Leaf," and Chaucer's "Dream," the genuineness has been admitted by some and denied by others. We need not take up space

[1] It has been doubted, apparently on insufficient evidence, whether this translation was by Chaucer.

[2] "English Poets," p. 19.

with the consideration of such questions, which can only be profitably discussed by those who have a very ripe knowledge of the literature of the period. It shows the versatility of Chaucer's intellect that he was the author of a translation of Boëthius on the "Consolation of Philosophy," a very popular book in the Middle Ages, and that he wrote in 1391 a treatise "On the Astrolabe" for the use of his little son Lewis.

Having thus enumerated the chief minor works of Chaucer, we pass on to the consideration of the "Canterbury Tales," to which alone we propose to confine our attention. Chaucer's other writings, excellent though many of them are, and interesting though they all are, partly for philological reasons, partly as indicating his mental growth, may be passed over by readers whose time is short; but the "Canterbury Tales" is of perennial importance, invaluable alike to the student of poetry, to the historian who aspires to delineate the social life of the period, and to the philologer. The plan of the "Canterbury Tales," a series of stories prefixed by a prologue and linked together by a framework, was probably derived by Chaucer from Boccaccio's "Decamerone," though there are other sources from which he might have borrowed the scheme. But there is a wide difference, greatly in favour of the English writer, between the "Decamerone" and the "Canterbury Tales." Boccaccio's connections between the stories might have been omitted and his book have been none the worse; there is no dramatic propriety in the tales which he puts in the mouth of the several speakers. One of the great attractions of the "Canterbury Tales," on the other hand, is that Chaucer, with the true instinct of genius, took care that each of the stories should be such as the speaker would naturally have told. In the "Prologue" he has hit off the points of the several characters with unrivalled grace and dexterity. "I see all the pilgrims in the 'Canterbury Tales,'" said Dryden, "their humours, their features, and their very dress, as distinctly as if I had supped with them at the Tabard in Southwark." A strangely mixed and jocund company they were who set forth on the pilgrimage, then a very common one for

Londoners, to the shrine of St. Thomas at Canterbury. We see before us the chivalrous Knight; the young Squire, "embroidered as a mead," and "as fresh as is the month of May;" the Yeoman, so careful of his accoutrements; the tender-hearted Prioress, who spoke French "after the school of Strat ford-atte-Bowe;" the Monk, who was so fond of hunting, and whose bridle "jingled in the air as clear and eke as loud as doth the chapel bell;" the Friar, who thought that instead of weeping and of prayers "men ought to give silver to the poor friars;" the Merchant, who sedulously attended to his business, and "spoke his reasons full pompously;" the Clerk of Oxford, who preferred books to any other earthly pleasure, and who would gladly learn and gladly teach; the Sergeant of Law, who "ever seemed busier than he was;" the Franklin, at whose house it "snowed of meat and drink;" the Shipman, who "of nice conscience took no keep;" the Doctor of Physic, whose "study was but little in the Bible;" the gaily-attired buxom Wife of Bath; the poor Parson and his brother the Ploughman, who, if it lay in his power, was always ready to work for the poor without hire; the stout Miller, who was not over honest, and who carried with him a bagpipe which he could "blow and sound;" the Reeve, "a slender, choleric man;" the Summoner, with his "fire-red cherubim's face;" the Pardoner, with his wallet full "of pardons come from Rome all hot;" and a good many other equally typical specimens of humanity, notably the jovial host of the Tabard, a fit predecessor to "mine host of the Garter" and to Boniface. "It is the first time in English poetry that we are brought face to face, not with characters, or allegories, or reminiscences of the past, but with living and breathing men, men distinct in temper or sentiment as in face, or costume, or mode of speech; and with this distinctness of each maintained throughout the story by a thousand shades of expression and action. It is the first time, too, that we meet with the dramatic power which not only creates each character, but combines it with its fellows, which not only adjusts each tale or jest to the temper of the person who utters it, but fuses all into a poetic unity. It is life in its largeness, its variety, its complexity, which surrounds us in the 'Canterbury Tales.' In some of the stories, indeed, composed no doubt at an earlier time, there is the tedium of the old romance or the pedantry of the schoolman; but, taken as a whole, the poem is the work not of a man of letters, but of a man of action. He has received his training from war, courts, business, travel—a training not of books, but of life. And it is life that he loves—the delicacy of its sentiment, the breadth of its farce, its laughter and its tears, the tenderness of its Griseldis, or the Smollett-like adventures of the miller and the schoolboy. It is this largeness of heart, this wide tolerance, which enables him to reflect man for us as none but Shakespeare has ever reflected it, but to reflect it with a pathos, a shrewd sense and kindly humour, a freshness and joyousness of feeling, that even Shakespeare has not surpassed." [1]

Pilgrimages to Canterbury seem to have been joyous affairs, in which merriment and not devotion held the foremost place in the minds of those who took part in them. "They will ordain with them before," says an old writer indignantly, "to have with them both men and women that can sing wanton songs, and some other pilgrims will have with them bagpipes; [2] so that every town they come through, what with the noise of their singing, and with the sound of their piping, and with the jangling of their Canterbury bells, and with the barking out of the dogs after them, that they make more noise than if the king came thereaway with all his clarions and many other minstrels. And if these men and women be a month in their pilgrimage, many of them shall be a half year after great janglers, tale-tellers, and liars." The "gentle" portion of Chaucer's company must have been not a little scandalised by the riotous behaviour of such "roistering blades" as the Miller, the Summoner, and the Cook, and by the grossly indecorous nature of some of the stories

[1] Green's "Short History of England," chap. v.

[2] The Miller carried his bagpipes with him.

told. For this indecorousness Chaucer makes a characteristic apology:—

> "And, therefore, every gentle wight I pray,
> For Goddës love deemeth not that I say
> Of evil intent; but for I must rehearse
> Their talës all, be they better or worse,
> Or ellës falsen some of my matter.
> And, therefore, whoso list it not to hear,
> Turn over the leaf and choose another tale;
> For he shall find enowë great and small
> Of storial thing that touches gentilesse,
> And eke morality and holiness,
> Blameth not me, if that ye choose amiss.
> The Miller is a churl, ye know well this;
> So was the Reeve, and other many mo,
> And harlotry they tolden bothë two.
> Aviseth you, and put me out of blame;
> And eke men shall not maken earnest of game."

It is easy to see that Chaucer is here laughing in his sleeve. The excuse he gives will not hold water. But we can forgive much to the man who, whatever his occasional license of language, was capable of delineating the finer qualities of human nature and the most tender of human feelings as none but one who really deeply sympathised with them could have done. A man who had seen much of the world, and had taken part in several of these diplomatic transactions which are not supposed to raise one's estimate of humanity, Chaucer yet preserved, amid all his frolicsome gaiety, a childlike simplicity of spirit which made him prompt to reverence worth, and gentleness, and mercy. There was nothing of the cynic in his composition. He took the world as he found it, and was very well contented with it. He was not a "good hater;" there is no trace of bitterness in his satire, nothing at all akin to the fierce misanthropy of Swift. Yet perhaps his sly touches of satire are none the less pungent on that account. There are few people who would not prefer being bitterly railed at to being good-humouredly laughed at. His penetrating accuracy of observation is perhaps best shown in what he says about women. Though, as many passages prove, he had a high and chivalrous estimate of women, he was well aware of their weak points, and from his works a choice anthology might be compiled of innuendoes or open sarcasms directed against the sex. This must be partly attributed to the custom of age; very probably it is in greater measure to be attributed to Chaucer's experience of married life, which is thought to have been far from a happy one. A pleasing feature in Chaucer is his want of all exaggerated reverence for rank and his total freedom from cant. Sprung from the people himself, he knew that it is neither long descent, nor high position, nor great wealth, that constitutes a gentleman :—

> " Look, who that is most virtuous alway,
> Privy and open, and most intendeth aye
> To do the gentle deedës that he can,
> Take him for the greatest gentleman."

His freedom from cant, and his contempt for those poetical commonplaces which form the stock-in-trade of minor versifiers, are shown by such passages as the following :—

> " Till that the brightë sun had lost his hue,
> For th' orison had reft the sun his light,
> (This is as much to sayen as 'it was night')."

What were Chaucer's religious views? The question is not very easy to answer. That he was fully aware of the abuses of the prevailing ecclesiastical system is conclusively proved by his pictures of the Monk, the Friar, the Pardoner, and others. On the other hand, his fine portrait of the " Poor Parson of a Town," who

> " —— Waited for no pomp and reverence,
> Nor made himself a spiced consciénce;
> But Christë's lore and His Apostles' twelve
> He taught, but first he followed it himself,"

has every appearance of being a representation of a Wiclifite priest. Hence some have rashly inferred that Chaucer himself was a Wiclifite. "Chaucer," wrote John Foxe, "seems to have been a right Wyclevian, or else there never was any; and that all his works almost, if they be thoroughly advised, will testify." But portions of the "Parson's Tale" are inconsistent with this supposition, which, indeed, other facts do not seem to corroborate. Chaucer was not a man to hold very pronounced religious views. Like many other people of his time, he was disgusted with the insolence and avarice of the ecclesiastical dignitaries, and, with his genuine appreciation of human excellence, could not look but with sympathy and admiration on the faithful pastors like the "Poor Parson," whom he saw amid discouragement and poverty striving to do their duty, and animated by a genuine religious spirit. But it is not likely that he ever desired or looked for an overthrow of the power of the Church of Rome in England: he was not the stuff of which reformers are made.

Though Chaucer was always a popular poet, as is proved by the many existing manuscripts of the "Canterbury Tales," by the fact that Caxton (who declares that "in all his works he excelleth, in mine opinion, all other writers in our English") issued two editions of his works, and by the numerous respectful allusions made to him by the poets of succeeding generations, his versification was a puzzle to his readers when the language had become fixed in substantially its present form. "The verse of Chaucer," wrote Dryden, "I confess is not harmonious to us. They who lived with him, and some time after him, thought it musical, and it continues so, even in our judgment, if compared with the numbers of Lydgate and Gower, his contemporaries: there is a rude sweetness of a Scotch tune in it, which is natural and pleasing." Waller went further:—

> "Chaucer his sense can only boast,
> The glory of his numbers lost!
> Years have defaced his matchless strain,
> And yet he did not sing in vain."

Chaucer himself perceived that he lived at a period when the language was in a state of transition. Towards the close of "Troilus and Cresside" he says:—

> "And since there is so great diversity
> In English, and in writing of our tongue,

I pray to God that none may miswrite thee,
Nor thee mismetre, for default of tongue,
And wheresoe'er thou mayst be read or sung
That thou be understood, God I beseech."[1]

He was, however, "mismetred" till the publication, in 1778, of Tyrwhitt's "Essay on the Language and Versification of Chaucer," which paved the way for what has been done since for the restoration of the text of Chaucer and the accurate knowledge of his language. The student may now, with very little trouble, acquaint himself with rules which regulate Chaucer's versification and grammar, and so be able to read him with a much fuller and clearer appreciation than such a man as Dryden could have done. The small expenditure of time necessary in order to do so will be recompensed a hundredfold by the pleasure derived from the study of the first English classic.

The appearance of Chaucer in our literature was compared by Warton to a premature day in an English spring, after which the gloom of winter returns, and the buds and blossoms which have been called forth by a transient sunshine are nipped by frosts and scattered by storms. The fifteenth century was a period of the deepest gloom, morally, materially, and intellectually. The wretched civil wars which devastated the country proved fatal to the muse: no great English poet arose within the period; no poet worthy even of a high place in the second rank. It is to Scotland, bleak, wild, barren, but full of men of high spirit and indomitable tenacity of purpose, that we must turn if we wish to find a writer who inherited the genius of Chaucer in any tolerable measure. James I. of Scotland, who has been styled the best king among poets and the best poet among kings, during his long captivity in England, which extended from 1405 to 1424, had the advantage of receiving an excellent education and of familiarising himself with the works of the best English poets. Though poems of a humorous nature, "Peebles to the Play" and

[1] Here and elsewhere the extracts from Chaucer have been modernised.

"Christ's Kirk of the Green," are generally supposed to have been written by him, his fame mainly rests on his "King's Quhair" [Book], a poem in six cantos, in which the influence of Chaucer is very apparent. It describes, in allegorical fashion, the attachment which, while a prisoner in Windsor Castle, he formed to a young English princess whom he saw walking in an adjacent garden. This lady is supposed to have been Lady Jane Beaufort, whom he afterwards married; but more probably the account given of her appearance is a pure poetical fancy. If rather deficient in originality—for it is impossible to believe that the "King's Quhair" would ever have been written if the works of Chaucer had not been already in existence—James I. had a fine poetical spirit, and were it not for the many difficulties of dialect which it presents, his poem would be much more generally read than it is. The unfortunate author, who was born in 1394, affords a bright example of the union of a poetical temperament with great practical powers. When he came to his kingdom, he found it in a state of anarchy through the lawless conduct of those turbulent nobles who were for many generations the curse of Scotland. "Let God but grant me life," he is reported to have said, "and throughout my dominions I shall make the key keep the castle and the furze-bush the cow, though I should lead the life of a dog to accomplish it." He was in a fair way to redeem his promise when he perished by assassination in 1437.

A poet of less tender and grateful fancy than the royal bard, but of more original genius, was William Dunbar, who has been called the Scotch Chaucer, a designation which recalls Coleridge's remark on hearing Klopstock styled the German Milton, "A very *German* Milton indeed." Dunbar, who was born in 1460, was educated at the University of St. Andrews, and in early life became a Franciscan friar—not a particularly suitable calling for him, if one may judge from the frequent license of his muse. By James IV. he was employed as a clerk to foreign embassies, and received numerous gratuities from the king in response to numerous supplications, for Dunbar was not a man to want money if it could be got for the asking.

His principal poems are the "Golden Targe," the target being Reason as a protection against the assaults of Desire, and his "Dance of the Seven Deadly Sins," a poem which, in its wild, reckless spirit, may be compared to the "Jolly Beggars" of Burns. The poetry of Dunbar has been described by Irving in his "Lives of the Scottish Poets" with something of a Scotchman's partiality to his countryman. "In the poetry of Dunbar," he says, "we recognise the emanations of a mind adequate to splendid and varied exertion—a mind equally capable of soaring into the higher regions of fiction, and of descending into the humble walk of the familiar and ludicrous. He was endowed with a vigorous and well-regulated imagination, and to it was superadded that conformation of the intellectual faculties which constitutes the quality of good sense. In his allegorical poems we discover originality and even sublimity of invention, while those of a satirical kind present us with striking images of real life and manners. As a descriptive poet he has received superlative praise. In the mechanism of poetry he evinces a wonderful degree of skill. He has employed a great variety of metres; and his versification, when opposed to that of his most eminent contemporaries, will appear highly ornamental and varied." The date of Dunbar's death is uncertain, but is supposed to have occurred about 1520. The "Golden Targe" was printed in 1508.

Gawain Douglas (1475–1522), Bishop of Dunkeld, is memorable as having been the author of the first metrical translation into English of a Latin author. He translated, with spirit and felicity, but with great diffuseness, the "Æneid" of Vergil in 1513. To each book he prefixed a prologue, and these prologues are commonly considered the most favourable specimens of his genius. His chief original poem is the "Palace of Honour," an allegory in which he maintains the theses that virtue is the only true chivalry. Like all the old Scottish poets, Douglas was permeated with a love for nature, which constitutes one of the great sources of his inspiration.

The last of the old school of Scottish poets was Sir David Lyndsay of the Mount, whose name is familiar to many who know nothing of his works by the ringing lines about him in Scott's "Marmion:"—

"He was a man of middle age;
In aspect manly, grave, and sage,
  As on king's errand come;
But in the glances of his eye
A penetrating, keen, and sly
  Expression found its home;
The flash of that satiric rage,
Which, bursting on the early stage,
Branded the vices of the age
  And broke the keys of Rome.
. . . .
Still is thy name in high account,
  And still thy verse hath charms,
Sir David Lindesay of the Mount,
  Lord Lion King-at-arms."

Lyndsay of the Mount (his family estate in Scotland) was no less a man of action than a poet: indeed it is mainly because he devoted his poetical talent to practical ends that his verses attained the wide popularity they long enjoyed among his countrymen. He was born in 1490, and rose to high office in the court of James V., with whom he was a great favourite. He had acted as gentleman-usher to that King in his youthful days, and the relations between master and pupil seem to have been unusually affectionate. Three of his poems, the "Dream," the "Complaint to the King," and the "Testament of the King's Papyngo," have for their purpose the exposure of abuses prevalent in church and state. Most of his works to a greater or less degree point in the same direction. His "Satire of the Three Estates," which was represented before the King at Linlithgow in 1539, having been first acted in 1535, is a morality play, having for its *motif* the fall of Cardinal Beaton, and stigmatising the crimes which led to that fall. In his last work, the "Monarchie" (1553), he continued in a graver tone than had been adopted in his earlier performances to protest against the abuses which had crept into the state. Different though their characters were, Lyndsay shares with Knox the honour of being one of the leaders of the Reformation. A clear-sighted, practical man, with considerable humour and much satirical power, he had great influence in stirring up the people to a sense of the wrongs which they endured and in bringing these wrongs under the attention of those in authority.

We now turn to our early prose writers. Prose is a much more artificial and mechanical mode of literary expression than verse: the poet's song (if it be a genuine song) is the outpouring of his heart in the metrical form which seems to him best adapted to the subject with which he deals: "he sings but as the linnets do," from the uncontrollable force of his genius. The prose writer, who has to handle all sorts of themes, uses, indeed, a much more commonplace instrument—for we all talk in prose—but before that instrument is adapted for literary purposes many refinements have to be adopted, and many expedients tried. The talk of an uneducated person, with its repetitions, its wanderings from the point, its innumerable accessory circumstances heedlessly thrown in at the most unsuitable places, its linking together of the most incongruous subjects, its want of clearness and precision, conveys a good idea of the style of our early prose-writers, who wrote before the language was fully formed and before the pathway to the art of English prose composition had been trodden smooth by the steps of innumerable wayfarers. With regard to the merely *mechanical* part of style, literary genius has not much to do: it may, in great measure, be acquired as grammar is acquired. A schoolboy would be ashamed of himself who could not express his meaning in a form less awkward and cumbrous than that used by Milton in his prose works.

The "first writer of formed English" is commonly said to have been Sir John Mandeville (1300–1371), and though the general opinion of experts now is that he was not the author of the English translation of the book of "Travels" which bears his name, thac book, whoever translated it, is the first English prose composition which deserves to be called literature. Of his own life, he says: "I, John Maundevylle, Knyght, alle be it I be not worthi, that was born in Englond, in the Town of Seynt Albones, passed the See in the Zeer of our Lord Jesu Crist MCCCXXII., in the day of Seynt Michelle; and hidre to have ben longe tyme over the See, and have seyn and gon thorghe manye dyverse Londes, and many Provynces and Kingdomes, and Iles, and have passed thorghe Lybye, Caldee, and a gret partie of Tartarye, Percye, Ermonye the litylle and the grete; thorghe Ethiope; thorghe Amazoyne, Inde the lasse and the more, a gret partie; and thorghe out many othere Iles, that ben abouten Inde; where dwellen many dyverse Folkes, and of dyverse Maneres and Lawes, and of dyverse Schappes of Men." Mandeville's "Travels" is believed to have been translated into English in 1356, and its popularity is proved by the fact that many copies of it circulated in manuscript. It is a strange and amusing book. A good deal of what he relates is somewhat of the Baron Munchausen order; but it is fair to say that the most extraordinary things told by the old traveller are given by him as having been stated by some one else, and not as the results of his own observation. Distant countries were then nearly as much a *terra incognita* to Englishmen as the mountains of the moon are to us; and ready credence was given to the most outrageous fables.

The great reformer John Wiclif (1324–1384), the stirring narrative of whose active life belongs more properly to the political than to the literary history of England, was, if tradition may be credited, a very extensive author. But it is now generally believed that his name was often made use of by other writers as a means of attracting attention to what they had to say. "Half the English religious tracts of the fourteenth and fifteenth centuries have been assigned to him in the absence of all external, and in defiance of all internal evidence." It is as the translator of the Bible into English that we mention Wiclif here. His version, which was finished in 1380, is a remarkable one from a literary point of view, and justifies his being called the first writer of later English prose, as Chaucer was the first writer of later English poetry. Wiclif is believed to have received some assistance in the translation of the Old Testament; but the translation of the New Testament is thought to have been entirely the work of his own hand. His translation of the New Testament was eclipsed by that of William Tyndale (1484–1536), which is the parent of all succeeding versions. It was first published at Antwerp in 1526. "Tyndale's translation of the New Testament," says Marsh, "is the most important philological monument of the first half of the sixteenth century, perhaps I should say of the whole period between Chaucer and Shakespeare, both as an historical relic and as having more than anything else contributed to shape and fix the sacred dialect, and establish the form which the Bible must permanently assume in an English dress. The best features of the translation of 1611 are derived from the version of Tyndale, and thus that remarkable work has exerted, directly and indirectly, a more powerful influence on the English language than any other single production between the ages of Richard II. and Queen Elizabeth." Besides the New Testament, Tyndale translated the Pentateuch, and published it in 1530. In 1536 he was martyred at Antwerp, on account of his heresy; and in the same year his version of the New Testament was for the first time published in England. The next English Bible was that issued by Miles Coverdale, who followed Tyndale closely in his translation of the New Testament published in 1535. It is from this version that the Psalms still used in the Book of Common Prayer are taken. A second edition, with the royal imprimatur, was published in 1537. Another translation, commonly called "Matthew's Bible," founded chiefly on the labours of Tyndale and Coverdale, appeared in the same year. It was the work of John Rogers, memorable otherwise as having been the first victim of the savage persecution of Protestants in the reign of Mary. Cranmer's Bible, the "Great Bible" as it was called, which is substantially the same as "Matthew's," was published in 1539. Then came, in 1611, the "Authorised Version," the influence of which, even looked at from a purely literary point of view, has been incalculable. Whether the "Revised Version" issued in 1881 is destined to supersede it, it is yet too early to say. The Authorised Version did not establish itself in public favour till it had encountered much severe opposition.

We have been led beyond our chronological limits, and must now retrace our steps. Attention in recent times has been much drawn to the "Morte d'Arthur" of Sir Thomas Malory, who flourished about 1470, by the fact that Mr. Tennyson has used it as the groundwork for much of his "Idylls of the King." The work, which is a condensation of the numerous floating legends about King Arthur and his Knights of the Round Table, was published by Caxton, the first English printer, in 1485. It is said that Mr. Tennyson first chanced upon a copy of it when little more than a boy: the story kindled his enthusiasm, and the vision of a great poem rose before him. Caxton (1420–1492) himself cannot be passed over in a history of literature. It is needless to enlarge on the results which followed the introduction of the printing press: how books have increased and multiplied till in our own day many are inclined to cry "Hold, enough;" how it has made literature accessible to all and attractive to all, how it has swept away thick mists of ignorance and prejudice; and how, by its means, journalism, "the Fourth Estate," has become more powerful for good or for evil than the other three Estates put together. Caxton was no vulgar tradesman; he had a keen interest in literature; was an industrious translator; and delighted to issue fine editions of the old English poets.

Sir Thomas More is a great figure both in political and in literary history. He was born in 1480, the son of a judge of the Court of King's Bench. At Oxford he made the acquaintance of Erasmus, an acquaintance which soon deepened into great mutual friendship. With a keen love of literature, and filled with enthusiasm for those classical studies, the interest in which was then beginning to revive in England, More concealed under a gay and cheerful exterior an almost ascetic piety, and at one time thought of becoming a monk. Instead of doing so, however, he began the study of law, and in 1529 was appointed by Henry VIII. successor to Wolsey in the Lord Chancellorship. A man of versatile genius, of gentle disposition, and of impregnable integrity, More may justly be reckoned one of the most lovable men of his time. It has been well remarked that one of his most striking characteristics was his infinite variety. "He could write epigrams in a hair shirt at the Carthusian convent; and pass from translating Lucian to lecturing on Augustine in the church of St. Lawrence. Devout almost to superstition, he was light-hearted almost to buffoonery. One hour we see him encouraging Erasmus in his love of Greek and the new learning, or charming with his ready wit the supper tables of the Court, or turning a debate in Parliament; the next at home, surrounded by friends and familiar servants, by wife and children, and children's children, dwelling among them in an atmosphere of love and music, prayer and irony—throwing the rein, as it were, on the neck of his most careless fancies, and condescending to follow out the humours of his monkey and the fool. His fortune was almost as various. From his utter indifference to show and money he must have been a strange successor to Wolsey. He had thought as little about fame as Shakespeare, yet in the next generation it was an honour to an Englishman throughout Europe to be his countryman." In advance of his age in many respects, More yet shared its persecuting tendencies. A staunch Romanist, "this most upright and merciful man became a persecutor of men as innocent, though not of such great minds as himself." To the Reformers he showed no mercy; and mercy was in turn denied him when he came to need it. He was beheaded in 1535, because he would not take the oath affirming the validity of the King's marriage with Anne Boleyn. "The innocent mirth," says Addison in a passage which has been universally admired, "which had been so conspicuous in his life, did not forsake him to the last. His death was of a piece with his life; there was nothing in it new, forced, or affected. He did not look upon the severing of his head from his body as a circumstance which ought to produce any change in the disposition of his mind, and as he died in a fixed and settled hope of immortality, he thought any unusual degree of sorrow and concern improper."

More's "Utopia" (1516), the picture of an imaginary commonwealth, in describing which he finds an opportunity for giving his views upon various social and political problems, such as education, the punishment of criminals, &c., was written in Latin and does not concern us here. It was translated into English by Ralph Robinson in 1551, and by Bishop Burnet in 1684. His chief English work is his "Life and Reign of Edward V.," which gives him a title to be considered the first Englishman who wrote the history of his country in its present language. It is believed to have been written in 1513, but was not printed till 1557. "The historical fragment," says Sir James Mackintosh, "commands belief by simplicity, and by abstinence from too confident affirmation. It betrays some negligence about minute particulars, which is not displeasing as a symptom of the absence of eagerness to enforce a narrative. The composition has an ease and a rotundity which gratify the ear without awakening the suspicion of art, of which there was no model in any preceding writer of English prose."

A man as admirable as More, though of very different temperament, was Hugh Latimer, the great Reformer. He was born about 1491 at Thurcaston in Leicestershire. His father was a yeoman in comfortable circumstances. Seeing the "ready, prompt, and sharp wit" of his son, he wisely determined, says Foxe, "to train him up in erudition and knowledge of good literature, wherein he so profited in his youth, at the common schools of his own country, that at the age of fourteen years he was sent to the University of Cambridge." In due time he obtained a fellowship there, and having been led to embrace Protestantism by the arguments of a certain "Maister Bylney," began, with characteristic impetuosity, to utter his protest against the doctrines of the Church of Rome. The University authorities brought his "heresies" under the notice of Cardinal Wolsey, but he was triumphantly acquitted. In 1530, he says, "I was called to preach before the King, which was the first sermon that I made before his Majesty; and it was done at Windsor, where his Majesty, after the sermon was done, did most familiarly talk with me in the gallery." The King seems to have liked the fearless outspoken spirit of the man, who never hesitated to speak out his mind either to prince or to peasant. In 1535 Latimer was appointed Bishop of Worcester, an office he did not long retain, being deprived of it in 1539, because he refused to sign the "Act of the Six Articles." For some time he suffered imprisonment in the Tower, and during the rest of Henry's reign was "commanded to silence." On the accession of Edward VI., in 1546, he again had an opportunity, of which he took full advantage, of exercising his gifts as a preacher. When Mary came to the throne in 1553, the tide again turned. Soon after her accession, Latimer was thrown into the Tower. In 1555 he was burned at the stake at Oxford. "Be of good cheer, Master Ridley," he said to his fellow-martyr, "and play the man: we shall this day light such a candle by God's grace in England, as (I trust) shall never be put out."

Latimer's sermons, of which that on "The Ploughers," delivered at St. Paul's in 1549, is the most famous, show that he possessed in an extraordinary degree the highest gift of the preacher—that of arousing men's consciences, and of impressing them with the belief that what he says is really true. He is not a seeker after fine phrases: the homeliest illustrations and the homeliest expressions are welcomed by him provided they clearly express the meaning he wishes to convey. A scorner of conventionality, he talked to his hearers as one plain man might talk to another, never mincing matters, and always anxious to set forth his subject in the most lucid way. He did not hesitate to address his remarks to individual hearers when he thought himself called upon to do so, careless if his remarks gave offence or not, so long as he did his duty. Latimer was no sour ascetic: he loved a racy anecdote or a humorous saying, and was ready to make use of them even when dealing with the most serious subject. A true Englishman, somewhat of the "John Bull" type, frank, manly, honest, courageous, he exerted a wonderful influence over the minds of his contemporaries, and his sermons, though their diction is occasionally rather startling, are still well worth reading as the utterances of a brave, thoroughly sincere man.

The story of Latimer's martyrdom, and of the other persecutions suffered by Protestants, was touchingly related by John Foxe (1517–1587) in his "Book of Martyrs" as it is commonly called, a title better expressing the nature of the work than its original one, "History of the Acts and Monuments of the Church." Foxe himself had to flee to the Continent to escape persecution during Mary's reign, and his "Book of Martyrs" was written on his return. It has great literary merit, but is often inaccurate and prejudiced. He lived too near the time with which he deals to write with impartiality.

We now quit the regions of the dawn, to enter on the broad effulgence of the Elizabethan period.

II.

THE ELIZABETHAN ERA.

Ascham; Wyatt and Surrey; Spenser; Sidney, Hooker, Raleigh, Lyly; The Elizabethan Dramatists: Lyly, Marlowe, Greene, Peele, Shakespeare, Chapman, Ben Jonson, Beaumont and Fletcher, and others.

IN this chapter we have to deal with what is, upon the whole, the greatest period in our literature. In it flourished Sidney and Hooker, Spenser and Shakespeare, and a crowd of writers, inferior, indeed, to these great names, but possessed of so much fertility and spontaneity of genius, of so much vehement energy and native talent, that in any other era they would have won for themselves a foremost place. Under the rule of the Maiden Queen, the pulse of the nation beat high; all human energies were cultivated to the utmost; the seas were scoured by daring buccaneers; enterprising travellers penetrated to distant places, bringing back accounts of the wonderful things they had seen and heard; English commerce increased to an unexampled extent; and the comparative isolation in which Protestant England stood apart from the Catholic nations of the Continent, made her proudly defiant and confident in her own resources. The love of gorgeous apparel and of splendid pageants which then prevailed is an apt symbol of the unpruned luxuriance, the wealth of high-coloured phrases and extravagant expressions which pervaded the literature. Men lived intensely, thought intensely, and wrote intensely.

Between the Elizabethan literature proper and the writers

of the preceding age, there are two or three authors who form as it were connecting links. Great poets and great prose-writers are always preceded by others, by far their inferiors in genius it may be, but in whose works we can trace the beginnings of the literary tendency which pervades their successors. We shall begin with a prose-writer, who might with equal propriety have been included among the authors mentioned in the preceding chapter, were it not for his close connection with Queen Elizabeth. Roger Ascham (1515–1568) lived in the reign of Henry, of Edward, of Mary, and of Elizabeth, and, more fortunate than many of his contemporaries, held comfortable offices under all those sovereigns. A cautious, conciliatory man, of no very pronounced religious opinions, he took care never to give offence; while his polished manners and cultivated mind made him a very attractive companion to his royal patrons. His first work, "Toxophilus," published in 1545, is a dialogue on archery, praising the national weapon, the bow, and advocating its use with the enthusiasm of one who was himself a proficient in the art.[1] No one is likely to find fault with Ascham for being fond of archery, but his love of cock-fighting, which, we are told, was his pastime in old age, was certainly reprehensible. Ascham's most famous work, the "Schoolmaster," was published in 1570, two years after his death. It is a very sensible, meritorious performance, abounding in digressions, but containing much advice, which is worth attending to, even in this era of universal education. The numerous anecdotes and reminiscences with which he diversifies his work, add greatly to its attractiveness. "Old Ascham," wrote Carlyle, "is one of the freshest, truest spirits I have met with; a scholar and writer, yet a genuine man."[2]

In the preceding chapter we have seen that the old Scottish poets derived their main impulse from Chaucer, whom they reverenced as their master. The same was the case with Chaucer's English successors. But a new epoch in the history

[1] Fuller quaintly describes Ascham as "an honest man and a good shooter."

[2] Correspondence of Macvey Napier, p. 77.

of English poetry dawned in the reign of Henry VIII. Foreign travel was becoming common among the higher classes, and the nobility, headed by a king who valued his learning not the least among his accomplishments, began to pride themselves as much upon their literary taste as upon their proficiency in manly exercises. It was from Italy, then the queen of the intellectual world, that the new school of poets obtained their inspiration—from Dante, Ariosto, Tasso, and Petrarch. Two courtly gentlemen who "had travelled into Italy and thus tasted the sweet and stately measures and style of the Italian poesy," introduced into England an entirely new fashion of writing, which took root and flourished. These were Sir Thomas Wyatt, and Henry Howard, Earl of Surrey, whose names are generally linked together. Their poems appeared in the collection known as "Tottel's Miscellany," which was published in 1557, and which contained poems by other versifiers. Wyatt (1503–1541), the elder of the two, was a man of grave and sombre genius, prone to look upon the dark side of things. His love-sonnets and songs have none of that lightness and gaiety which we are apt to associate with such verses, but they contain much subtle thought, and bear the appearance of expressing a genuine passion. Surrey (1516–1547) was a personage of different character. Impetuous and headstrong, he led a stirring and adventurous life, holding commands in Scotland and France, and being one of the most prominent figures at Court. He was executed for high treason in 1547. "Compared with Wyatt, Surrey strikes one as having much greater affluence of words—the language is more plastic in his hands. When his mind is full of an idea he pours it forth with soft voluble eloquence; he commands such abundance of words that he preserves with ease a uniform measure. Uniformity, indeed, is almost indispensable to such abundance: we read him with the feeling that in a 'tumbling metre' his fluency would run away with him. Such impetuous affluent natures as his need to be held in with the bit and bridle of uniformity. A calm composed man like Wyatt, with a fine ear for varied melodies, may be trusted to elaborate tranquilly irregular and subtle rhythms; to men like Surrey there is a danger in any medium between 'correctness' and Skeltonian license."[1] Surrey was a much more lively and gay-hearted singer than Wyatt; we have in his works, instead of the dolorous strains of a lover, the cruelty of whose mistress has really sunk deep in his heart, rather the affected passion of a poet who makes it his business to write love-verses. One of Surrey's best titles to remembrance is his introduction of blank verse. In this metre he translated the second and fourth books of Vergil's "Æneid." His blank verse is neither harmonious nor metrically correct; but the first user of an instrument cannot be expected to employ it with the same facility and precision as those who come after him.

We now come to the second of England's great poets—Edmund Spenser. A greater contrast to Chaucer it would be difficult to imagine. Spenser "dwelt in a world ideal;" the visionary sights and beings which fill the land of Faerie floated round him continually; his imagination rose above the rough practical world in which he lived to take refuge with the allegorical beings who occupied his thoughts. Chaucer, on the other hand, as we have seen, was very well satisfied with this world, enjoying heartily the frolics, the eccentricities, the virtues, nay even the vices of its inhabitants, ready always to laugh with those who laughed, and to weep with those who wept. There is, as will be admitted even by his warmest admirers, a want of human interest about Spenser's works; it is just their deep human interest which makes Chaucer's works so constantly attractive in spite of their antique dialect, and the fact that they refer to a condition of society which can now be conceived only by an effort of the imagination. Like Wyatt and Surrey, Spenser derived his chief impulse from Italy. He knew and admired Chaucer and the other old English poets, but his real masters were Ariosto and Tasso.

Spenser was born in London about 1552. He was distantly

[1] Minto's English Poets, p. 163.

connected with the noble family of the Spensers, a fact in which he took not a little pride, and which is referred to by Gibbon, when he says, "The nobility of the Spensers has been illustrated and enriched by the trophies of Marlborough; but I exhort them to consider the 'Faery Queen' as the most precious jewel in their coronet." Spenser was educated at Cambridge, where he graduated M.A. in 1576. After leaving the University he seems to have resided for some time as a tutor in Lancashire. On the advice of his college friend Gabriel Harvey, he returned to London in 1578, and was introduced by Harvey to Sir Philip Sidney and the Earl of Leicester, who took the poet under their patronage. Next year appeared Spenser's first publication, "The Shepherd's Calendar," a collection of twelve pastorals, one for each month of the year. The work is not very easy to criticise. It indubitably proved that Spenser was the greatest English poet then living; but would his name now have been more familiar to readers in general than that of Wyatt or of Surrey if he had written nothing else? We are inclined to think not. There is a certain artificiality about all pastoral poetry which prevents it from ever being popular, except among cultured readers. "The shepherds of Spenser's 'Calendar,'" says Campbell in his "Specimens of the British Poets," a work containing much sound and excellent criticism, "are parsons in disguise, who converse about heathen divinities and points of Christian theology." The antique language of the pastorals, which was adopted by Spenser of set purpose, was condemned by his patron Sidney, and Ben Jonson went so far as to say that the author in affecting the ancients had written no language at all. The mysterious commentator on the "Shepherds' Calendar," who is generally believed to have been the poet himself, and who, at any rate, certainly was inspired by Spenser, thus refers to the antique phraseology. "And first," he says, "of the words to speak, I grant they be something hard, and of most men unused, yet both English, and also used of most excellent authors and most famous poets. In whom whereas this our poet hath been much travelled and thoroughly read, how could it be (as that worthy orator said) but that, walking in the sun, although for other causes he walked, yet needs he mought be sun-burnt; and, having the sound of these ancient poets still ringing in his ears, he mought needs in singing hit out some of their tunes." He then goes on at considerable length to defend this practice of the poet, but his defence is not very convincing.

In 1580 Spenser went to Ireland, as secretary to the Viceroy, Lord Grey of Wilton. There he remained, with the exception of two visits to England, for eighteen years, holding various offices and writing the "Faerie Queen," which had been begun ere he quitted England. In 1586 he obtained, by the intercession of his friends, a grant of three thousand acres of land from the forfeited estates of the Earl of Desmond at Kilcolman, near Cork. In this beautiful and romantic district, through which flowed the river Mulla which has obtained an eternity of poetic fame by its frequent mention in Spenser's works, he was visited in 1589 by Sir Walter Raleigh, who listened with admiration to the portion of the "Faerie Queen" already written. This visit is thus, in figurative language, commemorated by Spenser:—

"'One day,' quoth he, 'I sate (as was my trade)
  Under the foot of Mole, that mountain hoar,
Keeping my sheep amongst the cooly shade
  Of the green alders by the Mulla's shore;
There a strange shepherd chanced to find me out,
  Whether allured with my pipe's delight,
Whose pleasing sound yshrilled far about,
  Or thither led by chance, I know not right;
Whom when I asked from what place he came,
  And how he hight, himself he did ycleepe
The Shepherd of the ocean by name,
  And said he came far from the main-sea deep."

In 1590 Spenser accompanied Raleigh to England, carrying with him the three first books of the "Faerie Queen." They were published in that year, and at once received with favour. Elizabeth bestowed on the poet an annual pension of £50, no mean sum in the sixteenth century. In 1591 Spenser returned to Ireland, and in the same year appeared a volume of minor poems from his pen, of which the most noticeable is "Mother Hubbard's Tale," a pleasing imitation of Chaucer. In 1595 appeared at different times his "Colin Clout's Come Home Again," from which the verse above cited is taken, and which describes his voyage to England and his reception there; his "Amoretti," love-sonnets which do not add materially to his fame; and his "Epithalamion," that magnificent marriage song, in which he celebrates in triumphant and richly jewelled verse the successful termination of his wooing. It has been called "the most glorious love-song in the English language," nor is this praise too high. In the following year, Spenser returned to London and published the last three books of the "Faerie Queen," and certain minor poems. In 1598 the Irish Rebellion took place; Spenser's castle was sacked and burned, and he and his household had to fly to England for their lives. He died in London in January 1599, in very destitute circumstances if tradition may be trusted. His only prose work (if we accept the lucubrations of "E. K.," the commentator on the "Shepherds' Calendar") was a dialogue entitled "A View of the State of Ireland," written in 1596, but not published till 1633.

Of Spenser's personal characteristics much cannot be said with certainty. It is difficult to believe that he was a happy man; he had none of Chaucer's broad geniality, and could never have described the Canterbury Pilgrims with any approach to dramatic impartiality. That he was vain is proved by the remarks on him put in the mouth of his *alter ego*, "E. K.," and it is probable that he was proud also. He was an extremely learned poet, acquainted with the best models not only in English, but in Greek, Latin, Italian, and French. His appearance is thus described by Mr. Kitchin in the Clarendon Press edition of the "Faerie Queen:" "Short curling hair, a full moustache, cut after the pattern of Lord Leicester's, close-clipped beard, heavy eyebrows, and under them thoughtful brown eyes, whose upper eyelids weigh them dreamily down; a long and straight nose, strongly developed, answering to a long and somewhat spare face, with a well-formed sensible-looking forehead; a mouth almost obscured by the moustache, but still showing rather full lips, denoting feeling, well set together, so that the warmth of feeling shall not run riot, with a touch of sadness in them—such is the look of Spenser as his portrait hands it down to us."

The "Faerie Queen" was intended to have extended to twelve books, but only six books and two cantos were written—at least that is all which has survived. Whether it is a matter for regret that the poem is incomplete may be disputed. Ardent admirers of the bard who sang of "heavenly Una and her milk-white lamb," who revel in his luxuriant descriptions and in his "linked sweetness long drawn out," who, like Christopher North, find something attractive even in such passages of his as are most repellent to the ordinary mind, may sigh when they think that half of the poetical feast which they might have enjoyed has been denied them. But it may well be doubted whether Spenser's popularity among readers in general would not have been diminished had the "Faerie Queen" extended to twelve books. Macaulay expressed the opinion of thousands when he said, "One unpardonable fault, the fault of tediousness, pervades the whole of the 'Fairy Queen.' We become sick of cardinal virtues and deadly sins, and long for the society of plain men and women. Of the persons who read the first canto not one in ten reaches the end of the first book, and not one in a hundred perseveres to the end of the poem. Very few and very weary are those who are in at the death of the Blatant Beast. If the last six books, which are said to have been destroyed in Ireland, had been preserved, we doubt whether any heart less stout than that of a commentator would have held out to the end." This extract (which proves that Macaulay, indefatigable reader though he was, had not been able to hold out to the end of the "Faerie Queen," for the Blatant Beast does not die) doubtless appears to those whose admiration of Spenser's beauties blinds them to a sense of his faults, one of the many proofs of Macaulay's deficiencies as a literary critic. Nevertheless the majority of readers will agree that in this instance Macaulay was substantially right. Books are written to be read; and surely a poem, which many who love poetry can with difficulty finish, is liable to the charge of tediousness. Now tediousness is so serious a fault that it needs many surpassing excellences to compensate for it. These excellences Spenser possesses. Perhaps no poet ever had so truly poetical a spirit—the power of viewing everything in a poetical light. "His command of imagery," writes Campbell, "is wide, easy, and luxuriant. He threw the soul of harmony into our verse, and made it more warmly, tenderly, and magnificently descriptive than it ever was before, or, with a few exceptions, than it has ever been since. It must certainly be owned that in description he exhibits nothing of the brief strokes and robust power which characterise the very greatest poets, but we shall nowhere find more airy and expansive images of visionary things, a sweeter tone of sentiment, or a finer flush in the colours of language than in this Rubens of English poetry."

If we wish fully to understand the "Faerie Queen," and to appreciate Spenser's mode of literary workmanship, we must note carefully the allegory which runs through the poem. This is no easy task, for not only are virtues and vices personified, but the personifications are made also to represent personages of Spenser's time, whom he wished to compliment or the reverse. Fortunately, however, the beauties of the poem may be felt though the allegory is disregarded, and perhaps the best advice to give to one reading Spenser for the first time is to let the allegory alone altogether. Spenser is a poet to be read leisurely: we must fully surrender ourselves to his spell before we can feel its power; and nothing is more apt to break the spell than to pause in the middle of some fine passage and endeavour to find out, either from commentators or from one's own resources, what Spenser meant to typify in the passage, and what living character, if any, was therein personified. Impatient readers, who wish for something clear and definite, must seek for it elsewhere than in the shadowy dreamland of the "Faerie Queen."

To the fastidious critics of Queen Anne's time, to whom "correctness" and good taste seemed the highest virtues of poetry, Spenser, if they read him at all, must have proved a terrible stumbling-block. Keen as was his sense of beauty, he sometimes draws pictures which, to present-day readers at any rate, are intolerably repulsive. Such are his description of Error, and, in an even higher degree, the picture of Duessa unmasked. Burke is said to have admired the former, disgusting though it be, and in his old age repeated it to Sir James Mackintosh as reminding him "of that putrid carcase, that mother of all evil, the French Revolution." That Burke should have been fond of the passage appears less singular when we remember that his own speeches are now and again stained by similar violations of good taste.

The language of the "Faerie Queen," like that of the "Shepherd's Calendar," is more archaic than that in general use at the time when it was written. The antique phraseology employed is not displeasing in a poem of the kind; perhaps upon the whole it rather adds to its attractiveness. The metre in which it is written, the "Spenserian stanza," as it is called, has been employed by so many great poets in great poems as to conclusively prove how admirably it is adapted for certain kinds of metrical effect. It is the stanza adopted by Thomson in the "Castle of Indolence;" by Burns in the "Cottar's Saturday Night;" by Campbell in "Gertrude of Wyoming;" by Scott in "Don Roderick;" by Wordsworth in the "Female Vagrant;" by Shelley in the "Revolt of Islam;" by Keats in the "Eve of St. Agnes;" and by Byron in "Childe Harold."

Spenser's patron, Sir Philip Sidney, may be taken as a typical example of all that was greatest and best among the courtiers of Queen Elizabeth. Handsome in appearance, richly cultivated in mind, a proficient in all manly exercises, of unimpeachable courage, and great skill in the management of affairs, he was regarded by the aspiring young noblemen of his time as a model whom they would do well to emulate;

while his courtesy to inferiors, his liberal benefactions, and his early and melancholy death, threw a halo around his name which even yet has not grown dim. He was born in 1554 at Penshurst, and was the son of Sir Henry Sidney, nephew of the Earl of Leicester, and of Mary Dudley, daughter of the Duke of Northumberland. Sidney is a good illustration of the axiom that the child is father of the man. From his earliest years he exerted his faculties to the utmost, striving to improve himself in every available way. He never seems to have been a boy. His friend, Fulke Greville, who was with him at Shrewsbury School, tells us that though he knew him from a child, he never knew him other than a man, with such staidness of mind, lovely and familiar gravity, as earned grace and reverence above greater years. He goes on to say that Sidney's talk was ever of knowledge, and his very play tending to enrich his mind, so that even his teachers found something in him to admire and learn above what they usually read and taught. It must not be supposed from this that Sidney was a mere plodding bookworm, buried in his studies, and with all the freshness and elasticity of youth crushed out of him. On the contrary, he cultivated his body as carefully as his mind, and attained high excellence in all the athletic sports which then prevailed. Spenser describes him as—

> "In wrestling nimble, and in running swift;
> In shooting steady, and in swimming strong;
> Well made to strike, to throw, to leap, to lift,
> And all the sports that shepherds are among.
> In every one he vanquished every one,
> He vanquished all, and vanquished was of none."

From Shrewsbury Sidney proceeded to Oxford, which he quitted at the age of seventeen to undertake a prolonged tour on the Continent. He visited Paris, where he was during the terrible massacre of St. Bartholomew, the horrors of which no doubt did something to confirm him in his strongly Protestant principles, and afterwards went to Frankfort, Vienna, Padua, and other places. Everywhere his accomplishments and courtesy made him sure of a kind reception; and he formed a close friendship with some of the most eminent men of the Continent. On his return to England in 1575, he was received with enthusiasm at Court, and won the favour of Queen Elizabeth, who was pleased to address him as "her Philip." In 1577 he was employed on a diplomatic mission, in which he acquitted himself so well as to excite the admiration of William the Silent, who pronounced him one of the ripest and greatest counsellors of state in Europe. On his return to England, Sidney for eight years devoted himself mainly to literary pursuits, associating with men of letters, who found in him a bountiful patron, and writing his "Sonnets," the "Arcadia," and the "Apologie for Poetry." He did not neglect politics altogether, however, although he held no public appointment; on the contrary, he actively exerted himself in endeavouring to provide measures in defence of the Protestant religion and to thwart the power of Spain. In 1585 came the crowning event of his life. He was sent to the Netherlands as Governor of Flushing along with an army under Leicester. There he soon distinguished himself by his valour and his prudence, but his bright career was destined to be a brief one. In October 1586, at a skirmish at Zutphen he received a mortal wound. As he rode from the battle-field occurred the touching incident which has done more than either his writings or his contemporary fame to keep Sidney's memory alive. "Being thirsty with excess of bleeding, he called for drink, which was presently brought him; but as he was putting the bottle to his mouth, he saw a poor soldier carried along, who had eaten his last at the same feast, ghastly, casting up his eyes at the bottle, which Sir Philip perceiving, took it from his head before he drunk and delivered it to the poor man with these words, 'Thy necessity is greater than mine.'"

None of Sidney's works were printed in his lifetime, though, as he was well known to be an author, writings of his were probably rather extensively handed about in manuscript. His most famous work is the "Arcadia," written in 1580, and dedicated to "Sidney's sister, Pembroke's mother," the illustrious Countess of Pembroke. It was not published till 1590. It is a pastoral romance, "containing discourses on the affections, passions, and events of life, observations on human nature, and the social and political relations of men, and all the deductions which a richly endowed and cultivated mind had drawn from actual experience." Such is an admirer's view of the "Arcadia." Hear now what Hazlitt, who never did a thing by halves, says of it: "It is to me one of the greatest monuments of the abuse of intellectual power upon record. It puts one in mind of the court dresses and preposterous fashions of the time, which are grown obsolete and disgusting. It is not romantic, but scholastic; not poetry, but casuistry; not nature, but art, and the worst sort of art, which thinks it can do better than nature. . . . In a word, and not to speak it profanely, the 'Arcadia' is a riddle, a rebus, an acrostic in folio; it contains about 4000 far-fetched similes, and 6000 impracticable dilemmas, about 10,000 reasons for doing nothing at all, and as many against it; numberless alliterations, puns, questions, and commands, and other figures of rhetoric; about a score good passages, that one may turn to with pleasure, and the most involved, irksome, unprogressive, and heteroclite subject that ever was chosen to exercise the pen or the patience of man." This is half-humorous exaggeration, but it must be confessed that the "Arcadia," though full of sweetness and gentle feeling, is tedious, and not likely to be ever much read, except in extracts. The "Apologie for Poetry," written, it is supposed, in 1581, and printed in 1595, is valuable both for its intrinsic merits and as an indication of the literary taste of the period. It is Spenser's best work in literature, and shows that he had a fine natural taste in poetry, and possessed a high degree of skill in warding off the objections of opponents.

Sidney was a considerable poet, but he was not a great one. Like Spenser's friend, Gabriel Harvey, he was very fond of trying to introduce new metres, particularly Greek and Latin ones, into the English language; but his efforts in this way do not call for much praise beyond what may be due to their ingenuity. The "Astrophel and Stella" sonnets, his most famous poems, were first published, perhaps surreptitiously, in

1591. Astrophel represents Sidney; Stella, Lady Penelope Devereux, sister of the Earl of Essex, whom he had loved and was to marry. The match, however, was broken off, and "Stella" married Lord Rich, a brutal and ignorant man, from whom she was afterwards divorced. Sidney's sonnets, which were addressed to her after her marriage, show cultivated taste and refinement of expression, and more impassioned emotion and deep personal feeling than is generally found in the love sonnets of that age, which were often written rather to exhibit the writer's talent than to express his love. One of the finest of Sidney's sonnets is the following, which would deserve to be called perfect were it not for the awkward transposition in the last line:—

"With how sad steps, O Moon, thou climb'st the skies!
How silently, and with how wan a face!
What! may it be that even in heavenly place
That busy archer his sharp arrows tries?
Sure, if that long-with-love-acquainted eyes
Can judge of love, thou feel'st a lover's case;
I read it in thy looks; thy languisht grace
To me, that feel the like, thy state descries.
Then, even of fellowship, O Moon, tell me
Is constant love deem'd there but lack of wit?
Are beauties there as proud as here they be?
Do they above love to be loved, and yet
Those lovers scorn whom that love doth possess?
Do they call *virtue* there—*ungratefulness*."[1]

Sidney's prose is distinctly superior to that of any preceding writer: it is clear, copious, and easy, containing few obsolete words; but it is frequently languid and diffuse, and wants the great quality of strength. The full resources of the English language as an instrument of prose composition were first distinctly shown by Richard Hooker, the "judicious Hooker," as he is called. Like many other great men, Hooker has suffered from the panegyrics of rash admirers. "So stately and graceful is the march of his periods," said Hallam, "so various the fall of his musical cadences upon the ear, so rich in images, so condensed in sentences, so grave and noble his diction, so

[1] Meaning, "Do they call ungratefulness virtue there."

little is there of vulgarity in his racy idiom, of pedantry in his learned phrases, that I know not whether any later writer has more admirably displayed the capacities of our language, or produced passages more worthy of comparison with the splendid monuments of antiquity." Hallam was not apt to sin on the side of over-praise, but here he undoubtedly does so, and thus, perhaps, has been the means of causing some writers to err on the opposite side. John Austin, no mean judge, spoke of the first book of the "Ecclesiastical Polity" as "fustian." The truth, as is usual in such cases, lies between the two extremes. Hooker's style is undoubtedly heavy, but it is also stately and powerful; he is no safe model for a student of English composition to follow, as his sentences are formed too exclusively upon Latin models, but the sonorousness and dignity of many of his periods will always give him a high place in literature.

The story of Hooker's life has been related by Isaac Walton with his usual quaint felicity. He was born at Heavitree, near Exeter, in 1553. His parents were poor, but Hooker's industry and talents early attracted the attention of his schoolmaster, who persuaded them to use every effort to give the promising boy a liberal education. "The good schoolmaster," as Walton calls him, also applied to a rich uncle of Hooker's to do something for his relative. The application was so far successful. The uncle spoke about the lad to Jewel, Bishop of Salisbury, who, after examining the youthful prodigy, "gave his schoolmaster a reward, and took order for an annual pension for the boy's parents, promising also to take him under his care for a future preferment." This promise he fulfilled by sending him to Oxford in 1567, and specially recommending him to the care of Dr. Cole, the President of Corpus Christi College. In 1571 Hooker lost his patron, but his fortunes were not impaired thereby, for Dr. Cole promised to see that he should not want; and nine months later he was appointed tutor to Edwin Sandys, son of the Bishop of London, who had heard Hooker warmly praised by Jewel. Soon after George Cranmer (nephew's son to the Archbishop) and other pupils came under his care.

In 1577 Hooker became a Fellow of his College, and two years later was appointed to read the public Hebrew lecture in the University. The period of his residence at Oxford was probably the happiest of his life. The quiet, regular life of a Fellow was well adapted to one of his retiring disposition; he had ample opportunities of gratifying to the full his love of study; and he could enjoy the company of men of similar tastes to himself. But less happy days were at hand. He took orders in 1581, and in the same year was appointed to preach one of the sermons at Paul's Cross in London. This visit of Hooker's to London is a striking instance of important results arising from trivial causes. He arrived at London very tired, and afraid that he would not be able to preach, but the careful attentions of the woman in whose house he lodged restored him, and he was able to perform his duty. Seeing that his constitution was feeble, the woman persuaded him that he ought to marry a wife who would attend to his comforts. He assented, and asked her to find him such a wife. She provided for him her daughter Joan, "who had neither beauty nor portion," and who proved lacking in the yet more essential qualities of good temper and love to her husband. After his marriage, Hooker settled with his wife in the living of Drayton-Beauchamp, near Aylesbury, where for about a year he led a very miserable life, owing to the shrewishness of his wife, who tyrannised over her meek-spirited husband in the most merciless manner. While in this wretched situation he was visited by his old pupils Sandys and Cranmer. The former, pitying his distress, spoke about it to his father, then Archbishop of York, at whose recommendation Hooker was in 1585 appointed Master of the Temple. In his new office Hooker found another source of vexation. The afternoon lecturer at the Temple, Walter Travers, defended the Presbyterian form of Church government, Hooker defended Episcopacy; so that, as Hooker preached in the forenoon and Travers in the afternoon, "the pulpit spoke pure Canterbury in the morning and Geneva in the afternoon." From verbal controversy the advocates of the opposing systems proceeded to a paper war, of which Hooker soon became heartily tired, and wrote to the Archbishop of Canterbury, asking to be removed to some quiet place in the country. His request was granted, and in 1591 he obtained the living of Buscombe, near Salisbury. There he elaborated the first four books of his "Ecclesiastical Polity," which were published in 1594. In the following year he removed to the living of Bishopsgate, near Canterbury, where he died in 1600. The fifth book of the "Ecclesiastical Polity" was published in 1597, the three remaining books being issued posthumously. The latter were suspected by some to have been tampered with by the Presbyterians, but there is no certain evidence of this.

Walton has given a graphic description of Hooker's appearance and disposition: "An obscure harmless man; a man in poor clothes, his loins usually girt in a coarse gown or canonical coat; of a mean stature and stooping, and yet more lowly in the thoughts of his soul: his body worn out, not with age, but study and holy mortifications; his face full of heat pimples, begot by his unactivity and sedentary life. And to this true characteristic of his person let me add this of his disposition and behaviour: God and nature blessed him with so blessed a bashfulness, that as in his younger days his pupils might easily look him out of countenance, so neither then, nor in his age, did he ever willingly look any man in the face: and was of so mild and humble a nature, that his poor parish-clerk and he did never talk but with both their hats on, or both off, at the same time: and to this may be added, that though he was not purblind, yet he was short or weak-sighted; and where he fixed his eyes at the beginning of the sermon, there they continued till it was ended." The circumstances of his marriage alone would suffice to prove that Hooker was not a man of much worldly wisdom, and that he was ill fitted for an active life. From Walton's account we gather that he was a timorous, sickly man, finding his only pleasure in study, and content to be "put upon" by any one. It is seldom that men of this kind are distinguished by remarkable talents; Hooker's genius and eloquence as a writer contrast strangely with his feebleness and incapacity in the ordinary affairs of life.

The object of the "Ecclesiastical Polity" is to defend the Episcopalian form of Church government. This is done without any partisan heat, with far-reaching scholarship, and with a studious desire to do justice to opponents. The sonorous roll of the sentences is well adapted to the dignity of the subject, and makes the work attractive to many who care little for the arguments it contains, but who read it for purely literary reasons. It is very seldom that a work of controversial theology (for so Hooker's may be called) can, like the "Ecclesiastical Polity," claim a permanent place in literature. Such works may be interesting to the historian of the history of opinion or to the theological student, but they are "caviare to the general."

Sir Walter Raleigh (1552–1618), one of those dashing, adventurous courtiers who surrounded the throne of Elizabeth, and who by their half-exploring, half-piratical voyages did much to make the name of England terrible on the seas and to advance its prosperity, found time, in the course of his chequered career, to acquire a rich store of book knowledge and to cultivate his naturally fine literary taste. If he had devoted a larger portion of his time to literature, and had chosen themes of more enduring interest, he would probably have occupied a place next to Hooker as the greatest prose-writer of the Elizabethan era. Raleigh's principal work is his "History of the World," composed during his long imprisonment in the Tower by King James. Though only a fragment, it is a gigantic fragment, comprising the history of the world from the creation to about a century and a half before the birth of Christ, a period of nearly four thousand years. A considerable part of the work is rather theological and philosophical than historical, dealing with such topics as the being and attributes of God, the origin of government, the personages of Scripture as compared with the personages of heathen mythology, &c. The finest passage by far in the work is the conclusion :—

"It is therefore death alone that can suddenly make man to know himself. He tells the proud and insolent that they are but abjects, and humbles them at the instant; makes them cry, complain, and repent; yea, even to hate their forepassed happiness. He takes the account of the rich, and proves him a beggar; a naked beggar that hath interest in nothing but in the gravel that fills his mouth. He holds a glass before the eyes of the most beautiful, and makes them see therein their deformity and rottenness, and they acknowledge it.

"O eloquent, just, and mighty Death! whom none could advise, thou hast persuaded; what none hath dared, thou hast done; and whom all the world hath flattered, thou only hast cast out of the world and despised: thou hast drawn together all the far-stretched greatness, all the pride, cruelty, and ambition of man, and covered it all over with those two narrow words, *Hic jacet.*"

This magnificent apostrophe to death has been universally admired; but his disappointment would be great who began to read the "History of the World" expecting to find it all of the same texture as this familiar passage. A great proportion of it is bald and dry enough. Raleigh's other chief works are his "Discovery of the Large, Rich, and Beautiful Empire of Guiana," and his "Advice to his Son." The former, which contains passages showing considerable descriptive power, was very unjustly described by Hume as "full of the grossest and most palpable lies that were ever attempted to be imposed on the credulity of mankind." Hume ought to have observed that all the more marvellous particulars are related by Raleigh solely upon the authority of Spanish writers. The character of Raleigh's "Advice to his Son" was very well given by Carlyle: "Worldly wise, sharp, far-seeing. The motto, 'Nothing like getting on.'"

The last prose-writer of the Elizabethan era that we shall mention deserves notice rather, perhaps, as a curious literary phenomenon than on account of his instrinsic merits. John Lyly (1554–1606), "the only rare poet of that time, the witty, comical, facetiously quick and unparalleled," as he was described, adopted, by the publication of his "Euphues, the Anatomy of Wit" (1579), a species of writing which at once found favour among fashionable circles, who loved elaborate phraseology and playing upon words. The first part was followed in 1580 by a second, called "Euphues and his England." The work describes the travels of Euphues, a young Athenian, first in Naples and afterwards in England, and contains discourses on education, friendship, love, and such-like subjects. In many ways it is a pleasing book: "as brave, righteous, and pious a book," said Charles Kingsley, "as any man need desire to look into." But it is also full of affectation; sense is sacrificed to sound, similitudes and parallels of all sorts are lugged in whether or not they are relevant to the matter in hand. Alluding to Lyly's use of comparisons ransacked from every quarter, Drayton compliments Sidney as the author that

> "Did first reduce
> Our tongue from Lyly's writing, then in use;
> Talking of stones, stars, plants, of fishes, flies,
> Playing with words and idle similes,
> As the English apes and very zanies be
> Of everything that they do hear or see."

Like More's "Utopia," Lyly's "Euphues" gave a new word to the language. "Euphuism," by which is generally meant an affected mode of writing, full of verbal ingenuities, forced comparisons, and painful elaboration of style, was common among the court circles of Elizabeth's time, having, it is thought, been imported from Italy by travelled scholars.[1] Lyly can scarcely claim to have originated the style; he merely gave it literary form, and linked it to matter of considerable permanent value. Euphuism was ridiculed by Shakespeare in "Love's Labour's Lost," in which he good-humouredly laughs at the affected love-phraseology then current; and Scott, in his character of Sir Piercie Shafton, endeavoured to reproduce the forgotten dialect, with, however, very slender success.

Besides his prose works, Lyly wrote several plays, being, indeed, one of the most distinguished of the pre-Shakespearean group of dramatists. As in Greece, so in England, the drama

[1] According to Professor F. Landmann, in his essay "Euphuismus" (Giessen, 1880), Euphuism was simply an adaptation of the *alto estilo* of Guevara, a Spanish writer, all of whose books were translated in English in Queen Elizabeth's time; and Lyly adapted his "Euphues" from Guevara.

had its origin in religion. During the fourteenth and fifteenth centuries, Miracle plays and Mysteries afforded one of the favourite entertainments of the common people. "Miracle plays, in the strict sense of the term, were dramatic representations of miracles performed by saints; Mysteries of incidents from the New Testament and elsewhere, bearing upon the fundamental principles of Roman Catholicism." The distinction, however, was not strictly observed. Monks were the authors of these plays, and they were acted "in the churches, or on stages erected in the churchyard or in the fields, or, as at Coventry, on movable stages wheeled from street to street." The actors were sometimes the brethren of a monastery, sometimes the members of a trade guild. Though Miracle plays were no doubt written with a moral purpose, we often find that in their desire to be amusing and instructive at the same time, the writers of them permitted the amusing element to overbalance the instructive one. The liberty often taken with Scriptural personages for the sake of comic effect, and the frequent buffoonery and ribaldry found in the plays, strange though they seem to modern readers, were no doubt eminently attractive to the rude crowd that witnessed the performances; but they can scarcely have tended to its edification or improvement. "So far," writes Professor Minto, "from helping to make demons more terrible, the Mysteries embodied the hideous ideals of the popular imagination, and raised temporary laughter by making them ridiculous—treated them for the time being as so much ludicrous capital. If superstitious fears had been absolutely bodiless before then —if the Mysteries had been the means of clothing the devil in popular imagination with claws, hoofs, horns, and tail—it might have been argued that they did add to the dreadful attributes of his fallen majesty. And even as it is, it may reasonably be maintained that the actual representation of the hideous being had a permanent effect of terror. I am inclined, however, to believe that the Mysteries left the fear of the devil where they found it, and simply provided the vulgar with a good day's sport."

From the Miracle play it was an easy transition to the Morality, in which the characters were personified virtues and vices, such as Folly, Repentance, Avarice, &c. By degrees the vices and virtues came to be represented by persons who stood for a type of these, Brutus representing Patriotism, Aristides, Justice, and so on. Plays of this description and Moralities were largely taken advantage of by both Catholics and Protestants to enforce their several views. It is obvious that it is only a single step from Moralities in their latter form to the regular drama; though whether the true modern drama arose out of them or from the Latin classical drama may be doubted. At any rate, the first English comedy was written by a classical scholar, who found his model in Terence, and owed nothing to the writers of Moralities. Nicholas Udall, sometime headmaster of Eton, and renowned for the thorough manner in which he had laid to heart Solomon's maxim about sparing the rod and spoiling the child, was its author. It is called "Ralph Roister Doister," and was first printed in 1566, but is known to have been written several years previously. Divided into acts and scenes, and furnished with a regular plot, it marks a great advance upon the plays which had hitherto gratified the thirst of the people for dramatic representation. It is written in rough verse, and is pervaded by a sort of schoolboy fun, which would seem to suggest that it was originally written for representation by the author's pupils. The first English tragedy, "Gorboduc," mainly the work of Thomas Sackville, was represented in 1562. It, too, is framed upon classical models. In literary merit it is superior to "Ralph Roister Doister;" its blank verse is grave and weighty, and of considerable poetical merit; but it is difficult to believe that it could ever have been popular as an acting play; the unmerciful length at which many of the characters speak alone must have been a severe trial to the strength of the actors and the patience of the auditors.

We now come to those who laid the foundations of the modern stage. Of these, the ingenious author of "Euphues" was the first. He was the author of no fewer than nine pieces, all of which show his peculiar vein of talent : his often happy verbal ingenuities, his love of punning (in which he found a frequent imitator in Shakespeare), and his occasional grace and tenderness of fancy. But Lyly was not a great writer: no one need read his plays who does not wish to make a special study of the Elizabethan drama, and it is not, therefore, requisite that we should go into detail regarding his productions. The first of Shakespeare's predecessors who possessed really great dramatic and poetical genius was Christopher Marlowe. Like too many of his contemporary playwrights, he lived a wild, reckless, dissolute life, at one time indulging in gross debauchery, at another time writing plays which, though disfigured sometimes by mere bombast, bear on them the imperishable stamp of genius. He was born at Canterbury in 1564. His father followed the humble calling of a shoemaker, but, perhaps owing to the liberality of some wealthy relation, Marlowe received a liberal education, graduating M.A. at Cambridge in 1587. Some three years before this date he is supposed to have come to London and commenced his career as a writer for the stage. None of his plays were printed in his lifetime, and their order of production can only be conjectured. "Tamburlaine the Great" is believed to have been the first; then came "Doctor Faustus," "Jew of Malta," "Edward II.," and "Massacre at Paris." In 1593 he lost his life in a wretched tavern brawl. Had he lived longer, it is very probable that he would have been the greatest of the Elizabethan dramatists, next to Shakespeare. As the hot ferments of youth subsided, his genius would have become more temperate, and his rich prodigality of fancy would have been turned into more profitable channels than the piling up of high-sounding words, too often signifying nothing.

In Marlowe's plays we find all the wantonness of imagination, all the colossal rant, all the prodigality of fancy, characteristic of a hot and fevered youth unrestrained by law, and of a mind ill at ease yet conscious of and aspiring after better things. "There is a lust of power in his writings," writes Hazlitt, "a hunger and thirst after unrighteousness, a glow of the imagination, unhallowed by anything but its own energies. His thoughts burn within him like a furnace with bickering flames, or throwing out black smoke and mists that hide the dawn of genius, or, like a poisonous mineral, corrode the heart." In many respects he resembles Byron: both lived wild and passionate lives; both possessed an energy and strength which cover a multitude of literary sins; both died young, just as they seemed on the eve of accomplishing better things. Marlowe's finest play is "Doctor Faustus," founded on the legend which also gave birth to the greatest work of the greatest modern poet, Goethe's "Faust." Nothing could well be imagined more different than the treatment by these two great dramatists of the same subject. In Goethe's play we find the genius of a great poet united with the wisdom, the self-restraint, the knowledge of the world possessed by a clear, cold, elaborately cultivated mind; in Marlowe's we find also the genius of a great poet, but disfigured by the want of self-restraint, the extravagance and the turbulence of a fiery and ill-regulated mind. But the general conception of his work is very powerful and striking, and passages of great beauty occur not unfrequently. Take, for example, the following, which we make bold to say has been matched by none of the Elizabethan dramatists save Shakespeare. It is the address of Faustus to the apparition of Helen—

"*Faustus.* Was this the face that launch'd a thousand ships,
And burnt the topless tow'rs of Ilium?
Sweet Helen, make me immortal with a kiss.
Her lips suck forth my soul! See where it flies.
Come, Helen, come, give me my soul again.
Here will I dwell, for Heav'n is in these lips,
And all is dross that is not Helena.
I will be Paris, and for love of thee,
Instead of Troy shall Wittenberg be sack'd;
And I will combat with weak Menelaus,
And wear thy colours on my plumed crest;
Yea, I will wound Achilles in the heel,
And then return to Helen for a kiss.
—Oh! thou art fairer than the evening air,
Clad in the beauty of a thousand stars:

> Brighter art thou than flaming Jupiter
> When he appear'd to hapless Semele;
> More lovely than the monarch of the sky
> In wanton Arethusa's azure arms;
> And none but thou shall be my paramour."

If Marlowe was dissipated, Greene and Peele, the two other most famous pre-Shakespearean dramatists, were yet more so. Greene, born at Norwich about 1560, was, like Marlowe, a Cambridge man, graduating M.A. at Clare Hall in 1583. He then travelled in Spain, Italy, Germany, and other countries of the Continent. From his own account he did not benefit by his tour, for he tells us that he acquired in Italy luxurious, profligate, and abominable habits. Settling in London, he became "an author of plays and a penner of love pamphlets." He was also an actor, and indeed appears to have been ready to turn his hand to anything in order that he might acquire the wherewithal to gratify his vicious desires. He died in 1592, in the most abject poverty, in the house of a poor shoemaker, who had pity on him, and took him in and nursed him. Before his death he seems to have sincerely repented of his sins, and wrote two pamphlets, "A Groatsworth of Wit bought with a Million of Repentance" and the "Repentance of Robert Greene," setting them forth. The former we shall have occasion to refer to in dealing with Shakespeare. His last letter was to his wife, whom he had deserted for six years: "Doll, I charge thee by the love of our youth and my soul's rest that you will see this man paid; for if he and his wife had not succoured me I had died in the streets.—ROBERT GREENE." Greene's best productions are the lyrics interspersed through his works, which show a fine ear for verse and a delight in beauty and innocence strange to find in a man of his character. One of his tales, "Dorastus and Fawnia," supplied the plot for Shakespeare's "Winter's Tale."

George Peele, a gentleman by birth, was born in Devonshire in 1558. He graduated M.A. at Oxford in 1579, and went to London in 1581. There, as was very common in those days, he united the occupations of poet, dramatist, and actor. He seems to have been a shifty, unscrupulous man, "without the faintest desire to use honest means in procuring a livelihood," always anxious to get his purse filled, and caring little or nothing by what means he did so. His best work is "The Arraignment of Paris," full of sprightly wit. He died about 1592.

Passing over the other dramatists who flourished about the time when Shakespeare came to London, we come to Shakespeare himself, the greatest writer the world has ever seen, or is ever likely to see. Of his personal history we know little compared to what we should like to know; yet the laborious accumulation of small facts, and the patient sifting of the traditions regarding him, have furnished us with information sufficient to enable us to judge with some degree of accuracy. We know, or at least we have some degree of certainty, that his youth was wild and passionate; that his marriage was not a very happy one; that when the ferments of youth had subsided he became prudent and industrious; that his manners were amiable and his conversational powers great; that he was rather looked down upon by college-bred contemporaries as having "small Latin and less Greek;" that he frequently felt bitterly the hardships and indignities of an actor's career; that he shared to the full the ordinary English dislike of being cheated of anything which was his due; that he was careless of literary fame; that his chief ambition, like Sir Walter Scott's, was to be the founder of a family; that he spent the closing years of his life in happiness and prosperity; and that before his death he had come to be generally recognised as the greatest living writer. We know, too, from his portraits, that he was an eminently handsome man, with a sweet serene face, full of intellect, yet also full of gentleness and kindliness. The bare facts of his life, when disinterred from the mounds of conjecture and disputation in which successive commentators have buried them, are soon told.

William Shakespeare was born at Stratford-on-Avon on or about April 23, 1564. His father, John Shakespeare, was a prosperous burgess there, carrying on business as a glover, and engaged also, it would seem, in corn-dealing or farming. His mother, Mary Arden, whom his father had married in 1557, was the daughter of a substantial yeoman in the neighbourhood, at whose death she became heiress to a small farm called Ashbies. William, the third child and eldest son of his parents, was, in all probability, educated at the Free Grammar School of Stratford, where he acquired the "small Latin and less Greek" Ben Jonson speaks about, and where doubtless he was a prominent figure in all schoolboy sports and amusements. At the earliest date at which Shakespeare could have entered the school—his seventh year—his father had attained the summit of municipal ambition by being appointed chief alderman. For some six or seven years after this John Shakespeare continued prosperous, but about 1577 his fortunes began to decline. In that year half his borough taxes were remitted; in 1578 his wife's property of Ashbies was mortgaged; in 1579 he was returned as a defaulter for not paying a certain tax. Bad luck steadily pursued him for many years; in 1592 he was set down in a list of those who did not come to church through fear of "process for debt." Owing to his father's pecuniary difficulties Shakespeare was, it is likely, withdrawn from school about his fourteenth year. What occupation he engaged in after he left school affords matter for boundless conjecture, as nothing certain is known about it. One tradition says that he became a schoolmaster; another that he was bound apprentice to a butcher; another that he entered a lawyer's office. The last hypothesis was strongly advocated by Lord Campbell, with whom Mr. Furnivall agrees. "That he was so at one time of his life," writes Mr. Furnivall, "I, as a lawyer, have no doubt. Of the details of no profession does he show such an intimate acquaintance as he does of law. The other books in imitation of Lord Campbell's prove it to any one who knows enough law to be able to judge. They are just jokes; and Shakespeare's knowledge of insanity was not got in a doctor's shop, though his law was (I believe) in a lawyer's office." But, as has often been said, the difficulties in which his father was involved must have early given Shakespeare an unfortunate experience of legal documents, and a clever boy under such circumstances would not be long in picking up and knowing the meaning of many terms of the law.

In 1582 occurred a very important event in Shakespeare's life—his marriage. His marriage bond to Anne Hathaway, daughter of a yeoman who lived near Stratford, is dated November 28, 1582, and their first child, Susanna, was born on May 26 of the following year—significant facts. Anne was eight years older than her husband, and their union does not seem to have been so happy as to afford any contradiction to the popular opinion that it is a foolish thing for a youth to marry a woman much older than himself. The facts of Shakespeare's life, and incidental allusions scattered through his works, alike go far to prove that his married life was not one of unbroken sunshine. It is difficult to believe that Shakespeare was not thinking of his own experience when he put in the mouth of the Duke in "Twelfth Night" the words—

> ". . . Let still the woman take
> An elder than herself; so wears she to him,
> So sways she level in her husband's heart.
> For, boy, however we do praise ourselves,
> Our fancies are more giddy and unfirm,
> More longing, wavering, sooner lost and worn,
> Than women's are."

About 1586 Shakespeare left his wife and family, increased by the birth of twins in 1585, and went up to London to seek his fortune. The immediate cause of his leaving Stratford is thus related by his first biographer, Rowe:—"He had, by a misfortune common enough to young fellows, fallen into ill company; and, amongst them, some that made a frequent practice of deer-stealing, engaged him more than once in robbing a park that belonged to Sir Thomas Lucy, of Charlecote, near Stratford. For this he was prosecuted by that gentleman, as he thought, somewhat too severely, and in order to avenge the ill-usage, he made a ballad upon him. And though this, probably the first essay of his poetry, be lost, yet it is said to have been so very bitter, that it redoubled the prosecution against him to that degree, that he was obliged to leave his business and family in

Warwickshire for some time and shelter himself in London." In this tradition there is very likely a basis of truth, though the details are not to be depended on. It is supposed that Shakespeare went up to London with a company of players. From his sixth year he had been familiar enough with the representation of plays, for the Queen's company, Lord Leicester's company, Lord Worcester's company, and others, had performed at Stratford. Whether he took to the stage because he had a strong natural bent to it, or because it afforded him the readiest means for earning a livelihood, it is impossible to say.

A London theatre was then a very different place from what it is now. Modern theatrical managers would save thousands of pounds if audiences were content to put up with as meagre scenery and as uncomfortable accommodation as satisfied the Londoners who listened to Shakespeare's plays or saw the great dramatist act. The first theatre in London was not erected till 1576. Until that time actors had been content to give their performances in inn-yards or any other suitable place that offered. After 1576 other theatres sprung up, but they were all very comfortless edifices, judged according to modern ideas. The following description of an Elizabethan theatre and its surroundings gives a sufficiently accurate notion of how plays were represented in the golden age of the English drama :—

"The building itself was a large circular edifice of wood, on the top of which a flag was hung out during the time of performance. The pit or yard was open to the sky (excepting in the private and winter theatres, which were enclosed), but galleries, with boxes beneath them, ran round the building, and these with the stage were roofed in. The wits, critics, and gallants were allowed to sit or recline at length on the rushes with which the stage was strewed, while their pages handed them pipes and tobacco ; and the audience generally, as in the tavern-theatres and singing saloons of our own day, enhanced the enjoyment of the intellectual pleasures of dramatic representation by the physical solaces of smoking, drinking ale, and eating nuts and apples. The performances commenced at three o'clock in the afternoon. Movable scenery was unknown till after the Restoration,[1] when it was introduced by Sir William Davenant, but curtains called *traverses* were drawn across when required, and the stage was hung with coarse tapestry. To point out the place or scene in which the events of the play were supposed to take place, a board, painted or written in large letters, was hung prominently forward; and a few chairs and tables, a couch, a rude imitation of a tomb, an altar, a tree, or a tower, constituted the theatrical 'properties.' A sort of balcony at the back of the stage served to represent a raised terrace or the platform of a castle, on which, in particular scenes, the characters in the play might be understood to be walking. Much, therefore, had necessarily to be left to the imagination of the spectators; but there can be no doubt, as Mr. Collier remarks, that to this very poverty of stage appliances we are indebted for many noble passages in the works of our earlier dramatists, who found themselves called on to supply, by glowing and graphic description, what in aftertimes was more commonly left to the touch of the scene-painter. In the department, however, of stage costume, the managers of the theatres in the time of Elizabeth displayed great magnificence and expended large sums. The actor who spoke the prologue, entering after the third sounding of the trumpet, usually wore a cloak of black velvet, and we hear of twenty pounds, an immense sum in those days, being occasionally given for a splendid mantle. When tragedies were performed, the stage was sometimes hung with black and covered with matting. Music, singing, and dancing relieved the pauses between the acts; the clown was allowed great latitude in the way of extemporary buffoonery to amuse the 'groundlings,' as the audience in the pit was termed; and at the close of the piece he delivered a rhyming rhapsody, called a *jig*, composed with reference to the popular topics of the day, in which he accompanied himself with the pipe and tabor, and which he occasionally varied by a dance."

[1] Actresses also appeared first on the stage after the Restoration. In the early days of the drama female parts were acted by young lads. In Charles I.'s time, women occasionally acted; but the practice was not at all common till the Restoration.

The first years of Shakespeare's life in London are shrouded in obscurity. Doubtless he had a hard struggle, and much bitter experience of the spurns which patient merit of the unworthy takes. Actors are a jealous race, and the playwrights in favour at the time would look with no kindly eye upon the young Warwickshire man, who, though deficient in scholastic learning, knew better than any of them how to delineate human life, and how to touch the springs of emotion. The earliest undoubted literary allusion to Shakespeare occurs in poor Robert Greene's "Groatsworth of Wit," published in 1592. There we read of "An upstart crow beautified with our feathers, that with his 'tiger's heart wrapt in a player's hide,'[1] supposes he is as well able to bombast out a blank verse as the best of you, and being an absolute *Johannes Factotum*, is in his own conceit the only *Shake-scene* in a country." This shows that by 1592 Shakespeare's fame had at least advanced far enough to make him an object of jealousy. Greene's pamphlet was published after his death by his executor, Henry Chettle, also a playwright. Both Marlowe and Shakespeare took offence at the allusions to them contained in it; and in his "Kind Hart's Dream," published about three months after Greene's pamphlet, Chettle made his apologies to Shakespeare. "With neither of them that take offence," he says, "was I acquainted, and with one of them [Marlowe], I care not if I never be; the other [Shakespeare], whom at that time I did not so much spare as since I wish I had, for that as I have moderated the heat of living writers, and might have used my own discretion, especially in such a case, the author being dead, that I did not I am as sorry as if the original fault had been my fault, because myself have seen his demeanour no less civil than he excellent in the quality he professes; besides, divers of worship have reported his uprightness of dealing, which argues his honesty, and his facetious grace in writing, that approves his

[1] A line from an old play, "The True Tragedy of Richard, Duke of York;" also found in the "Third Part of Henry VI.," a recast of the "True Tragedy."

art." Valuable testimony this, proving that Shakespeare was beginning to be appreciated both as a man and as an author.

In 1593 Shakespeare published the first work to which he put his name, "Venus and Adonis," a poem full of youthful passion, rich in colour, and showing an exuberant imagination and delight in country sights and sounds. It was dedicated to Henry Wriothesley, Earl of Southampton, a gallant and accomplished nobleman, well known as a patron of men of letters. To him was also dedicated the "Rape of Lucrece," published in the following year. By 1594 he is also supposed to have written several of his plays. "Titus Andronicus," "Henry VI.," Parts I., II., and III., the "Two Gentlemen of Verona," the "Comedy of Errors," "Love's Labour's Lost," "Romeo and Juliet," "Midsummer Night's Dream," "Richard II.," and "Richard III.," are conjectured to belong to about this period. Their dates cannot be assigned with any approach to certainty. Probably Shakespeare began his work by retouching old plays, as he is supposed to have done in the case of "Titus Andronicus" and the first part of "Henry VI." Certainly neither of these dramas are distinguished by such excellence as to make us desirous to prove them the work of Shakespeare alone.

From 1595 to 1601, during what is called the second period of his dramatic activity, the following plays are supposed by Mr. Furnivall to have been produced by Shakespeare :—"King John," the "Merchant of Venice," the "Taming of the Shrew" (an old play only retouched by Shakespeare), "Henry IV.," Parts I. and II., the "Merry Wives of Windsor," "Henry V.," "Much Ado About Nothing," "As You Like It," "Twelfth Night," "All's Well that Ends Well." During this period Shakespeare attained entire mastery over his art : in none of these plays do we find the slips and flaws incident to the work of a "prentice hand."

To Shakespeare's third period, extending from 1601 to 1608, belong all his great tragedies. In it are believed to have been written "Julius Cæsar," "Hamlet," "Measure for Measure," "Othello," "Macbeth," "King Lear," "Troilus and Cressida," "Antony and Cleopatra," "Coriolanus," and "Timon of

Athens." This seems to have been a gloomy period in Shakespeare's life; disgust with his profession and other troubles led him to look on the dark side of things; "the burden and the mystery" of this unintelligible world weighed heavily on him; and, perplexed by the enigmas of fate, he found relief for his overburdened soul, as so many great artists have done, by shadowing forth in the creatures of his imagination his own doubts and difficulties.

After the tempest came calm and sunshine. In the plays belonging to what is called Shakespeare's fourth period we find a sweet grave tenderness: the blessings of forgiveness and domestic love are set forth: himself escaped from turmoil and sorrow, the dramatist looks with lenient eye upon the frailty of mankind, regarding with fond sympathy their errors and shortcomings, their struggles and trials. To this period, extending from 1609 to about 1613, belong "Pericles" (only in part Shakespeare's), the "Tempest," "Cymbeline," the "Winter's Tale," and "Henry VIII.," part of which is thought to have been written by Fletcher.

We have left unnoticed the work which, from a biographical point of view, is by far the most interesting that Shakespeare ever wrote—the Sonnets. They were not published till 1609, but were probably written between 1595 and 1605. Round perhaps no book do so many literary problems centre. Almost every one who has written about Shakespeare has had some new theory regarding them. The first difficulty meets us before we begin their perusal. By Thomas Thorpe, the publisher, they were thus dedicated: "To the onlie begetter of these insuing Sonnets, Mr. W. H., all happiness, and that Eternitie promised by our ever-living poet, wisheth the well-wishing adventurer in setting forth, T. T. [Thomas Thorpe]." Now who was this Mr. W. H.? Many have been the conjectures as to this, and very likely none of them are correct, but the most probable one is that "Mr. W. H." signifies William Herbert, Earl of Pembroke. Many little facts, not very striking individually, but tolerably convincing collectively, point to this conclusion. When we look at the Sonnets themselves, we find that they fall into two divisions; the first, from 1 to 126, addressed to a man; the other, 127–154, to a woman, and indicating apparently that Shakespeare had unwisely loved and had been betrayed in his love by the friend to whom the first series of sonnets is addressed. Other divisions of the Sonnets have been suggested, but they do not seem to have any great claims to consideration. Mr. Fleay, strangely enough, supposes that the latter division of the Sonnets was addressed by Shakespeare to his wife. Professor Minto is inclined to think that they are a *tour de force*, written to show Shakespeare's contempt for the exaggerated tone adopted by the sonnet-writers of the period—an interpretation which many who admire Shakespeare would gladly accept, but which almost certainly is not correct. Of another difficulty in the Sonnets Professor Minto was the first to suggest what is now generally accepted as the true solution. In Sonnets 76–86 we find the poet complaining that his friend favours a rival writer. In Sonnet 86 he speaks of—

> ——"the proud full sail of his great verse,
> Bound for the prize of all too precious you;"

of "his spirit, by spirits taught to write above a mortal pitch," of his "compeers by night" that gave him aid, and of "that affable familiar ghost which nightly gulls him with intelligence." The rival thus spoken of was formerly supposed to be Marlowe, but there are good reasons for believing that he cannot have been meant. All who have read any of George Chapman's translation of the "Iliad" will admit that "the proud full sail of his great verse" applies admirably to its sonorous Alexandrines; and there are other indications, such as that Chapman "advanced fervent claims to supernatural inspiration" ("by spirits taught to write"), which lead to the conclusion that he was the rival poet indicated.

We know little of the tenor of Shakespeare's life while he went on producing his wonderful series of dramas. He became a partner in the profits of the Globe Theatre in 1599, and, before and after that event, worldly prosperity shone on him, as, in spite of all that is said about the caprice of fate, it generally does upon those who work diligently and are ready to take at the flood the tide that leads on to fortune. In 1596 John Shakespeare, doubtless at his son's instigation, applied at the Heralds' College for a grant of arms. In 1597 Shakespeare bought for £60 a fine house, New Place, in Stratford. In 1602 he purchased for £320 a hundred and seven acres in the parish of Old Stratford. In the same year he bought a second and smaller property. In 1605 he bought a thirty-one years' remainder of a lease of tithes in Stratford, Old Stratford, Bishopton, and Wilcombe for £440. Many other particulars indicative of his increasing wealth have been exhumed from old documents. Unlike most poets, Shakespeare seems to have attended to the maxim about taking care of the pence. No doubt his father's difficulties made him more careful about financial matters than he might otherwise have been. It is evident that he had a sharp eye for business. In 1604 he brought an action at Stratford for £1, 15s. 10d., and in 1609 he strenuously pursued for a debt of £6 and 24s. costs a certain John Addenbrooke. These are curious facts, well worth pondering by those who think that men of genius are generally fools as regards money matters.

About 1612 Shakespeare returned to his native town, "a prosperous gentleman." Rowe's account of the last years of his life may be accepted as substantially correct. "The latter part of his life was spent, as all men of good sense wish theirs may be, in ease, retirement, and the conversation of his friends. He had the good fortune to gather an estate equal to his occasions, and in that to his wish; and is said to have spent some years before his death at his native Stratford. His pleasurable wit and good nature engaged him in the acquaintance, and entitled him to the friendship, of the gentlemen of the neighbourhood." His hopes of founding a family, if he ever entertained such, had fallen to the ground by the death of his only son, Hamnet, in 1596.

Shakespeare died on April 23, 1616. Two days later his remains were deposited in the chancel of Stratford Church, where his grave is marked by a flat stone, bearing the famous inscription—

> "Good frend, for Jesus sake forbeare
> To digg the dust encloased heare:
> Blest be ye man y^t^ spares thes stones,
> And curst be he y^t^ moves my bones."

In spite of numerous temptations to the contrary, the adjuration of the epitaph has proved effectual: no sacrilegious hand has interfered with Shakespeare's "honoured dust."

Though his life in London was a successful one, we know from the Sonnets that Shakespeare often felt bitterly regarding his position as an actor. In Sonnet 110 he says—

> "Alas! 'tis true, I have gone here and there,
> And made myself a motley to the view,
> Gored mine own thoughts, sold cheap what is most dear,
> Made old affections of offences new."

Probably his desire to acquire the means of escaping from what he regarded as an irksome servitude, and to obtain "independence, that first of earthly blessings," gave many a fresh spur to his exertions to acquire a competence. Those who reproach Scott for "selling his brains for money," for writing hastily in order to amass a fortune, often forget that Shakespeare is liable to a precisely similar reproach, if reproach it be, which we do not think it is. In not a few respects indeed a curious parallel might be drawn between Scott and Shakespeare. Both cared little for fame: Shakespeare allowed some of his best plays to appear in pirated editions, regardless what might be their eventual fate. Both were men of genial, kindly disposition, conscious of their own great powers, we cannot doubt, but perhaps because of that very consciousness wisely tolerant of others, and totally free from arrogance or contempt. Both were men of great prudence, with a large fund of common sense, which would have made them prosperous and respected though they had not been men of genius. Immeasurably superior though Shakespeare is to Scott in genius and width of range, there are many points of resemblance between them in their mode of literary workmanship. Both possessed the power of depicting all classes of society with equal sympathy and equal discernment; both were equally great in describing the tragic and the comic aspects of life; both, amidst higher qualities, are full of maxims on conduct and character showing great natural shrewdness developed by wide experience of men and affairs.

It is impossible for us to enter upon any minute account of Shakespeare's plays, or to discuss the order of their appearance, the sources from which their plots are drawn, &c. To do so would require a volume, not a few pages. Neither do we propose to attempt any estimate of his genius. So much has been written on this topic, that he would be a bold writer who should attempt to say anything new regarding it. We therefore content ourselves by quoting Dryden's eulogy, one of the finest, and one of the most discerning. It appeared in his "Essay of Dramatic Poesy:"—"To begin, then, with Shakespeare. He was the man who of all modern, and perhaps ancient poets, had the largest and most comprehensive soul. All the images of nature were still present to him, and he drew them not laboriously but luckily: when he describes anything, you more than see it—you feel it too. Those who accuse him to have wanted learning give him the greater commendation: he was naturally learned; he needed not the spectacles of books to read nature; he looked inwards and found her there. I cannot say he is everywhere alike; were he so, I should do him injury to compare him with the greatest of mankind. He is many times flat, insipid; his comic wit degenerating into clenches, his serious degenerating into bombast. But he is always great when some great occasion is presented to him."

Among people who know them only by report, there is an impression that Shakespeare's contemporaries were just inferior copies of the myriad-minded dramatist; that in their works we can trace the same characteristics as we find in his. Of course it is true that they are inferior; indeed it is a case of "Eclipse first and the rest nowhere;" for great as many of the Elizabethan dramatists were, none of them approached Shakespeare's surpassing greatness. But the difference between Shakespeare and the other dramatists is not merely one of degree, it is one of kind. There is a delicacy and grace, an ethereal flavour difficult to describe but easily felt by every student, about Shakespeare which none of the others has any pretensions to. Indeed one scarcely realises fully his sovereign position till one has read some of the other great Elizabethan dramatists, such as Marlowe, Ben Jonson, and Fletcher.

Among the greater contemporaries or immediate successors of Shakespeare, George Chapman (1559–1634), already mentioned as the rival poet of the "Sonnets," occupied in his lifetime a prominent place. But his principal claim to remembrance now is his translation of the "Iliad," full of genuine Homeric fire, and still perhaps the best translation of that often-translated poem.[1] Passing over Marston, whose chief excellence consisted in passionate declamation, we come to Ben Jonson, as striking and vigorous a personality as his namesake Samuel. Ben was born in London in 1573. He was educated at Westminster School, where he was the celebrated Camden's favourite pupil, and went from it to Cambridge. Unable to find means for his support there, he returned to London, and worked as a bricklayer for about a year. Becoming tired of this uncongenial occupation, he joined the army as a volunteer in the expedition to Flanders, and in a brief campaign there greatly distinguished himself by his bravery. His first play, "Every Man in his Humour," was acted in 1596. Others speedily followed. His best comedies, "Volpone, or the Fox," and "The Alchemist," were produced in 1605 and 1610 respectively; his best tragedy, "Sejanus," in 1603. His plays were not popular, and he did not realise much money by them, but for many years he found a lucrative source of income in the preparation of masques for the Court. Ben died in 1637, after he had by his talents and his self-assertion fought his way, amidst much poverty and many trials, to a literary dictatorship; not so generally recognised, indeed, but as despotic as that held by Samuel Johnson in the eighteenth century. He was a strong-minded, vain

[1] Keats's noble sonnet "On first looking into Chapman's Homer" shows the impression made by this translation on one possessed of the finest poetic susceptibilities.

man, prone to quarrel with any one who did him a real or a fancied injury; confident in his own powers, and not too ready to recognise the powers of others. Yet, passing over one or two expressions which may be referred to a not unnatural jealousy, he was warm in his praise of Shakespeare; and, like Samuel Johnson, concealed much genuine kindliness of heart beneath a rough and self-asserting exterior. He is by far the most learned of the dramatists; indeed his plays are overlayed by the curious erudition which he was too fond of displaying. The title of his first play indicates his main fault as a dramatist. All his characters are mastered by some special tendency of the mind or *humour*. "They do not represent men and women," says Barry Cornwall, "with the medley of vices and virtues common to human nature about them, but each is the personification of some one single humour, and no more. There is no fluctuation, no variety or relief in them. His people speak with a *malice prepense*. They utter by rote what is set down for them, each one pursuing one leading idea from beginning to end, and taking his cue evidently from the prompting of the poet. They speak nothing spontaneously. The original design of each character is pursued so rigidly that, let what will happen, the one single humour is ever uppermost, always the same in point of force, the same in its mode of demonstration, instead of being operated on by circumstances, increased or weakened, hurried or delayed, or turned aside, as the case may require." Ben Jonson's finest pieces are the songs, many of them exquisite, scattered through his masques.

Literary partnerships were not uncommon among the Elizabethan dramatists. Marston, Chapman, and Ben Jonson wrote a play, "Eastward Ho," together; Shakespeare (if the surmises of critics be correct) wrote only part of "Timon" and "Henry VIII.;" but the standing examples of united authorship are Beaumont and Fletcher. Beaumont's share in the plays which bear the joint name is believed to have been small. He died in 1616, at the age of thirty. Fletcher, born in 1579, died in 1625. Both were of gentle birth. Written in the reign of James I., their plays form a transition stage to the Restoration drama. They (perhaps we should rather say Fletcher) were the founders of the comedy of intrigue, afterwards fully developed by Wycherley and Congreve. In "studious indecency" they are surpassed by none of the dramatists, which is saying a great deal.

Of John Webster, of whose life almost nothing is known, the chief works are "Vittoria Corombona," published in 1612, and the "Duchess of Malfi," published in 1623, two tragedies deeply tinged with terror and sorrow. In the delineation of characters affected by crime, misery, and remorse, he has few equals. John Ford (1586–1640), too, excelled in dealing with the darker emotions of the heart. His chief plays are "Perkin Warbeck," reckoned the best historical drama after Shakespeare, and the "Broken Heart." Philip Massinger (1584-1640) was also a man of sombre genius, but in his case it was united with considerable humorous power. His finest play, "A New Way to Pay Old Debts," has one very powerfully drawn character, Sir Giles Overreach, an incarnation of selfishness and self-will. James Shirley (1596–1667) was the last of the great race of dramatists, "all of whom," says Lamb, "spoke nearly the same language, and had a set of moral feelings and notions in common." He was not a great writer, but he was a very prolific one, having written nearly forty plays previous to 1641. In 1642 the theatres were closed, not to be reopened again till about the time of the Restoration, when a totally new species of dramatic art came into vogue.

We have left altogether unnoticed many of the Elizabethan dramatists, and have passed very lightly over most of the others. This is not because they have less literary merit than many other writers dealt with more fully in this book, but because it is nearly impossible to describe their characteristics without lengthy quotations. Excellent introductions to their study will be found in Hazlitt's "Lectures on the Literature of the Age of Elizabeth," an exceedingly brilliant, if occasionally misleading book, and in Charles Lamb's "Specimens," which was one of the first works to call attention to their beauties.

III.

THE SUCCESSORS OF THE ELIZABETHANS.

Bacon; Fuller, Jeremy Taylor, Baxter, Bunyan; Walton; Browne; Clarendon; Hobbes; Lovelace, Suckling, Herbert, Herrick; Milton; Donne, Cowley, Denham, Waller.

IN this chapter we purpose to deal with the period between the accession of James I. and the Restoration. The ground we shall have to traverse is one of the greatest interest to students of English history, full of momentous events and great constitutional changes. In literature, also, it is important. With one illustrious exception, no poet of the first order of merit flourished during this epoch; but that illustrious exception was John Milton, who, by common consent, occupies a place in the brilliant galaxy of English poets second only to that of Shakespeare. In prose writers of great excellence the period was rich. Some of these we can notice only very briefly; others we shall be obliged to omit altogether. Even amid the agitating and perilous times of the Civil War, two or three writers on religious subjects appeared, who, by the fervour of their devotional feeling or the splendour of their imperial eloquence, earned for themselves an imperishable name. Though only fifty-seven years elapsed between the beginning of the reign of James I. and the Restoration, English prose made vast progress during the interval. From a powerful but unwieldy machine, it grew to be a handy, serviceable instrument, still capable, indeed, of great improvement, but infinitely more shapely and methodical than before. The prose of Cowley and Hobbes might, so far as clearness and sentence-arrangement are concerned, have been written in our own day. Many writers, it is true, and these among the greatest, neglected the mechanical part of style; still it was gradually beginning to be much more studied than hitherto.

To this period belong most of the works of Francis Bacon, who, if we ranked authors strictly according to date of birth, would have been placed among the Elizabethans. He was born in London in 1561, the son of Sir Nicholas Bacon, Lord-Keeper of the Great Seal. When a child, his precocious sagacity so attracted Elizabeth that she "delighted much to confer with him, and to prove him with questions; unto which he delivered himself with that gravity and maturity above his years, that her Majesty would often term him 'the young Lord-Keeper.'" At the age of twelve he was sent to Cambridge, where he remained for two years and a half. Even at that early period he is said to have conceived a dislike to the philosophy of Aristotle, as "a philosophy only strong for disputations and contentions, but barren of the production of works for the benefit of man." After leaving the University he resided for more than two years in Paris, from which he was recalled by the sudden death of his father in 1579. He was left poor, and after in vain soliciting his uncle Burleigh to obtain for him some sinecure office under Government, devoted some years to the study of the law. At twenty-three he became a member of the House of Commons, where his eloquence and ability soon made his name widely known; but he was unfortunate enough to incur the resentment of Elizabeth by his opposition to her demand for a subsidy, and though he endeavoured to atone for his error in policy by servile apologies, he was never forgiven, and high offices were steadily denied him. His cause was warmly espoused by Lord Essex, whose indiscreet advocacy probably did him more harm than good. He befriended Bacon generously, however, and when, in 1594, he failed to procure for him the vacant office of Attorney-General, he consoled him for his disappointment by the present of an estate of considerable value. Bacon in vain endeavoured to persuade Essex to desist from the course of policy which ended in his execution; but there his gratitude towards his benefactor ended. When Essex was brought to trial for a conspiracy against the Queen, Bacon, as Queen's Counsel, appeared against his old friend, employing all his powers of oratory and argument to substantiate against him the charge of treason; and, after the Earl's execution, wrote, at the Queen's request, "A Declaration of the Practices and Treasons attempted and committed by the Robert, Earl of Essex." It is easy to say that Bacon in his conduct in this matter did not exceed the duties appertaining to him as Queen's Counsel, and that he could not have acted otherwise with prudence; but the fact remains that no high-minded or generous man would have done as he did. After all has been said that can be said to extenuate the part he took in this matter, it remains the great blot on his memory.

During the life of Queen Elizabeth, Bacon's efforts to advance his fortunes were constantly thwarted, but in the succeeding reign he attained the summit of his ambition. In 1603 he was knighted, in 1607 he became Solicitor-General, in 1613 Attorney-General, and in 1618 Lord Chancellor. He was also created Baron Verulam, and at a late period Viscount St. Albans. In 1621 he was charged before the House of Lords with corruption in the exercise of his office. He pleaded guilty, was deprived of the Great Seal, disqualified from holding any public office in future, fined £40,000, and condemned to imprisonment in the Tower during the King's pleasure. He was released from confinement after a single night, and his fine was commuted by the King; but his public career was for ever at an end. His guilt, rightly viewed, does not seem to have been great; if, as regards receiving gifts from successful litigants, he was no better than the majority of his contemporaries, he was no worse. He died in 1626 from the effects of a chill he had caught while making an experiment as to the preservative qualities of snow.

We have related the story of Bacon's life very briefly, partly because, in spite of the labours of the late Mr. Spedding, who devoted a lifetime of painstaking industry to its elucidation, portions of it are still matter of dispute; partly because to enter into details about his public career would have led us greatly beyond our limits. He was a little, square-shouldered, nervous-looking man, with a finely intellectual head and small features. Speaking of his powers as an orator, Ben Jonson says, "No man ever spake more neatly, more pressly, more weightily, or suffered less emptiness or less idleness in what he uttered. No member of his speech but consisted of his own graces. His hearers could not cough or look aside from him without loss. He commanded where he spoke, and had his judges angry or pleased at his devotion. No man had their affections more in his power. The fear of every man that heard him was lest he should make an end." "My conceit of his person," writes the same authority, "was never increased towards him by his place or honours; but I have and do reverence him for his greatness that was only proper to himself, in that he seemed to me ever by his work one of the greatest men, and most worthy of admiration, that had been in many ages. In his adversity I ever prayed that God would give him strength; for greatness he could not want." Ben Jonson is not an impartial witness; nevertheless what he says is sufficient to prove that Bacon was a man whose intellectual power impressed strongly those with whom he came into contact.

Of Bacon's most generally read work, the "Essays," the first edition, containing only ten, appeared in 1597. In 1612 the second edition, containing thirty-eight, appeared; and in 1625 the complete edition, containing fifty-eight, was published. There is not much room for difference of opinion regarding these productions. They contain little or nothing to gratify any high moral ideal; people who think, with John Wesley, that one of the first things a Christian ought to pray to be delivered from is prudence, will not find much in Bacon's "Essays" to please them. They are the counsels of a shrewd, politic man of the world, who has looked with eager and penetrating eye upon mankind as it appears in the senate-house, in courts of law, in the commercial world; of a man who is firmly convinced that self-interest is the actuating principle of humanity. Even when treating of themes which might have made a more enthusiastic writer rise to flights of poetry and warm human feeling, Bacon remains cold and unimpassioned. The severe terseness of the style of the "Essays," in which every sentence is packed with as much matter as it can possibly hold, makes their intelligent perusal at first a task of some difficulty; but fresh perusals reveal their inexhaustible wealth of matter,—indeed, as Dugald Stewart said, after the twentieth perusal, one seldom fails to remark in them something overlooked before.

The chief other English works of Bacon are the "Advancement of Learning;" "History of Henry VII.," a very masterly piece of work of its kind, and, as has been elaborately demonstrated, wonderfully accurate in all its leading statements; the "New Atlantis," a philosophical romance; and "Sylva Sylvarum," a treatise on natural history, which was the last work of his life. His great philosophical work, the "Novum Organum," which is written in Latin, appeared in 1620. "It would be presumptuous to attempt anything like an exact valuation of Bacon's intellectual power. We state only what lies upon the surface when we say that the character and products of intellect are very often as much over-estimated upon one side as they are under-estimated upon another. He is frequently praised as if he had originated and established the inductive method, as if he had laid down the canons appealed to in modern science as the ultimate conditions of sound induction. This is going too far. Bacon was an orator, not a worker; a Tyrtæus, not a Miltiades. He rendered a great service by urging recourse to observation and experiment rather than to speculation; but neither by precept nor by example did he show *how* to observe and experiment well, or so as to arrive at substantial conclusions. Not by precept; for if modern inductive method were no better than Bacon's inductive method, Macaulay's caricature of the process would not be so very unlike the reality. Nor by example; for the majority of his own generalisations are loose to a degree. To call Bacon the founder of scientific method is to mistake the character of his mind, and to do him an injustice by resting his fame upon a false foundation. Unwearied activity, inexhaustible constructiveness—that, and not scientific accuracy or patience, was his characteristic. He had what Peter Heylin calls "a chymical brain;" every group of facts that entered his mind he restlessly threw into new combinations. We over-estimate the man upon one side when we give him credit for scientific rigour; his contemporary, Gilbert, who wrote upon the magnet, probably had more scientific caution and accuracy than he. And we under-estimate him upon another side when we speak as if the Inductive Philosophy had been the only outcome of his ever-active brain. His projects of reform in Law were almost as vast as his projects of reform in Philosophy. In Politics he drew up opinions on every question of importance during the forty years of his public life, and was often employed by the Queen and Lord Burleigh to write papers of State. All this was done in addition to his practical work as a lawyer. And yet his multiplex labours do not seem to have used up his mental vigour; his schemes always outran human powers of performance. His ambition was not to make one great finished effort and then rest; his intellectual appetite seemed almost insatiable."[1]

Passing over many authors of less importance, we come to a writer whose genius and character were as far removed from Bacon's as it is possible to imagine. The vast intellect of "high-browed Verulam" commands our respectful admiration, but it is icy and ungenial; we cannot bring ourselves to love the man, however much we may venerate the writer. Not so with witty Thomas Fuller (1608–1661). Even now, after the lapse of more than two centuries, it is impossible for any reader of his works not to conceive a feeling approaching to affection for one so full of the milk of human kindness, so re-

[1] Professor Minto's "Manual of English Prose Literature," p. 238. A very able and careful work, showing a large amount of original labour and thought.

dolent of harmless wit, so free from any taint of malice or bitterness. He lived at a time when the venom of party-spirit permeated every section of society, breaking family ties and putting an end to the closest friendships; yet, though a staunch Royalist, and ready to suffer for the cause of the King, he remained moderate in his sentiments, and was willing to acknowledge the virtues of the Puritans. Fuller was born at Aldwinkle in Northamptonshire, where his father was Rector. At twelve years of age he was sent to Cambridge, where he took his degree of M.A. in 1628. In 1631 he was made a prebendary of Salisbury and vicar of Broad Windsor in Dorsetshire, where his first prose work, the "Holy War," was written. It was published in 1640, and had been preceded by a poem, of which nothing is now remembered but the title, which shows the love of alliteration which then prevailed. The title was, "David's Heinous Sin, Hearty Repentance, and Heavy Punishment." On the outbreak of the great Civil War, Fuller obtained a chaplaincy in the royal army, and while following the forces from place to place, employed himself in collecting materials for his "Worthies of England." During the prolonged siege of Exeter, he resumed his interrupted studies, and ministered regularly to the citizens of the besieged town. When Exeter capitulated, Fuller removed to London, where, in 1655, he received from Cromwell special permission to preach. On the Restoration he received sundry ecclesiastical honours; and his death, which occurred in 1661, happened just when he was on the eve of being appointed a bishop.

Fuller's chief works are "The Holy State" (1642), commonly bound up with "The Profane State" (1648); "Good Thoughts in Bad Times" (1644-45); "Good Thoughts in Worse Times" (1649); "Pisgah Sight of Palestine," a very quaint book on the geography of the Holy Land, illustrated with plates as amusing as the text (1650); "Abel Redivivus," a collection of lives of martyrs, and so on (1651); "Church History of Britain" (1656); "Mixed Contemplations in Better Times" (1660); and the "Worthies of England," which was published in the year after his death. There is no occasion to consider his books separately. Whatever the subject, they one and all bear the impress of the same inventive, confident, good-humoured, and pre-eminently witty mind. We read a page of his on a topic on which we look for serious treatment, and nothing but serious treatment. Suddenly we find in the middle of it some quaint conceit, some ingenious pun, which at once raises a smile if not a laugh. His wit is a perennial fountain, bubbling up continually in the most unexpected places. A few examples may be cited: "Anger kept till the next morning, with manna, doth putrify and corrupt; save that manna, corrupted not at all (and anger most of all), kept the next Sabbath. St. Paul saith, 'Let not the sun go down on your wrath,' to carry news to the antipodes in another world of thy revengeful nature. Yet let us take the apostle's meaning rather than his words, with all possible speed to depose our passion; not understanding him so literally that we may take leave to be angry till sunset; then might our wrath lengthen with the days, and men in Greenland, where day lasts above a quarter of a year, have plentiful scope of revenge." Speaking of the charity of the Jesuits, he says, "Such is the charity of the Jesuits, that they never owe any man any ill-will, making present payment thereof." "Aphek, whose walls falling down, gave both death and gravestones to 27,000 of Benhadad's soldiers." Of the celebrated Selden he remarks, "Mr. Selden had some coins of the Roman emperors, and a good many more of our English kings." Hundreds of such instances might be given. But his effervescent wit, as is perhaps generally the case, was accompanied with shrewd practical wisdom and great fertility of intellectual resource. Coleridge, with characteristic exaggeration, said, "Next to Shakespeare, I am not certain whether Thomas Fuller, beyond all other writers, does not excite in me the sense and emotion of the marvellous; the degree in which any given faculty, or combination of faculties, is possessed and manifested, so far surpassing what one would have thought possible in a single mind, as to give one's admiration the flavour or quality of wonder." Coleridge's judgments upon favourite authors must, like Charles Lamb's, be accepted with great reservations; but to the literary epicure, who loves to read books that have infused into every page of them the genius of a singular and original mind, few volumes are likely to be more attractive than the works of Thomas Fuller.

With all his many excellences, Fuller, it must be owned, never touches, even in his finest passages, the highest chords of our nature. Witty, ingenious, inventive, he was not imbued with a poetic spirit, and those who desire rich strains of devotional feelings must seek for them elsewhere. They will find them in abundance in the works of Bishop Jeremy Taylor, whose writings, though marred by very complicated sentence-arrangement and unpruned luxuriance of imagination, still rank among the best religious classics in our language. On the whole, he was the greatest prose writer of his time, and, as was said above, the period was rich in prose writers of great excellence. Taylor was born in 1613 at Cambridge, at which University he received his education. Taken under the patronage of Archbishop Laud, who had been greatly impressed by his eloquence, he was, at the age of twenty, placed at All Souls' College, Oxford, where he obtained a fellowship, and was appointed one of the Archbishop's chaplains. A year or two later, Juxon, Bishop of London, presented him to the rectory of Uppingham, in Rutlandshire. On the outbreak of the Civil War, he embarked his fortunes with the Royalists, and composed a work in favour of Episcopacy, which obtained for him the degree of D.D. from the King—an honour more than compensated for by the sequestration of his rectory of Uppingham by the Presbyterians, who were now rapidly gaining strength. Of Taylor's history during the Civil War not much is certainly known. In 1643 we find him residing with his mother-in-law in Wales; and in the following year, his fortunes having again brought him into connection with the royal army, he was taken prisoner in the battle fought near Cardigan Castle. He was soon released, but preferred remaining in the comparatively safe solitudes of Wales to again risking the loss of his liberty. In conjunction with two friends he opened a school, and also busied himself in the composition of his first great work, "The Liberty of Prophesying," a plea for tolerance, which would not now be considered very liberal, but which was far in advance of the opinions then entertained by most on that subject. In the dedication to that work he says, alluding to his imprisonment, "In the great storm which dashed the vessel of the Church all in pieces, I had been cast on the coast of Wales, and in a little boat thought to have enjoyed that rest and quietness which in England, in a far greater, I could not hope for. Here I cast anchor, and thinking to ride safely, the storm followed me with so impetuous violence, that it broke a cable, and I lost my anchor. And here again I was exposed to the mercy of the sea, and the gentleness of an element that could distinguish neither things nor persons; and but that He that stilleth the raging of the sea, and the noise of the waves, and the madness of His people, had provided a plank for me, I had been lost to all opportunities of content or study; but I know not whether I have been more preserved by the courtesies of my friends or the gentleness and mercies of a noble enemy." He soon found a patron in the Earl of Carbery, at whose seat, Golden Grove, he wrote his "Life of Christ" and his "Golden Grove," and his most popular work, "Holy Living and Dying," besides several minor performances. Some expressions in the "Golden Grove" gave offence to Cromwell, and in the years between 1654 and 1658 Taylor more than once suffered imprisonment. In 1658 his friends obtained for him an alternate lecturership at Lisburne, in the north-east of Ireland, where he lived in tranquillity and happiness till the Restoration. About this time he composed his most elaborate work, the "Ductor Dubitantium" (Guide to the Scrupulous). His most important works, besides those already mentioned, are his treatise on "Repentance" and his sermons. After the Restoration the sunshine of Court favour shone upon him. He was appointed Bishop of Down and Connor, and afterwards Bishop of Dromore, and had besides several minor dignities bestowed upon him. He died in 1667.

Taylor has been called the Shakespeare of English prose; and although his position as a prose writer is not at all comparable to that occupied by Shakespeare as a poet, there is a good deal of truth in the designation. Like Shakespeare, his superabundant fancy occasionally gets the better of his good taste, and he pours forth the riches of his imagination with a profusion which is more to be wondered at than admired. Like Shakespeare, too, he seems to have "written right on," careless of minute accuracy in the grammatical construction of his sentences. He possessed the typical poetic temperament: tender, full of love for all that is beautiful, impassioned, and impetuous. Another characteristic of Taylor is his width of learning, which is distributed over his works with the same careless abundance as the flowers of his fancy. Thus in writings intended for popular perusal, he speaks of hard students "being as mute as the Seriphian frogs;" of "garments made of the Calabrian fleece, and stained with the blood of the *murex;*" of "the tender lard of the Apulian swine;" and so on. This pedantry (for it can be called by no better name) is no doubt to be in part attributed to the fashion of the time; but Taylor carries the practice further than any of his contemporaries. His quotations from classical authors, which are frequent, are, as has been several times shown, often inaccurate to an astonishing degree. He was also a great coiner of new words, using "respersed" for "scattered;" "deordination" for "confusion;" "clancularly" for "secretly;" "immorigerous" for "disobedient;" "ferity" for "fierceness;" "intenerate" for "render soft," and many others of the same kind. With all his faults (many of which, after all, are faults that a man of less copious genius could not have committed), Taylor was a writer of astonishing power, who can in no wise be passed over by any one aspiring to even a fair knowledge of English literature. "He was," said Coleridge, "a man constitutionally overflowing with pleasurable kindliness, who scarcely even in a casual illustration introduces the image of a woman, child, or bird, but he embalms the thought with so rich a tenderness as makes the very words seem beauties and fragments of poetry from a Euripides or a Simonides." In occasional passages he reaches surpassing heights of eloquence. Take the following description of the "Day of Judgment":—

"Then all the beasts and creeping things, the monsters, and the usual inhabitants of the sea shall be gathered together, and make fearful noises to distract mankind: the birds shall mourn and change their song into threnes and sad accents; rivers of fire shall rise from east to west, and the stars shall be rent into threads of light, and scatter like the beards of comets; then shall be fearful earthquakes, and the rocks shall rend in pieces, the trees shall distil blood, and the mountains and fairest structures shall return into their primitive dust; the wild beasts shall leave their dens, and shall come into the companies of men, so that you shall hardly tell how to call them, herds of men or congregations of beasts; then shall the graves open and give up their dead, and those which are alive in nature and dead in fear shall be forced from the rocks whither they went to hide them, and from the caverns of the earth where they would fain have been concealed; because their retirements are dismantled and their rocks broken into wild ruptures, and admit a strange light into their secret bowels; and the men being forced abroad into the theatre of mighty horrors, shall run up and down distracted and at their wits' end; and then some shall die, and some shall be changed; and by this time the elect shall be gathered together from the four quarters of the world, and Christ shall come along with them to judgment."

But it is not alone in sublime description that Taylor excels. In pathos he has few equals; and had we space, many passages from his writings might be quoted full of the most touching grace and tenderness.

Two other theological writers of the period may be briefly mentioned. One of these was Richard Baxter (1615–91), who, originally ordained in the Church of England, afterwards joined the Parliamentary party. Of his many works—he is said to have written one hundred and sixty-eight in all—two still remain popular, the "Saint's Rest" and the "Call to the

Unconverted," and merit their popularity not so much because of any great charm of style as because they express in homely language the thoughts of a most sincere, heavenly minded, and excellent man. The other, John Bunyan, is one of our greatest authors, and may be taken as the typical prose writer of Puritanism, as Milton is its typical poet. The story of his early years, as related by himself in his "Grace Abounding to the Chief of Sinners," is a very touching one. The son of a tinker, he was born at Elstow, near Bedford, in 1628. More fortunate than most children born in so low a rank, he was sent to school and taught to read and write. He must have been a thoughtful and imaginative child, for when only about nine years old he began to be tormented with those fearful thoughts which caused him such agony for several years. "I would," he says, "be greatly troubled with the thoughts of the fearful torments of hell-fire; still fearing that it would be my lot to be found at last among those devils and hellish fiends who are there bound down with the chains and bonds of darkness unto the judgment of the great day." As he grew older these terrible impressions wore nearly off; he became, according to his own account, "a very ringleader in all manner of vice and ungodliness." A very exaggerated statement, it would seem, for the only sins he specifically mentions are Sabbath-breaking and swearing: there is no reason to believe that his conduct was worse than that of other young men belonging to the same class. When about eighteen he married. His wife's relations were pious, and she brought with her as her only portion some religious books. Influenced by them and by his wife's conversation, Bunyan soon became a Pharisee of the Pharisees. He went to church twice a day, and did "there very devoutly both say and sing as others did," and regarded all connected with the church with the utmost reverence. But Bunyan was not the sort of man to find peace of mind in the observation of forms and ceremonies. One by one he gave up the sports and sins in which he had indulged,—swearing, Sabbath-breaking, dancing, bell-ringing, and so on. Still, while his neighbours were praising him for his spotless morality, he felt that he was but a whited sepulchre. In vain he tried to obtain inward peace of mind. At one time he was overwhelmed by doubts whether he was one of the elect, at another he suffered unspeakable agonies from the thought that he had committed the unpardonable sin. At length peace dawned upon his troubled soul; but it was several years before his shattered nerves recovered their tone.

Five or six years after his conversion, Bunyan, who had joined a Baptist society at Bedford, "was desired, and that with much earnestness, that he would be willing at some times to take in hand at one of the meetings to speak a word of exhortation unto them." Very reluctantly he assented, and his ministrations soon became so popular that he "was more particularly called forth, and appointed to a more ordinary and public preaching of the word." For five years he continued to preach with increasing popularity, when, in 1660, "I was," to use his own words, "indicted for a maintainer of unlawful assemblies and conventicles, and for not conforming to the Church of England; and after some conference there with the justices, they taking my plain dealing with them for a confession, as they termed it, of the indictment, did sentence me to a perpetual banishment because I refused to conform. So, being again delivered up to the gaoler's hands, I was had to prison, and there laid a complete twelve years, waiting to see what God would suffer these men to do with me." In vain his persecutors told him that if he promised to abstain from preaching he would at once be liberated. "If you let me out to-day," was his reply, "I will preach again to-morrow." His trials and privations sat lightly on him; no agony that man could inflict was equal to the mental tortures he had come through. While in prison he supported himself by making tagged thread laces; he gave religious instructions to his fellow-captives; he studied over and over again his two favourite books, the Bible and Foxe's "Book of Martyrs;" and he engaged in religious controversy, writing against the Quakers and the Liturgy of the Church of England. During the last six years of his imprisonment, when he was treated with great leniency, he hit upon the vein of writing for which his genius was adapted. Before his release he began that allegory to which he owes his fame. "'The Pilgrim's Progress,'" writes Macaulay in his admirable "Encyclopædia Britannica" sketch of Bunyan, "stole silently into the world. Not a single copy of the first edition is known to be in existence. The year of publication has not been ascertained. It is probable that during some months the little volume circulated only among poor and obscure sectaries. But soon the irresistible charm of a book which gratified the imagination of the reader with all the action and scenery of a fairy tale, which exercised his ingenuity by setting him to discover a multitude of curious analogies, which interested his feeling for human beings, frail like himself, and struggling with temptations from within and from without, which every moment drew a smile from him by some stroke of quaint yet simple pleasantry, and nevertheless left on his mind a sentiment of reverence for God and of sympathy for man, began to produce its effect. In puritanical circles, from which plays and novels were strictly excluded, that effect was such as no work of genius, though it were superior to the 'Iliad,' to 'Don Quixote,' or to 'Othello,' can ever produce on a mind accustomed to indulgence in literary luxury. In 1678 came forth a second edition with additions, and then the demand became immense."

In 1687, when the penal laws against the Dissenters were relaxed, a chapel was built for Bunyan at Bedford, where his powerful though uncultivated eloquence and his wonderful acquaintance with the workings of conscience, won by much hard-bought experience, attracted crowds of hearers from the districts around. In the summer of 1688 he caught cold from exposure incurred during a ride through heavy rain to visit an angry father whom he wished to reconcile to his son. A few days after he died. Bunyan is a man on whose character much might be written. Of a morbidly keen conscience and of strong imagination, his faults assumed gigantic size in his eyes, and were felt by him with proportionate intensity. Totally free from hypocrisy, he, while in his stormy youth almost worshipping good people, found no relief by endeavouring to imitate their mode of life, while feeling that he was only playing a part. His vehement, impulsive nature was a source of trouble to him long after his more terrible agonies had disappeared. He often felt an almost uncontrollable desire to utter words which he ought not to utter, just as some people cannot stand on the brink of a lofty precipice without wishing to throw themselves over. Thus at his first communion after he had joined the Baptist society at Bedford, he with difficulty refrained from imprecating destruction on his brethren while the cup was passing from hand to hand; and sometimes when he was preaching he was "violently assaulted with words of blasphemy, and strongly tempted to speak the words with his mouth before the congregation." Yet all these peculiarities did not prevent him from being a man of sound common-sense, with a clear and half-humorous insight into the ways and thoughts of the different types of humanity. The fact that he was often employed as a mediator in family quarrels—the most difficult and dangerous diplomatic office any man can undertake—is a conclusive proof of his tact and skill in the management of men; and many of the characters in the "Pilgrim's Progress" are evidently drawn from the life, with such accuracy and spirit as show Bunyan to have been a first-rate observer of human nature.

Mr. Froude is probably correct in thinking that the "Pilgrim's Progress" has affected the spiritual opinions of the English race in every part of the world more powerfully than any book or books except the Bible. The simplicity of its style, combined with the interest of its allegory, and its touches of genuine eloquence and pathos, admirably adapt it for all classes of readers—for the poor and uneducated as well as for the rich and cultivated, for the man of letters and for the humble peasant, for the child just setting out on life's journey, and for those who are nearing the gates of the Celestial City. Macaulay declares that during the century which followed his death, Bunyan's fame was entirely confined to religious families of the middle and lower classes, and that very seldom during that time was his name mentioned with respect by any writer of great literary eminence. This seems rather an overcharged statement. Johnson, it is well known, praised Bunyan highly, saying that "his 'Pilgrim's Progress' has great merit, both for invention, imagination, and the conduct of the story; and it has had the best evidence of its merit, the general and continued approbation of mankind. Few books, I believe, have had a more extensive sale." If Johnson's opinion of the "Pilgrim's Progress" had been different from that generally prevalent in literary society, we may be pretty sure that Boswell, who records the above, would have drawn attention to the fact. Bunyan's chief works besides the "Pilgrim's Progress" are the autobiographical "Grace Abounding" already mentioned and the "Holy War," an allegorical account of the fall and redemption of mankind under the figure of a war carried on by Satan ("Diabolus") for the possession of the city of Mansoul.

Izaak Walton (1593–1683) is best known as the author of the "Complete Angler" (1653), a delightful book even to those who have no skill in the art with which it deals, full of sweet pictures of pastoral scenery, and having, as it were, the fresh air of the country blowing over every page. His Lives of Donne, Wotton, Hooker, Herbert, Sanderson, written at various times between 1640 and 1678, are among our first good biographies, appreciative, affectionate, and truth-telling. In a fine sonnet Wordsworth has celebrated their excellence:—

"There are no colours in the fairest sky
So fair as these. The feather whence the pen
Was shaped that traced the lives of these good men
Dropped from an angel's wing. With moistened eye
We read of faith and purest charity,
In statesman, priest, and humble citizen.
Oh! could we copy their mild virtues, then
What joy to live, what blessedness to die!
Methinks their very names shine still and bright,
Apart—like glow-worms on a summer night;
Or lonely tapers when from far they fling
A guiding ray; or seen, like stars on high,

Satellites burning in a lucid ring
Around meek Walton's heavenly memory."

Walton was a retired London linendraper, who, having amassed a competent fortune in business, spent his latter days in the pursuits that pleased him best, reading and writing occasionally, enjoying the society of good men, and wandering about the country in the pursuit of his favourite art.

A man of much more unique genius than Walton was Sir Thomas Browne, who has written passages of such fine, organ-like rhythm as it would be difficult to parallel save in the pages of De Quincey. The son of a rich merchant, he was born in London in 1605, educated at Winchester, and afterwards at Oxford, where he studied medicine. He then travelled for some time on the Continent, taking the degree of doctor of physic at Leyden in 1633. On his return to England he practised for a short time at Halifax, after which he settled at Norwich, where he remained till his death in 1682. He was knighted, "with singular marks of consideration," by Charles II. in 1671. Browne's first work, "Religio Medici" (the Religion of a Physician) was published in 1643. This little work, which was at once successful, being "very eagerly read in England, France, Italy, Belgium, and Germany," is divided into two parts, the first containing an account of his religious opinions and feelings, and the second of his human feelings. Grave and musical in style, the book besides possesses that peculiar attractiveness which is always found in the self-portraiture of a gifted and original mind. We may quote one passage as showing the width of Browne's learning, and the odd mixture of vanity and humility which characterised him :—"I thank God," he says, "amongst these millions of vices I do inherit and hold from Adam, I have escaped one, and that a mortal enemy to charity, the first and father sin, not only of man, but of the devil—pride; a vice whose name is comprehended in a monosyllable, but in its nature not circumscribed by a world. I have escaped it in a condition that can hardly avoid it. Those petty acquisitions and reputed perfections that advance and elevate the conceits of other men add no feathers unto mine. I have seen a grammarian tower and plume himself over a single line in Horace, and show more pride in the construction of one ode than the author in the composure of the whole book. For my own part, besides the jargon and *patois* of several provinces, I understand no less than six languages; yet I protest I have no higher conceit of myself than had our fathers before the confusion of Babel, when there was but one language in the world, and none to boast himself either linguist or critic. I have not only seen several countries, beheld the nature of their climes, the chorography of their provinces, topography of their cities, but understood their several laws, customs, and policies; yet cannot all this persuade the dulness of my spirit into such an opinion of myself as I behold in nimble and conceited heads, that never looked a degree beyond their nests." In a similar half-deprecating, half-conceited way he goes on to describe his attainments in astronomy and botany. Three years after the "Religio Medici" appeared the "Pseudodoxia Epidemica," commonly known as "Browne's Vulgar Errors," devoted to the refutation of many beliefs current in the seventeenth century, such as the legends about the phœnix, that a man hath one rib less than a woman, that crystal is nothing else but ice strongly congealed, that a wolf first seeing a man begets a dumbness in him. Browne's finest effort is his "Hydriotaphia" (1658) (Urn Burial), a discourse founded upon the discovery of certain sepulchral urns found in Norfolk. The concluding chapter, in which he speaks of the shortness of life and of posthumous fame, is one of the noblest examples in English literature of solemn, impassioned eloquence. "It is," wrote Carlyle in his Diary for Dec. 3, 1826, "absolutely beautiful: a still, elegiac mood, so soft, so deep, so solemn and tender, like the song of some departed saint flitting faint under the everlasting canopy of night; an echo of deepest meaning from the great and famous nations of the dead. Browne must have been a good man." Browne's greatest fault as a writer is his excessive fondness for words derived from the Latin. His highly Latinised style no doubt adds to the diginity and sonorous swell of his sentences, but it detracts from their general intelligibility. He was also an extensive coiner of new words, a fault common with the writers of his time.

Only one historian of any eminence appeared during the period with which we are dealing. This was Edward Hyde, Earl of Clarendon, a prominent actor in the events which he recorded. He was born in 1608 at Dinton, in Wiltshire, the son of a country gentleman. Destined for the Church, he turned aside to the study of the law, and in 1640 began his public career as member of Parliament for Wootton Basset. By his caution and prudence he soon rose to high favour; in 1643 he was knighted and made Chancellor of the Exchequer. In 1646 he went with the Prince of Wales to Jersey, where he began his "History of the Rebellion." He afterwards accompanied the Prince and the Queen Mother to France, returning to England at the Restoration, which he had no inconsiderable share in bringing about. He was made Earl of Clarendon and Lord Chancellor in 1660; but his prosperity did not continue long. In 1667 he was impeached of high treason by the Commons and ordered to quit the kingdom. He never returned to England, dying at Rouen in 1674. He completed his "History of the Rebellion" during his second exile, writing besides his "Life and Continuation of the History," published from his manuscripts in 1759; the History having appeared previously in 1707. No active partisan can be a fair chronicler of a movement in which he was himself engaged. It is therefore not surprising that though many facts are to be found in Clarendon's account of the Great Civil War which add to our knowledge of that struggle and the men who figured in it, it is often exceedingly incorrect and prejudiced. Its main excellence consists in its noble gallery of portraits, drawn with great skill and with much discernment of character. The style of the history, looked at from what may be called the mechanical point of view, is exceedingly bad, prolix and tautological, full of parentheses and endless involutions.

That English style was, however, advancing in the right direction is proved by the writings of one of Clarendon's contemporaries, Thomas Hobbes (1588–1679), in which we find, with much less literary genius, an infinitely larger portion of that clearness and accuracy which are the note of modern prose. "A permanent foundation for his fame," writes Sir James Mackintosh, "consists in his admirable style, which seems to be the very perfection of didactic language. Short, clear, precise, pithy, his language has never more than one meaning, which never requires a second thought to find. . . . He had so thoroughly studied the genius of the language, and knew so well to steer between pedantry and vulgarity, that two centuries have not superannuated probably more than a dozen of his words. His expressions are so luminous, that he is clear without the help of illustration." This extravagant eulogium, which bears all the marks of Sir James's over-laudatory disposition, must not be understood to mean more than that Hobbes wrote with a lucidity and precision rarely found in philosophers. During his long life, Hobbes mingled in much of the best society, intellectual and social, both of England and the Continent. In his earlier years he was secretary to Bacon, and was, we are told by the antiquary Aubrey, "beloved by his Lordship, who was wont to have him walk in his delicate groves, where he did meditate; and when a notion darted into his mind, Mr. Hobbes was presently to write it down. And his Lordship was wont to say that he did it better than any one else about him; for that many times when he read their notes he scarce understood what they writ, because they understood it not clearly themselves." Hobbes was also greatly in favour with the Cavendish family, acting as tutor to two successive Earls of Devonshire, with whom he wandered over a large part of the Continent, making acquaintance with the more prominent literary men there. Hobbes's literary career began with a translation of Thucydides, designed to show the evils of popular rule. From 1640 to 1660 appeared the works on which his fame as a thinker rests: "De Cive;" "Treatise on Human Nature;" "De Corpore Politico;" "Leviathan, or the Matter, Power, and Form of a Commonwealth, Ecclesiastical and Civil;" and "De Corpore."

The latter years of his life were embittered by a controversy on certain mathematical points, in which he got decidedly the worst of it. At the age of eighty-six, the versatile old man published translations of the "Iliad" and "Odyssey," not remarkable save as literary curiosities. Hobbes's philosophical theories had immense influence on the Restoration period. He became the philosopher *par excellence* of the court and the society which surrounded it. His selfish theory of morals and his theory of government, which, though setting out with the statements that the origin of all power was in the people, and that the end of all power was for the common weal, practically inculcated a sort of divine right, were very acceptable to King and courtiers. As frequently happens, Hobbes's followers often carried his views to an extreme length, and the name "Hobbism" was given to doctrines which Hobbes himself would have been the last to countenance.

With the great exception already mentioned, the poets of the era preceding the Restoration do not compare favourably with the prose writers. It is a sad contrast to leave the magnificent efflorescence of the Elizabethan era and to study the works of the many poetasters who flourished about the time of Charles I. Even those who tower above the common herd, and have not long since been consigned to obscurity, are now remembered chiefly by a few happy verses, and not by their writings as a whole. Such is the case with the unfortunate cavalier Richard Lovelace, who died in 1658 at the age of forty. Two or three of his lyrics are perfect gems, to be committed to heart and conned over by all who care anything about poetry, but his genius was the reverse of prolific, and "rubbish" is the only fit epithet by which to characterise most of what he wrote. Much the same may be said about Sir John Suckling (1608–1641). A few sprightly society verses, of which the well-known and justly celebrated "Ballad on a Wedding" is the best, is all of his work that can in any sense be said to live. Of even "Holy George Herbert," whose "Temple," published in 1633, has received warm praise from some of the best judges of poetry, can it be said that he is at all generally known or appreciated save in select extracts? Beautiful as his devout earnestness is, and poetical and striking as are many of his thoughts, his quaint conceits prove an insuperable stumbling-block to many. "Neither their intrinsic excellence," says Mr. Ruskin, "nor the authority of those who can judge of it, will ever make the poems of George Herbert popular in the sense in which Scott and Byron are popular, because it is to the vulgar a labour instead of a pleasure to read them; and there are parts in them which to such judges cannot but be vapid and ridiculous." If Mr. Ruskin had said that parts of them *are* vapid and ridiculous, he would, we think, have approached nearer the truth; though to not a few whose opinion is worthy of all respect it will appear something little short of profanity to say so. The "Hesperides" of Robert Herrick, which was published in 1648, has supplied many choice flowers to our poetical anthologies. In a similar way the works of Wither, of Carew, and others have been laid under contribution. To all these Campbell's criticism on Herrick may, with the requisite modifications, be applied: "Herrick, if we were to fix our eyes on a small portion of his works, might be pronounced a writer of delightful anacreontic spirit. He has passages where the thoughts seem to dance into numbers from his very heart, and where he frolics like a being made up of melody and pleasure, as when he sings—

> 'Gather ye rosebuds while ye may,
> Old Time is still a-flying;
> And this same flower that blooms to-day,
> To-morrow will be dying.'

In the same spirit are his verses to Anthea, concluding—

> 'Thou art my life, my love, my heart,
> The very eyes of me;
> And hast command of every part,
> To live and die for thee.'

But his beauties are so deeply involved in surrounding coarseness and extravagance, as to constitute not a tenth part of his poetry; or rather, it may be safely affirmed that of 1400 pages of verse which he has left, not a hundred are worth reading."

Herrick, Lovelace, and their fellow-lyrists belonged to the Cavalier party, but Puritanism, which produced the greatest statesmen and soldiers of the age, produced its two greatest imaginative writers, Milton and Bunyan; a rather curious fact when we remember that the Royalists prided themselves on having a monopoly of the arts, which the austere Puritans were apt to regard with ill-judging contempt. John Milton, England's greatest epic poet, in comparison to whose organ tones the voices of his contemporary singers seem as penny-whistles, was born on December 9, 1608, at a house in Bread Street, Cheapside. His father, a cultivated man, of puritanical tendencies, but fond of music and the arts, was a well-to-do scrivener, a calling uniting part of the work now done by attorneys and law-stationers. Milton's early education was sedulously attended to: he was, to use his own words, "exercised to the tongues and some sciences as my age would suffer, by sundry masters and teachers both at home and the schools." Very early he applied himself to study with that intense eagerness which he retained through life; from the twelfth year of his life, he tells us, he very rarely went to bed without studying to midnight, thus, as he believed, laying the seeds of that weakness in his eyes which developed into blindness. To the period of Milton's school-days belong the first poems of his which have been preserved, Paraphrases of the cxiv. and cxxxvi. Psalms, verses well described by Johnson: "They raise no great expectations; they would in any numerous school have obtained praise but not excited wonder."

From St. Paul's School, where he had been for some years, Milton, early in 1625, went to Cambridge, where he was enrolled as a lesser pensioner of Christ's College. Rooms there, venerable from their association with his name, are still pointed out to visitors. After his enrolment he returned to London, where he remained till his matriculation in April of the same year. For seven years, barring vacations, visits to his parents, &c., Milton remained at Cambridge, not leaving it till he took his

M.A. degree in 1632, having previously graduated B.A. in 1629. By the undergraduates he was nicknamed "The Lady," on account of his "fair complexion, feminine and graceful appearance, and a certain haughty delicacy in his tastes and morals." At first he was not popular among his associates; nor is there any reason to wonder that he was not so. It is easy to imagine with what scorn the youthful poet, self-restrained, self-conscious, haughty, and of purity approaching to asceticism, must have regarded the rough fun, the practical jokes, the noisy gatherings, the jovial conversation which are the delight of undergraduates possessed of high animal spirits. A want of humour, with its usual concomitant, a want of power to do justice to men of different type from himself, was Milton's great defect through life. As time wore on, however, he seems to have made himself more agreeable to his associates; and he certainly was distinguished for his learning and accomplishments. "'Twas," says Anthony Wood, speaking of Milton's Cambridge life, "usual with him to sit up till midnight at his book, which was the first thing that brought his eyes into the danger of blindness. By his indefatigable study he profited exceedingly — performed the academical exercises to the satisfaction of all, and was esteemed a virtuous and sober person, yet not to be ignorant of his own parts." At the outset of his university career, in 1626, he had a quarrel with his tutor, which led to his temporary rustication: he is even said on this occasion to have suffered the indignity of corporal punishment. However this may be, Milton certainly looked back to his university life with no great liking or respect for his *Alma Mater*.

The following is a list, with dates, of the English poems composed by Milton during his Cambridge life. We omit the Latin ones, as not properly coming within the scope of a book on English literature:—"On the Death of a Fair Infant" (1626); "At a Vacation Exercise in the College" (1628); "On the Morning of Christ's Nativity" (1629); "Upon the Circumcision;" "The Passion;" "On Time;" "At a Solemn Music;" Song on May Morning;" "On Shakespeare" (1630);

"On the University Carrier;" "Epitaph on the Marchioness of Winchester;" "Sonnet to the Nightingale;" "Sonnet on Arriving at the Age of Twenty-three" (1631). Of these, the most interesting, for different reasons, are the "Ode on the Nativity," which, despite some fantastic conceits which Milton's maturer judgment would have rejected, is an excellent specimen of a class of poetry of which very few excellent specimens exist; the lines on Shakespeare, prefixed, along with other verses, to the second folio edition, published in 1632, and thus the first printed of Milton's English poems, which show that Milton had not yet become fully imbued with the spirit of Puritanism, and could look on all forms of art with a more catholic spirit than he afterwards showed; and the epitaph on Hobson, the University carrier, which proves how totally destitute Milton was of humour. His witticisms, as has been more than once remarked, resemble the gambollings of his own "unwieldy elephant," who,

> "To make them mirth, used all his might, and wreathed
> His lithe proboscis."

Lastly, the "Sonnet on Arriving at the Age of Twenty-three" is of deep personal interest. It was accompanied by a letter to an unknown friend, explaining why Milton declined to enter the Church, the profession for which he had been destined by his friends, and which he himself had at one time intended to pursue.

On leaving the University, Milton went to reside at Horton, a small village in Buckinghamshire, where his father, having retired from business, had taken a country-house. There he remained for five years, "wholly intent," he writes, "through a period of absolute leisure, on a steady perusal of the Greek and Latin writers, but still so that I occasionally exchanged the country for the city, either for the purpose of buying books, or for that of learning anything new in mathematics or in music, in which I then took delight." During his seclusion in this pretty pastoral spot, surrounded by woods, orchards, cornfields, streams, and all country sights and sounds, Milton wrote the finest of his smaller poems—the "Allegro" and "Penseroso," the "Arcades" and "Comus." The dates of the three former poems are not quite certain; "Comus" was represented in 1634. The "Allegro," beginning with morn and ending with night, represents things as they appear to a man of cheerful mood; the "Penseroso," beginning with night and ending with morn, represents things as they appear to a man of melancholy mood. Both poems are triumphs of versification; rarely or never was sense better linked to sound than in some of their lines. The "Arcades," part of a masque presented before the Countess-Dowager of Derby at Hanfield, does not call for special notice. Much more remarkable is "Comus," both for its intrinsic merits, and as throwing light on Milton's tone of thought. The dignity of its blank verse, weighted with deep thought, the beauty of the lyrics interspersed, the almost passionate praise of purity, the scorn manifested for those who indulge in sensual delights, sufficed to prove that a new poet, unique alike in his imaginative and in his moral power, had arisen in England. It was published anonymously by Milton's friend Lawes, the musical composer, in 1637. Sir Henry Wotton's opinion of it was doubtless that of most cultivated men into whose hands it came: "A dainty piece of entertainment, wherein I should much commend the tragical part, if the lyrical did not ravish me with a certain Doric delicacy in your songs and odes, whereunto I must plainly confess to have seen yet nothing parallel in our language."

"Lycidas," the last poem of Milton's Horton period, was written in 1637. It commemorates the death of a college companion of his, Edward King, who met his death by shipwreck while crossing the Irish Sea, and was published in 1638 in a volume of memorial verses by various writers, designed to commemorate the sad event. In form it is a pastoral; first there is an introduction, then the monody of the shepherd lamenting his lost friend, then an epilogue. There are no traces in the poem of such deep emotion as we find in "In Memoriam;" the careful artist is more visible in it than the sorrowing friend. Many writers, especially those who have an intimate acquaintance with the ancient classics, have agreed with Lord Macaulay in regarding the appreciation of "Lycidas" as a test of one's insight into the most poetical aspects of poetry. But this may reasonably be doubted. It has been well remarked that minds trained upon the old models seem incapable of understanding how cold and artificial sounds the strain to uneducated but not unpoetical persons which treats of Arethuse and Mincius in speaking of a gentleman drowned in the Irish Channel, and which describes a Fellow of Christ's College as tending flocks and singing for the edification of old Damœtas. In "Lycidas" Milton at length appears as a Puritan full-fledged; "he has thrown away the last relics of Church and State, and is Presbyterian." The scathing passage in which he denounced—

——"Such as, for their bellies' sake,
Creep, and intrude, and climb into the fold!
Of other care they little reckoning make
Than how to scramble at the shearers' feast,
And shove away the worthy bidden guest.
Blind mouths! that scarce themselves know how to hold
A sheep-hook, or have learnt aught else the least
That to the faithful herdman's art belongs,"

doubtless found an echo in many a stern heart in England at that time, when Laud and his policy were causing widespread revolt.

In 1638 Milton took that journey to the Continent which he had long meditated. Taking letters of introduction with him, he passed through Paris (where he saw Grotius), Nice, Genoa, Leghorn, Pisa, and settled at Florence, where he remained for two months. There he made the acquaintance of many learned men, some of them well known in Italian literary history, and "found and visited the famous Galileo, grown old, a prisoner to the Inquisition for thinking in astronomy otherwise than the Franciscan and Dominican licensers thought." From Florence he went to Rome, where also he received a very warm reception from cultivated society.

After staying about two months there, he spent a short time in Naples. From Naples it was his intention to travel to Italy and Greece, but the sad news of the Civil War in England called him back; "for I thought it base that I should be travelling abroad for pleasure while my fellow-countrymen at home were fighting for liberty." He returned to England by slow stages, arriving there in August, 1639. Soon after his father's household at Horton was broken up, and Milton took lodgings in St. Bride's Churchyard, where he acted as tutor to his two nephews, John and Edward Phillips, and busied himself in literary projects—amongst others, in drafting schemes for a poem on the subject of "Paradise Lost." But stirring times had now arrived, and Milton was not the man to see his countrymen struggle for liberty and quietly remain buried in literary meditations. For twenty years, from 1640 to 1660, his life is not that of a poet, but of a strenuous combatant, constantly engaged in controversy, the most exhausting, the most hurtful, the most evanescent of all modes of composition.

Is this to be regretted? From a literary point of view undoubtedly it is. There are splendid passages in Milton's prose works—passages where we are carried away by torrents of gorgeous eloquence; but in prose, as he himself said, "he had only the use of his left hand;" and the natural acerbity of his temper, quickened by the insults of his assailants, often led him to indulge in the most vulgar railing. "For the mass of his prose treatises, *miserable discussions* is the final and right word," says Mr. Matthew Arnold, who quotes with approbation the remarks on them by the distinguished French critic M. Scherer:—"In all of them the manner is the same. The author brings into play the treasures of his learning, heaping together testimonies from Scripture, passages from the Fathers, quotations from the poets; laying all antiquity, sacred and profane, under contribution; entering into subtle discussions on the sense of this or that Hebrew or Greek word. But not only by his undigested erudition, and by his absorption in religious controversy, does Milton belong to his age; he belongs to it too by the personal tone of his polemics." But there are other than literary grounds from which the question ought to be regarded. If Milton thought that by the services his pen could render, the cause of justice, and liberty, and good government could be advanced, most assuredly he did well to use it as he did during those twenty eventful years.

Milton's prose writings, and the circumstances which led to their publication, we can only very briefly touch on. He began his career as a controversialist by five pamphlets against the Episcopal form of Church government, all published in 1641 and 1642. The preface to the second book of the fourth of these, "The Reason of Church Government urged against Prelacy," is one of the finest pieces of Milton's prose, besides being of high biographical importance. He there gives a sketch of his life, of his work, and of his aim at some future period, when quieter times came, to produce a work "which the world would not willingly let die." "Neither do I think it shame," he says, "to covenant with any knowing reader that for some few years yet I may go on trust with him towards the payment of what I am now indebted, as being a work not to be raised from the heat of youth or the vapours of wine, like that which flows at waste from the pen of some vulgar amourist or the trencher fury of a rhyming parasite; not to be obtained by the invocation of Dame Memory and her siren daughters, but by devout prayer to that Eternal Spirit who can enrich with all utterance and knowledge, and sends out His seraphim with the hallowed fire of His altar to touch and purify the lips of whom He pleases: to this must be added industrious and select reading, steady observation, insight into all seemly and generous arts and affairs; till which in some measure be compassed, at mine own peril and cost I refuse not to sustain this expectation from as many as are not loth to hazard so much credulity upon the best pledges which I can give them." From this proud self-confidence a great result might have been augured, and a great result was achieved, for that result was "Paradise Lost."

The second series of Milton's pamphlets was written with a purely personal object. About Whitsuntide 1643, Milton, with his nephew Phillips, "took a journey into the country, nobody about him certainly knowing the reason, or that it was any more than a journey of recreation; but home he returns a married man that went out a bachelor, his wife being Mary, the eldest daughter of Mr. Richard Powell, then a justice of the peace, at Foresthill, near Shotover, in Oxfordshire." The circumstances connected with this marriage have never been clearly explained. The Powells were Royalists; Mary was only seventeen, whereas her husband was thirty-five; and altogether it seems to have been as ill-assorted a union as could well be imagined. After the newly married pair had lived together for a month, Mary Powell went back to her friends, promising, however, to return at Michaelmas. Milton, like Carlyle, was "gey ill to live wi';" his studious habits, his solitary life, and his austere disposition were doubtless very repellant to a young girl accustomed to "a great house and much company and jollity." She did not return at Michaelmas, and for a very good reason. Before that time Milton had published the first of those strange pamphlets in which he advocated freedom of divorce on very easy conditions. This raised a tempest of opposition against him, but single-handed he undauntedly continued to maintain his thesis in three other pamphlets, the last of which appeared early in 1645. When, however, the Powell family, later on in that year, fell into difficulties, and his wife returned to him and asked his forgiveness, Milton granted it, and again received her into favour.

Between the publication of the first and the last pamphlet on Divorce appeared Milton's tract on Education (1644), and his "Areopagitica," published in the same year, the first formal plea for the liberty of the press. It is the most generally known of Milton's prose works, and there is little need to dwell on its surpassing eloquence; none but a poet and a very great one could have written it. Meanwhile Milton's writings on Divorce had lost him the favour of the Presbyterians, many of whom bitterly assailed him; and he began to think that "new Presbyter is but old Priest writ large." From about

1646, he favoured Independency so far as he favoured any form of church government; but in religious matters he was a law unto himself, going to no church, and joining no communion.

The year 1646 is memorable as having been that in which the poems written by Milton up to that date were collected and published together. "Let the event guide itself which way it will," wrote Moseley, the publisher, in the preface to the collected edition; "I shall deserve of the age by bringing into the light as true a birth as the Muses have brought forth since our famous Spenser wrote, whose poems in these English ones are as rarely imitated as sweetly excelled." Three years after, in 1649, Milton again entered into controversy by publishing a pamphlet defending the execution of Charles I. Then came his Latin controversy with the great Leyden scholar Salmasius, over whom he obtained a brilliant victory. His exertions in this battle cost him his eyesight: in 1652 he became totally blind. Some consolation for his blindness was to be derived from the fact that his replies to Salmasius had caused Europe to ring with his fame from side to side. About 1654 his wife died, leaving behind her three daughters. He married again in 1656, but his second wife only lived fifteen months, dying in childbirth in 1658.

On the death of Cromwell, Milton in vain endeavoured to stem the tide of popular feeling in favour of the restoration of the monarchy, writing five pamphlets with this end in view, and fighting for what was clearly a hopeless cause till the very last moment. All in vain: on the 8th of May Charles II. was proclaimed, and on the 29th he entered London in triumph. Milton, who had been the foremost advocate of Republicanism, who had defended the execution of the King, who had acted as Latin secretary during the Protectorate, whose name was famous throughout Europe as the champion of the Commonwealth and the contemner of kings, now indeed found himself fallen on evil days and evil tongues. It is a wonder that he escaped death: if any man deserved it, the Royalists might plausibly have argued, it was the stern old blind man who had fought strenuously against them till the very last. For about two months he lay in hiding, till, in August 1660, the Act of Indemnity passed. He was then for some time in custody, but was soon released, at the intercession, according to an old tradition, of Sir William Davenant, for whom he had performed a similar good office during the Commonwealth.

Now "in darkness and with dangers compassed round," Milton, after twenty years spent in the arid deserts of controversy, again girt his singing robes around him. A few old friends remained faithful to him, but his daughters, to whom he was a harsh parent, were undutiful, and his domestic infelicity for a time was great. Affairs were, however, put on a more comfortable footing by his marriage to Elizabeth Minshull, an excellent woman, who did her duty well to him and his daughters. In 1667 "Paradise Lost," begun in the year before the close of the Protectorate, was published. Four years later, in 1671, "Paradise Regained" and "Samson Agonistes" appeared. Busy to the last, he also published various minor prose works, a "Latin Accidence," a "History of Britain," a "Tract on True Religion," &c. The most important work of his later years, however, was his Latin "Treatise on Christian Doctrine," which is very valuable for the light which it throws on his theological opinions. After the manuscript of it had been lost for many years, it was at length found in an old brown paper parcel that had been lying in the State Paper Office since 1675; and its publication, along with an English translation, by Bishop Sumner in 1825, gave occasion to Macaulay's famous *Edinburgh Review* essay.

On November 8th, 1674, Milton died. Four days later he was buried in the chancel of St. Giles, Cripplegate, attended to the grave by "all his learned and great friends in London, not without a friendly concourse of the vulgar." His personal appearance is well known from his portraits. In his youth he was eminently beautiful, with something of feminine delicacy in his appearance; and even in his old age, when blind and careworn by many trials, his features retained a sort of greatness and nobleness. "His domestic habits, so far as they are known, were those of a severe student. He drank little strong drink of any kind, and fed without excess in quantity, and in his earlier years without delicacy of choice. In his youth he studied late at night, but afterwards changed his hours, and rested in bed from nine to four in the summer, and five in the winter. The course of his day was best known after he was blind. When he first rose, he read a chapter in the Hebrew Bible, and then studied till twelve; then took some exercise for an hour; then dined; then played on the organ, and sang, or heard another sing; then studied to six; then entertained his visitors till eight; then supped, and, after a pipe of tobacco and a glass of water, went to bed."* The "Notes" of Richardson supply a graphic and touching picture of Milton in his closing years. "An aged clergyman of Dorsetshire," he says, "found John Milton in a small chamber hung with rusty green, sitting in an elbow-chair, and dressed neatly in black; pale, but not cadaverous; his hands and fingers gouty, and with chalkstones. He used also to sit in a grey coarse cloth coat at the door of his house near Bunhill Fields in warm, sunny weather, and so, as well as in his house, received the visits of people of distinguished parts as well as quality." His character, after all deductions have been made, was a very noble one. Not amiable, irritable, exacting, vindictive, he was totally free from anything deserving the name of vice; conscientious, high-minded, dignified, courageous.

"Paradise Lost," as originally published, consisted of ten books. For the manuscript Milton received £5; and it was arranged that he should receive £5 after each of the first four editions, which were to consist of 1300 copies each. In 1669 Milton gave the publisher, Simmons, a receipt for £5, so that he received for the first edition just £10. The second edition appeared in 1674. In it the two longest books of the first edition, Books VII. and X., were each divided into two, and some other trifling alterations were made. In 1678 the third edition appeared, for which, in 1680, Simmons paid Milton's

* Johnson.

widow £5, and for £3 more purchased all interest in the copyright. All circumstances considered, the sale of the book was not bad, and Simmons must have made a tolerably good thing of his purchase. It would be presumption to attempt to criticise a work so great and so well known as "Paradise Lost." The most salient objections to its plan and execution are given in Johnson's unappreciative but very able criticism. Such trifling faults as he mentions are but as a feather in the balance when weighed against the wonderful majesty, the consummate art, the strength and dignity, of England's greatest epic. The theme of the poem is one so vast, so transcending human faculties, so full of difficulties, as to require a poet of Milton's massive genius to grapple with. It may be granted at once that "Paradise Lost" is overlaid with learning; that it is occasionally prolix; that it is sometimes even (as in the case of the war in heaven) grotesque; but no poem, taken as a whole, is so uniformly grand, or soars up into such splendid regions of eloquence. The verse, as in all poems of first-rate excellence, is an echo to the sense. "Perhaps no man," writes Dr. Guest, a great authority on such matters, "ever paid the same attention to the quality of his rhythm as Milton. What other poets effect as it were by chance, Milton achieved by the aid of science and art; he *studied* the aptness of his numbers, and diligently tutored an ear which nature had gifted with the most delicate sensibility. In the flow of his rhythm, in the quality of his letter sounds, in the disposition of his pauses, his verse almost ever *fits* the subject, and so insensibly does poetry blend with this—the last beauty of exquisite versification—that the reader may sometimes doubt whether it be the thought itself, or merely the happiness of its expression, which is the source of a gratification so deeply felt."

"Paradise Regained" had its origin in a suggestion of Ellwood the Quaker. Visiting Milton in 1665, the poet gave him the MS. of "Paradise Lost" to read. When it was returned, Milton asked, "How I liked it, and what I thought of it, which I modestly but freely told him; and, after some further discourse about it, I pleasantly said to him, 'Thou hast said much here of Paradise lost, but what hast thou to say of Paradise found?' He made me no answer, but sat for some time in a muse; then brake off that discourse and fell upon another subject. After the sickness was over, and the city well cleansed, and become safely habitable again, he returned thither. And when, afterwards, I went to wait on him there, which I seldom failed of doing whenever my occasions drew me to London, he showed me his second poem, called 'Paradise Regained,' and in a pleasant tone said to me, 'This is owing to you, for you put it into my head by the question you put to me at Chalfont [where Milton was staying while the plague raged at London], which before I had not thought of.'"

Milton's alleged preference of "Paradise Lost" to "Paradise Regained" is very often given as an example of the incorrect judgments which authors are apt to form of their own works. As a matter of fact, however, there is no evidence that he did so prefer it; the sole foundation for that statement being a remark of Philips's that "Paradise Regained" was generally thought to be much inferior to "Paradise Lost," though Milton could "not hear with patience any such thing when related to him." That it is greatly inferior is indisputable, though some passages, such as the description of Greece, are eminently beautiful. In majesty and sublimity it cannot be compared to "Paradise Lost."

"Samson Agonistes" is one of Milton's most characteristic poems. The subject was one upon which his thoughts had long dwelt, but in his old age it came back to him with renewed intensity when his own lot seemed to have so many points in common with that of the ancient hero. Like Samson, he was blind; like Samson, he had fallen into the hands of the Philistines; like Samson, he was a Nazarite, shunning wine and strong drink; like Samson, he had incurred much misery by his marriage to a Philistine woman. The drama is formed upon Greek models, and imitates them in the strong simplicity of its style. It would be difficult to mention any equally great poem so bare of ornament, so ruthlessly stripped of conventional poetic phrases and imagery.

One of the strangest and most undiscerning criticisms of Johnson on Milton is that on the Sonnets. "Of the best," he writes, "it can only be said that they are not bad; and perhaps only the eighth and twenty-first are truly entitled to this slender commendation." The fact is that they are among the finest sonnets in the language, unsurpassed in strength and dignity save by some of Wordsworth's. In Milton's hand, as Wordsworth says in his Sonnet on the Sonnet—

> "The thing became a trumpet, whence he blew
> Soul-animating strains, alas! too few."

The rage for playing upon words and ideas which is found in many writers of the Elizabethan era, and most prominently in Lyly, culminated in the poets called the metaphysical school, a name which was given to them by Johnson, and which, though not very appropriate, has adhered to them. Of this school, of which Lyly was the true progenitor, the characteristics are pointed out by Johnson in a very masterly way. "The metaphysical poets were men of learning, and to show their learning was their whole endeavour; but unluckily resolving to show it in rhyme, instead of writing poetry they only wrote verses, and very often such verses as stood the trial of the finger better than of the ear; for the modulation was so imperfect that they were only found to be verses by counting the syllables.

"If the father of criticism has rightly denominated poetry *τεχνη μιμητικη*, an imitative art, those writers will, without great wrong, lose their right to the name of poets, for they cannot be said to have imitated anything; they neither copied nature for life; neither painted the forms of matter, nor represented the operations of intellect."

Of the "metaphysical" school, John Donne [1573–1631] may be said to have been the founder. He was the first to make fanciful similitudes, remote analogies, and verbal subtleties not only a competent part, but actually the main feature of his verse. A very learned man, of much original power, and endowed with a real though not a powerful vein of poetical genius, he was totally unable, or at any rate unwilling, to curb that fantastic spirit which appears equally in his sermons, which were very famous in their day, and in his poetry. His works are stiff reading, the windings of his perverted ingenuity being often difficult to trace. Many other writers followed the affected strain adopted by Donne, but they are now nearly all forgotten with the exception of Abraham Cowley [1618–1667]. He was born in London, and educated at Westminster and at Cambridge. While very young he read and admired Spenser's "Faerie Queen," a poem which has exercised a vast influence over many juvenile bards, and was so fascinated with it that its perusal made him, as he says, irrecoverably a poet. When only fifteen years of age he published a volume of poems, which, if its abstract merits are not great, at any rate bears witness to the wonderfully precocious nature of his genius. At Cambridge, where he pursued his studies with great zeal, he wrote the greater part of his "Davideis," an unreadable epic, and two or three forgotten comedies. Ejected from Cambridge in 1643, on account of his Royalist opinions, by the Puritan visitors, he went to Oxford, where he gained great favour among prominent members of the King's party, "by the warmth of his loyalty and the elegance of his conversation." When Oxford surrendered to the Parliament, "he followed the Queen to Paris, where he became secretary to Lord Jermyn, afterwards Earl of St. Albans, and was employed in such correspondence as the royal cause required, and particularly in ciphering and deciphering the letters that passed between the King and Queen, an employment of the highest confidence and honour." In 1647 appeared his "Mistress," a collection of amorous verses, making no pretence to genuine passion, and full of conceits, often highly ingenious, but very unsuitable to anything aspiring to the name of poetry. In 1656 he returned to England, where he was arrested as being in communication with the exiled party, but was soon liberated on bail. In the same year he published his poems, with a preface expressing his earnest desire "to forsake the world for ever, by retiring to some of the American plantations." He then applied himself to the study of medicine; and received the degree of Doctor of Physic in 1657, but never practised. He had, however, a considerable interest in natural science, particularly in botany, and was one of the first members of the Royal Society. After the Restoration his loyalty was rewarded by the grant of certain lands of the annual value of about £300. He then retired to Chertsea, where he passed the evening of his life in the solitude he had so often longed for, without, however, finding that retirement had all the advantages which his imagination had pictured it to possess.

Some of Cowley's shorter poems show that if he had not been under "metaphysical" influence he might have acquired great and permanent fame, if not in the higher walks of poetry, at any rate as a writer of gay songs and occasional verses. He had a highly inventive and ingenious intellect; his works convey a strong impression of great intellectual powers misused and wasted. His prose writings, which go into a very small volume, are excellent, and have none of the faults of his poems. "No author," says Johnson, "ever kept his verse and his prose at a greater distance from each other. His thoughts are natural, and his style has a smooth and placid equability, which has never yet obtained its due commendation. Nothing is far sought or hard laboured, but all is easy without feebleness, and familiar without grossness."

Among the "metaphysical" poets Denham and Waller are included by Johnson. But they can scarcely be said to belong to that school; occasional passages in their works may show its influence, but they are not pervaded by it. Denham [1615–1668] is remembered chiefly as the author of "Cooper's Hill," one of the earliest and one of the best of our descriptive poems. Waller [1605–1687] was one of the many men who shamefully changed sides at the Restoration, employing his pen first in commemorating the virtues of Cromwell, and then in panegyrising Charles II. "Elegant" is the term by which his verses, dealing largely with trifling subjects, may be best characterised. In the technical accuracy of his style, the smoothness of his numbers, and the conventional tone of his sentiments he preluded the school of Dryden and Pope, which long reigned paramount in English poetry.

IV.

THE RESTORATION.

Butler; Dryden; Wycherley, Congreve, Vanbrugh, Farquhar, Sheridan; Otway, Lee, Rowe; Barrow, Tillotson, Stillingfleet, Sherlock, South; Gilbert Burnet; Locke; Newton.

NEVER was a monarch welcomed with more general and heartfelt joy than was manifested when, in May, 1660, Charles II. landed at Dover. Not only those staunch cavaliers who through evil report and through good report had remained steadfast in their allegiance to the "good old cause," but the nation at large felt as glad to be relieved from the iron sway of Puritanism as a school-boy, wearied of tasks and punishments, is when the long-wished-for holiday-time comes at last. All the numerous class of men who make a point of adhering to the winning side, whatever it may happen to be, hastened to abjure Puritanism, and added their voices to the general shout of delight which hailed the arrival of King Charles. "It is my own fault," said the King, "that I had not come back sooner; for I find nobody who does not tell me that he has always longed for my return." Immediately the fierce reaction against the enforced moralities and decencies of the Commonwealth set in. The stern moroseness of the Puritans had made their very virtues so odious, that it was considered that a loyal gentleman could not better show his detestation of the Commonwealth and his joy at the Restoration than by indulging in vice openly and unashamed. The king himself, dissolute, cool, clever, ready to sacrifice anything to the pursuit of pleasure, and never making even the faintest attempt to cover his excesses with a cloak of outward decency, was a fair specimen of the courtiers who surrounded him; not so heartless and brutal as some, but as sensual, and as destitute of honour and conscience as the worst of them could be. The new literature was a fair reflex of the prevalent social morality. The shameless indecency of some of the noble versifiers of the period was more than surpassed by the deliberate obscenity, the gross pandering to vicious tastes, the heartless immorality of the comic drama, which aspired to be, and no doubt was, a faithful representation of the fashionable society of the time. In a moral atmosphere so fetid and unhealthy, literature of the highest kind could not be expected to flourish, yet even during this age we find not a few writers whose works the world would not willingly let die.

About the close of 1662 appeared a poem which in striking and witty fashion gave forcible expression to the long-accumulated hatred of the Puritans which thousands had nourished in their breasts during the time of the Commonwealth. The work was admirably adapted to suit the prevailing taste, and its success was instantaneous. The King read it and was much amused by it; in all the coffee-houses its merits were discussed by the wits; everywhere it was applauded as the most successful of the many assaults made on the fallen party. This poem was the first part of the "Hudibras" of Samuel Butler, who, though a man of fifty, had not, till the time of its publication, given any evidence of his talents as a writer. Of the story of his life not very much is known. He was born in 1612, the son of a farmer in Worcestershire, and received a good education at the cathedral school of that town. It is not known for certain whether he was ever sent to either of the universities. In his youth he acted as secretary to Thomas Jefferies, a justice of peace in Worcestershire, and he afterwards held a similar office in the household of the Countess of Kent in Bedfordshire. In the latter situation he had the advantage of an excellent library, when, doubtless, he amassed a large store of that curious erudition which we find in "Hudibras." There also he enjoyed the conversation of the learned Selden, then steward of the Countess's estates. About 1651 (the precise date is uncertain) he became secretary to Sir Samuel Luke of Cople Hoo, also in Bedfordshire, which seems a strange situation for a man of Butler's Royalist opinions to have occupied, as Sir Samuel was one of the leading Presbyterians in the county, and had been a colonel in the Parliamentary army during the Civil Wars. After the Restoration Butler was, perhaps on account of his known loyalty, promoted to the office of secretary to the Earl of Carbery, Lord President of the principality of Wales. This situation he held for about a year, quitting it some months before the publication of the first part of "Hudibras," which, though bearing on its title-page the date 1663, was really issued in November 1662. A good indication of the avidity with which the satire was received is afforded by an entry in the amusing diary of Samuel Pepys, that delightful book of gossip, which constitutes our most valuable memorial of the social life of the period over which it extends (1660–69). "To the wardrobe," we find Samuel writing on the 26th of December 1662, "and hither came Mr. Battersby; and we falling into discourse of a new book of drollery in use called 'Hudibras,' I would needs go find it out, and met with it at the Temple: cost me 2s. 6d. But when I come to read it, it is so silly an abuse of the presbyter knight going to the wars, that I am ashamed of it; and by and by meeting at Mr. Townsend's at dinner, I sold it to him for 18d." Finding that as time went on "Hudibras" was as much talked of as ever, Pepys soon repented that he had disposed of the book so hastily. "To Lincoln's Inn Fields," he writes on February 6, 1663, "and it being too soon to go home to dinner, I walked up and down, and looked upon the outside of the new theatre building in Covent Garden, which will be very fine; and so to a bookseller's in the Strand, and there bought 'Hudibras' again, it being certainly some ill-humour to be so against that which all the world cries up to be an example of wit; for which I am resolved once more to read him, to see whether I can find it or no." The great success of the first part of "Hudibras" evoked a crowd of imitations and spurious continuations, but these were all put in the shade when, late in 1663, the genuine "Second Part" appeared. The desire to see the Puritans satirised was still as strong as ever, and since, in point of wit and drollery, the new part was in no way inferior to its predecessor, it was received with equal enthusiasm. Fourteen years after, in 1678, the poem was completed. By this time the nation was beginning to realise that the rigour and gloom of Puritanism were, after all, preferable to debauchery and prodigality, and probably the conclusion of "Hudibras" was not so universally applauded as the two preceding parts. Butler died in 1680, a poverty-stricken, neglected, disappointed man.

> "On Butler who can think without just rage,
> The glory and the scandal of the age?
> Fair were his hopes when first he came to town,
> Met everywhere with welcome of renown.
> . . . .
> But what reward had he for all at last,
> After a life in dull expectance past?
> The wretch, at summing up his misspent days,
> Found nothing left but poverty and praise:
> Of all his gains by verse he could not save
> Enough to purchase flannel and a grave.
> Reduced to want, he in due time fell sick,
> Was fain to die, and be interred on tick;
> And well might bless the fever that was sent
> To rid him hence, and his worse fate prevent."

These vigorous lines are by John Oldham (1653–83), a contemporary satirist. They do not exaggerate the facts of the case. Charles and his courtiers praised Butler and left him in indigence. Perhaps this was partly owing to Butler's peculiar temperament: he was a shy, eccentric, unpliable man, not likely to put himself about to gain the favour of any one. But none the less was it disgraceful of the victorious party to leave unrewarded the author of the most telling and pungent satire on their opponents. The inexhaustible wit of "Hudibras," its exuberant wealth of fancy, its frequent happy expressions and flashes of sound sense amid all its comic extravagances, have saved it from the common fate of political satires. The idea of the poem is borrowed from "Don Quixote," but otherwise the work is entirely original; there is nothing in English literature which has any close resemblance to it. Of course it is exceedingly unjust to the Puritan party, violating facts so grossly as to represent them as cowards; but in such productions we do not look for impartiality. The jolting octo-syllabic verse in which it is written lends itself admirably to the odd turns and queer rhymes in which Butler delights. Like Mr. Browning in our own day, Butler had a sort of genius for finding out rhymes the most unexpected and out of the way. The great fault of "Hudibras" is that it is too long; there are few even of those who enter most thoroughly into the spirit of the poem whose attention does not begin to flag before they reach the end. In 1659, many years after his death, Butler's "Genuine Prose Remains" were published. They possess much of the coarse vigour of his poetry. We append a few specimens, which have a decidedly Hudibrastic flavour. "Hudibras" itself, it may be mentioned, was to some extent composed from prose hints which the author had jotted down as they occurred to him.

"One that is proud of his birth is like a turnip—there is nothing good of him but that which is underground."

"His (the courtly fop's) tailor is his creator, and makes him of nothing; and though he lives by faith in him, he is perpetually committing iniquities against him."

"A proud man is a fool in fermentation."

"When he (a versifier) writes, he commonly steers the sense of his lines by the rhyme that is at the end of them, as butchers do calves by the tail."

"He (the amateur of science) is like an elephant, that though he cannot swim, yet of all creatures most delights to walk by the riverside."

"Hudibras" could not be adequately described or criticised unless large extracts from it were given. Except his hatred of the Puritans and the clearness of his style, Butler had not many features in common with his contemporaries; in his mode of literary treatment he neither influenced nor was influenced by them to any great extent. The representative man of the Restoration era is John Dryden, who in all respects was pre-eminently the child of his age. It has been truly said that the literary history of England for nearly a century and a half centres round three personalities, each in his day the focus of all that was said or written that was either wise or witty. "He who knows minutely the lives of Dryden, of Pope, and of Dr. Johnson, with their sayings and doings, their friendships and their enmities, knows intimately the course of English letters and poetry from the Restoration to the French Revolution." Of Dryden especially it is true that by tracing the course of his literary activity we may form a very fair notion of all the characteristics and tendencies of the literature of his epoch. Dryden was born in 1631 at the Vicarage of Aldwinkle All Saints, in Northamptonshire. He was of good descent, his father being the son of Sir Erasmus Dryden, a baronet whose family originally came from the neighbourhood of the Border. Of Dryden's youth very little is known: indeed the information we possess respecting him at all periods of his life is not nearly so copious or so trustworthy as could be wished. About 1642 he entered Westminster School, of which the then head-master was Busby, whose flogging propensities have been widely celebrated. With all his severity, Busby was a most successful teacher, and Dryden, who seems to have been a favourite with him, always regarded him with affectionate respect. From Westminster, Dryden, in 1650, went to Cambridge, where he remained about seven years. During the earlier part of his residence there he got into trouble with the university authorities, and he does not appear to have afterwards cherished very kindly feelings towards his *alma mater*. In one of his prologues to the University of Oxford, he, in an indirect manner, shows his dislike to the sister university:—

"Oxford to him a dearer name shall be
Than his own mother university;
Thebes did his green unknowing youth engage,
He chooses Athens in his riper age."

Leaving Cambridge in 1657, Dryden settled in London, and attached himself to his cousin, Sir Gilbert Pickering, who was high in the favour of the Protector. Though over twenty-seven years of age, he had as yet given very slender evidences of his literary power. A few occasional verses, in which it is hard to discern any indications of genius, were all that he had written. The earliest of these, a poem lamenting Lord Henry Hastings, who died of small-pox in the last year of Dryden's residence at Westminster, shows, in an amusing way, how Dryden's receptive mind had been impressed by the conceits of Cowley and the other poets of the metaphysical school. Describing the manner of his Lordship's death, the youthful poet says—

> "Each little pimple had a tear in it,
> To wail the fault its rising did commit,
> Which, rebel-like, with its own lord at strife,
> Thus made an insurrection 'gainst his life.
> Or were these gems sent to adorn his skin,
> The cabinet of a richer soul within?
> No comet need foretell his change drew on
> Whose corpse might seem a constellation."

This was out-heroding Herod; the metaphysical poets, with all their curious fancies, never reached a greater height of absurdity than this; and Dryden, though it was many years later before he altogether abandoned such conceits, never again indulged in them so extravagantly. In 1658 he published his first poem of merit, the heroic stanzas on the death of Cromwell. The metre of the poem, dignified but rather cumbrous and difficult to handle, is imitated from the "Gondibert" of Sir William Davenant, a poet and playwright of considerable merit, who became Laureate after the Restoration. When Charles became king, Dryden employed the pen which had panegyrised the Protector in panegyrising the new monarch. For this sudden change of opinion the best excuse that can be given is that stated by Johnson: "The reproach of inconstancy was, on this occasion, shared with such numbers that it produced neither hatred or disgrace; if he changed, he changed with the nation." "Astræa Redux," a poem celebrating the return of Charles, appeared in 1660, the "Panegyric on the Coronation" in 1661, and the "Epistle to the Lord Chancellor" (Clarendon) in 1662. All these poems are in the heroic couplet, the form of verse over which Dryden was afterwards to gain such a mastery. In 1663 appeared the "Epistle to Dr. Charleton," which Hallam very unjustly thought was the first of Dryden's works that possessed any considerable merit.

At the close of 1663, Dryden married Lady Elizabeth Howard, the eldest daughter of the Earl of Berkshire. This union is thought, though on no very certain evidence, to have been an unhappy one. Some months before his marriage, Dryden's first play, the "Wild Gallant," was acted. During the Commonwealth the drama had lived in a stealthy and precarious kind of way, forbidden by the law and frowned upon by all who wished to stand well with the Puritans. At the Restoration it revived, and became, in fact, the best market which a man of literary talents could carry his wares to. It may be safely asserted that a writer, possessed like Dryden of a versatile genius, will, in almost every case, employ himself mainly in the kind of work which he finds most remunerative, even though it may not be the kind of work for which he is best adapted. It is idle, therefore, to lament that so much of Dryden's time should have been occupied in the composition of plays, none of which is of such value that it would be any serious loss to literature to be deprived of it, and which several writers of his time could have written almost, if not quite, as well. But we have good cause to lament that he should have prostituted his genius by, in his comic dramas, pandering shamelessly and recklessly to the licentious tastes of his audience. Altogether he wrote twenty-eight plays, the first appearing, as above stated, in 1663, the last, "Love Triumphant," in 1694. In his comedies, indecency frequently takes the place of wit, and their merit in other respects is small. "I know," wrote Dryden himself, "I am not so fitted by nature to write comedy. My conversation is slow and dull, my humour saturnine and reserved. So that those who decry my comedies do me no injury except it be in point of profit; reputation in them is the last thing to which I shall pretend." Dryden's serious dramas fall into two well-marked divisions. The earlier of them are written in the pompous heroic style which had been made fashionable in England by Sir William Davenant, and the tragic portions are, like the similar parts of Davenant's plays, written in rhyming couplets. A good specimen of Dryden's dramas of rhymed declamation, as they may be called, is afforded by the "Conquest of Granada" (1670). The sublime rants of its hero, Almanzor, are difficult to regard in other than a humorous light, though, singularly enough, they seem to have inspired Dr. Johnson with a sort of admiration. "All the rays of romantic heat," he says, "whether amorous or warlike, glow in Almanzor by a kind of concentration. He is above all laws; he is exempt from all restraints; he ranges the world at will, and governs wherever he appears. He fights without inquiring the cause, and loves in spite of the obligations of justice, of rejection by his mistress, and of prohibition from the dead. Yet the scenes are, for the most part, delightful; they exhibit a kind of illustrious depravity and majestic madness, such as, if it is sometimes despised, is often reverenced, and in which the majestic mingles with the astonishing." In 1668 Dryden had defended rhymed tragedies in an "Essay on Dramatic Poesy," which first showed his skill in prose composition and his power of acute and discerning criticism. He did not, however, remain steadfast to the practice he then advocated. In 1671 appeared the famous burlesque called the "Rehearsal," which inflicted a severe blow on the popularity of rhymed tragedies. This very amusing play, which will bear reading even by those whose knowledge of the literature of the age is not sufficient to enable them to appreciate all its allusions, was the work of the Duke of Buckingham, assisted by Samuel Butler, Thomas Sprat, afterwards made a bishop, and Martin Clifford, the head-master of the Charterhouse. Though it contained allusions to several other dramatists of the time, the main object of the "Rehearsal" was to caricature Dryden, who is represented under the name of Bayes, a nickname which stuck to him throughout life. Not only his literary but his personal peculiarities, his dress, his voice, his gesture, his habit of taking snuff, his favourite expletives are mercilessly ridiculed. This attack Dryden bore very stoically, making no reply, and continuing to write rhymed tragedies as before. At length his own good sense showed him that it would be better to abandon the practice, and return to the form of verse which had been employed with such eminent success by the Elizabethan dramatists. About 1678 appeared "All for Love," his first drama in blank verse, and one of his best plays from every point of view. There was something of audacity in writing a play on a subject which had already been handled by the greatest dramatist the world has ever seen in "Anthony and Cleopatra." Yet with such vigour and force is "All for Love" written, that it can sustain comparison with the work of Shakespeare, and still be admired. Dryden's other most famous play in blank verse is "Don Sebastian" (1689), one scene in which, the altercation between Sebastian and Dorax, used to be very often given in books of extracts.

Having thus briefly dealt with Dryden as a dramatist, we now return to trace the course of his life. "Annus Mirabilis" appeared in 1667, which, from a literary point of view, is one of the most important years of the seventeenth century. It witnessed the publication of "Paradise Lost," the death of Denham, Cowley, and Jeremy Taylor, and the birth of Swift and Arbuthnot. "Annus Mirabilis," which is written in the same metre as "Astræa Redux," commemorates the events of the "wonderful year" 1666, the great fire of London, and the Dutch war. Though frequently disfigured by "metaphysical" conceits, it is a powerful piece of writing, and at once made Dryden the most illustrious poet of the day, Milton of course excepted. His "Discourse on Dramatic Poesy" raised him to similar rank as a prose writer; and in 1670 his merits in both capacities were recognised by his being appointed historiographer-royal and poet laureate. In the latter capacity he succeeded Sir William Davenant, who died in 1668. The two offices brought him a salary of

£200 a year, to which was afterwards added a pension of £100 bestowed on him by Charles. The income thus derived was, however, to a considerable extent a nominal one; for Charles was a very bad paymaster, and Dryden's salary was frequently in arrear. Nevertheless his financial position about this time was tolerably prosperous. He had a small estate worth about £80 a year, which he had inherited from his father; and from his dramas, and a lucrative contract he entered into with the players, he obtained a considerable revenue. For fourteen years after the publication of "Annus Mirabilis" Dryden employed himself in dramatic work, adding little to his permanent fame, but acquiring, by prolonged and laborious practice, a consummate mastery of the heroic couplet. In 1681, when party spirit ran very high about the Exclusion Bill, he gave the first specimen of his wonderful power of reasoning in verse and his extraordinary talent for satire by the publication of "Absalom and Achitophel." The plan of the poem is not original, but the mode of treatment is eminently so. In vigorous couplets he gives us a matchless series of political portraits, strong, mordant, incisive, and always having the crowning merit of keeping sufficiently close to actual fact to save them from having the semblance of caricature. Interspersed with these are occasional speeches relating the sentiments of the different characters from Dryden's point of view. Dryden never surpassed this his first essay in the field of satire: the energy of genius, it has been well said, has transformed a party pamphlet in verse into a work which men of all ages and of all opinions have agreed to recognise as a masterpiece. When, on the acquittal of Shaftesbury, who had been tried on a charge of high treason, a medal was struck by the joyful Whigs to commemorate the event, Dryden followed up "Absalom and Achitophel" by another satire, "The Medal," in which "he hurled at Shaftesbury and his party a philippic which, for rancorous abuse, for lofty and uncompromising scorn, for coarse, scathing, ruthless denunciation, couched in diction which now swells to the declamatory grandeur of Juvenal, and now sinks to the homely vulgarity of Swift, has no parallel in literature."[1] Of the innumerable replies and attacks on the author which "Absalom and Achitophel" and "The Medal" called forth, Dryden took no notice, till Thomas Shadwell, a dramatist of no inconsiderable talents but of infamous life, assailed his private character in terms so gross and libellous as to imperatively demand a rejoinder. Of him Dryden determined to make a terrible example. This he did in "MacFlecknoe," which was published late in 1682. Richard Flecknoe, an Irish priest, who died in 1678, and who had been the favourite butt of many satirists, is represented as having chosen Shadwell for his successor as King of the Realms of Nonsense in a mock-heroic strain which must have been infinitely galling to the subject of ridicule. Shadwell's coronation is then described, and the poem concludes with a ferocious assault which bears too many traces of personal bitterness. About a month after "Mac-Flecknoe" appeared the second part of "Absalom and Achitophel." Most of it was written by Nahum Tate, a worthy though dull man, but two hundred and fifty lines are entirely from Dryden's pen, and traces of his hand may be perceived in other parts of the poem. In the portion which is wholly his he returned to the attack on Shadwell, and also took the opportunity of gibbeting Elkanah Settle, a worthless versifier and playwright, who had occupied a rather prominent place among his numerous assailants.

In the same year, 1682, the "*annus mirabilis*" of his genius, Dryden took a new departure. In that year he published "Religio Laici," which Scott has described as one of the most admirable poems of the language. "It is," says Mr. George Saintsbury, in his excellent little book on Dryden, "also one of the most singular. That a man who had never previously displayed any particular interest in theological questions, and who had reached the age of fifty-one with a

[1] *Quarterly Review*, October 1878, art. "Dryden," one of the ablest and most vigorous Review articles of the kind which has appeared for many a year. Bating its opinions, it might very well have been written by Macaulay. It is, we believe, by Mr. J. Churton Collins.

reputation derived, until quite recently, in the main from the composition of love-plays, should appear before his public of pleasure-seekers with a serious argument in verse on the credibility of the Christian religion and the merits of the Anglican form of doctrine and church government, would nowadays be something more than a nine days' wonder. In Dryden's time it was somewhat less surprising. The spirit of theological controversy was bred in the bone of the seventeenth century." "Religio Laici" is a fine specimen of Dryden's talent for reasoning in verse; but he was soon to show that the arguments in it as to the superiority of the Church of England over other ecclesiastical institutions had not convinced himself. In 1685 Charles II. died, and James II. ascended the throne. Every one knows how sincere a Catholic the new sovereign was, and how assiduously he strove that all around him should conform to his own faith. In 1686 Dryden joined the Church of Rome.

It was so obviously Dryden's interest, both from pecuniary and from other points of view, to become a Catholic at this time, that the sincerity of his conversion has naturally been much discussed. Some critics have thought they discovered in the "Religio Laici," where he says—

> "Such an omniscient Church we wish indeed,
> 'Twere worth both Testaments cast in the Creed,"

an indication of dissatisfaction with the Church of England; but this is very doubtful. The true explanation of Dryden's sudden change of religion seems to be that, prompted at first by self-interest to favour the Church of Rome, he at length became really attached to it. With characteristic readiness he now set himself to defend Catholicism. The "Hind and the Panther," in which he defends his newly adopted faith so well that Hallam declares that no candid mind could doubt the sincerity of one who could argue so powerfully and subtly in its favour, appeared in 1687. It is an allegory; "the milk-white hind, unspotted and unchanged," representing the Church of Rome; "the panther, sure the noblest, next the hind, and fairest creature of the spotted kind," the Church of England; a bear, the Independents; a boar, the Baptists, and so on. When the Revolution came, in 1688, Dryden had an opportunity of proving the sincerity of his convictions. Had he apostatised, there is little doubt that he might have retained his offices of historiographer-royal and poet laureate; but, to the credit of his fair fame, he remained constant to the faith he had adopted. His prospects were now gloomy enough, and he was obliged to labour hard to earn a living by his pen. In 1697 he published his translation of Virgil, the result of three years' toil. Previous to its publication he had translated Persius and part of Juvenal, as well as other scattered pieces, but these efforts were thrown into the shade by his Virgil, which, though freely translated and very little imbued with the spirit of the original, is nevertheless a noble achievement. The chief works of the remaining years of Dryden's life are the well-known ode commonly called "Alexander's Feast" and his "Fables," stories paraphrased from Chaucer and Boccaccio, interesting not only on account of their intrinsic merits, which are in many respects great, but also as showing the extraordinary versatility of Dryden's genius, which enabled him, when an old man of sixty-eight, to win laurels in a new field of literature. They were published in 1699, a few months before his death, which occurred in April 1700. The splendid literary services which he had rendered to his country were recognised by his being buried in Westminster Abbey, where he was laid in Poet's Corner, beside Chaucer and Cowley.

"We are enabled, from the various paintings and engravings of Dryden, as well as from the less flattering delineations of the satirists of his time, to form a tolerable idea of his face and person. In youth he appears to have been handsome and of a pleasing countenance; when his age was more advanced, he was corpulent and florid, which procured him the nickname attached to him by Rochester ['Poet Squab']. In his latter days, distress and disappointment probably chilled the fire of his eye, and the advance of age destroyed the animation of his countenance. Still, however, his portraits bespeak the look and features of genius; especially that in which he is drawn with his waving grey hairs."[1] During his lifetime and afterwards, Dryden's moral character was fiercely assailed by a crowd of opponents, including Bishop Burnet, who went so far as to describe him as "a monster of impurity of all sorts." Very little credence, however, is to be placed in such statements; and there is every reason to believe that Dryden's life compared very favourably with that of most of his literary contemporaries. Of his habits not much has been related. He was fond of snuff, in which he indulged largely. Fishing was the only sport which he practised, and in it he attained considerable proficiency. After spending the morning in study, he would adjourn to Will's Coffee-house, where he occupied the same undisputed pre-eminence which Addison afterwards held at Button's, and where his dicta as to the literary matters of the day were eagerly listened to and carefully treasured up. In his disposition he was kind and generous, "ready and gentle," says Congreve, "in his correction of the errors of any writer who thought fit to consult him, and full as ready and patient to admit of the reprehension of others in respect of his own oversights and mistakes."

Dryden was the first poet and the first prose writer of his time. There is no other English author of whom this could be said, but it is strictly and literally true of him. As a poet, indeed, he stood so far above his contemporaries that there is none fit to be mentioned in the same breath with him. Satire was his peculiar province, but he also won distinction in other fields. His didactic poems are among the best of their kind, and his odes, especially the one "To the Memory of Miss Anne Killegrew" (1686), which Johnson called the noblest in the language, as perhaps it was in his time, and "Alexander's Feast," are fine pieces of concerted music. There was in Dryden's nature a certain coarseness of moral fibre, very disagreeably apparent in his plays, which occasionally detracts from the value of his poems; but this is atoned

[1] Scott.

for by his masculine strength, his width of range, and his rich command of expression. As a prose writer, his works of most abiding value are the "Essay on Dramatic Poesy," already mentioned, and the prefaces which he almost invariably added to his publications.

> "Read all the prefaces of Dryden,
> For these the critics much confide in,
> Though only writ at first for filling,
> To raise the volume's price a shilling."

These doggerel lines of Swift show the esteem in which the critical remarks on his art with which Dryden was wont to enrich his poems were held by his contemporaries. Occasionally they are found embedded in the very fulsome dedications with which, after the fashion of his age, he addressed his patrons, occasionally in explanatory or apologetic prefaces. Dryden's criticisms are often inconsistent; he wrote hastily, and was apt to put down whatever occurred to him at the moment, without reflecting that he had elsewhere expressed different opinions; but they are generally excellent, and his admiration of Shakespeare and Milton at a time when their praise was not, as now, in every one's mouth, shows his good taste and discernment. His style is clear, easy, and flexible; rather unmethodical, but quite free from the involutions and long-windedness which had almost invariably marked the prose of the preceding generations. "At no time that I can think of," says Mr. Saintsbury, "was there any Englishman who, for a considerable period, was so far in advance of his contemporaries in almost every branch of literary work as Dryden was during the last twenty years of the seventeenth century. . . . But his representative character in relation to the men of his time was almost more remarkable than his intellectual and artistic superiority to them. Other great men of letters, with perhaps the single exception of Voltaire, have usually, when they represented their time at all, represented but a small part of it. With Dryden this was not the case. Not only did the immense majority of men of letters in his later days directly imitate him, but both then and earlier most literary Englishmen, even when they did not imitate him, worked on the same lines and pursued the same objects. The eighteen volumes of his works contain a faithful representation of the whole literary movement in England for the best part of half a century; and what is more, they contain the germs and indicate the direction of almost the whole literary movement for nearly a century to come."

Bearing in mind these remarks as to Dryden's representative character, the reader will readily infer, from what has been said as to Dryden's comedies, the leading features of the "dramatists of the Restoration," as they are somewhat loosely styled. Of these, Wycherley, Congreve, Farquhar, and Vanbrugh were the chief, and Congreve the greatest. Charles Lamb, in his amusing and paradoxical essay "On the Artificial Comedy of the Last Century," mentions a characteristic of Congreve's plays which applies also to the plays of all the other members of the group. "Judged morally, every character in these plays [he is speaking of the Restoration comedy generally]—the few exceptions are only *mistakes*—is alike essentially vain and worthless. The great art of Congreve is especially shown in this, that he has entirely excluded from his scenes—some little generosities on the part of Angelica perhaps excepted—not only anything like a faultless character, but any pretensions to goodness or good feelings whatsoever. Whether he did this designedly or instinctively, the effect is as happy as the design (if design) was bold. I used to wonder at the strange power which his 'Way of the World,' in particular, possesses of interesting you all along in the pursuit of characters for whom you absolutely care nothing—for you neither hate nor love his personages—and I think it is owing to this very indifference for any that you endure the whole. He has spread a privation of moral light, I will call it, rather than by the ugly name of palpable darkness, over his creations; and his shadows flit before you without distinction or preference. Had he introduced a good character, a single gush of moral feeling, a revulsion of the judgment to actual life and actual duties, the impertinent Goshen would have only lighted to the discovery of deformities, which now are none because we think them none." This is not intended for censure, yet what a censure it is! It is this moral darkness, this heartlessness, this cynical contempt for virtue, or rather unbelief in its existence, which, more than their frequent license of language, make the Restoration dramatists a synonym for unhealthy literature. That they had great talents, that their wit was often brilliant, is undeniable; but though no literary history can altogether pass them over, a full account of them would be out of place here, and we shall accordingly make haste to escape from their polluted atmosphere.

William Wycherley, the coarsest, but not the least gifted, of the dramatists of the Restoration, was born in 1640, the son of a Shropshire gentleman of good family. Sent to France at the age of fifteen to receive his education, he there acquired the manners of a fine gentleman, and became a convert to Roman Catholicism. When the Restoration came, he once more turned Protestant, and became a member of Queen's College, Oxford. Leaving Oxford without taking a degree, he entered the Temple, where he soon distinguished himself among the gay young men about town by the elegance of his manners and by his strikingly handsome appearance. In 1672 his first play, "Love in a Wood," was acted. His two most famous plays, the "Country Wife" and the "Plain Dealer," appeared in 1675 and 1677. Wycherley's life was a sad one enough. After basking for some years in the sunshine of royal favour, he fell into disgrace, and, imprisoned for debt, languished for seven years in the Fleet, "utterly forgotten, as it should seem, by the gay and lively circle of which he had been a distinguished ornament." At length he owed his release to the favour of James II., who paid his debts and granted him a pension of £200 a year. Macaulay suspects that this munificence was the price of Wycherley's apostasy: it is certain, at any rate, that before his death Wycherley a second time joined the Church of Rome. In 1704 he published a folio volume of miscellaneous verses, very immoral and very worthless. He died in 1715 a wretched, worn-out rake, who had outlived his talents and accomplishments. The desire of literary fame was strong in him to the last, and he called in the aid of young Mr. Pope, the most rising genius of the time, to amend his doggerel verses. This Pope did with such unfailing rigour of criticism, such cruel minuteness, that poor Wycherley at length found his advice so unpalatable that he withdrew his papers from him. Coarse vigour and no small show of humour as well as wit are the great characteristics of Wycherley as a dramatist.

The names of Wycherley and Congreve are generally placed together, but there are wide differences between them, both as regards their natural capabilities and their mode of literary treatment. Wycherley was a child of the Restoration with its roistering coarseness; Congreve was rather a child of the Queen Anne period with its low moral ideals united to outward polish and refinement. Hence it is not surprising to find that the comedies of Congreve, if perhaps equally immoral, are not nearly so much disfigured by grossness as Wycherley's. Congreve was born in 1670 at Bardsey, near Leeds. His father, a scion of an ancient Staffordshire family, settled in Ireland soon after the Restoration, and there Congreve received his education. He afterwards came to London to study law; but he was more ambitious to cut a brilliant figure in fashionable society than to accumulate a store of forensic knowledge. His first work was a novel—one of those insipid and affected romances with which our ancestors were compelled to beguile their leisure in the absence of anything better. In 1693 his first comedy, "The Old Bachelor," was acted with great success. The merits of the gifted young author were at once recognised by the generous Montagu, then one of the Lords of the Treasury, who bestowed on him offices of which the salary was more important than the duties. In 1694 Congreve's second play, the "Double Dealer," was produced; in 1695 came "Love for Love," and in 1697 the "Mourning Bride," a tragedy containing one famous passage, which Johnson was accustomed to praise extravagantly in conversation, and which, in his "Lives of the Poets," he declares that he considered the most poetical paragraph in the whole mass of English poetry. Here it is:—

> "*Alm.* It was a fancied noise; for all is hushed.
> *Leo.* It bore the accent of a human voice.
> *Alm.* It was thy fear, or else some transient wind
> Whistling through hollows of this vaulted isle;
> We'll listen.
> *Leo.* Hark!
> *Alm.* No, all is hushed and still as death.—'Tis dreadful!
> How reverend is the face of this tall pile,
> Whose ancient pillars rear their marble heads,
> To bear aloft its arched and ponderous roof,
> By its own weight made steadfast and immoveable,
> Looking tranquillity! It strikes an awe
> And terror on my aching sight; the tombs
> And monumental caves of death look cold,
> And shoot a chillness to my trembling heart.
> Give me thy hand, and let me hear thy voice;
> Nay, quickly speak to me, and let me hear
> Thy voice—my own affrights me with its echoes."

In 1700 Congreve produced what is perhaps his best play, the "Way of the World;" it failed, for some reason or other, and the indignant author took his leave of the stage. He died in 1728. Congreve was a man both of wit and learning, but he was anxious to be distinguished rather as an accomplished gentleman than as a talented writer. When Voltaire called on him, he disclaimed the character of a poet, and declared that his plays were trifles produced in an idle hour. "If," said the great Frenchman, disgusted by what Johnson truly calls this despicable foppery, "you had been only a gentleman, I should not have come to visit you." By his contemporaries Congreve was much looked up to. Dryden gave him in large profusion the weighty tribute of his praise and respect; Pope dedicated to him his translation of the "Iliad;" everywhere among young authors his esteem was courted and his advice sought. It is only as a dramatist that Congreve has any title to fame: his miscellaneous poems are singularly poor productions. "Congreve," says Hazlitt, a very acute if somewhat too partial critic, "is the most distinct from the others, and the most easily defined, both from what he possessed and from what he wanted. He had by far the most wit and elegance, with less of other things, of humour, character, incident, &c. His style is inimitable, nay, perfect. It is the highest model of comic dialogue. Every sentence is replete with sense and satire, conveyed in the most polished and pointed terms. Every page presents a shower of brilliant conceits, is a tissue of epigrams in prose, is a new triumph of wit, a new conquest over dulness. The fire of artful raillery is nowhere else so well kept up. . . . It bears every mark of being what he himself in the dedication to one of his plays tells us that it was, a spirited copy taken off and carefully revised from the most select society of his time, exhibiting all the sprightliness, ease, and animation of familiar conversation with the correctness and delicacy of the most finished composition."

Two years before the publication of Congreve's last play, the Restoration comedy received what proved to be its death-blow. In 1798, Jeremy Collier, a nonjuring clergyman of High Church and High Tory proclivities, published his "Short View of the Profaneness and Immorality of the English Stage." Collier was a keen controversialist, harsh, firm, and unbending; a man of considerable learning (his "Ecclesiastical History" is still in some sort a standard work), and possessed of a vigorous and telling style. Though disfigured by much irrelevant, and indeed absurd matter, the "Short View" was on the whole so just an indictment of the license which the dramatists had allowed themselves, that its effect was very great. "His onset was violent," says Johnson; "those passages which, while they stood single, had passed with little notice, when they were accumulated and exposed together excited horror; the wise and the pious caught the alarm, and the nation wondered why it had so long suffered irreligion and licentiousness to be taught at the public charge." Dryden, who was the most prominent object of attack, had the good sense to kiss the rod. "I shall say the less of Mr. Collier," he wrote in the preface to his "Fables," "because in many things he has taxed me justly, and I have pleaded guilty to all thoughts and expressions of mine which can be truly argued of obscenity, profaneness, or immorality, and retract them. If he be my enemy, let him triumph; if he be my friend, as I have given him no personal occasion to be otherwise, he will be glad of my repentance. It becomes me not to draw my pen in the defence of a bad cause, when I have so often drawn it for a good one." Many of Dryden's fellow-offenders were not so prudent. Congreve entered the lists in defence of the dramatists, and, with the usual ill-fortune which attends controversialists in behalf of a bad cause, instead of assailing the parts of Collier's production which were really open to attack, argued with so little ability as to expose himself to a crushing rejoinder. It would be foolish to attribute the influence exerted by the "Short View" to Collier's ability alone. It owed its success in great measure to the fact that it chimed in with a wide-spread public sentiment.

Among the authors of replies to Collier was Sir John Vanbrugh (1666?–1726), the most distinguished architect of his day, and one of the wittiest dramatists. As an architect, his principal achievements were the noble erections of Blenheim and Castle Howard; as a dramatist, the "Relapse" and the "Provoked Wife," which were produced about 1697. His plays are full of fun, and its ordinary accompaniment in those days—indecency. He has little or nothing of the refined art of Congreve. "Van," Pope truly said, "wants grace who never wanted wit;" but there is about him a flavour of jovial high spirits and comic power, which makes his plays (apart from the defect mentioned) very pleasant reading.

A writer in many ways resembling Vanbrugh was George Farquhar, a gay Irishman of lively fancy and much vivacity. He was the son of a clergyman, and was born at Londonderry in 1678. He quitted Trinity College, Dublin, where he had fallen into some scrape, and, while still a mere boy, became an actor. At the age of eighteen he bade farewell to the boards, having obtained a commission in the army from the Earl of Orrery. When only twenty years old he won credit by his first play, "Love and a Bottle," and steadily improved in his art till the close of his brief life in his thirtieth year. His best plays are his two last, the "Recruiting Officer" (1706) and the "Beaux Stratagem" (1707). In the first, scenes of low life, evidently drawn from actual observation, are described with great humour and fidelity to nature. The second, which was written in the short space of six weeks, contains the admirable portrait of Boniface, the landlord, which has become as classical in its way as that of Mr. Pickwick or any other hero of fiction.

This is the proper place in which to mention the last great writer of the prose comedy of manners. Though many years separate Richard Brinsley Sheridan from Wycherley, Congreve, Vanbrugh, and Farquhar, he is animated by their spirit, though happily he has none of their license of language. Sheridan was born in Dublin in 1751. His father, a man of some note in his day, is now chiefly remembered as the theme of certain of Johnson's most pungent sarcasms. "Why, sir," said the Doctor on one occasion, "Sherry is dull, naturally dull; but it must have taken him a great deal of pains to become what we now see him. Such an excess of stupidity is not in nature." Sheridan was educated at Harrow, and his first production was a translation of a worthless Greek writer, done in conjunction with a friend whose acquaintance he had formed there. While still a very young man, without fortune and without any high position in society, he married the beautiful Miss Linley, who had been courted by many wealthy and titled admirers. In 1775 he produced his first comedy, "The Rivals," an admirable piece of writing, carefully elaborated, and one blaze of wit from beginning to end. In 1777 appeared his masterpiece, the "School for Scandal," which is still, after so many years, always welcomed on the stage. In 1779 was produced the farce of "The Critic," the idea of which is borrowed from the "Rehearsal," but which is nevertheless a most admirable and mirth-provoking performance. Besides these, he wrote, in 1775, a slight farce called "St. Patrick's Day," and "The Duenna," containing some songs which are excellent of their kind. "His table-songs," says Leigh Hunt, "are always admirable. When he was drinking wine he was thoroughly in earnest." He also wrote two serious dramas, but they are of no value. In 1780 Sheridan became a member of Parliament, and though the faults of his private life told greatly against him, he soon became noted as one of the most eloquent speakers in an assembly which contained Burke, and Fox, and Pitt. "Whatever Sheridan has done or chosen to do," said Byron, "has been, *par excellence*, the best of its kind. He has written the best comedy ('School for Scandal'), the best drama ('The Duenna,' to my mind far beyond that St. Giles lampoon, the 'Beggar's Opera'), the best farce ('The Critic,' it is only too good for a farce), and the best address (Monologue on Garrick); and, to crown all, delivered the very best oration (the famous Begum speech) ever conceived or heard of in this country." This is absurdly over-laudatory; but Sheridan was certainly a man of brilliant abilities, and, with all his love of dissipation, could labour strenuously when he had made up his mind to achieve any design. His comedies are a continual running fire of wit; not true to nature and utterly destitute of that highest kind of humour which approaches pathos, but full of happy turns of expression and admirably constructed with a view to stage representation. He is the last of our playwriters who have produced works both excellent as literature and also good acting dramas. Sheridan lived a shifty and vagabond existence, constantly in debt and constantly harassed by duns, whose demands he, by long experience, acquired unrivalled dexterity in evading. In the closing years of his life his wealthy and titled friends forsook him, and he was reduced to sore straits. He died in 1816.

Only three good writers of tragedy appeared in the period with which we are dealing. Thomas Otway (1651–1685) possessed more of the fire and passion of the great Elizabethans than any of his contemporaries. His chief plays, "The Orphan" and "Venice Preserved," show great powers of pathos, and, although too inflated in style, are more impressive and of deeper interest than the dramas of any other tragedian of the time. The unfortunate poet died in a state of wretched poverty. In the plays of Nathaniel Lee, who was subject to attacks of insanity, we find considerable genius for tragedy united with a propensity to indulge freely in bombast and fustian. The "Rival Queens" and "Lucius Junius Brutus" are his best plays. He died in 1692. Nicholas Rowe (1673–1718), who also deserves remembrance as having been the first editor and biographer of Shakespeare, was the author of two tragedies which were at one time much admired, the "Fair Penitent" and "Jane Shore." In the former appears the "gallant, gay Lothario," the prototype of Richardson's Lovelace and of innumerable romance-heroes of a similar description. Rowe, who was a very estimable man, had his death commemorated by the following epitaph of Pope, which shows the extent of his popularity among his contemporaries:—

> "Thy relics, Rowe, to this sad shrine we trust,
> And near thy Shakespeare place thy honoured bust;
> Oh! next him, skilled to draw the tender tear,
> For never heart-felt passion more sincere;
> To nobler sentiment to fire the brave,
> For never Briton more disdained a slave.
> Peace to thy gentle shade and endless rest!
> Blest in thy genius, in thy love, too, blest!
> And blest that timely from our scene removed,
> Thy soul enjoys the liberty it loved."

As already stated, Dryden in force and elegance of style stands at the head of the prose writers of this period, which does not contain many authors whose fame has outlived their own time. Nevertheless there are a few great names, notably some divines of the Church of England, whose works are still reckoned classics. Of these, Dr. Isaac Barrow is especially memorable, not only for his literary gifts, but for his varied learning. Born in 1630, the son of a linendraper in London, he entered the University of Cambridge when very young. There at first his attention was turned to the study of physical science, and after he had obtained the degree of Bachelor of Arts he applied himself to the study of medicine. Disappointed in the hopes he had formed of obtaining the Greek professorship, he determined to go abroad, and spent some years in travelling in France, Italy, Germany, Turkey, and Holland. On his return to England he took orders, and in 1660 was elected professor of Greek in the University of Cambridge. Two years after he was appointed professor of geometry in Gresham College. In 1663 he became Lucasian professor of mathematics in Cambridge, and resigned both his other offices. In 1669, having resolved to devote himself to the study of theology, he resigned his chair in favour of Isaac Newton. In 1670 he was made D.D. by royal mandate; two years after he was appointed master of Trinity College, and in 1675 he was chosen vice-chancellor of the University. He died in 1677. Barrow is the author of numerous mathematical publications in Latin, and of three folio volumes of English works, published posthumously in 1685. They consist for the most part of sermons. Barrow was in his day a very popular preacher, though his sermons were of unusual length even for that age. He seldom employed less than an hour and a half in delivering a discourse, and on one occasion, when preaching before the Lord Mayor and Aldermen of London, spoke for three hours and a half. Being asked on coming down from the pulpit whether he was not tired, he replied, "Yes, indeed, I began to be weary with standing so long." Barrow's mathematical keenness and ingenuity of intellect is well shown by his famous definition of wit, which has been so often quoted. It also shows his fertility of illustration and his habit of dealing fully with all sides of a subject. Occasionally in his writings we meet with happy phrases, such as "A straight line is the shortest in morals as well as in geometry;" but such epigrammatic turns are rare. In one place he describes with considerable felicity the general literary character of his period: "All reputation appears now to vail and stoop to that of being a wit. To be learned, to be wise, to be good, are nothing in comparison thereto; even to be noble and rich are inferior things, and afford no such glory. Many at least, to purchase this glory, to be deemed considerable in this faculty, and enrolled among the wits, do not only make shipwreck of conscience, abandon virtue, and forfeit all pretences to wisdom, but neglect their estates and prostitute their honour; so, to the private damage of many particular persons, and with no small prejudice to the public, are our times possessed and transported with this humour."

John Tillotson, also born in 1630, became after the Revolution the most admired preacher in London, and was a special favourite of Queen Mary. He was born in Yorkshire of Puritan parents, but in 1662 submitted to the Act of Uniformity. After holding various ecclesiastical appointments, he removed to London, where his sermons soon attracted attention. After the Revolution he obtained from King William the deanery of St. Paul's, and in 1691 was appointed Archbishop of Canterbury. He died in 1694. Tillotson was a tolerant, open-minded man, without a trace of ecclesiastical bigotry, always more willing to conciliate than to crush opponents, and fondly cherishing schemes to draw the Nonconformists within the pale of the Church of England. His popularity is shown by the high price obtained for his sermons, which were published posthumously in three folio volumes. They were, says Macaulay, "bought by the booksellers for the almost incredible sum of two thousand five hundred guineas, equivalent, in the wretched state in which the silver coin then was, to at least three thousand six hundred pounds. Such a price had never before been given in England for any literary copyright. About the same time Dryden, whose reputation was then in its zenith, received thirteen hundred pounds for his translation of all the works of Virgil, and was thought to have been splendidly remunerated." Dryden, it may be mentioned, is said "to have owned with pleasure that if he had any talent for English prose, it was owing to his having often read the writings of Archbishop Tillotson." But Dryden had written excellent prose before Tillotson appeared as an author, and long before he became famous; nor indeed is there any noticeable resemblance between their styles. The merits of Tillotson's style are its ease and simplicity; but he is tautological and diffuse in no ordinary degree. Not only does he ring the changes on ideas—a very common fault in sermons —but he is apt to heap together synonymous words in a rather irritating way. The following extract, which is a fair sample of his style, shows this peculiarity:—"Truth is always consistent with itself, and needs nothing to help it out; it is always near at hand, and sits upon our lips, and is ready to drop out before we are aware; whereas a lie is troublesome, and sets a man's invention upon the rack, and one trick needs a great many more to make it good. It is like building upon a false foundation, which continually stands in need of props to shore it up, and proves at last more chargeable than to have raised a substantial building at first upon a true and solid foundation; for sincerity is firm and substantial, and there is nothing hollow or unsound in it, and because it is plain and open, fears no discovery; of which the crafty man is always in danger; and when he thinks he walks in the dark, all his pretences are so transparent that he that runs may read them." Tillotson probably presents more examples than any author of passages wherewith to exercise the skill of the student of English composition in weeding out their superfluous words and phrases.

Three other notable divines, all ardent controversialists, were Stillingfleet, Sherlock, and South. Edward Stillingfleet (1635–1699) defended with considerable vigour and acrimony the doctrines of the Church of England, attacking all her opponents, Atheists, Unitarians, Papists, and Dissenters. In 1686 he had a controversy with Dryden, who had been employed to defend the reasons of conversion to the Catholic faith by Anne Hyde, which were said to have been found in Charles II.'s strong-box. In this controversy he had decidedly the best of it, but he was signally worsted in a dispute with Locke on the doctrine of the Trinity, and the mortification he then sustained is said to have hastened his death. William Sherlock (1641–1707) "entered warmly into dispute with the most busy sectaries of the time, the Solifidians and Antinominans, who appeared in the reign of

Elizabeth; with the Catholics and Nonconformists, the latter of whom he was very anxious to bring back to the Established Church." Sherlock is now chiefly remembered by his "Discourse Concerning Death," published in 1690. His "Vindication of the Doctrine of the Trinity" was fiercely attacked by Robert South (1633–1716), who has been very unjustly called "the wittiest of English divines." No doubt he displays a great command of satirical wit, but his wit was neither so spontaneous nor so affluent as Fuller's. South, who had a brilliant university career, was an extreme Anglican, adhering firmly to the doctrine of passive obedience and the divine right of kings. At the Revolution, though, after some delay, he took the oaths to the new Government, he steadily declined preferment, declaring, "that notwithstanding he, for his part, saw nothing that was contrary to the laws of God and the common practice of all nations to submit to princes in possession of the throne, yet others might have their reasons for a contrary opinion; and he blessed God that he was neither so ambitious nor in want of preferment as for the sake of it to build his rise upon the ruin of any one father of the Church, who for piety, good morals, and strictness of life, which every one of the deprived bishops were famous for, might be said not to have left their equal." His solid erudition, united to his command of language and his frequent flashes of wit, give his sermons high literary value; but the intolerant spirit which animates all his works contrasts very unfavourably with the conciliatory tone and forbearance of Tillotson.

Another divine, of great popularity as a preacher, but whose fame is grounded upon his historical works, was Gilbert Burnet, a prominent figure in the history of the Revolution of 1688. He was born at Edinburgh in 1643, and educated at Marischal College, Aberdeen, which, in accordance with the ridiculous fashion of the time, he entered when he was ten years old, graduating when he was fourteen. He then applied himself to the study of civil law, but soon turned aside from this pursuit to devote himself to theology. In 1669 he was made professor of divinity at Glasgow, which office he held about four years, resigning in 1673, when he went to London. There he soon attracted attention as a preacher and as a man of liberal opinions. During the troubled reign of James II. he went abroad, and after a tour through various parts of the Continent, was invited to the Hague by the Prince and Princess of Holland. He afterwards accompanied the Prince in his expedition to England as his chaplain, and took a leading part in the politics of the Revolution. In 1689 he was appointed Bishop of Salisbury. So attractive were his pulpit ministrations, that he was often, says Macaulay, "interrupted by the deep hum of his audience, and when, after preaching out the hour-glass, he held it up in his hand, the congregation clamorously encouraged him to go on till the sand had run off once more." We doubt very much if there is any preacher now living whose congregation would listen to him with attention and sympathy for two hours; but sermons were more popular in those days, when reading was not a universal accomplishment. Burnet died in 1715, having spent a very industrious, active, and useful life. He was an honest, courageous man, rather disposed to be fussy and interfering, but a faithful and steady friend to those whose cause he had adopted, and not disposed to keep up malice against his enemies. He was the author of many writings, of which the most noteworthy are "An Account of the Life and Death of the Earl of Rochester" (1680), a book which Dr. Johnson declared "the critic ought to read for its elegance, the philosopher for its arguments, and the saint for its piety," though, as he once said in conversation, the "death" is better than the "life;" a "History of the Reformation of the Church of England," in three volumes, of which the first appeared in 1679, gaining for him the thanks of Parliament; and the "History of my Own Times," which was published posthumously. The last is his most valuable work, though his "History of the Reformation" contains a great store of information. "Burnet's 'History of His Own Times,'" Johnson is recorded to have said, "is very entertaining; the style, indeed, is mere chit-chat. I do not believe that Burnet intentionally lied; but he was so much prejudiced that he took no pains to find out the truth. He was like a man who resolves to regulate his time by a certain watch, but will not inquire whether the watch is right or not." This is somewhat unjust as regards both Burnet's accuracy and his style. All things considered, the History is wonderfully accurate; and the many character-portraits it contains are masterpieces of shrewd description.

The greatest philosopher of the period was John Locke, who besides did good work in helping forward the cause of toleration. He was born in 1632 in Somersetshire, where his father, who had been a captain in the Parliamentary army during the Civil Wars, had a small estate. He was educated at Westminster, and afterwards at Christ Church, Oxford, where he took the degree of B.A. in 1655. About this time his inclinations led him to study medicine, and he acquired sufficient knowledge of physic to earn the praise of the great Sydenham. He remained at Oxford till 1664, when he accompanied, as secretary, Sir Walter Vane, the envoy sent by Charles II. to the Elector of Brandenburg during the Dutch war. Two years afterwards he became acquainted with Lord Ashley, afterwards Earl of Shaftesbury, who was so captivated by his society that Locke became an inmate of his house, where he mingled freely with the best society of the time. By Shaftesbury, in 1692, he was made secretary of prosecutions, but ill-health prevented him from holding this office long, and induced him to visit France, where he resided for several years. On Shaftesbury's fall from power Locke came to be looked on with suspicion by the Government, and had to take refuge in Holland. There he wrote, in Latin, his first "Letter on Toleration," which appeared in 1689. In 1690–1692, he published two other letters on the same subject, replying to objections which had been urged against his doctrines. After the Revolution Locke's defence of liberal principles was rewarded by his being made Commissioner of Stamps, and afterwards one of the Commissioners of Trade. In 1689 and 1690 he published "Two Treatises of Government," the first containing a reply to the ridiculous theories of Sir Robert Filmer, who, in his "Patriarchia" (1680), upheld the divine right of kings in its extremest form, the other treating of the true original, extent, and end of civil government. In 1690 also appeared his famous "Essay on the Human Understanding" and his interesting tractate on Education. He died in 1704. His "Essay on the Conduct of the Understanding" was published posthumously. It is very highly praised by Hallam, who declares that he cannot think any parent or instructor justified in neglecting to put this little treatise in the hands of a boy about the time his reasoning faculties become developed. "It will give him a sober and serious, not flippant or self-conceited, independency of thinking; and while it teaches how to distrust ourselves and watch those prejudices which necessarily grow up from one cause or another, will inspire a reasonable confidence in what he has well considered, by taking off a little of that deference to authority, which is the more to be regretted in its excess, that, like its cousin-german, party-spirit, it is frequently found united to loyalty of heart and the generous enthusiasm of youth." Locke's style is simple and graceful; he was called by Landor the most elegant of prose writers. He is a great name in the history of philosophical thought, and his writings on Toleration and Government had considerable political influence.

The establishment of the Royal Society dates from about the time of the Restoration. It was incorporated by royal charter in 1662. Its germ was a society which, in 1645, during the turmoil and agitation of the Civil Wars, had been formed in London by some quiet, studious men, of whom the most notable were Dr. Ward, Dr. Wallis, and Dr. Wilkins. "Our business," says Wallis, "was (precluding matters of theology and state affairs) to discourse and consider of philosophical inquiries, and such as related thereto, as Physick, Anatomy, Geometry, Astronomy, Navigation, Staticks, Magneticks, Chymicks, Mechanicks, and Natural Experiments, with the state of these studies and their cultivation at home and abroad. We then discoursed of the circulation of the blood, the valves in the veins, the venæ lacteæ, the lymphatic vessels, the Copernican hypothesis, the nature of comets and new stars, the satellites of Jupiter, the oval shape of Saturn, the spots on the sun and the turning on its own axis, the inequalities and selenography of the moon, the several phases of Venus and Mercury, the improvement of telescopes and grinding of glasses for that purpose, the weight of air, the possibility or impossibility of vacuities and Nature's abhorrence thereof, the Torricellian experiment in quicksilver, the descent of heavy bodies and the degrees of acceleration therein, with divers other things of like nature, some of which were then but new discoveries, and others not so generally known and embraced as now [1696] they are; with other things appertaining to what has been called the New Philosophy, which, from the times of Galileo at Florence, and Sir Francis Bacon (Lord Verulam) in England, hath been much cultivated in Italy, France, Germany, and other parts abroad, as well as with us in England." This comprehensive survey well shows the growing interest taken in science. Charles II. was fond of dabbling in chemistry, and his courtiers followed suit, till it became considered gentlemanly to have a tincture of scientific knowledge. The increased orderliness and method of English style which now began to prevail may in some measure be attributed to the scientific spirit abroad, which was intolerant of confusion and carelessness of arrangement. To this period belongs the greatest name in the history of science, Sir Isaac Newton (1642–1727), who cannot be altogether omitted even in a purely literary history. He succeeded Barrow, whose pupil he had been, as Lucasian professor of mathematics at Cambridge, and published his great work, the "Principia," in 1687. It was written in Latin. Besides his scientific works, he found time to write on ancient chronology, on the Scripture prophecies, and "An Historical Account of Two Notable Corruptions of Scripture." These were published posthumously, and are interesting for the light they throw on his religious opinions. Their style is not specially remarkable in any way.

V.

THE WITS OF QUEEN ANNE'S TIME.

Swift, Addison, Steele, Arbuthnot, Bolingbroke, Berkeley, Butler; Pope, Prior, Gay, Young, Churchill, Gray, Collins, and Akenside.

DURING the reign of Queen Anne and the two first Georges, the government of England was in a very unsettled condition. Jacobitism, till finally crushed in 1745–46, flourished among men who held high places of trust, and was so prevalent among the community at large that the restoration of the Stuart line was looked upon by all sagacious observers as no unlikely event. It was a time of the grossest political immorality, when men shifted sides unhesitatingly for the most selfish motives, and when both the great political parties lived in constant fear of having their secrets betrayed by traitors. Party spirit ran high, and Whigs and Tories alike strained every nerve to win the voice of the public to their side. Both employed armies of hack writers to advocate their cause, and both were ready to shower gifts and offices upon any writer of mark and talent who should employ himself in their defence. The pen was then a much more powerful political agent than it is now. Parliamentary reporting was forbidden, and thus the speech delivered in Parliament, which in our day, by the reports of it in the newspapers, affects the minds of millions, could at the best only influence the three or four hundred members who might happen to hear it. Recess oratory and great political manifestoes at party gatherings were little practised, nor would they have been attended by any widespread results though they had been practised, for there was not yet such a thing as copious newspaper reports of speeches. A well-written pamphlet, or a series of vigorous articles in one of the political periodicals which came into fashion in Queen Anne's time, was as powerful an auxiliary in either averting the ruin of a ministry or in hastening it to its fall as a great oration defending his policy by a Prime Minister or a scathing denunciation of the plans of the Government by an Opposition leader is in the present day. Under these circumstances, and considering the munificent rewards popular and telling party writers often had bestowed upon them, it is not surprising that the literature of the time with which we are now dealing should have been pre-eminently a party literature. Almost every eminent prose writer of the period—Defoe, Swift, Addison, Steele, and others—ranged himself on the side of the Whig or the Tory party, and employed his pen in its defence. The effect of this on prose style was on the whole favourable, giving it greater energy, precision, and lucidity than it had yet possessed. But it had also its evil results. Something of the want of moral elevation and breadth of view which distinguished the politics of the age communicated itself to the literature: with all its many good qualities, the so-called Augustan period of English literature has about it a worldly air and an absence of any spiritual insight.

Among the men of letters who entered the bustling arena of political controversy was the greatest and most original writer of his time, Jonathan Swift, one of the most powerful, most imperious, and most puzzling figures our literary history presents. He was born in Dublin in 1667. It was only by the accident of birth that he was an Irishman. He was descended from an old Yorkshire family, and had no Irish blood in his veins. Even he, though wiser and more far-sighted in regard to Ireland than almost any of his contemporaries, always spoke of the native Irish with that indiscriminating contempt which has since born such bitter fruit. Swift was a posthumous child, and his mother having been left very slenderly provided for, the expenses of his education were defrayed in what appears to have been a sufficiently grudging fashion by his uncle Godwin. He was educated at the school of Kilkenny, and then at Trinity College, Dublin, where he obtained his degree *speciali gratia* in 1685. In 1689 he became private secretary to Sir William Temple, whose wife was a relative of his mother's. All things considered, Swift entered the world under very promising auspices. Temple (1628–1699) was a veteran diplomatist and statesman, who had taken a leading part in negotiating the Triple Alliance, and he was universally looked up to and consulted in his old age as one of the most wary, sagacious, and politic of men. As an author he ranks high, not so much because his works show great power or genius, as because he was one of the first to obtain a mastery over the great and difficult art of English prose composition. "Sir William Temple," Johnson is reported to have said, "was the first writer who gave cadence to English prose. Before his time they were careless of arrangement, and did not mind whether a sentence ended with an important word or an insignificant word, or with what part of speech it was concluded." In the household of Temple at Moor Park, Swift had ample opportunity for increasing his store of knowledge, and, besides, he was admitted behind the scenes of political life, and even had the honour on one occasion of acting as Temple's mouthpiece in advising King William regarding the policy he should pursue as to the Triennial Bill. Yet he felt his position very galling. He was a dependant, his proud, imperious, self-confident nature chafed bitterly against the chains of servitude, however richly gilded they might be; and Temple, a man of cold, selfish, precise disposition, was a master whose behests it was not always easy to obey with cheerfulness. With but a brief interval, during which, apparently in despair of ever obtaining any lay promotion from his patron, he committed the great mistake of his life by taking orders, Swift remained with Temple till his death in 1699. It was during his residence at Moor Park that he first became acquainted with the woman, then a little girl, whose name is indissolubly connected with his. Esther Johnson, better known as Stella, was only about six years old when Swift saw her first. He constituted himself her tutor, "directing," he says, "what books she should read, and perpetually instructing her in the principles of honour and virtue, from which she never swerved in any one action or moment of her life."

In 1699 Swift went to Ireland with Lord Berkeley as private chaplain. From him he expected high ecclesiastical promotion, but his hopes were, as usual, doomed to disappointment. To his bitter grief and mortification, he had to be content with the livings of Laracor and Rathbeggin in the county of Meath, to which he was appointed in 1700. He performed his duties as a clergyman in a manner which, if it would now be considered perfunctory, was probably more exemplary than was then usual, though he often left his "parish, with an audience of half a score," to go to England, there to advance his fortunes by becoming acquainted with wits and statesmen. His first publication, "A Discourse on the Contests and Dissensions between the Nobles and Commons at Athens and Rome," which appeared in 1701, had a political intent, being meant to check the impeachment of Somers, Halifax, Oxford, and Portland for their share in the Partition Treaty. When he visited England in 1702, he avowed the authorship of this tract, and thus won the regard of the leading Whig statesmen and their political allies. In 1704 he published anonymously the "Tale of a Tub," which appears to have lain for about seven or eight years in MS. His authorship of it was never acknowledged, but it was generally known that he was the writer, and the work proved the one insurmountable obstacle to his professional preferment. In vigour and poignancy of satire, in grave irony, in masculine force and intensity, the "Tale of a Tub" has never been surpassed. On one occasion, when in his old age he happened to come across a copy of the work, Swift exclaimed, "Good God! what a genius I had when I wrote that book!" But it was thought to have an irreligious tendency, and Swift's natural love of obscenity appears strongly in many parts of it, so that while it made him known as a man of genius, it also caused him to be regarded with suspicion as an ecclesiastic. The three sons, Peter, Jack, and Martin, who figure in the allegory, are intended to represent Popery, Presbyterianism, and Episcopalianism, and the story of their adventures is so related as to favour Episcopalianism, for Swift was always strongly attached to the Anglican Church. Along with the "Tale of a Tub" was printed the "Battle of the Books," which had been written at Moor Park in behalf of Temple, who had taken a prominent part in a very foolish controversy as to the relative merits of ancient and modern literature. It does not show the same condensation and elaboration as distinguish Swift's later satires. During the years 1708–9 he published several tracts, of which the most noticeable is his famous "Argument against the Abolishing of Christianity," an admirable specimen of his gravely ironical style, and his "Predictions of Isaac Bickerstaff," a squib upon the astrological almanac-makers of the time, in which, among other things, he predicted that John Partridge, one of the chief members of the body, would die on a certain specified date. In his almanac for 1709, Partridge proclaimed that he "was still living, and in health, and all were knaves who reported otherwise." Swift replied in a very amusing pamphlet, "The Vindication of Isaac Bickerstaff," in which he argued that Partridge was quite mistaken, and that he really was dead. "The jest," says Mr. Forster, "had by this time diffused itself into so wide a popularity that all the wits became eager to take part in it; Rowe, Steele, Addison, and Prior contributed to it in divers amusing ways, and Congreve described, under Partridge's name, the distresses and reproaches Squire Bickerstaff had exposed him to, insomuch that he could not leave his door without somebody twitting him for sneaking about without paying his funeral expenses. The poor astrologer himself meanwhile was continually advertising that he was *not* dead."

We now come to the most active and exciting period of Swift's career. Till 1710 he had supported the Whigs—not so strenuously, it is true, as he afterwards supported the rival party, but still with considerable zeal. His services had not been rewarded, and there can be no doubt that the personal neglect with which he was treated was the main reason why he, in 1710, transferred his talents to the Tory ministry of Harley and St. John. By his new associates he was received with open arms. "We were determined to have you," said St. John; "you were the only one we were afraid of." Till the fall of the Tory ministry in 1714, Swift occupied a position which for real power and influence was probably unsurpassed. "He held probably," writes Mr. Hannay,[1] "the most potent position that a writer ever held in this country, but all the while held it in a dubious unrecognised way. He was the patron of men of letters; got them places and got them money. He 'crammed' the ministers; and his pen was not employed in quizzing hoops or patches, or sneering at City people—it was an engine of power over all England. He used it as an orator does his tongue,—to *do* something with. In a word, he was a power in the State; and, indeed, it is one of the few pleasant things to read about in the records of these days, how those who, in their hearts, tried to despise him as an 'Irish parson,'—how, I say, they dreaded him; how they flattered and courted him; and how they felt that he was their master." During this period Swift wrote his most telling political pamphlets, the "Conduct of the Allies," the "Letter to the October Club;" and the *Examiner*, a weekly periodical which had been started in support of the new ministry, and which he conducted for seven months, assailing the enemies of his party with the intensest virulence and the most trenchant ridicule. Of more permanent value than his political writings is his ever-charming "Journal to Stella," which he wrote during the years of his residence in London: "that wonderful journal," says Mr. Forster, "that unrivalled picture of the time, in which he set down day by day the incidents of these momentous years; which received every hope, fear, or fancy in its undress as it rose to him; which was written for one person's private pleasure, and has had indestructible attractiveness for every one since."

[1] "Satire and Satirists," p. 160.

"Stella" had removed to Ireland shortly after Swift received the living of Laracor, and now lived there, along with Mrs. Dingley, a relation of the Temple family.

The fond expectations cherished by Swift that his Tory friends would reward his great exertions in their favour by a bishopric fell to the ground as completely as his former hopes of preferment. Queen Anne would not make a bishop of the author of the "Tale of a Tub;" all the advancement he received was being made Dean of St. Patrick's in 1713. On the death of the Queen the Whigs again returned to power; and Swift, a soured and disappointed man, went back to Ireland to pass the remainder of his days with dire scorn and indignation gnawing at his heart. By the publication in 1720 of the tract proposing the "Universal Use of Irish Manufactures," and still more by his famous "Drapier's Letters" (1723) written against Ward's patent for a copper coinage, he raised himself to unexampled popularity in Ireland; his name was in every mouth as the saviour of his country, and so great was the commotion excited that the patent had ultimately to be withdrawn. His success did nothing to cheer him: he still remained the same gloomy and misanthropic man. In 1726–27 he published "Gulliver's Travels," his most generally read work, the last part of which shows to how terrible an extent he carried what he believed to be his virtuous indignation against the "villanies and corruptions of mankind." In his latter years a settled melancholy spread over him. When parting with a friend he would say with a sigh, "I hope I shall never see you again." The melancholy gradually darkened into madness. During the last three years of his life he is known to have spoken only once or twice. At length, in October 1745, death came to his release. He bequeathed the bulk of his fortune to found and endow an asylum in Dublin for lunatics and idiots.

Stella had died before him in 1727. How truly and tenderly he loved her, the thousand endearing expressions in the "Journal" amply show. But the dark cloud which overshadowed all Swift's life, overshadowed his relations with her also. Mr. Forster, whose unfinished Life of Swift is, with all its wordiness and tediousness, a splendid tribute to this great satirist's memory, could see no sufficient evidence for the story that Swift became united to her by a private marriage. However this may be, they certainly always lived apart. Of his relations with Vanessa (Hester Vanhomrigh) we need not say much. He became acquainted with her in London, where she made him an offer of marriage, which he declined, without, however, breaking off his intercourse with her; followed him to Ireland; and died of a broken heart on becoming acquainted with his intimacy with Stella.

Had Swift been born in such a position as to give him an independent fortune, his life might have been a happy one. Nay, if he had not entered the Church, but had risen (an event quite within the range of possibility) like Addison to high office in the State, it is very probable that we should never have heard so much of his misanthropy and cynicism. Impatient of control, proud, contemptuous of inferiority, and intolerant of stupidity, he never found a proper field wherein to exercise his vast and daring genius. For literary fame, except as a stepping-stone to what he considered higher ends, he cared little or nothing: the finest fruits of his mind, "Gulliver" and the "Tale of a Tub," were flung carelessly, unacknowledged, upon the world. That there were noble and generous tendencies in Swift's nature can scarcely be doubted by any one who has studied him with impartiality. Strictly economical in his personal expenses, he could, when occasion required, give largely: like many who take care of the pence, he sometimes dispensed the pounds with a bounteousness which put to shame the charity of his apparently more free-handed contemporaries. That he was often sullen, rude, insolent, and disdainful cannot be denied. But some of his fugitive pieces, and especially the "Journal to Stella," show that beneath his outward misanthropy and harshness lay a vein of playfulness, tenderness, and affection. The fact that he was a general favourite with women is a further proof in the same direction. In spite of the large literature which has accumulated round Swift's name, the key which shall enable us to solve the many enigmas about his life and character, which have baffled so many inquirers, still remains to be found. He stands alone, a unique and portentous figure, to whom the eyes of men will long be directed, some with pity and even affection, some with aversion and distrust, all with wonder and great admiration. Swift's outward appearance corresponded to the character of him which we gather from his writings and from other sources. He was, says Scott, "in person tall, strong, and well made, of a dark complexion, but with blue eyes, black and bushy eyebrows, nose somewhat aquiline, and features which remarkably expressed the stern, haughty, and dauntless turn of his mind."

As an author, Swift was prominent within his own range, but his range was not very wide. For the sublime and pathetic in composition he had no turn. His verses, of which he wrote many, are clever, lively, and spirited, but they are not poetry in any high sense of the word. His intellect was not at all of an ethereal order: it was solid, massive, and intense, but of the earth, earthy. Satire was his peculiar province; there his genius got full scope in expressing the fierce indignation which lacerated his heart. Hating insincere sentiment, he was too apt to believe that all sentiments to which his nature did not respond were insincere; the baser qualities of men stood out much more prominently before his eyes than their virtues; and he often fell into the common error of satirists of supposing that the anger which arose simply from his own jaundiced imagination was the wrath of a good man disgusted with the wickedness he saw around him. His style is simple, nervous, terse, disdainful of gaudy ornament, yet often surprising us by happy turns of expression and felicitous illustrations. As his "Drapier's Letters" and other political writings show, he could adapt himself admirably to any class to which he appealed, never hesitating to use homely expressions, and picking out with great skill the facts which best suited his purpose. His love of gross allusions and filthy images is the great stain on his literary fame. It no doubt arose, in part at least, from the degraded notions he entertained of humanity.

To turn from the contemplation of Swift's dark and tempestuous life to the calm, prosperous, happy career of Addison is like viewing some sweet, tranquil spot in the sunny South, with its delicately perfumed flowers and its luxuriance of fruits and foliage, after looking on a wild mountain-pass, with its rocks and gloomy recesses, its grand desolation, and its fierce and gurgling streams rushing on unseen. True, Addison had for a time to bear the burdens and trials of poverty, but it was only for a short period, and poverty, where it does not last so long as to sour one's temper and embitter one's views of life, is an excellent schoolmaster if its lessons be viewed in a proper spirit. It teaches forethought, self-reliance, sympathy with the mass of humanity, industry and patience under difficulties. None of these qualities was wanting in Addison: he is the "model boy" of the school; the most blameless, irreproachable of the wits of Queen Anne's time. The correct and virtuous lad who receives the prize for good conduct, though commended by his tutors and regarded with admiring hope by his parents, is not, it is to be feared, always a popular character; he is often destitute of those generous excesses, those fine spontaneous impulses of a free and liberal nature, which make us forgive not a few departures from the path of strict decorum. Something of this is true about Addison. Though no serious fault can be laid to his charge, he was a little selfish, a little cold-hearted, had somewhat too keen an "eye to the main chance," and sometimes carried prudence to the verge of meanness.

Joseph Addison was born in 1672, the son of the Rev. Lancelot Addison, Rector of Milston in Wiltshire, who afterwards rose to be Dean of Lichfield. He was educated at the Charterhouse, and afterwards at Magdalen College, Oxford, where he distinguished himself in the studies then most valued there, acquiring a competent knowledge of the Latin poets, and writing Latin verse with fluency and elegance. In his twenty-second year he addressed some English verses to Dryden, and soon after published a translation of the greater part of Virgil's fourth Georgic. Addison's early poetical performances in Latin and in English do not merit much notice. After the fashion of the time, he made them the vehicle of conveying compliments to a good many persons whose patronage might be of value to him: he praised Charles Montagu, he praised Somers, and he praised King William. His encomiums were not bestowed in vain. Montagu dissuaded him from the design he had entertained of entering the Church, declaring that the State could not at that time afford to spare to the Church such a man as he was. A Government pension of £300 a year was obtained for him in order that he might travel, and in the summer of 1699 Addison set out for the Continent. The design of his journey probably was to enable him to acquire such a knowledge of French as to qualify him for acting as a diplomatist.

After travelling in France and Italy for about three years, Addison returned to England on the death of King William, which, by depriving his political friends of power, had stopped his pension. Soon after, in 1704, he published an account of his travels in Italy, with a dedication to Lord Somers. The character which Johnson gives of this work may be accepted as substantially correct: "As his stay in foreign countries was short, his observations are such as might be supplied by a hasty view, and consist chiefly in comparisons of the present face of the country with the descriptions left us by the Roman poets, from whom he made preparatory collections, though he might have spared the trouble had he known that such collections had been made twice before by the Italian authors." About this time he wrote his "Dialogues on Medals," which was not published till after his death. Like the "Travels in Italy," it shows that Addison was what was then called an "elegant scholar:" to anything like profound erudition he could lay no claim, but he knew well those departments of classical literature which were most esteemed in polite society. After his return from the Continent he had to endure for a short period the hardships of poverty, when, in 1704, a fortunate accident opened up to him the path to power and riches. The great victory at Blenheim had roused the nation to the utmost enthusiasm, but none of the versifiers who had attempted to celebrate it had talents sufficient to do justice to the occasion. By the advice of Montagu (now Lord Halifax) Addison was applied to, and readily undertook the proposed task. When the poem was about half finished, it was carried to Lord Treasurer Godolphin, who was so pleased with the famous simile of the angel, that Addison was immediately appointed to a Commissionership worth £200 a year. This "famous simile of the angel," which proved such a fortunate stroke to Addison, is now, we imagine, little known. It runs as follows:—

"But, O my muse! what numbers wilt thou find
To sing the furious troops in battle joined?
Methinks I hear the drum's tumultuous sound,
The victors' shouts and dying groans confound;
The dreadful burst of cannon rend the skies,
And all the thunders of the battle rise.
'Twas then great Marlborough's mighty soul was proved,
That in the shock of charging hosts unmoved,
Amidst confusion, horror, and despair,
Examined all the dreadful scenes of war:
In peaceful thought the field of death surveyed,
To fainting squadrons lent the timely aid,
Inspired repulsed battalions to engage,
And taught the doubtful battle where to rage.
So when an angel by divine command,
With rising tempests shakes a guilty land
(Such as of late o'er pale Britannia passed),
Calm and serene he drives the furious blast;
And, pleased the Almighty's order to perform,
Rides on the whirlwind and directs the storm."

Certainly these lines do not show any high poetical genius: they are, in truth, commonplace enough; nevertheless they are as good as anything Addison ever wrote in verse, with the exception of a few hymns, to which their fine religious fervour lends a perennial attractiveness. Shortly after "The Campaign," Addison wrote the opera of "Rosamond," which, after it had failed on the stage, he published, with a dedication to the Duchess of Marlborough; "a woman," says Johnson, "without skill, or pretensions to skill, in poetry or literature. His dedication was therefore an instance of servile absurdity. We need not criticise severely Addison's conduct in sometimes dedicating his writings in very adulatory fashion to persons whom he must have known to be unworthy of his praises. His exploits in this direction turn pale before those of Dryden, a greater man. It was the fashion of the time—a fashion productive of much lying and sycophancy, but which was undoubtedly often efficacious in filling the pockets of a needy author with gold. It was to single individuals, not to the general public, that literary men looked for support, and what wonder though they sometimes strained a point in their endeavour to please their patrons? In our own time, do we not too frequently see writers of great power becoming untrue to their genius, and writing works unworthy of them, to please the capricious taste of *their* patrons, the public?

Addison's promotion from a comparatively humble position to the highest offices of State was very rapid. In 1706 he was made Under Secretary of State. In 1708 he became a member of Parliament, and in the same year was appointed to go to Ireland, of which Wharton had become Lord-Lieutenant, as Chief Secretary. Along with his secretaryship, he obtained a patent appointing him keeper of the Irish records for life, with a salary of over £300 a year. This wonderful success in life was no doubt largely owing to Addison's tact and discretion, as well as to his abilities. He was a conciliatory man, not ready either to give or to take offence; his political creed was of the most orthodox description—where his party went he was ready to go too; and his shrewd powers of observation and insight into the character of men must have made him an adept in the difficult art, so useful to Government officials, of managing people without letting them know that you are managing them.

It was during his residence in Ireland that Addison first attempted that species of composition in which he reigns supreme. But here our story requires us to go back a little, and to bring a new character on the scene.

Among the little senate of admirers to whom Addison gave

laws, and who reverenced him as the greatest and wisest man of the day, he had no more devoted henchman than Dick Steele, a stout, jovial, kind-hearted man, of good principles and bad practices, who had passed a haphazard, reckless, and not unhappy life, sinning one day and repenting the next, working strenuously when he did work, but ever ready, on the slightest temptation, to fling aside his pen, and sally forth to engage in the pursuit of pleasure. Steele was a year older than Addison, having been born in Dublin in 1671. His mother was Irish; whether his father was so or not is uncertain. At the age of twelve he was sent from Dublin to the Charterhouse, where he first made the acquaintance of Addison. Thackeray, whose lecture on Steele[1] is full of that peculiar sympathy which he always felt for men of his type of character, says, doubtless with much truth, "I am afraid no good report could be given by his masters and ushers of that thick-set, square-faced, black-eyed, soft-hearted, little Irish boy. He was whipped deservedly a great number of times. Though he had very good parts of his own, he got other boys to do his lessons for him, and only took just as much trouble as should enable him to scuffle through his exercises, and by good fortune escape the flogging-block." From the Charterhouse Steele went to Oxford, where he seems to have been very idle. He left it without taking a degree, though not without having given some evidence of his literary capacity, for while there he wrote a comedy and a poem. At this period of his life, however, his taste ran in the direction not of a literary but of a military life, and his friends refusing to buy him a commission, he enlisted as a private in the Horse Guards. He obtained from Lord Cutts, whose private secretary he became, an ensign's commission; not, we may suppose, granted him on account of his attention to his duties, but because he was a likeable man, whose wit and generous

[1] In his "English Humourists of the Eighteenth Century," the notes to which—not the least interesting or valuable part of the amusing volume—are, it may be worth mentioning, by James Hannay, author of "Singleton Fontenoy," &c.

disposition made him a general favourite. At this, as at all other periods of his life, Steele sowed wild oats profusely, and reaped their customary harvest of remorse and repentance frequently, and with great intensity. Unfortunately, however, he always soon grew tired of the latter occupation, and broke off in the middle of it to sow wild oats again with as great industry as ever. It was during his temporary fits of repentance that he wrote his first book, "The Christian Hero," which appeared in 1701. Though its intent was good, the difference between the preaching and the practice of the writer was productive of a good deal of irreverent laughter among his comrades. In the following year he wrote a comedy, "The Funeral," which met with a fair share of success. In 1703 and 1704 he wrote two other plays, "The Tender Husband" and "The Dying Lover," of which the first succeeded, while the other failed—on account of its piety, Steele boasted; on account of its dulness, said others. About this time he quitted the army, having received through the influence of his friends the appointment of Gazetteer, with a salary of £300 a year. He now became a politician and a man of letters by profession, and entered freely into the literary society of the period. In 1709 the happiest notion of his life occurred to him. Under the name of Isaac Bickerstaff, which Swift had made popular, he resolved to edit a periodical of somewhat the same kind as the *Review* begun by Defoe in 1704, but, unlike it, excluding party politics. This was the *Tatler*, of which the first number was published on April 12, 1709. It was published three times a week, and "was intended, in some respects, to serve the purpose of a newspaper, as well as to supply a series of brief essays on life and literature, or any topic, in short, that the quick-witted author could, in the language of the day, entertain the town with." Addison soon discovered, by a passage in the sixth number containing a remark on Virgil which he had made in the course of conversation, that "Isaac Bickerstaff," the editor of the *Tatler*, was none other than his old companion Dick Steele, and he lent him the invaluable assistance of his pen, not very frequently at first, but more often when the work was pretty far advanced. "This good office," said Steele, with his usual generosity and freedom from jealousy, "he performed with such force of genius, humour, wit, and learning, that I fared like a distressed prince who calls in a powerful neighbour to his aid. I was undone by my auxiliary; when I had once called him in, I could not subsist without dependence on him." In so saying he perhaps overstated the case. If Addison had the more subtle, delicate, and cultured mind, Steele had more originality, and in the *Tatler*, as elsewhere, he showed that fine chivalrous instinct which runs like a thread of gold through all his writings.

The *Tatler* was, after a prosperous career, brought to a close on January 2, 1711. On the 1st of March in the same year appeared the first number of another periodical, also conducted by Steele, of somewhat the same character. "No trace of the newspaper or gazetteer was to be admitted; it was to be altogether literary in its character; it was to fulfil the functions of the modern magazine; it was, in fact, the complete inauguration of periodical literature. Brief essays, tales, imaginary correspondence, imaginary conversations, strictures on the manners and the morals of the day—there was nothing new in any of these; but a publication which should present some one of these every morning on the breakfast-table was a novel and bold undertaking." The *Spectator*—for such was the name of this new periodical—appeared daily, and was carried on without intermission for about a year and nine months, ceasing on December 6, 1712. In 1714 it was revived for a brief period, the papers then published constituting the eighth volume in the old editions. To the *Tatler* Steele was the most prominent contributor; it is the name of Addison, on the other hand, which is inseparably connected with the *Spectator*. Many good papers were contributed by Steele, and occasional essays by other writers, some of whose names would now be buried in oblivion had they not gained a sort of immortality through their association with men of genius; but it is to Addison that the *Spectator* owes the major part of its fame. His best and most generally read papers in it are, of course, those descriptive of men and manners. "He walks about the world," writes Thackeray, "watching their petty humours, fashions, follies, flirtations, rivalries, and noting them with the most charming archness. He sees them in public, in the theatre, or the assembly, or the puppet-show; or at the toyshop higgling for gloves and lace; or at the auction, battling together over a blue porcelain dragon or a darling monster in Japan; or at church eying the width of the ladies' hoops; or the breadth of their laces as they sweep down the aisles; or he looks out of the window at the Garter in St. James's Street at Ardelia's coach, as she blazes to the drawing-room with her coronet and six footmen; and remembering that her father was a Turkey merchant in the City, calculates how many sponges went to purchase her earrings, and how many drums of figs to build her coachbox; or he demurely watches behind a tree in Spring Gardens as Saccharissa (whom he knows under her mask) trips out of her chair to the alley where Sir Fopling is waiting." His delicate satire and "gay malevolence," as Johnson calls it, give his sketches a precision, a neatness, an epigrammatic point which are wanting in Steele's more clumsy and more good-humoured delineations. The delightful papers relating to Sir Roger de Coverley, of which Steele wrote eight, well show the distinctive differences between the two friends. Addison's papers are better written, they contain more fine touches and subtle strokes of humour than Steele's; but to Steele belongs the merit of having introduced most of the features in the good knight's character which make him so lovable. In one point, his just appreciation of women, Steele was far in advance not only of Addison, whose general tone towards the sex is that of quiet contempt, but of his age generally. On Addison's critical papers, those on the "Pleasures of the Imagination," Milton's "Paradise Lost," &c., little remark is necessary. They strike us now as barren and insipid; they show no depth or power of analysis; his descriptions of the fine passages in Milton are such as, apart from the elegance of their style, might be written by any clever schoolboy. But considering the time when they were written, they possess considerable merit, and even boldness. At a period when the artificial school of poetry was in vogue, it was a daring thing to praise the fine old ballad of "Chevy Chase," as Addison did. How such pieces of poetry were generally regarded then and for many years afterwards is well shown by Johnson's comment on Addison's disquisition. "In 'Chevy Chase,'" he says with commendable candour, "there is not much of either bombast or affectation; but there is chill and lifeless imbecility. The story cannot possibly be told in a manner which shall leave less impression on the mind."

It is now time to resume our account of Addison's life. In 1713 he secured one of the greatest triumphs of his career. While travelling in Italy he had projected a tragedy on the subject of Cato's death, and, it would seem, had written part of it. For several years he had had the first four acts of it finished, and such of his friends as saw the manuscript were unanimous in urging him to complete it. Some of them thought it would be best for him to print it; others thought that it should be brought out on the stage. After much demurring and hesitation, he finally agreed to adopt the latter plan. Pope furnished a prologue, Garth an epilogue, and in 1713 "Cato" was acted at Drury Lane Theatre. Officious, enthusiastic Dick Steele had taken care that the fame of his friend Mr. Addison should not be endangered by its reception. The house was carefully packed with an audience willing to applaud it to the echo, and it obtained an almost unequalled success. "The Whigs," says Johnson, "applauded every line in which liberty was mentioned, as a satire on the Tories; and the Tories echoed every clap to show that the satire was unfelt." During a whole month "Cato" was performed to crowded houses; and when it was printed, it was received with well-nigh universal approval. Its pompous monotony was taken for dignity, and its strict adherence to the critical rules then accepted was preferred by Addison's contemporaries to the truth and nature of Shakespeare. In it the dramatic unities—unity of place, unity of time, and unity of action—are observed with a completeness which leads to some rather ridiculous results; all the characters go through their actions and their speeches with the utmost conventional correctness; but it does not contain a passage which shows genuine poetic feeling, or indeed high artistic skill of any kind. It lives now, if it lives at all, by a few happy lines which have become stock quotations.

Amidst the general chorus of praise which hailed the production of "Cato," one dissentient voice made itself heard with considerable vehemence. Old John Dennis, a bitter and vindictive critic, who railed at any successful production with intense malignity and some acuteness, attacked it in a pamphlet, considerable specimens of which are preserved by Johnson in his Life of Addison. The fact that many of his strictures were just did not make them any more palatable, but Addison made no rejoinder. Pope, however, partly by way of courting Addison's favour, partly because he saw, as he thought, a good opportunity of wiping off sundry old scores of his own, published his "Narrative of the Frenzy of John Dennis," a rather coarse and unskilful performance. No doubt he thought he was doing Addison a service, but Addison, whose conduct in the matter does not seem to have been generous, thought otherwise, and caused Dennis to be informed that he was sorry for the insult. This was the beginning of a long literary feud between Pope and Addison. Both appear to have hated each other cordially; and Addison has never been wholly acquitted of the charge of having, by various sly intrigues, endeavoured to injure Pope's reputation. Pope took revenge in the finest piece of satire he ever wrote, the stinging lines on Atticus, with which everybody is, or ought to be, acquainted.

On the death of Queen Anne, Addison was appointed Secretary to the Regency. In 1715 he obtained a seat at the Board of Trade. In the following year he married the Countess Dowager of Warwick, whom he had long courted, and whom he at length obtained, "on terms much like those on which a Turkish princess is espoused, to whom the Sultan is reported to pronounce, 'Daughter, I give thee this man for thy slave.'" This union added nothing to his happiness. He would often escape from the uncomfortable grandeur of Holland House, where he had resided since his marriage, to the ease and freedom of his favourite coffee-house, Button's, there to enjoy himself in tranquil conversation with old friends, and would afterwards adjourn to a tavern, where he indulged somewhat freely in wine. In 1717 he was made one of the chief Secretaries of State; but as his constitutional timidity prevented him from being a ready or effective speaker, the office was not well suited to him, and he was soon glad to retire on a pension of £1500 a year. He died in June 1719.

In the company of one or two intimate friends, with whom he could be at freedom, Addison talked long and excellently. "He was," says Steele, "above all men in that talent called humour, and enjoyed it in such perfection, that I have often reflected, after a night spent with him apart from all the world, that I had the pleasure of conversing with an intimate acquaintance of Terence and Catullus, who had all their wit and nature, heightened with humour more exquisite and delightful than any other man ever possessed." Pope, no partial witness, confessed that Addison's conversation had something in it more charming than was to be found in that of any other man. But it was only when with one or two old associates that Addison displayed his conversational talents: in a large company he sat silent, partly from natural bashfulness, partly from fear lest he should compromise his dignity. Alluding to his fluency of composition compared with his deficiencies as a ready talker, he used to say that he could draw bills for a thousand pounds, though he had not a guinea in his pocket.

Addison's principal political writings were a pamphlet published in 1707 on the "Present State of the War," the *Whig Examiner*, a periodical written in opposition to Swift's *Examiner*, of which only five numbers appeared, and which Johnson praises very highly, and the *Freeholder*, which appeared twice a week during part of 1715-16. The last contains the famous sketch of the Tory Fox-Hunter, one of his best compositions. It is sad to have to relate that before Addison's death political differences led to an estrangement between him and Steele.

Addison was one of the sort of politicians dear to party-leaders, who follow their chiefs submissively wherever they may lead them, and who have no hobbies of their own, no strong opinions which they are determined to act up to whether their colleagues are opposed to them or not. The reverse is true of Steele. He was ardent and impetuous in politics as in everything else; and when a measure was introduced of which he did not approve, he opposed it strenuously, even though it was a measure introduced by the ministry to which he owed his appointments. When, in 1719, the Whigs brought forward their Peerage Bill, by which they proposed to limit the number of the Peers, Addison supported the Ministers, while in a paper called the *Plebeian* Steele vehemently attacked them. This opposition led to mutual recriminations; and the death of Addison soon after prevented a reconciliation.

The leading events of Steele's life, from the foundation of the *Spectator* till his death, may be briefly summed up. In 1713 he began the publication of a daily periodical called the *Guardian*, which continued to be published during about eight months, and to which Addison contributed largely. In 1714 the publication of two violent political pamphlets, the "Englishman" and the "Crisis," led to his being expelled from the House of Commons. His numerous productions on the topics of the day it would be useless to enumerate. The "Conscious Lovers," his best comedy, appeared in 1722. In 1715 he was appointed surveyor of the royal stables at Hampton Court; and about the same time received the honour of knighthood. He afterwards held other appointments, and during the latter years of his life was patentee of Drury Lane Theatre, which brought him a considerable income. He died in 1729 at Langunnor, near Carmarthen, where he had retired some time before his death. "I was told," a friend of his related, "that he retained his cheerful sweetness of temper to the last, and would often be carried out of a summer's evening when the country lads and lasses were assembled at their rural sports, and with his pencil he gave an order on his agent, the mercer, for a new gown for the best dancer." It is pleasing to learn that the close of his life was so tranquil and pleasant.

Steele was described by the merciless Dennis as being "of a middle stature, broad shoulders, thick legs, a shape like the picture of somebody over a farmer's chimney—a short chin, a short nose, a short forehead, a broad flat face, and a dusky countenance." The many letters which he wrote to his wife, "dearest Prue," all of which that worthy and much-tried woman carefully preserved, give one an excellent idea of his genial, impulsive, hasty, affectionate, and reckless temperament. Johnson, with whom Macaulay agrees,[1] praises Addison because he employed wit on the side of virtue and religion. "He not only made the proper use of wit himself, but taught it to others; and from this time it has been generally subservient to the cause of reason and of truth. He has dissipated the prejudice that had long connected gaiety with vice, and easiness of manners with laxity of principles. He has restored virtue to its dignity, and taught innocence not to be ashamed." If this praise be due to Addison, as it certainly is, it is also due to Steele. However wild his conduct may have occasionally been, in his writings he never swerved from upholding the cause of purity and goodness; and in many respects his moral precepts were of a less conventional kind, and reached a higher spiritual level than Addison's.

It was during the reign of Queen Anne that the writing of correct and polished English prose first became a general accomplishment. Many writers who flourished about this period, though of infinitely less original power than their predecessors of fifty or a hundred years ago, are much more pleasant to read, simply because they had acquired the knack of expressing themselves in clear, well-ordered sentences, free from the cumbrousness and involution which, till the time of Dryden, are usual characteristics of our prose writers. Three of these may be mentioned. Dr. John Arbuthnot

[1] It is very well worth while to read Johnson's 'Life of Addison' and Macaulay's 'Essay on Addison' together. There is scarcely a critical idea in Macaulay's essay of which the germ is not to be found in Johnson's.

(1667–1735) was a Scotchman, who, coming up to London, attained great reputation as a medical man, and was the intimate associate of many of the foremost writers of his time. His "History of John Bull," a political satire, and other writings, mostly of a controversial or satirical nature, have much the same characteristics as Swift's—clearness, force, and incisiveness. He seems to have been a most excellent man. "He has more wit than we all have," said Swift, "and his humanity is equal to his wit;" and again, "If the world had a dozen Arbuthnots in it, I would burn my 'Travels.'" Arbuthnot wrote little, and there is no collected edition of his works; but the little that he did write shows that if he had used his pen more freely he could have won for himself a very high position in literature. Henry St. John, Viscount Bolingbroke (1678–1751), whose meteoric career still sheds a sort of lustre round his name, wrote, when his political life was brought to an end by the discovery of his intrigue with the Pretender, a number of works, "Letters on the Study of History," "Letter on the Spirit of Patriotism," the "Idea of a Patriot King," &c., in a style artificial and somewhat stilted, but emphatic, striking, and often epigrammatic. On the whole, it may be said that the reader who, finding how much Bolingbroke was admired by his contemporaries, is led to study his works, will not find much to reward him, except a few happy sentences, such as "Don Quixote believed, but even Sancho doubted." George Berkeley (1684–1753), Bishop of Cloyne, whose work belongs to the history of philosophy, deserves mention here as having possessed a style, simple, sweet, and melodious in an eminent degree. He could write with equal elegance on the most subtle philosophical theories and on the virtues of tar-water. Pope's well-known line, which attributes "to Berkeley every virtue under heaven," shows how he was regarded by his contemporaries.

During the early part of the eighteenth century was waged the somewhat barren "Deistical Controversy," in which a great number of writers, including nearly all the leading theologians of the day, took part. It produced one book of permanent value, the "Analogy of Religion" of Bishop Butler (1692–1752), a work full of weighty thought, though its style is very awkward and complex. "It came (1736) towards the end of the Deistical period. It is the result of twenty years' study—the very twenty years during which the Deistical notions formed the atmosphere which educated people breathed. The objections it meets are not new and unseasoned objections, but such as had worn well, and had borne the rub of controversy, because they were genuine. And it would be equally hard to find in the 'Analogy' any topic in reply which had not been suggested in the pamphlets and sermons of the preceding half century. Like Aristotle's physical and political treatises, it is a *résumé* of the discussions of more than one generation."[1]

We now turn to the poetical literature of the beginning of the eighteenth century. This finds its highest representative in Alexander Pope. The correctness and finish which all the poets of his age were endeavouring to attain, he attained more completely than any; and though before his death new influences were beginning to be at work which ended in the overthrow of the school of which he was the accepted leader, he influenced very strongly the poets of the two generations which succeeded him. Pope was born in London in 1688. After he had risen to eminence and was taunted with the lowness of his birth, he circulated some rather fabulous stories about the exalted pedigree of his father, an honest and successful merchant, who acquired by his industry a fortune which in those days was reckoned a large one. Both his parents were Catholics, and Pope, in spite of considerable temptations to the contrary, always remained constant to the faith of his fathers. He was deformed and weakly from his birth, a dwarfish and precocious child, with a sweet voice and a quick intellect. He was taught to read at home, and early learned to write by imitating printed books. When about eight years old his

[1] Mr. Mark Pattison's "Tendencies of Religious Thought in England, 1688–1750," in "Essays and Reviews," an essay containing an admirable account of the current of theological thought during the time with which it deals.

education was intrusted to a Catholic priest, through whom he acquired the elements of Latin and Greek. He afterwards had other instructors, but the most valuable part of his education was that which he obtained without the aid of any master. He was a voracious reader, and if his knowledge, like that of most self-educated men, was destitute of minute accuracy, it was, at any rate, much wider than is at all common. He had a good knowledge of Latin, a fair share of Greek, knew French well, and at one time studied Italian to some extent.

His crooked frame and weak health debarred Pope from the usual sports of childhood; and when, in his early years, his father retired to Binfield in Windsor Forest, where he had purchased a small estate, the ambitious boy began earnestly the practice of that art which was to be the toil and the pleasure of his life. When little more than twelve he commenced an epic poem, of which he wrote about four thousand verses. Other compositions preceded and followed this large undertaking, all of which were submitted to his father, who, when he found them defective, would request him to "new-turn them," saying, "These be not good rhymes." When very young he managed to become acquainted with some of the leading men of letters in London, to whom he wrote carefully composed letters in the artificial style then prevalent, and by whom he seems, in spite of his youth, to have been regarded as an equal. Among these was Wycherley, who submitted some verses to the revision of the youthful critic, who pointed out their faults with such unsparing rigour that Wycherley was not unnaturally offended. Another was Walsh, "Knowing Walsh," as Pope calls him, a poetaster of the day, who was much esteemed as a critic. Having read some of Pope's verses, he advised him to aim especially at correctness, for, said he, "We have had several great poets, but we never had one great poet who was correct." This well-meant advice was never forgotten by Pope. In 1709 Pope published his first poems, the "Pastorals," which had been for some time handed about among poets and critics. They were well received at the time, Walsh declaring "that 'tis no flattery at all to say that Virgil had written nothing so good at his age;" but they are now generally regarded as Pope's poorest compositions, being artificial, absurd, and wearisome. Two years after came the "Essay on Criticism," which shows a great advance in more ways than one. The versification is exact and polished, the style clear and epigrammatic, the illustrations various and well selected. As regards the value of the subject-matter of this poem, critics have differed widely. "If he had written nothing else," says Johnson, "this would have placed him among the first critics and the first poets, as it exhibits every mode of excellence that can embellish or justify didactic composition—selection of matter, novelty of arrangement, justness of precept, splendour of illustration, and propriety of digression." De Quincey, on the other hand, thought it "the feeblest and least interesting of Pope's writings, being substantially a mere versification, like a metrical multiplication table, of commonplaces the most mouldy with which criticism has baited her rat-traps." The truth is, that our judgment of the poem will depend upon the point of view from which we regard it. Pope's precepts are not original, though they are generally sound enough; but they are so well and strikingly put that they come home to us with a new force. A wanton attack on Dennis, under the name of "Appius," in the "Essay on Criticism," brought on the first of the long series of literary squabbles in which Pope was implicated. Dennis rejoined in a furious pamphlet, in which, alluding to Pope's deformed figure, he declared that "he may extol the ancients, but he has reason to thank the gods that he was born a modern; for had he been born of Grecian parents, and his father consequently had by law had the absolute disposal of him, his life had been no longer than that of one of his poems, the life of half a day." If opinions have differed as to the merits of the "Essay on Criticism," there has been but one judgment on the "Rape of the Lock." It was published in 1712,[1] and, as is well known, was founded on a frolic of Lord Petre's, who had cut off a lock of Miss Arabella

[1] The version published in 1712 is only a fir t sketch. It appeared in a volume of miscellaneous poems.

Fermor's hair. His gallantry offending the lady and breaking off the intercourse of the two families, Pope was asked by a common friend to do something to effect a reconciliation. The result of this request was the best mock-heroic poem in the language. The first edition wanted the supernatural machinery, one of the greatest attractions of the work, and some excellent passages which were added in the second edition (1714). It is perhaps Pope's most universally pleasing performance—light, easy, graceful, full of delicate satirical touches, never flagging in interest, and having the additional merit of giving us an accurate picture of the fashionable society of Queen Anne's time. "Pope's adaptation of his airy refulgent sylphs to the ephemeral trivialities of fashionable life, the admirable art with which he fitted his fairy machinery to the follies and commonplaces of a giddy London day, the poetic grace which he threw around his sarcastic narrative, and which unites with it as naturally as does the rose with its thorny stem, are all unborrowed beauties, and consummate in their kind." Not long after the "Rape of the Lock," Pope wrote a poem in a very different style, the "Epistle of Eloisa to Abelard," which is also one of the brightest jewels in his poetic crown. We do not look to Pope for the successful expression of deep, passionate feeling; he is pre-eminently a poet of artificial society, of nature as seen in clubs and coffee-houses and in fashionable town assemblages. Yet it cannot be denied that in the "Epistle of Eloisa" he shows himself possessed of a vein of genuine pathos and tenderness. The hand of the artist is, indeed, a little too apparent in its smooth couplets and neatly turned phrases, but it is, at any rate, always the hand of a master of his art.

In 1713 Pope, whose fame was now widespread, entered upon the most fortunate undertaking of his life, his translation of the "Iliad." It was with many doubts and fears that he began his task. "In the beginning of my translating Homer," he told his faithful chronicler, Spence, "I wished anybody would hang me a hundred times. It sat so very heavily on my mind at first that I often used to dream of it, and even do so sometimes still to this day. My dream usually was that I had set out on a very long journey, puzzled which way to take, and full of fears that I should never get to the end of it." De Quincey thinks that Pope's trepidation when he commenced translating the "Iliad" was owing to his defective knowledge of the Greek language, and this opinion is very probably correct. As the work advanced, practice brought facility, until at length he was able to translate fifty lines a day. It had been decided that the translation should be published by subscription, and Pope's friends exerted themselves to the utmost to procure subscribers. There is an amusing anecdote of how, in a coffee-house in 1713, Swift was seen informing "a young nobleman that the best poet in England was Mr. Pope (a Papist), who had begun a translation of Homer into English verse, for which he must have them all subscribe; 'for,' says he, 'the author shall not begin to print till I have a thousand guineas for him.'" In 1720, when Pope had reached his thirty-second year, the translation was completed. Its success surpassed all the high hopes that had been formed of it. Altogether the work produced £5320, which would now represent a purchasing power of at least double that amount. Of the worth of the translation, a sufficiently correct judgment was expressed by Richard Bentley, the greatest classical scholar England has ever seen. "It is a pretty poem, Mr. Pope," he is recorded to have said, "but you must not call it Homer." Pope's genius was, in truth, singularly un-Homeric; nothing can be imagined more different from his polished artificiality than the grand simplicity of the Greek bard. Yet, full as Pope's "Iliad" is of faults which jar against a pure literary taste, it may fairly claim to have done good service. To thousands unacquainted with Greek it has afforded at least a glimpse of the old heroic world painted by Homer, and even yet, though now surrounded by so many competitors, it is perhaps to the average reader the most attractive translation. Elated with his success, Pope determined to translate the "Odyssey" also. To aid him in his task he engaged two assistants, Broome and Fenton, by whom twelve books out of the twenty-four were translated. The work was finished in 1725, and was very profitable, though it did not realise nearly so much as the "Iliad." It is a striking proof of how usual an accomplishment the art of writing the heroic couplet had now become to find that it is difficult, if not impossible, to distinguish by internal evidence passages of the "Odyssey" translated by Broome and Fenton, from passages translated by Pope.

With the money acquired by his translation of the "Iliad," Pope bought the cottage at Twickenham, where he resided for the remainder of his days, and where he was often visited by the most notable men of the day, Swift, Bolingbroke, Arbuthnot, Lord Peterborough, and many others. In 1728 he published the "Dunciad," in which he lashed mercilessly the minor scribblers of his day, and discharged venomous shafts of ridicule against all who had at any time assaulted him. Between 1733 and 1738 he published the various pieces which, when his works were first collected, constituted the volume entitled "Satires and Epistles of Horace Imitated." These so-called "imitations" contain some of his most vigorous writing—the matchless portrait of Addison under the name of Atticus; the stinging and vindictive lines in which Lord Hervey is pilloried under the name of Sporus; and the touching passage which commemorates his filial piety. In his satires, Pope pretended to be inspired by a genuine indignation against vice. But it was not so in reality; he used satire as a means of gratifying private revenge, not because the villanies of mankind stirred him up to write. "Pope was contented enough," says De Quincey, "with society as he found it; bad it might be, but it was good enough for him. It was the merest self-delusion if, at any moment, the instinct of glorying in his satiric mission persuaded him that in his case it might be said, *Facit indignatio versum.* Pope having no internal principle of wrath boiling in his breast, being really in the most pacific and charitable frame of mind to all scoundrels whatsoever, was a hypocrite when he conceited himself to be in a dreadful passion with offenders as a body." One of the most common topics of his ridicule is poverty, which is certainly no fit theme for the exercise of the satirist's art. "He seems," says Johnson with melancholy scorn, "to be of an opinion not very uncommon in the world, that to want money is to want everything." How far mere personal indignation could lead him is shown by the fact that when, in 1741, he published a revised edition of the "Dunciad," to which the fourth book was added, he degraded Theobald from his former position as hero, and placed Colley Cibber, who had offended him in the interval between 1728 and 1741, in his stead. The change altered the "Dunciad" greatly for the worse. Theobald was really a very dull man; Colley Cibber, on the other hand, was decidedly lively and clever, so that the ridicule which was applicable enough to Theobald loses all its pungency when applied to him. Like many writers who are careless how much pain they may give to others, Pope felt any attack on himself with the intensest keenness. On one occasion, when a pamphlet of Cibber's against him came into his hands while Richardson the painter was with him, Pope turned to Richardson and said, "These things are my diversion." Richardson watched him as he perused it, and saw his features writhing with anguish!

In the "Essay on Man," published in 1732, Pope attempted to deal in verse with a philosophical topic which was then exciting much attention. The "Essay on Man," says Mr. Mark Pattison in the Introduction to his admirable edition of it, "was composed at a time when the reading public in this country were occupied with an intense and eager curiosity by speculation on the first principles of natural religion. Everywhere, in the pulpit, in the coffee-houses, in every pamphlet, argument on the origin of evil, on the goodness of God, and the constitution of the world was rife. Into the prevailing topic of polite conversation, Bolingbroke, who returned from exile in 1723, was drawn by the bent of his native genius. Pope followed the example and impulse of his friend's more powerful mind. Thus much there was of special suggestion; but the arguments or topics of the poem are to be traced to books in much vogue at the time." There is now a pretty general consensus of critical opinion as to the "Essay on Man."

Its philosophy is poor, borrowed, and inadequate. Pope did not understand what he was writing about, and mixed up incongruous statements; but it has kept and will keep its place in literature owing to its masterly execution, its many felicitous phrases, and the great beauty of occasional passages. When the "Essay" first appeared, many assailed it on account of its alleged heterodoxy. Pope was annoyed at the charge, and was therefore delighted when an unexpected auxiliary rushed to his aid in the person of William Warburton (1698–1779), who afterwards rose to be Bishop of Gloucester, and whose very paradoxical work, "The Divine Legation of Moses," is still remembered. By helping Pope in his difficulty, Warburton thought he saw an opportunity for advancing his own fame and fortune, and he therefore vindicated the orthodoxy of the "Essay on Man" in a series of articles which appeared in a monthly publication called *The Works of the Learned.* The substance of these articles was afterwards, at Pope's request, formed into a commentary—a very tedious and worthless production, it may be said in passing—and printed in the next edition of the "Essay." Pope never ceased to be grateful to Warburton for the service he had done him, and on the death of the poet, which occurred in 1744, Warburton found he had been appointed his literary executor. He discharged the duties of his office arrogantly, carelessly, and dishonourably.

The careful research of Pope's latest editors, and particularly of Mr. Whitwell Elwin, if it has not materially altered the estimate of Pope's private character which may be derived from the perusal of Johnson's Life of him, with its curious undertone of latent scorn, has proved beyond all possibility of doubt that he was frequently guilty of treachery, falsehood, and hypocrisy. Anxious to have his letters printed in his lifetime, and desirous of an excuse for so unusual an act, he contrived that an alleged surreptitious edition of these should be published, so as to give him a colourable pretext for printing an authentic edition. Great allowances are to be made for a man like Pope, with his deformed figure and his weak health, which debarred him from many of the common pleasures of mankind. It is only natural that such a man should be peevish, irritable, and, if possessed of talents, insatiate of praise and impatient of censure; but Pope's habitual duplicity cannot be condoned even by his most lenient judges. The most pleasing feature of his character is his unwearying tenderness to his parents, and the sincere affection and esteem which he appears to have felt for a large and brilliant circle of friends. "I never in my life," said Bolingbroke by his deathbed, "knew a man who had so tender a heart for his particular friends, or a more general friendship for mankind." This "general friendship for mankind" did not prevent him from traducing cruelly all who happened to offend him; but the statement of his love for his particular friends may be accepted without reservation.

Like the other writers of the time when his fame reached its zenith, Pope in all his works had "the town" in view when he wrote. All the chief authors of that period appealed in their style, their mode of treatment, their sentiments, their descriptions, their satires to an audience of Londoners. It is this which gives the poetry of the age its polish, neatness, and clearness; it is this also which gives it its artificiality, and which accounts for the absence from it of any deep emotional feeling, and for its poverty as regards natural description. Pope's poetry is the mirror of his age, as it presented itself before one who saw it with the eyes of a man to whom metropolitan society constituted the world. "He shows us the rise of woman as a controlling power in society and politics; the extension among the nobility of an Italian taste in painting and architecture; the hatred felt by the Catholics for the moneyed middle-class, which was the backbone of the Revolution, the mainstay of Whiggery, and the bulwark of Protestantism. In his satires, too, we see a mirror of the feelings of the Parliamentary Opposition directed by Bolingbroke and Pulteney; of their rancour against Walpole's foreign and domestic policy; of the relations between the court and the party of the Prince of Wales; of the popular dislike of the Hanoverian dynasty and of Low Church principles. Besides, we have suggestive glimpses of the interior of society at a time when St. James's was in the extreme west-end of London, and old Burlington House was but just built. The 'British youth' appear at their diversions at White's Chocolate House, Hockly-in-the-Hole, or Fig's Academy. Complaints are heard from polite society of the degradation of the stage in consequence of the public passion for spectacles. The penniless 'man of rhyme walks forth' from the Mint, and the dealings of the ill-lodged bard of Drury Lane with his aristocratic or commercial patrons are exposed in the full light of pitiless ridicule. As we read, the society of the past rises before us in its dramatic reality. The age in many respects may have had the defects of the poet, but, like him, it was not without its generous qualities; it is, at least, full of human and historical interest, whether it be regarded as the period when the British Empire first began to rise, or as the aristocratic stage of English society, in which the realities of character displayed themselves with a frankness wanting in our democratic times, when the individual is apt to disguise his natural impulses in deference to public opinion."

Among the poets who were contemporary with Pope, a few deserve notice. Matthew Prior (1664–1721) affords one of the most striking instances on record of the extraordinary rewards sometimes bestowed on literary merit in the reign of Queen Anne. He received a good education at Westminster School, and was then employed by his uncle, who kept a tavern near Charing Cross, as his assistant. In this uncongenial situation his love of literature did not forsake him, and one day the Earl of Dorset by chance found the vintner's boy reading Horace. This was the turning-point of Prior's fortunes. The Earl, who was celebrated for his patronage of genius, was so well pleased with Prior's proficiency, that he undertook the care and cost of his education. Prior passed through his academical career with credit, and soon after obtained great popularity by his authorship, in conjunction with Montague, of the "City Mouse and the Country Mouse," in ridicule of Dryden's "Hind and Panther." Upon the merits of this parody, which attained great celebrity at the time, opinions differ considerably. Mr. Saintsbury, a very acute critic, thinks that it has had the honour of being more overpraised than perhaps anything of its kind in English literature.[1] Soon after its publication Prior was taken into the service of the State, and rose to various high diplomatic appointments, justifying the choice of his patrons by his industry and dexterity. A happy retort of his, uttered when he was secretary to the English embassy at Paris, has been often quoted. When he was being shown the pictures of the victories of Louis XIV. painted on the walls of the apartments of Versailles, he was asked whether the King of England's palace had any such decorations. "The monuments of my master's actions," replied Prior, "are to be seen everywhere but in his own house." On the death of Queen Anne, Prior's diplomatic career came to an end, and for a time he laboured under considerable difficulties, from which, however, he was at length relieved by the success of a subscription edition of his poems, and by the generous assistance of the Earl of Oxford. Prior's serious poems are worthless and unreadable, but his songs and humorous pieces, though not over-delicate, are lively and spirited enough of their kind. "Johnson speaks slightingly of his lyrics," says Thackeray, "but with due deference to the great Samuel, Prior's seems to me among the easiest, the richest, the most charmingly humorous of English lyrical poems. Horace is always in his mind, and his song, and his philosophy, his good sense, his happy easy turns and melody, his loves and Epicureanism, bear a great resemblance to that most delightful and accomplished master. In reading his works, one is struck by their modern air, as well as by their happy similarity to the songs of the charming owner of the Sabine farm." This is too high commendation; but the fact that Prior's lyrical pieces obtained such praise from a man like Thackeray shows that, slight and somewhat artificial as they are, they possess a considerable degree of genuine excellence.

John Gay, who was born in the same year as Pope, was one of those ineffectual, helpless, likeable men, who pass through

[1] Monograph on Dryden, p. 97.

life as easily as possible, always looking to others for help and protection. Originally a silk-mercer's apprentice in London, he was in 1712 appointed secretary to the Duchess of Monmouth. "By quitting a shop for such service," says Johnson, "he might gain leisure, but he certainly advanced little in the boast of independence." Next year Gay published a poem on "Rural Sports," which, being dedicated to Pope, was the means of introducing him to the society of the wits, among whom he became a great favourite. Gay's chief works are his "Fables," which are ingenious and amusing; his "Trivia, or the Art of Walking the Streets of London," which gives a curious picture of scenes and customs which have now passed away; and the "Beggar's Opera," his best and most famous work. It was brought out in 1728, and was such a success that for some weeks the town talked of nothing else. Under the guise of a mock-heroic drama about pickpockets and informers, it contains a scathing and incisive satire on the politics and politicians of the day. When Gay produced the second part of the "Beggar's Opera," under the name of "Polly," the Lord Chamberlain refused to license it, no doubt because of its political intent. It has not nearly the merit of the first part; nevertheless, when it was published by subscription, it proved very successful, and brought the fortunate author a large sum of money. The songs interspersed through the "Beggar's Opera" are of great merit, melodious, sprightly, witty, and always (the highest excellence of such compositions) reading as if they had been made to sing. Gay died in 1732. For some years before his death, he lived in the household of the Duke and Duchess of Queensberry, who were very kind to him, taking charge of his money for him, and otherwise assiduously attending to his comforts.

One of the best examples of the pretty numerous class of works which are often referred to and almost never read is the "Night Thoughts" of Edward Young. Young (1681–1765) was one of the greatest sycophants of a very adulatory age; a self-seeking, greedy, worldly man. He entered into holy orders in 1728, and was appointed Rector of Welwyn in Hertfordshire, where, in 1742–44, he wrote his "Night Thoughts." Abounding in epigrams and quotable passages, and having about them a sort of gloomy grandeur, the "Night Thoughts" are often extravagant and tedious. Young wrote a great many other poetical works, satires, tragedies, odes, and epistles, "The Last Day," a paraphrase of part of the Book of Job, and a poem called "Resignation." Of these, the best is a rather vigorous satire entitled "The Love of Fame, or the Universal Passion." Another satirist of the school of Dryden and Pope was the unfortunate and dissipated Charles Churchill (1731–1764), who "blazed," as Byron says, "the comet of a season," between 1761 and 1764. His satires are coarse and vigorous, destitute of refinement and elaboration, but strong and manly.

Among the writers of Pope's time, with their preference for town life and their indifference to natural scenery, a voice made itself heard speaking of the aspects of country life, of the green fields, of the changes of the seasons, of the gloom of winter, the freshness of spring, the rich profusion of summer, and the russet-clad tints of autumn. This was James Thomson, a Scotchman, who, born in 1700, came up to London to seek his fortune in 1725. His poem of the "Seasons" appeared in four instalments in 1726–1730. Thomson is often careless and dull; his verse is disfigured by that pseudo-classicalism which delighted to speak of Ceres, Pomona, Boreas, &c., but he had a genuine love for nature, and his descriptions, despite their artificial dress, bear the stamp of reality. The fact that the "Seasons" was at once successful, shows that the taste for the poetry of town life was already beginning to decay. Thomson was a fat, lazy, good-natured, benevolent man, fond of lying in bed in the mornings, and of indulging in long-drawn reveries or in building luxurious castles in the air when he ought to have been actively exerting himself. He died in 1748, having had his latter years made very comfortable by a pension bestowed on him by the Prince of Wales, and a sinecure situation which he obtained through the influence of his patron Lyttleton. Besides his "Seasons," Thomson wrote some tragedies, which proved failures, a long and unreadable poem called "Liberty," several smaller pieces, and what is in the opinion of some of his critics his best work, "The Castle of Indolence," which appeared in the year of his death. In it "he has poured out the whole soul of indolence, diffuse, relaxed, supine, dissolved into a voluptuous dream, and surrounded himself with a set of objects and companions in entire unison with the listlessness of his own temper." To appreciate Thomson properly one must be prepared to read him in the same easy-going frame of mind as that in which he himself wrote; in a calm leisurely way, not constantly on the outlook for fine passages nor impatient of tediousness. Hazlitt, who thought very highly of him, is constrained to say that "the same suavity of temper and sanguine warmth of feeling which threw such a natural grace and genial spirit of enthusiasm over his poetry was also the causes of his inherent vices and defects. He is affected through carelessness, pompous from unsuspecting simplicity of character. He is frequently pedantic and ostentatious in his style because he had no consciousness of these vices in himself. He mounts upon stilts, not out of vanity but indolence. He seldom writes a good line but he makes up for it by a bad one. He takes advantage of all the most trite and mechanical commonplaces of imagery and diction as a kindly relief to his muse, and as if he thought them quite as good and likely to be quite as acceptable to the reader as his own poetry. He did not think the difference worth putting himself to the trouble of accomplishing."

Shortly after the death of Pope, the poems of Gray and Collins, in quite a different style from his, began to appear. They were formed on classical models, and we find in them nothing of that constant reference to contemporary life which is one of the notes of Pope's poetry. Thomas Gray, born in 1716, was, like Milton, the son of a London scrivener. He was educated at Eton and at Cambridge, where he became acquainted with Horace Walpole, whom, in 1739, he accompanied on a tour to France and Italy. Both were fastidious, "touchy" men, and it is not surprising to learn that they quarrelled during the journey and parted, each to pursue his own separate route. Soon after his return from the Continent in 1741, Gray settled down at Cambridge, where most of his subsequent life was spent. In 1768 he was appointed Professor of History there, an office for which he was well qualified, but he never discharged the duties of his situation, being too lazy to prepare a course of lectures. Gray was a literary voluptuary, refined, finical, indisposed to active exertions, and so terrified lest a faulty piece of work should go out of his hands that he wrote very little. He was an extensive and curious reader in all departments of literature, and prevented time from lying heavy on his hands by engaging in all those trifling occupations by which so many worthy indolent people try to persuade themselves that they are busy. He made annotations in the books which he read; he drew up (for his own edification) tables of chronology; during the chief part of his life he kept a *daily* record of the blowing of flowers, the leafing of trees, the state of the thermometer, the quarter from which the wind blew, the falling of rain, and other matters of the kind; and he delighted his friends by writing long and excellent letters, many of which have been published, and constitute his not least-enduring title to remembrance. They are unconstrained, natural, amusing effusions, and give us a pleasing picture of a man who was content "to let the world go by," so long as he was free to engage in the innocent intellectual pursuits which he loved. "Don't you remember," he says in one place, "Lord —— and ——, who are now great statesmen, little dirty boys playing at cricket? For my part, I do not feel a bit wiser, or bigger, or older than I did then." His wish to lie on a sofa and read eternal new romances of Marivaux and Crebillon has inspired many inveterate novel-readers with sympathy and regard for the placid poet who found such pleasure in their favourite class of literature.

Gray died in 1771. As already indicated, his poems were few and short—so few and short that, despite their excellence, he can scarcely be called a great poet. His most famous piece is, of course, the "Elegy in a Country Churchyard," which was written in 1749. There is no need to eulogise a poem which has excited universal pleasure. The patient industry of commentators has shown that there is scarcely an idea in it which can be regarded as original; but that in no way detracts from the merit of Gray, for consummate artistic skill, such as is shown in the "Elegy," is at least as rare a quality as original genius. Gray's "Odes," which were published at various times, never have been and never will be so popular as the "Elegy:" they contain many far-fetched allusions; their language is rather artificial, and they do not in general appeal to feelings which are the common property of humanity as the "Elegy" does. Gray's "classical coldness" and want of spontaneity has exposed him to the censure of many, including Johnson and Carlyle. Johnson declared that he was a "mechanical poet;" while Carlyle (in his essay on Goethe) says that his poetry is "a laborious mosaic, through the hard stiff lineaments of which little life or true grace could be expected to look; real feeling, and all freedom in expressing it, are sacrificed to pomp, cold splendour; for vigour we have a certain mouthing vehemence, too elegant indeed to be tumid, yet essentially foreign to the heart, and seen to extend no deeper than the mere voice and gestures. Were it not for his 'Letters,' which are full of warm exuberant power, we might almost doubt whether Gray was a man of genius, nay, was a living man at all, and not rather some thousand times more cunningly devised poetical turning-loom than that of Swift's philosophers in Laputa." This is extravagantly unjust; none but a man of true genius could have written the "Elegy" or the "Ode on a Distant Prospect of Eton College;" but it does hit a defect in Gray's poetry by indicating that its pomp and ceremony are sometimes felt oppressive, and its art is not of that perfect order which conceals itself.

The story of the life of William Collins, a poet who bears a strong resemblance to Gray, is a very sad one. He was born in 1720 at Chichester, where his father had a good business as a hatter. In 1733 he entered Winchester College, Oxford, and afterwards became a demi of Magdalen College, where he remained till he took his degree. While in residence there he published his "Oriental Eclogues" (1742), of which he used afterwards to speak contemptuously, as destitute of Orientalism, calling them his "Irish Eclogues." About 1744 he came to London, "with many projects in his head, and very little money in his pocket." Though depending for his means of support on the liberality of a relative, he was dissipated and profuse in his expenditure, and soon, like many another author of the day, knew what it was to be in the hands of a bailiff. Collins was a learned man, with a taste for reading and study, and could, no doubt, if he had exerted himself, have earned at least a fair competency by his pen. But he was one of the class of men who, like Coleridge, love much better to draw up magnificent projects which they intend to accomplish at some future time than to put their shoulder to the wheel and do the duty which lies nearest them. Among his plans was a "History of the Revival of Learning," of which he published proposals, but none of the work ever appeared, and very little of it was ever written. He also planned several tragedies, and on one occasion, when confined to his house lest he should be captured by a bailiff who was prowling in the street, entered into an engagement with the booksellers to execute a translation of Aristotle's "Poetics," for which he received as much money as enabled him to escape into the country. Soon afterwards he received a legacy of two thousand pounds, whereupon he repaid the booksellers the sum they had advanced him and abandoned the translation. His only publication besides the "Eclogues" was his "Odes," which appeared in 1746, and proved such a failure in point of sale, that the sensitive author purchased the remainder of the edition from the publisher and burned it. About 1751 he began to decay in body and in mind. "His disorder," says Johnson, who knew and liked him, "was no alienation of mind, but general laxity and feebleness, a deficiency rather of his vital than his intellectual powers. What he spoke wanted neither judgment nor spirit; but a few minutes exhausted him, so that he was forced to rest upon the couch, till a short cessation restored his powers, and he was again able to talk with his former vigour." He lingered on in this deplorable state for some years, till, in 1759, death relieved him from it. Once when, during his malady, Johnson called on him, he found the unfortunate poet reading the New Testament, which he always carried about with him. "I have but one book," said Collins, "but it is the best."

After Collins's death there was found among his papers a long ode on the "Superstitions of the Highlands," which has since been printed. His entire works form a very slender volume, but it is a volume which will always be dear to those who can appreciate real poetical genius. His brilliant personification of the Passions and his fine "Ode to Evening" show pure taste, deep poetic feeling, and a wide command of poetical diction. His contemporaries, including Johnson, were blind to his merits, but their neglect of him has been amply avenged by the honour paid to him by posterity.

We have only mentioned a few of the poets who flourished during the reign of Queen Anne and the first Georges. The list might be indefinitely extended; but it is idle to try to keep alive the memory of a crowd of versifiers, most of whose compositions are inferior to those which every day appear in the pages of our periodicals. Of all kinds of reading, that of bad or middling poetry is the most profitless. One or two of the poets who belong to the first half of the eighteenth century will be mentioned in a subsequent chapter, but we may here mention, as belonging to the school of Pope, Mark Akenside, whose "Pleasures of the Imagination" (1744) was inspired by Addison's papers in the *Spectator* on the same subject. This poem is in blank verse, and though frequently commonplace and wearisome, is not without dignity and force. But poems which aspire to treat such a theme in a poetical way are apt to prove failures unless in the hands of a great master of his art, and Akenside did not possess genius enough to grapple successfully with the many difficulties of his subject. Accordingly, although it deserves and will reward the attention of the student of English poetry, the "Pleasures of the Imagination" is now generally neglected.

VI.

OUR FIRST GREAT NOVELISTS.

Defoe; Richardson; Fielding; Smollett; Sterne.

SIR WALTER SCOTT, in the beginning of his "Essay on Romance," referring to the division of fictitious prose narratives into two classes, defines the *romance* as that in which the interest turns chiefly on marvellous and uncommon incidents, and the *novel* as that in which the events are accommodated to the ordinary train of human events and the modern state of society. The definitions are not, perhaps, altogether unexceptionable, but they indicate the distinction in a way sufficiently clear and broad for practical purposes. Romances of one kind or another, pastoral and heroic, were known in England from an early period—Sir Thomas Malory's "Morte d'Arthur," which Scott calls "indisputably the best prose romance the language can boast of," was written during the reign of Edward IV.; but as a rule they were very extravagant and of small literary merit. The novel, on the other hand, is of comparatively recent introduction into English literature. It seems strange to us, who live in a time when novels constitute by far the most generally attractive species of composition, when they are produced by thousands and read by tens of thousands, when more deft and gifted penmen employ themselves in this branch of literature than in any other, to think that we have not to go farther back for the beginnings of this fascinating species of composition than the early part of the eighteenth century. Its rise coincides pretty much with the decline of the drama. Education was beginning to be more widely diffused, and people were not only able to follow a story with interest as represented on the stage, but also to read it with pleasure.

Daniel Defoe, the first of our great writers of fiction, was scarcely a novelist in the modern sense of the word. His tales may be described as fictitious biographies, intended to be accepted as authentic; they have no carefully wrought out plot, so contrived as to keep the reader's attention enchained to the last. He wrote enormously—about 250 distinct productions it is said, and in all departments of literature—verse, history, fiction, politics, &c.—but his memory is now mainly kept alive by his incomparable "Robinson Crusoe," which has charmed the schoolboys of many generations, and bids fair to continue to charm them as long as the English tongue is spoken. Defoe, who had almost as stirring and chequered a career as any of the heroes he loved to celebrate, was born in 1661, the son of a wealthy butcher in St. Giles, Cripplegate. According to his own account, he was educated with a view to becoming a dissenting clergyman, and studied with this intent for about five years. However this may be, he seems by some means or other to have picked up a very unusual amount of learning, for he tells us in one of his *Reviews* that he had been master of five languages, and that he had studied mathematics, natural philosophy, logic, geography, and history. His education over, he entered into business, becoming a hosier, his enemies said; a trader, he himself said. While still a very young man he visited Portugal, and perhaps other parts of the Continent, and in 1683 he began his long and industrious career of political pamphleteering by writing on the war between the Turks and the Austrians. Defoe's life was so shifty and intricate, his own statements about it, despite their air of plausibility, have been proved to be so little trustworthy, so many parts of it are still in some degree matter of controversy, that here we cannot attempt to do more than indicate briefly some of its great outstanding features. He appears to have joined the Duke of Monmouth's party in 1685; he started many ingenious projects, and entered into some business speculations which proved unsuccessful; and in 1695 he was appointed accountant to the commissioners for managing the duties on glass, an office which he held till 1699, when he lost his situation owing to the suppression of the tax. In 1701 he won his way to royal favour by his satire "The True-Born Englishman," an enthusiastic eulogium on King William and the Revolution. His "Shortest Method with the Dissenters," an ironical pamphlet published in 1703, gave such offence that the unfortunate author was fined, pilloried, and imprisoned. In February 1704 he began the publication of *The Review*, a periodical publication which deserves remembrance in literature as the forerunner of the *Tatler* and the *Spectator*; and in the same year he began his profitable if somewhat dishonourable career of hack political writer in the pay of the Government, in which capacity he wrote dozens of pamphlets. In 1706–7 he was sent to Scotland to assist in promoting the Union. He died in 1731, writing steadily to the last. Defoe's personal appearance is thus described in a proclamation offering a reward for his capture after the publication of his "Shortest Way with the Dissenters:"—"He is a middle-sized, spare man, about forty years old, of a brown complexion, and dark brown coloured hair, but wears a wig, a hooked nose, a sharp chin, grey eyes, and a large mole near his mouth." His character presents few features, save his indomitable industry, calculated to win respect or regard. He appears to have been an habitual and shameless liar, and in the latter years of his occupation as a hired political writer he acted a treacherous part, insinuating himself into the staff of a Jacobite journal in order to mitigate the fierceness of its attacks on the Whig statesman by whom, of course, he was paid for his services.

As a writer of these political pamphlets, which were then nearly as powerful agents in the dissemination of political opinions as newspapers are now, Defoe has been ranked along with Swift. Both of them, by the studied simplicity of their style, the homeliness of their illustrations, the clearness and precision of their arguments, were admirably adapted for such work. In point of elegance Swift carries off the palm; but Defoe's frequent colloquialisms and rough and ready modes of expression were very well suited for the audience which he addressed. The fame of political writings, however, is generally shortlived, and it is not what he did in this way that gives him a title to be mentioned here. It was not till he was past the prime of life that Defoe began the series of works to which he owes his fame. "Robinson Crusoe" appeared in 1719, "Captain Singleton" in 1720, "Colonel Jack" in 1721, and the "Journal of the Plague" in 1722. These are only a few of the many long works which issued from his prolific pen; he wrote besides on religion, on success in business, on his own adventures, and several works of fiction, the latter for the most part dealing with characters from the lowest strata of society. In all his books we find the same characteristics: a style often incorrect and never rising into dignity or eloquence, but always clear, flowing, and graphic; a matter-of-fact imagination, which gives his productions a wonderful air of veracity; and a knowledge of different types of society, especially among the lower classes, such as has perhaps never been attained by any writer. His "Journal of the Plague" is so minute, so circumstantial, so exactly like reality, that it was believed by Dr. Mead to be the work of a medical man; and his "Memoirs of a Cavalier" (the precise date of the publication of which is unknown) was taken by Lord Chatham and many others for a real history. Of Defoe's minor novels we need not say much. The subjects with which they deal, and the elaborate minuteness with which scenes of vice are described in them, do not tend to edification. It is difficult to believe that Defoe was not led to the choice of his peculiar themes by a secret sympathy with roguery. He certainly had an extraordinary fondness for exploring in their minutest recesses the shady corners of life. In his novels, it has been said with much truth, "we rarely meet with anything more exalted or respectable than masters of trading vessels, dealers in small wares, supercargoes, or it may be pickpockets, pirates, candidates for the plantations, or *emeriti* who have already obtained that distinction. In the foreground we have the cabin, the night-cellar, the haunts of fraud, or the roundhouse; in the distance, Newgate or Execution Dock."

Infinitely healthier in tone, and superior also in literary skill, is Defoe's masterpiece, "Robinson Crusoe." Perhaps the universal fame of this work as a book for the young makes it more neglected than it should be by readers in general. The subject was one admirably adapted for Defoe's genius. The patient ingenuity with which he piles detail on detail, his thorough identification of himself with his hero, even the wearisome and commonplace religious meditations interspersed through the book, combine to give it such an appearance of reality that in reading it the insight and genius necessary to produce such a result fall out of view, and we imagine ourselves attending to the wonderful adventures of a veritable English sailor, rather prone to loquacity and moralising, but fertile in resources, and possessing more than an average proportion of the ordinary English faculty of adapting oneself with as good grace as possible to any situation. Robinson Crusoe is no hero of romance, destitute of the fears and weaknesses belonging to men in general, but simply a stout-hearted mariner, determined not to be vanquished by obstacles which there is any possibility of overcoming. "Is there any modern novelist, who, wishing to represent a very brave, adventurous young man, would have sufficient confidence in himself to make him beat his breast and sob and cry like a madman, trusting to his resources to prove that such conduct was a part of the bravest, hardiest, and most indomitable character that genius ever conceived? Defoe knew that courage is not a positive quality which some men have and others want; that it is that willingness to do disagreeable things which we have all acquired in some measure, but that there are acts of courage which the very bravest are only just able to do, and in which even they falter and tremble. How nobly is this brought out in Crusoe's behaviour on the island! At first he is in a passion of grief almost amounting to madness; 'but I thought that would do little good, so I began to make a raft,' &c. Little by little he calms down, often fairly giving way to the horrors of his situation, but always, after a time, setting to work manfully on whatever comes next to hand, until at last his mind grows into a state of settled content and cheerfulness, to which none but a man ribbed with tripled steel' could have attained. There is a fearless humility about the whole conception of Crusoe of which we have almost lost the tradition."[1] One of the great attractions of "Robinson Crusoe" is the boundless scope which it gives to the imagination of the reader in conjecturing what he would have done had he occupied Crusoe's position. This helps to give an interest to the smallest details, making us follow such passages as those in which he gives an account of his difficulties in getting a boat out to sea, the methods which he took to raise and preserve his crops, &c., with something of a personal interest. The fine and sublime conception of a shipwrecked mariner cast on a desert island is one which, to a writer with a genius less happily constituted for his subject than Defoe's, would have offered almost irresistible temptations to indulge in high-flown and philosophical meditations above the reach of the hero, and above the reach of humanity in general, thus, in great measure, taking away from the reader the power of, as it were, substituting himself for Crusoe, besides greatly diminishing the fascination of the story. The superiority of the first part of "Robinson Crusoe" is no doubt to be largely attributed to the excellence of the subject: the second part, where the solitude is broken in upon by a crowd of planters and ship-captains, is little if at all superior to Defoe's other novels.

A man of very different character from Defoe was our next great novelist, Samuel Richardson, the equable current of whose career is in striking contrast to Defoe's active and bustling life. In intellect, also, and in choice of subjects, the two men differ greatly, but there is some resemblance between their

[1] Fitzjames Stephen on "The Relation of Novels to Life," in "Cambridge Essays" for 1855, p. 188.

styles. Both loved great minuteness of detail, both were apt to deal too much in what may be called the "inventory" style of writing, omitting no fact or incident, even the least important, and both in consequence sometimes become intolerably long-winded, though there is a certain dramatic propriety about Defoe's tediousness which is wanting in Richardson's. An industrious, frugal, punctual man, attending carefully to business, and avoiding every kind of dissipation, Richardson passed a happy and blameless life, surrounded by a host of female admirers who were never tired of praising him. He drank in all their flattery with greedy ears; for he was a vain man, and, like most vain men, preferred the society of women to that of men. The story of his life presents no unusual or striking incidents, and need not detain us long. He was born in 1689, apprenticed to a printer in 1706, served his apprenticeship, worked for some years as a compositor, and then set up in business on his own account in Fleet Street. To the end of his life he continued to keep his shop, and was thus able to avoid the many hardships and privations which in his day were the common lot of men of letters. Perhaps in all London it would not have been possible to find a man who to the casual observer bore a more thoroughly commonplace appearance.

Yet in this man there was a spark of the divine fire of genius, and although he was well advanced in life before he thought of appearing as an author, it so happened that he had unintentionally from a very early period been training himself for the work which he was to accomplish. "As a bashful and not forward boy," he writes, "I was an early favourite with all the young women of taste and reading in the neighbourhood. Half-a-dozen of them, when met to work with their needles, used, when they got a book they liked, and thought I should, to borrow me to read to them, their mothers sometimes with them, and both mothers and daughters used to be pleased with the observations they put me upon making.

"I was not more than thirteen when three of these young women, unknown to each other, having a high opinion of my taciturnity, revealed to me their love secrets, in order to induce me to give them copies to write after, or correct, for answers to their lovers' letters; nor did any of them ever know that I was the secretary to the other. I have been directed to chide, and even repulse, at the very time that the heart of the chider or repulser was open before me, overflowing with esteem and affection, and the fair repulser, dreading to be taken at her word, directing *this* word or *that* expression to be softened or changed. One, highly gratified with her lover's fervour and vows of everlasting love, has said, when I have asked her direction, 'I cannot tell you what to write; but' (her heart on her lips) 'you cannot write too kindly;' all her fear was only that she should incur slight for her kindness."

Thus it was that Richardson began to acquire that knowledge of the depths and windings of the human heart which constitute his strength as a novelist. The occupation above described does not appear to be a very suitable one for a boy of thirteen, and it must be confessed that Richardson had in his character a good deal of the prig and not a little of the milksop. Yet it is to his engaging in this curious employment that we owe "Pamela" and "Clarissa." Having found out that he had a talent for letter-writing, Richardson continued to practise the art as much as his opportunities allowed, and thus acquired considerable facility in composition. About 1739 two booksellers asked him to write for them "a little book of familiar letters on the useful concerns of common life." He consented; the design gradually expanded under his hands; and "Pamela" was the result. The first two volumes appeared in 1741, and were received with a chorus of public approbation comparable to that which welcomed "Waverley" or the "Pickwick Papers." Dr. Sherlock recommended the work from the pulpit. Pope declared that it would do more good than twenty volumes of sermons. One enthusiastic gentleman went so far as to say that if all other books were to be burned, the Bible and "Pamela" should be preserved. Nor was the enthusiasm about the book confined to England. It was translated into French, and excited as great a *furore* on the other side of the Channel as here. This extraordinary blaze of popularity seems very strange to us. Besides the coarseness of many of the details, which may be excused, as the fashion of the age allowed an amount of plain speaking which we should now think quite intolerable, there is in the book a mawkish tediousness and a sort of canting virtue which tend to repel the reader. One great reason for its success no doubt was that it was a novel of quite a different character from any that had hitherto been published. "It requires," says Scott, "a reader to be in some degree acquainted with the huge folios of inanity, over which our ancestors yawned themselves to sleep, ere he can estimate the delight they must have experienced from the unexpected return to truth and nature."

A spurious continuation of "Pamela" led Richardson to add to it two additional volumes, but they shared the common fate of continuations in turning out a failure, and are now seldom if ever read even by Richardson's most enthusiastic admirers. For some years after this Richardson kept silence, revolving in his mind the plot of the work on which rests his most enduring claim to remembrance. This was the noble and tragic story of "Clarissa," which was published eight years after the appearance of "Pamela." Though, like all his works, too long-winded, there is in it a power and a depth of pathos which keep the reader who has once fairly entered on its perusal enchained to the end. Nowhere in either English fiction or poetry is there drawn a figure more beautiful, intense, and splendid than that of Clarissa. Mrs. Oliphant does not exaggerate when she says that in this figure Richardson added at least one character to the inheritance of the world, of which Shakespeare need not have been ashamed—the most celestial thing, the highest imaginative effort of his generation. When the first four volumes of "Clarissa" appeared, and apprehensions began to be entertained that the catastrophe was to be unfortunate, requests crowded upon the author to spare the high-souled creature whom he had called into being, and wind up his story with the stereotyped happy ending. To his credit be it said, Richardson steadfastly withstood all such importunities. He saw that if he were to save his heroine, he should inevitably degrade her, and thus ruin what is probably, with all its many defects, the grandest prose tragedy ever penned.

In Richardson's last great work, "Sir Charles Grandison," which was published in 1753, he sank below the level not only of "Clarissa," but even of "Pamela." At the instigation of some of his female admirers he set himself to portray the *beau ideal* of a "fine gentleman," who should unite in one person all excellences, mental, moral, and physical. The result is such as might have been apprehended. Sir Charles is "that faultless monster whom the world ne'er saw; a polite, moralising, irreproachable coxcomb," content to dwell in decencies for ever. "It is impossible for the reader to feel any sympathy with a hero whose worst trial is the doubt which of two beautiful and accomplished women, excellent in disposition and high in rank, sister excellences, as it were, both being devotedly attached to him, he shall be pleased to select for his bride, and this with so small a share of partiality towards either, that we cannot conceive his happiness to be endangered wherever his lot may fall, except by a generous compassion for her whom he must necessarily relinquish." "Sir Charles Grandison" now takes rank with the continuation of "Pamela," as utterly unreadable save by such omnivorous students as Macaulay, to whom every kind of literary food is palatable.

Richardson died in 1761, a much-respected, prosperous, and in the main worthy man. Vanity, the common vice of those who like him are contented to receive as infallible the opinions of their own petty circle of acquaintances, was his predominant failing. He could not, as Johnson expressed it in one of the many fine remarks which flashed from him in the heat of conversation, be contented to sail quietly down the stream of reputation without longing to taste the froth from every stroke of the oar. In company he had little to say except when the conversation turned upon his own works, about which he was always willing to talk. If he could revisit the earth, Richardson's vanity would receive a sad shock. His works, read and praised by thousands in this country, and applauded abroad by such men as Rousseau and Diderot, are now unknown, not only to the general public, but even to many whose knowledge of English literature is far from contemptible. Indeed, we are very much inclined to doubt if there are ten persons now living who could conscientiously affirm that they had read his three novels from beginning to end. This general neglect is not difficult to account for. His works are so enormously long, that the very appearance of the massive volumes in which they are contained is apt to frighten away a reader of these degenerate days. But their length is not the only obstacle to their perusal. All are written in the form of letters to and from the various characters who figure in them, a mode of storytelling which greatly aggravated Richardson's natural tendency to diffuseness. A not inconsiderable part of the letters is occupied with the commonplace forms of epistolary politeness, which we could very well have dispensed with, and, moreover, the same incident is sometimes related by different correspondents at unmerciful length. Add to this that the story moves so slowly that an old lady is said to have chosen "Sir Charles Grandison" to be read to her in preference to any other work, because she could sleep for half an hour at any time while it was being read, and still find the personages just where she left them, conversing in the cedar parlour, and we have said enough to account for the decline of Richardson's popularity. Even Johnson, who, probably from personal regard to the author, had an extravagantly high opinion of Richardson's novels, was compelled to own that "Were you to read Richardson for the story, your impatience would be so much fretted that you would hang yourself." "You must read him for the sentiment," he went on to say, "and consider the story only as giving occasion to the sentiment." But Richardson's sentiment and moral reflections have now a thoroughly antiquated flavour: he is no longer found capable of teaching "the passions to move at the command of virtue." Yet, acting on the sound critical principle that a writer ought always to be judged by his best performance, we are constrained to admit that the writer of "Clarissa," full of improbabilities and wearisome minutiæ as it is, deserves the conspicuous position which he still holds in the history of English literature, not only because he originated a new species of composition, but because he was a man of strikingly original genius. "Clarissa" belongs to the small class of works which, once read, never fail to leave a powerful and indelible impression on the memory.

"How charming, how wholesome Fielding always is! To take him up after Richardson is like emerging from a sick-room heated by stoves into an open lawn on a breezy day of May." Thus Coleridge spoke of Richardson's great contemporary and rival, Henry Fielding, who, after the lapse of more than a century and a half, still disputes with Scott and one or two others the proud position of the greatest of English writers of fiction. Richardson's novels are novels of *sentiment:* he draws men from the inside, as it were, portraying their passions, feelings, imaginations, and so forth. It was reserved to Fielding to inaugurate a new era in fiction by writing novels of *real life*, painting with graphic pencil the manners, fashions, and characters prevalent in English society at the time when he lived. Fielding was born in 1707 at Sharpham Park, Somersetshire, the son of a general who served under the Duke of Marlborough. He was descended from a lofty ancestry, being a great-grandson of the Desmond who was a son of the Earl of Denbigh, a circumstance which gave rise to Gibbon's stately sentence, which Thackeray was so fond of quoting: "Our immortal Fielding was of the younger branch of the Earls of Denbigh, who drew their origin from the Counts of Hapsburgh. The successors of Charles V. may disdain their brethren of England; but the romance of 'Tom Jones,' that exquisite picture of human manners, will outlive the palace of the Escurial and the imperial eagle of the House of Austria." Like many another scion of a noble family, Fielding found that his long-drawn pedigree was not attended by any very solid material advantages. Leaving Eton, where he amassed that stock of classical learning which he was rather too fond of displaying in his works, he went to Leyden to study civil law. There he remained for two years, when, at the age of twenty, he was compelled to return to England, owing to the inability of his father to supply him with funds. Settling in London, he found that he had no resource but, to use his own expression, to become a hackney-writer or a hackney-coachman. His father, it is true, granted him a nominal allowance of £200 a year, but, as his son used to say, "anybody might pay it who would." Of handsome exterior, great conversational powers, and free, reckless, jovial disposition, Fielding entered with zest into the many dissipations of the great city, earning a precarious income by dashing off rapidly play after play. We need not enter into details regarding Fielding's dramatic performances. Though they are not without merit, his name would now have been quite forgotten if he had written nothing else. Fielding himself seems to have viewed them with philosophic indifference. Garrick once asked him to erase a passage from one of his comedies, as he felt certain it would provoke opposition. "No," replied Fielding, "if the scene is not a good one, let *them* find *that* out." The play was accordingly brought out without alteration, and, as had been foreseen, was ill received. Garrick, alarmed at the hisses he met with, retired into the green-room, where the author sat drinking champagne. "What's the matter, Garrick?" said Fielding; "what are they hissing now?" "Why, the scene that I begged you to retrench, and they have so frightened me that I shall not be able to collect myself again the whole night." "Oh, they *have* found it out, have they?" was the cool reply.

About 1735 Fielding married Miss Cradock of Salisbury, a beautiful and amiable lady, with a fortune of £1500. About the same time he fell heir to a property of £200 a year. It must be remembered that these sums then represented a much larger purchasing power than they would do now. If managed with economy, they would have placed Fielding above the reach of sordid want for the rest of his life.

But unfortunately he was one of the pretty numerous class of men who, whatever their income be, always live beyond it. Setting up as a country squire, he kept a vast retinue of servants clad in costly yellow liveries; he exercised an unbounded hospitality, throwing open his doors to all comers, and indulged in profuse expenditure on horses and hounds. By these and such-like means he soon devoured his little patrimony, and was obliged to return to his old literary drudgery. The time he spent in the character of a country squire was not, however, altogether wasted. While apparently exceeding all his brother squires in folly, he was in reality noting with keen and vigilant eye all their peculiarities and little traits of manner, and thus storing up a vast variety of materials wherewith to enrich some of the most imperishable pages of English fiction.

On his return to London, Fielding, in order to escape from the miseries which surrounded a poor author, formed the valorous resolution of studying the law. He was called to the bar in 1740, and appears to have made considerable efforts to obtain success in his profession. Clients, however, came in slowly, and literature was, as formerly, his principal means of subsistence. Up to this time Fielding had been groping blindly about, without, it appears, the slightest knowledge of what province of literature his genius was peculiarly fitted to share in. Had Richardson never written "Pamela," Fielding, if known at all to our age, would have been known only as the author of some indifferent essays and plays. "Pamela" showed him the true path into which his powers should be directed. "He couldn't," to quote Thackeray, "do otherwise than laugh at the puny Cockney bookseller pouring out endless volumes of sentimental twaddle, and hold him up to scorn as a molly-coddle and a milksop." The result was "Joseph Andrews" (1742), the first English novel in which the author set himself to delineate the broad panorama of English life as it was moving before his eyes. Originally intended to be little else than a caricature of "Pamela," it soon passed into something much better than that. The character of Parson Adams, guileless, benevolent. child-like, with a touch of pedantry, and a touch of vanity (charmingly shown by his offering to walk ten miles to fetch his sermon on Vanity, merely to convince the friend with whom he was talking of his thorough contempt for that vice), is one of the finest portraits in that noble gallery where hang Dr. Primrose, My Uncle Toby, Mr. Pickwick, Colonel Newcome, The Antiquary, and other faithful and long-tried friends. Richardson never forgave Fielding for the slight put upon him by the publication of "Joseph Andrews," and to the end of his life continued to speak of him with a degree of contempt altogether unjustifiable. He declared that "he has little or no invention;" that "nothing but a shorter life than I can wish him can hinder him from writing himself out of date;" and that his knowledge of the human heart was "but as the knowledge of the outside of a clockwork machine!"

The interval between the publication of "Joseph Andrews" and Fielding's next great work may be briefly passed over. In 1743 he published by subscription three volumes of "Miscellanies," the more notable contents of which are the "Journey from this World to the Next," a clever *jeu d'esprit*, the interest of which falls off considerably towards the end, and "Jonathan Wild." The latter work, which well illustrates Thackeray's remark, that Fielding's wit flashes upon a rogue and lightens up a rascal like a policeman's lantern, may be compared to the "Barry Lyndon" of the former novelist. Roguery, and not a rogue, is, as the author himself said, the subject; and the fine satire, the contempt for and abhorrence of villany, which permeate the book, go far to compensate for the unpleasantness of the subject. Fielding at all times resembled Thackeray in having a thorough and healthy aversion for anything approaching to making a hero out of a blackguard, a practice more common in our day than in his. About the time when the "Miscellanies" was published, he sustained the great affliction of his life in the loss first of his daughter, and soon after of his wife, his affection for whom constitutes one of the finest traits of his manly and generous, if somewhat reckless and dissipated, character. Her death, we are told by one of his biographers, brought on such a vehemence of grief that his friends began to think him in danger of losing his reason. Mrs. Fielding left behind her a maid, whose expressions of grief at the loss of her beloved mistress so touched Fielding's heart, that he made her his second wife. He never had any reason to repent of having done so. In the last production of his pen, he commemorated her as a woman "who discharged all the offices becoming the female character—a faithful friend, an amiable companion, and a tender nurse."

In the end of 1748 Fielding accepted what was then considered the rather degrading office of a Bow Street Magistrate. These officials were termed Trading Justices, being repaid by fees for their services to the public. It deserves to be recorded to Fielding's honour that, in contrast to many of his brethren, he discharged his duties with strict honesty, thus, as he said, "reducing an income of about £500 a year of the dirtiest money upon earth to little more than £300; a considerable proportion of which remained with my clerk." In 1749 appeared his greatest work, "Tom Jones," the labour, he tells us, of some years of his life—a fact sufficiently well attested by its careful and masterly execution. It was so well received that within a month after its publication a notice appeared stating, that it being impossible to bind sets fast enough to answer the demand, those who pleased might have them in blue paper or boards; and the publisher, in consequence of the enormous sale, added £100 to the £600 agreed to be paid to the author. The skilful elaboration of the plot, the admirable drawing of the characters, and the shrewd and sensible remarks interspersed thickly throughout the work, combine to give "Tom Jones" a proud pre-eminence over all the other novels of the eighteenth century. Exception may, indeed, be taken to parts of it; one is sometimes tempted to think that Tom, who is evidently such a favourite with the author, was in reality not much better than an "accomplished blackguard," as Byron calls him, and that the beautiful Sophia was, to use Hazlitt's expression, merely a pretty simpleton; but there can be no question as to the general power, spirit, and fidelity to nature of the book. The character of Squire Western, the Tory fox-hunter, with his animalism, his coarseness, his prejudices, his instinctive love of his daughter, balanced by his equally strong love of the pleasures of the chase, is immortal and unsurpassed. Thackeray's Sir Pitt Crawley, who was evidently modelled on this unapproachable portrait, is only a feeble echo of it. The coarseness and indelicacy which too often pollute the pages of "Tom Jones" are what must be allowed for in all the novels of the time. Neither Richardson, nor Fielding, nor Smollett, nor Sterne is reading adapted *virginibus puerisque.* Nevertheless, we are decidedly of Mr. Ruskin's opinion, that, rightly viewed, Fielding is a thoroughly moral novelist. The absence from his works of all cant and insincerity, his love of truth, courage, and uprightness, his hatred and detestation of falsehood, malice, and depravity, give his novels a perennial air of freshness and health.

About three years after "Tom Jones," in December 1751, Fielding's last important work, "Amelia," was completed. It is on the whole the least excellent of the trio. Its construction is far inferior to the consummate art with which the plot of "Tom Jones" is worked out; and though in some ways considerably superior to "Joseph Andrews," it contains no shining character like Parson Adams, on whose memory one loves to linger. Nevertheless, the book had one great triumph. Dr. Johnson, who was always so scandalously unjust to Fielding, that one is tempted to suppose that he must have had some personal animosity towards him, read it through without stopping, and declared that Amelia was the most pleasing heroine in romance. Amelia, whose portrait Fielding drew from that of his second wife, has, indeed, been always a favourite character with readers; but the same cannot be said about her husband, Booth, who, we may suppose, was intended to represent Fielding himself. If so, the likeness which he drew is certainly not a flattering one. Thackeray preferred Captain Booth to Tom Jones, because he thought much more humbly of himself than Jones did, and went down on his knees and owned his weaknesses; but most will be inclined to agree with Scott, who declares that we have not the same sympathy for the ungrateful and dissolute conduct of Booth which we yield to the youthful follies of Jones. However, after all necessary deductions have been made, "Amelia" must be pronounced a wonderful work, full of that rich flow of humour and deep knowledge of human nature which charm us in "Tom Jones" and "Joseph Andrews."

Besides his plays and his novels, Fielding wrote a variety of other works. He was the conductor and principal writer of two or three periodical publications, in which he strenuously upheld his political opinions, which were strongly Protestant and anti-Jacobite, and assailed vigorously some of the more noted quacks of the day. He also, in connection with his duties as magistrate, wrote on such subjects as the best means for diminishing the number of robberies, making effectual provision for the poor, &c. His irregular life early undermined his naturally vigorous constitution, and in 1753 he was advised to endeavour to recruit his shattered frame by a voyage to a warmer climate. He sailed for Lisbon, but his health was too seriously impaired to be benefited by the change, and he expired on the 8th October 1754. He is buried in the English Cemetery at Lisbon, where a tomb erected to him in 1830 bears the following inscription :—

"HENRICUS FIELDING,
LUGET BRITTANIA GREMIO NON DATUM
FOVERE NATUM."

"I am sorry for Henry Fielding's death," wrote Lady Mary Wortley Montagu, "not only as I shall read no more of his writings, but because I believe he lost more than others, as no man enjoyed life more than he did. . . . His happy constitution, even when he had, with great pains, half demolished it, made him forget every evil when he was before a venison pasty or over a flask of champagne; and I am persuaded he has known more happy moments than any prince upon earth. His natural spirits gave him rapture with his cook-maid, and cheerfulness when he was starving in a garret. There was a great similarity between his character and that of Sir Richard Steele. He had the advantage, both in learning and, in my opinion, genius; they both agreed in wanting money, in spite of all their friends, and would have wanted it if their hereditary lands had been as extensive as their imagination; yet each of them was so formed for happiness, it is a pity he was not immortal." Her Ladyship's picture is a very graphic, and, as we know from other sources, a very correct one. Fielding was no hero. Ginger was hot in the mouth with him, and he was always apt to prefer the call of pleasure to the call of duty. But with all his vices and weaknesses, which it is not desirable either to palliate or excuse, he was so good-hearted, so courageous, so affectionate, so manly, that we cannot contemplate his character without a certain admiration as well as liking. The leading features of his novels have been already sufficiently indicated. There are greater depths in human nature than he ever sounded; he had less of the spirit of a poet than any other novelist of equal merit; and he had no skill in that subtle psychological analysis which—whether for good or for evil, we need not discuss—is such a prominent characteristic of some of our great recent writers of fiction. Moral problems never troubled him; he was content to take the world as he found it, with its mixture of good and evil, riches and poverty, laughter and tears. Perhaps it is the want of the subjective or retrospective element in Fielding's novels which has caused him to be unduly depreciated by some who ought to have known better. Harriet Martineau, for example, could see scarcely any merit in his works, and was quite at a loss how to account for his popularity.

Comparing his works with those of professed historians, Fielding said that in their productions nothing was true but the names and dates, whereas in his everything was true but the names and dates. There is more truth in this statement than may at first sight appear. "As a record of past manners and opinions, too," says Hazlitt, speaking of the English novelists, "such writings afford the best and fullest information. For example, I should be at a loss where to find in any authentic documents of the same period so satisfactory an account of the general state of society, and of moral, political, and religious feeling in the reign of George II., as we meet with in the adventures of Joseph Andrews and his friend Mr. Abraham Adams. This work, indeed, I take to be a perfect piece of statistics in its kind. In looking into any regular history of that period, into a learned and eloquent charge to a grand jury or the clergy of a diocese, or into a tract on controversial divinity, we should hear only of the ascendancy of the Protestant succession, the horrors of Popery, the triumph of civil and religious liberty, the wisdom and moderation of the sovereign, the happiness of the subject, and the flourishing state of manufactures and commerce. But if we really wish to know what all these fine-sounding names come to, we cannot do better than turn to the works of those who, having no other object than to imitate nature, could only hope for success from the fidelity of their picture."

The works of our next great novelist, Tobias Smollett, are like Fielding's in being of great value from an historical point of view, as depicting faithfully the social life of our ancestors. Although they differ in many respects, Fielding and Smollett resemble each other in this—they were both novelists who drew from real life, and filled their pages with such characters, incidents, and situations as were found in the England of their time. Smollett was born in Dumbartonshire in 1721. He came of a good family, being a grandson of Sir James Smollett of Bonhill. At an early age he was bound apprentice to John Gordon, an eminent surgeon of Glasgow, who seems to have appreciated the talents of his youthful pupil. Smollett was a tricky urchin, which caused some one to boast of the superior decorum and propriety of *his* youthful acquaintances. "It may be all very true," manfully replied Gordon, "but give me, before them all, my own bubbly-nosed callant with the stane in his pouch." To the end of his life, Smollett, in spite of his irritability and fretfulness, had something of a schoolboy's love of fun and frolic. It shines forth conspicuously in his novels, while it is almost totally absent from Fielding's.

When, after he had undergone the trials and privations of many years, he went to see his mother, he endeavoured to conceal his identity, but he could not so compose his countenance as altogether to refrain from smiling. His smile enabled his mother at once to recognise him. She afterwards told him that if he had kept his austere looks and continued to *gloom*, he might have escaped detection for some time longer, "but your old roguish smile betrayed you at once."

The death of his grandfather left Smollett, whose father had died early, totally unprovided for at the age of eighteen. He afterwards revenged his grandfather's neglect in making no provision for him, by consigning him to immortal disgrace as the old judge who figures in the early chapters of "Roderick Random." Armed with the "Regicide," a tragedy, Smollett in his nineteenth year set out for London to win fame and fortune by those talents of which he was always fully conscious. The tragedy, though at first patronised by Lord Lyttleton, whom Smollett afterwards described with perfect truth as "one of those little fellows who are sometimes called great men," was not appreciated by theatrical managers. Disappointed in his hopes of fame as a dramatist, Smollett embarked as surgeon's mate on board of a ship of the line, and served in the disastrous Carthagena expedition of 1741. Of his experience while thus employed he has left a faithful record in some of the most stirring and vigorous pages of "Roderick Random." It was at this period of his life that he acquired that accurate and intimate acquaintance with the habits of sailors to which we owe some of the most vivid and lifelike portraits in his novels. Smollett quitted the naval service in disgust in the West Indies, and after residing some time in Jamaica, returned to England in 1746. He then set up in London as a physician, but his success was very small, owing partly, it is said, to his haughty manners and irascible temper, which made him show very manifest signs of impatience when listening to prosy accounts of petty indispositions. In 1746–1747 he published two poetical satires, "Advice" and "Reproof," of no very great merit, but so bitter and unsparing as to greatly increase the number of his enemies. In 1747 he married Miss Lascelles, described as "beautiful and accomplished."

Such is a brief outline of the leading events of Smollett's life up to the publication, in 1748, of his first great work, "Roderick Random." In great part it is a record of his own personal experiences, and of the queer acquaintances whom he had fallen in with during his rather stormy life. In this respect it resembles all his other works of fiction. Thackeray is doubtless right in thinking that Smollett's novels are recollections of his own adventures, and that his characters are drawn from personages with whom he became acquainted in his own career of life. "He did not invent much, as I fancy, but had the keenest perceptive faculty, and described what he saw with wonderful relish and delightful broad humour." "Roderick Random" has very little plot: it is merely a collection of incidents and adventures very loosely strung together by a thread of autobiography, after the fashion of "Gil Blas." The hero is intended to stand for Smollett himself, just as Tom Jones stood for Fielding. In neither case is the portrait thus presented a pleasing one; but Tom Jones is as far superior to the selfish and low-minded Roderick Random, as the devoted and generous Strap, the follower of the latter, is superior to the lying and self-seeking Partridge, Jones's attendant. The finest character in "Roderick Random," and the one to which the reader turns with most affection, is undoubtedly Lieutenant Bowling, whose bluff kind-heartedness, honesty, and impulsiveness, are sketched with a masterly pencil. The fidelity to nature of all Smollett's accounts of life at sea is very marked. He never surrounds the hardships, toils, and dangers of a seaman's existence with that rose-coloured atmosphere which leads the unsuspecting reader of such books as Captain Marryat's novels to suppose that a sailor's life is largely one of joking and sport, diversified by hairbreadth escapes and romantic dangers.

"Roderick Random" was at once received with favour by the public, and Smollett's position as an author was now finally established. In 1750 he made a tour to Paris, where he gathered materials for future works, and where "Peregrine

Pickle" was chiefly written. It was published in the following year. It is a laughter-provoking book, with abundance of incident and "go," but it is occasionally indefensibly coarse, and not unfrequently shows that want of gentlemanly feeling which Smollett's admirers have too often to regret. Shortly after the publication of "Peregrine Pickle," Smollett endeavoured to establish himself at Bath as a physician, and, with a view to make his name known in this capacity, published in 1752 an "Essay on the External Use of Water." This second attempt to win success as a medical man failed as completely as the first. Campbell, in his "Specimen of the British Poets," remarks with much truth that the celebrity for aggravating and exposing personal follies which Smollett had acquired by his novels was rather too formidable to recommend him as a confidential visitant to the sick chambers of fashion. "To a sensitive valetudinarian," he goes on to say, "many diseases would be less alarming than a doctor who might slay the character by his ridicule, and might *not* save the body by his prescriptions." Having returned disappointed from Bath, Smollett fixed his residence at Chelsea, and never again seems to have thought of abandoning the career of an author. In 1753 he published the "Adventures of Ferdinand Count Fathom," a novel descriptive of the deepest depravity, unpleasing generally, and sometimes tedious, but containing one scene—the adventure in the hut of the robbers—equal if not superior in tragic intensity to anything he ever wrote. Two years later he gave to the world his translation of "Don Quixote," which, if in many ways not a faithful representation of Cervantes' immortal novel, is a lively and spirited production, showing Smollett's great command over language and power of fluent and vivacious narrative.

In 1756 Smollett became editor of the *Critical Review*, a Tory and High Church periodical. It was an evil day for his happiness and peace of mind when he undertook this office. Impatient of folly and stupidity, of a satirical and cynical temperament, he soon showed that he was determined not to spoil the author by a sparing use of the critical rod. Many excellent specimens of the "slashing" style of criticism, now happily gone altogether out of fashion, might be culled from Smollett's contributions to the *Review.* The result, of course, was that he speedily raised against himself a host of enemies, thus embittering his life with a long series of petty squabbles and disputations. One controversy in which he engaged carried with it very serious consequences. Reviewing a pamphlet in which Admiral Knowles vindicated his conduct in the secret expedition against Rochfort in 1757, Smollett declared that Knowles was "an admiral without conduct, an engineer without knowledge, an officer without resolution, and a man without veracity." This was strong language, though it seems to have been justified by the facts of the case; and Smollett being prosecuted for libel, was sentenced to pay a fine of £100, and to suffer three months' imprisonment. While confined in prison he occupied himself in writing the "Adventures of Sir Launcelot Greaves," which in 1760–1 appeared by instalments in the *British Magazine,* being one of the first of those serial tales which now form the staple of so many of our periodicals. It was republished in 1762. Sir Launcelot is a modern Don Quixote, and the story of his exploits is one of the least successful of Smollett's productions.

Besides the works by which his name is principally known, Smollett compiled or lent his name to a number of pieces of literary hackwork. Among these may be mentioned a collection of voyages (1757), and a History of England from the earliest period to 1748. This was published in 1758, in four quarto volumes, and is said to have been written in fourteen months—a feat of literary activity which, we should imagine, has never been surpassed. The narrative was afterwards brought down to 1765. Smollett does not rank high as an historian; the speed with which he wrote carried with it its inevitable fruits of carelessness and inaccuracy. "I spent much of the day over Smollett's History," writes Macaulay in his Diary (December 8, 1838). "It is exceedingly bad: detestably so. I cannot think what had happened to him. His carelessness, partiality, passion, idle invective, gross ignorance of facts, and crude general theories, do not surprise me much. But the style, wherever he tries to be elevated, and wherever he attempts to draw a character, is perfectly nauseous; which I cannot understand. He says of old Horace Walpole that he was an ambassador without dignity and a plenipotentiary without address. I declare that I would rather have my hand cut off than publish such a precious antithesis." This is too harsh a judgment; it errs as much on the side of severity as Scott's does on the side of lenity when he says that Smollett's History is written with uncommon spirit and correctness of language. Smollett could scarcely fail to render any subject he treated of readable at least; and though his facts are gathered with little care, his style is frequently attractive and vigorous. The latter part of his History is (or rather used to be) often printed as a continuation of Hume's.

In 1763, Smollett, broken down in health and much depressed in spirits by domestic affliction, undertook a journey to France and Italy, in which countries he resided for between two and three years. On his return to England in 1766 he published an account of his travels, which bears painful traces of how his bodily weakness and mental trials had affected his disposition. The "learned Smelfungus," says Sterne, alluding to Smollett, "travelled from Boulogne to Paris—from Paris to Rome,—and so on; but he set out with the spleen and jaundice; and every object he passed by was discoloured and distorted. He wrote an account of them, but 'twas nothing but an account of his own miserable feelings. I met Smelfungus in the grand portico of the Pantheon—he was just coming out of it. ''Tis nothing but a huge cockpit,' said he." The closing years of Smollett's life were spent in a very pitiful condition of weak health and often of severe pain. Like his great rival, Henry Fielding, he sought to regain his strength in a foreign climate, only to find there his grave. He set out for Italy in 1770, and drew his last breath in the neighbourhood of Leghorn in 1771. There is something peculiarly sad about the death of Smollett at the early age of fifty-one. In spite of his multifarious industry he left his family almost totally unprovided for. Had he lived a few years longer he would have inherited the estate of Bonhill, of the value of about £1000 a year, and thus have been enabled to end his days in comfort and affluence.

Shortly before his death, Smollett completed his last and best work, the "Expedition of Humphrey Clinker," "the most laughable story," says Thackeray, "that ever was written since the goodly art of novel-writing began." Humphrey Clinker himself, Winifred Jenkins, Matthew Bramble, Mrs. Tabitha Bramble, and above all Lismahago, are characters that none but a writer of first-rate humorous genius could have created. There is, too, a fine mellow flavour about "Humphrey Clinker," which makes it a fitting close to Smollett's literary life. There is in it, too, a vein of pathos, not uncommon in Smollett's novels, but never found in Fielding's. "I remember," said Carlyle to Mr. Moncure Conway, speaking about his early years, "few happier days than those in which I ran off into the woods to read 'Roderick Random,' and how inconsolable I was that I could not get the second volume. To this day I know of few writers equal to Smollett. 'Humphrey Clinker' is precious to me now as he was in those years. Nothing by Dante or any one else surpasses in pathos the scene where Humphrey goes into the smithy made for him in the old house, and whilst he is heating the iron, the poor woman who has lost her husband and is deranged comes and talks to him as to her husband, 'John, they told me you were dead. How glad I am you are come.' And Humphrey's tears fall down and bubble on the hot iron." Comparing Fielding's novels with Smollett's, Hazlitt said that the one was an observer of the characters of human life, the other a describer of its various eccentricities. The distinction is just. Smollett could not draw his characters without, like Dickens, adding to them a considerable touch of caricature, while Fielding painted men as they really were. There is, too, an air of culture and refinement about Fielding's novels which is absent from Smollett's. To relish Fielding properly one must have some literary taste and knowledge, while Smollett's riotous fun can be appreciated by any one who is able to read. On the other hand, in variety and originality of incident and character Smollett decidedly surpassed Fielding, and he was besides no contemptible poet, as his "Tears of Caledonia," written after the massacre of Culloden, and his "Ode to Independence," sufficiently show. As a man Smollett in many ways deserves to be held in kindly remembrance. Proud, frank, imprudent, he was a hard hitter, always ready to give a blow, and always ready to take one manfully. Good-hearted and generous, but petulant and sometimes revengeful, he made many enemies; but when he saw that he had done any one an injustice, he was always ready to make noble reparation. To his poor brethren of the quill, the ragged denizens of Grub Street, he, poor himself, gave bountiful aid, though he could not refrain from making fun of their eccentricities. In person he is said to have been remarkably handsome, "with a certain air of dignity that seemed to show that he was not unconscious of his own powers."

A writer of equal genius to Fielding or Smollett, but differing from them in almost every respect, was the last great novelist of the eighteenth century, Laurence Sterne. As a novelist he stands unique; for though many, inspired by his success, endeavoured to imitate him, they succeeded only in catching a portion of his peculiar mannerism: his subtle humour and his singular vein of sentiment were beyond their reach. Sterne's one work of fiction is not a novel of real life, neither has it any elaborately constructed plot: he seems, indeed, to have thought, with Bayes in the "Rehearsal," "what is a plot good for except to bring in good things?" He rambles on in the most incoherent and eccentric way, constantly indulging in digressions and meditations, so that through the whole long work the plot scarcely makes any material progress. It is by his finely conceived sketches of character and by the depth and tenderness of his humour that Sterne has won for himself an immortal name in literature. Sterne is one of the happily few men of genius whose character was such as to cause one to approach the study of their writings with a feeling of prejudice. He was born at Clonmel, Ireland, of English parents, in 1713. His father was a lieutenant, who was engaged in the wars in Flanders during the reign of Queen Anne; and Sterne thus spent rather a wandering childhood, following the sound of the drum as his father's regiment was ordered from place to place. When about ten years old he was sent to England, and put to school near Halifax, "with an able master," he says in the fragment of autobiography which he left behind him, "with whom I stayed some time, till, by God's care of me, my Cousin Sterne of Elvington became a father to me, and sent me to the University." One anecdote which he relates of his school-days would seem to show that his genius had been rather precocious. Upon the newly whitewashed ceiling of the schoolroom he wrote with a brush in large capital letters LAU. STERNE. For so doing he was severely whipped by the usher, but the head-master took Sterne's part strongly, and declared that his name should never be effaced, for he was a boy of genius, and sure to come to preferment. Sterne left school shortly after the death of his father, which occurred in a duel, and in 1733 entered Jesus College, Cambridge, where he took his degree of M.A. in 1740. On leaving the University he took orders, and through the interest of his uncle, a well-beneficed clergyman, obtained the living of Sutton and the Prebendary of York. In York he met with the lady whom he afterwards married. The account of his courtship shall be given in his own words: "I courted her for two years. She owned she liked me, but thought herself not rich enough or me too poor to be joined together. She went to her sister's in S——, and I wrote to her often. I believe then she was partly determined to have me, but would not say so. At her return she fell into a consumption; and one evening that I was sitting by her, with an almost broken heart to see her so ill, she said, 'My dear Laurey, I never can be yours, for I verily believe I have not long to live; but I have left you every shilling of my fortune. Upon this she showed me her will. This generosity overpowered me. It pleased God that she recovered, and I married her in the year 1741." It is a pity to have to relate, after this sentimental narrative, that within a few years after his marriage Sterne grew very tired of his wife, and neglected her shamefully. She brought him a small fortune, and soon after his marriage a friend of hers presented him with the living of Stillington, in Yorkshire. At this period of his life, Sterne relates that he had very good health, and amused himself by books, painting, fiddling, and shooting. At Skelton Castle, the library of his friend John Hall Stevenson, author of some tales the indecency of which is much more apparent than the wit, he found a large library, containing many old and curious books, in turning over which he amassed that store of out-of-the-way, if superficial and often secondhand, erudition which he was fond of parading. He was in no hurry to appear as an author. Two sermons preached at York were his only publications, till, in 1759, he astonished the whole reading public by the first two volumes of "Tristram Shandy." They were originally published at York, and were reprinted in London early in 1760.

By "Tristram Shandy" Sterne was elevated from the position of an obscure Yorkshire parson to that of a metropolitan lion of the first magnitude. When he went up to London, invitations to dinner showered thickly upon him, and he was welcomed in all societies of rank and fashion as the humorous, eccentric, sentimental "Mr. Yorick," who had bestowed on them that inestimable boon—a new sensation. Gray says in one of his delightful letters, that at dinners which were honoured by Sterne's presence, the company were invited a fortnight before. "Any man who has a name," said Johnson in a conversation recorded by Boswell, "or who has the power of pleasing, will be very generally invited in London. *The man Sterne*, I have been told, has had engagements for three months." "And a very dull fellow, too," replied Goldsmith, with perhaps a touch of jealousy. "Why, no, sir," said Johnson. Sterne wisely took advantage of his popularity to publish two volumes of sermons, which, as the production of the author of "Tristram Shandy," attracted an amount of attention which would certainly never have been vouchsafed to them on account of their intrinsic merits. "They are in the style," says Gray, "I think most proper for the pulpit, and show a strong imagination and a sensible heart; but you see him often tottering on the verge of laughter, and ready to throw his periwig in the face of his audience." Any one who from the latter part of this account may be induced to look over Sterne's sermons with the view of finding in them passages which recall "Tristram Shandy," will assuredly be disappointed. For the most part, they are barren and commonplace enough. To the two volumes of sermons published in 1760 Sterne afterwards added other four. The remaining seven volumes of "Tristram Shandy" appeared at intervals between 1761 and 1767. The latter volumes did not create the same sensation as the former ones: the novelty of the thing had worn off, and the numerous affectations and eccentricities of style began to repel rather than to attract. In 1764 Sterne went to Italy to recover his health, which had become greatly impaired. He returned in 1767, and in the following year published his "Sentimental Journey," giving an account, in his peculiar fashion, of his recent travels and of a former visit to France. The "Sentimental Journey" was received with the same rapturous avidity as the first volumes of "Tristram Shandy;" but Sterne was not destined to enjoy any longer the applause which was so sweet to him. He died in London on the 18th of March 1768, much in the manner in which he had wished to die—in hired lodgings and attended by strangers.

Sterne's figure was tall and slight, his face pale and haggard, his general expression penetrating, scrutinising, and satirical. His moral nature, which had, it is to be feared, always something rotten about it, was too weak to endure uninjured the continuous course, trying to all but very strong minds, of flattery and dissipation which his success as an author brought upon him. "He degenerated in London," said David Garrick, "like an ill-transplanted shrub; the incense of the great spoiled his head and their *ragouts* his stomach. He grew sickly and proud, an invalid in body and mind." In his writings the most tender-hearted and sentimental of men, he was in his conduct heartless, hypocritical, and unprincipled. "He preferred," as Byron said, "whining over a dead ass to relieving a living mother." His tainted character communicated itself in part, as it could not but do, to his books. Fielding and Smollett are coarse, but they are never indecent purely for the sake of indecency, as Sterne is. He mars his finest passages by an obscene insinuation or a ribald jest. Like Swift, he had in his nature an inherent love for allusions to subjects which most people are glad to banish from their thoughts. His affectation and his alleged plagiarisms from other writers are of little or no consequence in comparison with the dark stream of pollution which runs through his books. It was this grievous defect which caused Thackeray to exclaim, "The man is a great jester, not a great humourist." Never was a more thoroughly wrong-headed judgment uttered. Sterne is not only a great humourist, he is one of the greatest of all humourists. "Sterne comes next," writes Carlyle in his Essay on Richter, after mentioning Shakespeare, Swift, and Ben Jonson, "our last specimen of humour, and, with all his faults, our best; our finest, if not our strongest; for *Yorick*, and *Corporal Trim*, and *Uncle Toby* have yet no brother but in *Don Quixote*, far as *he* lies above them." In a style full of tenderness and sweetness he brings before us a series of family portraits, all original, all well marked, and all so delineated that one cannot but love them. The elder Shandy, with his irritability, his pedantry, and his theory about Christian names; Uncle Toby, full of loving-kindness and gentleness to all created beings, harmless and credulous as a child; Corporal Trim, devoted, faithful, and vigilant, are characters so full of graciousness and humanity that for their sake we can readily afford to forgive Sterne much. When we read about Uncle Toby and his bowling-green, with its fortifications, its ammunition, and its counterscarps, we feel inclined to mount behind him and ride his hobby along with him. Many of the best parts of "Tristram Shandy" devoted to Uncle Toby and Corporal Trim are reminiscences of Sterne's youth, when, following his father's regiment, he must have heard thousands of stories connected with the time when "our troops swore terribly in Flanders," and thus amassed a store of curious anecdotes, which remained in a memory tenacious of such things, and bore good literary fruit after many years.

The leading names in English fiction from the death of Sterne till the time of Sir Walter Scott may be very briefly dealt with. Of Goldsmith, the greatest of them all, some account is given in the following chapter. Sterne's pathos found a not very successful imitator in Henry Mackenzie, whose "Man of Feeling," published in 1771, is a very lackadaisical novel, though it had many readers at one time. Horace Walpole in his "Castle of Otranto" (1764), and Mrs. Radcliffe (1764–1823), wrote wild romantic tales, somewhat after the fashion of the old school of romance. Mrs. Radcliffe's works belong to a class of fiction that would now find favour only with children. After having led us to suppose that the wonderful effects which occur in her novels have been produced by supernatural agency, she systematically unravels her own spells, and shows how in reality they were the result of natural causes. William Beckford, whom Byron celebrates as "England's wealthiest son," published in 1784 his little Oriental romance called "Vathek," which is still read, owing to its originality and its fine description of the terrible Hall of Eblis. William Godwin's best novel, "Caleb Williams," which appeared in 1794, was intended to be "a general review of the modes of domestic and unrecorded despotism by which man becomes the destroyer of man." It was thus a "novel with a purpose," one of the first of that bad class; but the moral is not obtrusively thrust forward; indeed, had the author not told us, we should be rather puzzled to say what the moral really is. "Caleb Williams," inartistic though it often be, is a singularly powerful and fascinating novel, which, as Hazlitt says, can never be begun without being finished, or finished without stamping itself upon the memory of the reader. The work of recent times to which it bears the closest resemblance is the "Scarlet Letter" of Nathaniel Hawthorne. Hawthorne was master of an infinitely more polished and flexible style than Godwin, but the characteristics which give both books such a firm hold on the reader are the same. In both, the plot is so slight that it might easily be told in half a page; in both, the marvellous picture of the workings of the human mind, sombre and melancholy though it be, which they present, enchains the imagination of the reader.

Three lady writers, among the earliest of the numerous sisterhood who have obtained distinction as novelists, remain to be mentioned. Fanny Burney (Madame D'Arblay) introduced the fashion of writing studies of society, such as the majority of modern English novels are, by "Evelina," which appeared in 1778. She had, like most women, a keen perception of little traits of character and peculiarities of manner, and described them with sprightliness and a good deal of broad humour. Nor was she destitute of a real though slender vein of pathos. "Evelina" charmed Burke and Johnson, and if it is generally neglected now, that is not owing to its want of merit, but because it has been shelved aside by more modern works, which, though much talked of at present, will probably share its fate when they are a century old. "Cecilia," Miss Burney's second novel, which was published in 1782, is on the whole inferior to "Evelina;" it has not the same subcurrent of tender simplicity. The fame of Miss Edgeworth (1767–1849), an Irish lady, is now mainly grounded on her moral tales for juvenile readers, but her sketches of Irish life, such as "The Absentee," &c., show a shrewd and observant mind. Her chief characteristics are cool good sense, combined with a total absence of anything approaching enthusiasm. In society she was a general favourite, owing to her unassuming manners and freedom from pretension or affectation. A greater novelist than either Miss Burney or Miss Edgeworth was Miss Austen (1775–1817), among whose admirers may be reckoned such men as Macaulay, Archbishop Whately, Scott, and many others of equal celebrity. Her works are "Sense and Sensibility," "Pride and Prejudice," "Emma," "Mansfield Park," "Northanger Abbey," and "Persuasion." Macaulay praised them to excess, declaring that there were in the world no compositions which approached nearer to perfection, and that "Northanger Abbey" was worth "all Dickens and Pliny put together." These judgments, to be sure, are found in his Diary, where, of course, he did not weigh his words very carefully; but praise almost equally high is bestowed upon them in his published works, and he for some time intended writing an essay on Miss Austen to show how highly he esteemed her genius. Miss Austen's finished humour and clear-cut sketches of everyday life were as likely to attract Macaulay as her conventionality and absence of passion were likely to repel Charlotte Brontë. "Why do you like Miss Austen so very much?" wrote the latter to G. H. Lewes. "I am puzzled on that point. . . . I had not seen 'Pride and Prejudice' till I read that sentence of yours, and then I got the book; and what did I find? An accurate daguerreotyped portrait of a commonplace face; a carefully fenced, highly cultivated garden, with neat borders and delicate flowers; but no glance of a bright vivid physiognomy, no open country, no fresh air, no blue hill, no bonny beck. I should hardly like to live with her ladies and gentlemen in their elegant but confined houses." In her chosen walk of fiction, truthful pictures of the ordinary middle-class society we see around us, Miss Austen has no equal; and the extent to which she succeeds in interesting us in her annals of humdrum, commonplace English life is the highest tribute to her genius.

VII.

DR. JOHNSON AND HIS CONTEMPORARIES.

Johnson; Goldsmith; Burke; Boswell; Junius; Hume; Robertson; Gibbon.

THE accession of George III. to the throne in 1760 marks an important era in English political life. The young King, a man of good moral character, mediocre abilities, and inflexible obstinacy, determined to be the real, and not merely the titular sovereign of the country, to break in pieces the oligarchy which had borne sway in the name of his two predecessors, and to assert what he considered his just rights. How he succeeded in carrying out his purpose; how administration after administration was broken up, either because they would not obey his dictates, or because their policy was marred by the intrigues of the so-called "King's friends;" how his strenuous persistence in an illegal course elevated Wilkes into a popular hero of the first magnitude, and brought about demonstrations of public feeling that almost shook the throne; how his adherence to a foolish and wicked policy caused the American colonies to throw off their allegiance to Great Britain and exhausted the resources of the country, are facts familiar to all. In curious contrast to the troubled state of politics is the placid and anti-revolutionary spirit which animated literature during the earlier part of the reign of George III. Through all the many political changes and political crises of the first twenty-five years of his reign, the stream of English literature flowed quietly on in its accustomed channel; the influence of the school of Addison and Pope still remained paramount; poetry and criticism were still fettered by artificial restrictions and conventionality. Here and there, it is true, a voice might be heard that seemed to prophesy the advent of a new literary era; but such voices were few and far between, and were little attended to or rudely condemned in an age that was not yet prepared for them. It was not till the time of the greatest event in modern history—the French Revolution—that the adherents of the so-called romantic school, appealing to feelings that then more or less influenced the minds of all classes, began to establish themselves as a new and great power in literature.

The most prominent figure in the literature of the period with which we are now dealing is that of Samuel Johnson, and round him its history centres. Several of his contemporaries were greater writers than he, but none was so looked up to; none possessed his strong and intensely marked character; and none was so exactly typical of his age alike in his good and in his bad qualities. Born in 1709, the son of a bookseller in Lichfield, he early imbibed from his father those Tory and High Church prejudices which clung to him throughout life. Very early, too, were noticeable his other distinguishing characteristics—a bodily frame massive and powerful but diseased; a strong propensity to indolence united with an extraordinary capacity for strenuous exertion when compelled to work; a memory capacious, retentive, and exact; a spirit proud yet humble, irascible but forgiving, and combining outward harshness with a deep and genuine tenderness of heart. When at school, though his shortness of sight deprived him of the power of distinguishing himself in field-sports, his strength of intellect and character made him occupy among his class-fellows somewhat the same position as he afterwards held in London literary society. Certain of his companions used to attend him in the morning and carry him to school in a species of triumphal procession. "Sir," he once said to Boswell, speaking of his school-days, "they never thought to raise me by comparing me to any one; they never said 'Johnson is as good a scholar as such a one,' but 'Such a one is as good a scholar as Johnson;' and this was said but of one, but of Lowe: and I do not think he was as good a scholar." In his sixteenth year his school education came to an end. He then loitered at home for two years, "in a state," says Boswell, "very unworthy of his uncommon abilities." His time was not, however, altogether wasted. In his desultory way he read largely, "not voyages and travels, but all literature, sir," he told Boswell, "all ancient writers, all manly;" and tried his hand at poetical translations and original verses, not without success. In his nineteenth year he was entered at Pembroke College, Oxford, where he was very proud, very poor, and very miserable. His father was not wealthy enough to bear the expenses of his education at the University, so he must have received assistance elsewhere—from whom is not quite certain. Conscious of great abilities but crushed by poverty, Johnson during his University career, which lasted about three years, was far from happy. He left Oxford in 1731, without taking a degree. Almost the only distinction won by him was the praise he received for a Latin version of Pope's "Messiah," of which Pope himself declared, "The writer of this poem will leave it doubtful in after-times which was the original, his verses or mine."

In the same year in which Johnson left the University his father died, leaving his affairs in a state approaching to insolvency. Johnson was now compelled to do something to earn a living. At first he tried teaching—that rough apprenticeship through which so many men of letters have had to pass, with pain, but not, perhaps, altogether without profit. The few months during which he was thus engaged he always afterwards looked back to with a kind of shuddering horror. Then he turned his thoughts towards literature, "that general refuge for the destitute," as Carlyle once called it. Settling in Birmingham in 1733, he contributed essays to a local newspaper, and translated from the Latin Lobo's "Voyage to Abyssinia." It lies before us as we write, a volume of about four hundred pages of some two hundred and eighty words each. For this work, which was published in 1735, Johnson received the munificent sum of five guineas. It is remarkable that during his whole career, whether working as a Grub Street hack or whether writing in a blaze of popularity, the most distinguished author of his time, Johnson seems to have received less for his productions than almost any of his fellow literary craftsmen.

In 1736 Johnson married. The object of his choice was a widow named Porter, forty-eight years of age, and described as a coarse, vulgar, ugly woman, who painted herself, and who was fantastic both in dress and in manners. It is said (with what degree of truth is not known for certain) that she possessed a fortune of some £800. Johnson's shortness of sight concealed from him her bodily defects, and there is every reason to believe that he was speaking nothing but the truth when he declared, "Sir, it was a love match on both sides." His wife, whatever may have been her faults, appears to have had a genuine admiration of Johnson's intellectual powers; and we can easily imagine how sweet praise must then have been to the "uncourtly scholar," whose appearance was far from prepossessing, and who had at that time done nothing to show the vast powers that lay concealed beneath his rough and uncouth exterior. On her death, which happened in 1752, Johnson's grief was terrible; and to the end of his life he never ceased to cherish with fond regret the remembrance of his "dear Tetty."

As literature did not appear likely to be sufficiently remunerative to afford sustenance to himself and his wife, Johnson, in 1736, determined to again try schoolmastering. He opened a boarding-school at Edial, in Staffordshire, and announced his intention of instructing young gentlemen in the Greek and Latin languages. The enterprise was an unfortunate one. Johnson was ill-gifted to be a preceptor; and neither his manners nor his appearance were such as to conciliate parents. Few pupils came, and the school was abandoned. Along with David Garrick, Johnson, with little or no money, but with the manuscript of his tragedy "Irene" in his pocket, in 1737 set out for London.

From this point the real commencement of his literary career may be dated. It was begun at a bad time. If, indeed, he had become what he afterwards described as one of the lowest of all human beings, a scribbler for a party, he might possibly have obtained remunerative occupation; but Johnson was too high-spirited to turn his pen to such vile uses. The age of patronage, when a well-written dedication was often munificently rewarded, was passing away; the reading public was small; and journalism, which now gives employment to thousands of writers, was then, comparatively speaking, in its infancy. Moreover, we must remember (what appears to have been forgotten by many writers about Johnson) that even in our own day, when the avenues to a literary career are so much better and more numerous than in Johnson's time, a writer who came to London circumstanced as he was would have a very hard battle to fight. The fact that he had translated a book from the Latin, or that he had contributed articles to a provincial newspaper, was not likely to tell much in his favour with publishers; he had left the University without obtaining any distinction; and he was destitute of money, which might have enabled him to subsist while he wrote some work which might attract the attention of the public. He was obliged to live "from hand to mouth," as the saying is, and work done under such circumstances is rarely of much value. Into the details of Johnson's literary hack-work we need not enter. He wrote extensively in the *Gentleman's Magazine;* he executed various translations; he assisted Osborne in compiling the catalogue of the Harleian Library; and, from November 1740 to February 1742, he wrote in the *Gentleman's Magazine* an account of the debates in parliament, under the title of "The Senate of Lilliput." Parliamentary reporting was then not allowed, but persons were employed to attend the two Houses and take such notes as they could. These notes Johnson put into shape, often writing entirely imaginary speeches, and always "taking care that the Whig dogs should not have the best of it." He gave up the occupation when he found that many received the speeches as actual reports, declaring that he "would not be accessory to the propagation of falsehood."

In May 1738 appeared anonymously Johnson's first work of importance, "London," an imitation of the Third Satire of Juvenal. It was a considerable success, a second edition being called for within a week, and Pope, the reigning king of poetry, declaring that whoever the author was, he would soon be *déterré*. "London" was followed ten years later by a similar but more powerful poem, the "Vanity of Human Wishes," an imitation of the Tenth Satire of Juvenal, containing in dignified and impressive verse a declaration of Johnson's profound and lifelong conviction, that, upon the whole, the amount of misery in the world is greatly in excess of the amount of happiness. Johnson, as some of his shorter poems (for example, the noble and touching verses on Levett) show, possessed a real though a slender vein of poetical genius; but "London" and the "Vanity of Human Wishes" are mainly valuable, not on account of their intrinsically poetical qualities, but as expressing in verse which has the merits of dignity, honesty, and originality, the opinions on life which had been formed by a man of strong mind, who had read much and thought much. This remark applies especially to the "Vanity of Human Wishes." "'Tis a grand poem," wrote Byron in his Diary, "and *so true*." Sir Walter Scott found in Johnson's poetry something peculiarly attractive to his manly good sense. He once told Ballantyne that he derived more pleasure from Johnson's poetry than from that of any writer he could mention.

Among the many questionable acquaintances whom Johnson fell in with during his sojourn in Bohemia, or, as it was then called, Grub Street, was Richard Savage, a dissipated profligate, of whom it was generally believed (falsely, it would appear) that he was the illegitimate son of the Countess of Macclesfield, who refused to acknowledge him. During his chequered career Savage had seen a good deal of literary society, and although his principal poem, "The Wanderer," which Scott pronounced "beautiful," is by most found quite unreadable, he was a man of considerable abilities: in particular, he possessed that talent which Johnson was always disposed to admire—he was a ready and entertaining talker. For Savage, in spite of his many vices, which he both saw and disapproved of, Johnson formed what seems to have been the strongest friendship of his life. He delighted in his company, he admired his abilities, he sincerely pitied his misfortunes, and on his death, in 1743, he celebrated his memory in a memoir, which, though its rhetoric is somewhat ponderous, is one of the most forcible and interesting of Johnson's productions. Nowhere will there be found a better account of the misery and degradation to which many poor authors of that period were subjected. It was published in 1744, and attained considerable popularity.

We have already mentioned that when Johnson set out for London he carried with him the manuscript of his tragedy "Irene" in his pocket. For several years he in vain attempted to get it put upon the stage. At length in 1749 it was produced by his friend Garrick, who had become manager of Drury Lane. With difficulty it was kept alive for nine nights, when it was withdrawn, and was never again produced. "Irene" deserved to fail. It may be described as a kind of worse "Cato," rhetorical and unnatural to a degree, and interesting only as one of the many examples of the unfitness of a man of genius to judge of the particular line into which his talents should be directed.

In 1747 Johnson commenced the preparation of a work for which in many ways he was admirably adapted—a dictionary of the English language. He calculated that it would occupy him three years, but he greatly over-estimated his powers, for though he employed several assistants to do the mechanical part of the work, it did not appear till 1755. Etymology had not then attained the dignity of a science, and the derivations given in the "Dictionary" are consequently very defective; but the definitions are generally excellent—clear, concise, and logical, and the examples are selected with much care and good taste. The publication of the "Dictionary" led to Johnson's famous quarrel with Lord Chesterfield. The plan for writing it had been dedicated to that nobleman, who aspired to act the part of a literary Mæcenas, but he soon grew tired of Johnson, and treated him with marked neglect. When, however, the "Dictionary" was on the eve of publication, Chesterfield thought it would be a feather in his cap if he patronised a man capable of writing such a work, and accordingly inserted in a periodical called the *World* two papers recommending the "Dictionary" to the notice of the public. In that singularly masterly and dignified letter with which all are acquainted Johnson repelled his Lordship's patronage, "proclaiming," in the words of Mr. Carlyle, "into the ear of Lord Chesterfield, and through him of the listening world, that patronage should be no more."

While writing the "Dictionary," Johnson engaged in a work which elevated his literary position considerably. This was the *Rambler*, a periodical of somewhat the same nature as the *Spectator*, which was commenced in 1750 and carried on twice a week for two years. From 1758 to 1760 he wrote under the general title of the *Idler* a series of essays which appeared in a newspaper called the *Universal Chronicle*. Both the *Rambler* and the *Idler* are now found very heavy reading, and it would be idle to deny that a considerable proportion of them is little better than sonorous commonplace. Johnson had not the lightness of hand and dexterity of touch which enabled Addison to treat trivial topics gracefully and appropriately, and where he aspires to do so he generally fails lamentably. He appears to greater advantage in his tale "Rasselas," which appeared in 1759. It is a discourse on his old theme, the "Vanity of Human Wishes," eloquently and powerfully written, and bearing everywhere the marks of that gloom approaching to despair with which he habitually contemplated life.

"Rasselas" was the last work of importance written by Johnson purely for the sake of making money. In 1762 the great services to literature he had conferred by the "Dictionary" and his other works were recognised by Government granting him a pension of £300 per annum. He hesitated very much about taking it, as in his "Dictionary" he had defined "pension" as generally understood to mean "pay given to a state hireling for treason to his country;" but on being distinctly informed that it was granted without the slightest reference to political considerations, he consented to accept it. Henceforth he was able to gratify to the fullest extent his love of indolence and of society, excusing himself, in public, for writing little by saying he could do as much good by conversation as by composition, but in his private memoranda bitterly reproaching his self-indulgence. Always fond of clubs—to use his own expression, he was a very *clubbable* man—he in 1764 founded the Literary Club, where he talked long and excellently in the company of such men as Burke, Goldsmith, Gibbon, Beauclerk, Reynolds, Langton, and his admirable biographer, Boswell, who had, not without difficulty, obtained an introduction to him in 1763. It is a pleasing feature in Johnson's character that, in spite of his occasional sharp retorts and surliness of temper, he managed to maintain a firm friendship with a large circle of acquaintances, including some of the most celebrated of his contemporaries. In 1765 he became acquainted with Mr. Thrale, a wealthy brewer, a connection which proved one of the happiest events of his life. Thrale was a sensible, though by no means a brilliant man; his wife possessed more brilliancy but less sense; and both together did their best to make Johnson happy at their country-house in Streatham, where for several years he was considered almost as a member of their family. At his own house in Bolt Court he kept a number of poor dependants—Mrs. Williams, Mrs. Desmoulins, Robert Levett, Miss Carmichael, Blank Frank—who, but for his generous aid, would have been in abject poverty. Johnson, partly from natural impulse, partly, no doubt, because he remembered how severe had been his own struggle with poverty, was one of the most generous men that ever lived. "He loved the poor," said Mrs. Thrale, "as I never saw man love them."

While obliged to labour for his bread, Johnson had projected an edition of Shakespeare, a task for which he was very slenderly equipped, as he had read none of the contemporary dramatists. For many years he loitered over his task, constantly reproaching himself for his negligence, but at last, in 1765, it was completed. The main value of his edition consists in the Preface, a very able piece of work, which still ranks among the best of all the countless treatises that have been written on the subject. In 1772 his worshipper Boswell managed to induce the sage to accompany him in a tour to the Hebrides, of which, in 1775, Johnson published an account under the title of a "Journey to the Western Islands of Scotland." It is interesting to compare Johnson's ponderous but not uninteresting work with the volume in which Boswell, soon after the "great lexicographer's" death, gave such a *naïve* and amusing account of the adventures and conversations of himself and his great companion. During the latter part of his life Johnson entered the troubled arena of political controversy by publishing four pamphlets on questions that were then agitating the minds of men. These were "The False Alarm" (1770), "Thoughts on the Late Transactions Respecting Falkland's Islands" (1771), "The Patriot" (1774), and "Taxation no Tyranny, an Answer to the Resolutions and Address of the American Congress (1775)." All these pamphlets show Johnson's usual vigour of style, his unbending Toryism, and his utter incapacity to take a candid and impartial view of a political controversy. "Taxation no Tyranny," in particular, is a very characteristic production. Even George III. could have desired no more strenuous and unreasoning supporter of the right of Great Britain to tax the American colonies.

The last and by far the best of Johnson's works has yet to be mentioned. In 1777 the booksellers formed the design of publishing an edition of the English poets, to which they asked Johnson to prefix introductions containing a Life of each poet and a criticism of his works. He readily consented, for literary history was a subject which always specially interested him; and, on being asked to name a price, mentioned 200 guineas. This modest sum the booksellers afterwards raised to 300 guineas, a rate of remuneration excessively low when we consider the degree of fame to which Johnson had attained and the high prices some of his contemporaries obtained for their works. English poetry was then considered to begin with Cowley, so that Chaucer, Spenser, and other great names were omitted. In all, fifty-two poets were dealt with, of whom about a third are deservedly forgotten, being known only to curious students of literary history. As a critic and biographer, Johnson united great faults and great merits. Few have surpassed him in the power of giving a rapid and vivid sketch of the main features in a man's life and character; but he was careless of minute accuracy, and often omitted to correct errors even after they had been pointed out to him. As a critic he had no sense for the higher kinds of poetry; anything that did not square with the dictates of common sense he condemned as absurd; but he possessed the rare and signal merit of always saying what he really thought, and not what he fancied would be agreeable to the taste of the majority of readers. Of thousands who have yawned over "Paradise Lost," very few have had the courage to say, "None ever wished it longer. Its perusal is a duty rather than a pleasure." And of thousands to whom Nature has denied the faculty of appreciating the classic purity and grace of "Lycidas," very few have been daring enough to run the risk of general opprobrium by saying, "In this poem there is no nature, for there is no truth; there is no art, for there is nothing new. Its form is that of a pastoral; easy, vulgar, and therefore disgusting; whatever images it can supply are long ago exhausted, and its inherent improbability always forces dissatisfaction on the mind."

In 1784 Johnson died at his house in Bolt Court, full of years and full of honours. Looking over his life, he could truly declare that "no man had ever lived more independently by literature than he had done." His brave and manly career did much to relieve authors by profession from the stigma thrown on them by the "Dunciad." Purely by the force of his intellect and character, without flattering the great or seeking their patronage, he fought his way up till by well-nigh universal consent he came to be regarded as the leading man of letters of his time.

Before leaving Johnson, it is fit that something should be said about James Boswell (1740–1795), to whom he now mainly owes his fame. In the case of most authors, we read their biographies because we have read their works; in the case of Johnson, we read his works because we have read Boswell's Life of him. Boswell's character was such an odd combination, that it puzzled the majority of his contemporaries—it partly puzzles us still. "His cleverness, his tact, his skill in drawing forth those he was studying," writes Lord Brougham, "his admirable good-humour, his strict love of truth, his high and generous principle, his kindness towards his friends, his unvarying but generally rational piety, have scarcely been sufficiently praised by those who nevertheless have always been ready, as needs they must be, to acknowledge the debt of gratitude due for perhaps the book, of all that were ever written, the most difficult to lay down once it has been taken up." Macaulay describes him as "servile and impertinent, shallow and pedantic, a bigot and a sot, bloated with family pride, and eternally blustering about the dignity of a born gentleman, yet stooping to be a tale-bearer, an eavesdropper, a common butt in the taverns of London," and declares that "if he had not been a great fool, he would never have been a great writer." Something may, no doubt, be said on behalf of both these estimates; but Brougham comes much nearer the truth than Macaulay, to whose essay on Johnson Carlyle's article on the same subject forms practically a crushing refutation. That Boswell possessed a peculiar talent, almost amounting to genius, his Life of Johnson sufficiently proves; that, in spite of all his oddities and follies, he was good-humoured, a pleasant social companion, and had a genuine liking for and admiration of literature, the fact that he lived on familiar terms with many of his most celebrated contemporaries makes equally evident. He had a keen eye for character, was a matchless raconteur, possessed no contemptible share of wit and literature; and, in spite of the pride with which he contemplated his long-drawn pedigree, seems always to have preferred the society of men of genius and learning to that of those who had only their titles to boast of. The publication of the "Life of Johnson" in 1791 forms an era in the history of English literature. Until then, biographies (with the exception of Mason's far inferior "Life of Gray") had been mostly either rapid sketches of the kind of which Johnson was a master, or dreary dissertations on books and characters, with very little personal interest. Boswell, by copiously detailing Johnson's conversations, and by uniting his correspondence with the narrative of his life, showed how biography might be made one of the most amusing and instructive departments of literature, and paved the way for such excellent books as Moore's "Life of Byron," Lockhart's "Life of Scott," and Mr. Trevelyan's "Life of Macaulay."

Among the original members of the Literary Club which Johnson founded, was an Irishman, who delighted to deck out his odd little figure in gaudy attire, and whom all his friends liked, but whom none of them respected. Every one admitted his abilities, but his oddities and the poverty of his conversational powers made him generally laughed at. He had led a strange and vagabond existence. The son of a poor and warm-hearted clergyman in Ireland, he possessed in ample measure that careless and happy-go-lucky disposition characteristic of his countrymen. Some of his friends having thought they detected in him signs of genius, it was resolved to give him a liberal education, and in 1745 he entered Trinity College, Dublin. There his career was not a brilliant one. He acquired a fair knowledge of the classics, but he neglected mathematics, and got into various scrapes, for one of which he was thrashed by his tutor, who rejoiced in the name of the Rev. Theaker Wilder. Having obtained his degree, he left college with no fixed aim. At length he determined to follow his father's footsteps; but the bishop to whom he applied for ordination rejected him, mainly, it appears, because he chose to appear before his lordship attired in a pair of gorgeous red breeches. He next thought of studying the law, but he spent all the money with which it was intended he should pursue his studies at London among some jolly companions he fell in with at Dublin; so that scheme, too, was given up. As a last resource, he went to Edinburgh to study medicine, which he seems to have done in a sufficiently desultory fashion for two years, when it occurred to him that it was well he should perfect himself under the great physicians of the Continent. There he accordingly set out, and wandered through Switzerland, Italy, and France, supporting himself by playing on the flute and by various other contrivances; for the patience of his relatives was exhausted, and from them he could obtain no remittances. At length, having, according to his own account, procured the degree of Doctor of Medicine from the University of Louvain, he arrived in London in 1756, destitute of money, of friends, and of the means of earning a livelihood. Such were the early adventures of Oliver Goldsmith (1728–1774), one of the most graceful, gentle-minded, and pure writers our literature can boast of. Johnson did not in the least exaggerate when, in his Life of Parnell, he described Goldsmith as "a man of such variety of powers and such felicity of performance, that he always seemed to do best that which he was doing,—a man who had the art of being minute without tediousness, and general without confusion; whose language was copious without exuberance, exact without constraint, and easy without weakness."

After his arrival in London, Goldsmith tried various shifts before subsiding into his natural avocation, that of an author. He was assistant to an apothecary; he practised physic with very little success; and he was for some time an usher at a school kept by Dr. Milner at Peckham. Like Johnson, he always regarded the portion of his life spent in tuition with abhorrence. He is constantly alluding in his writings to the hardships of an usher's life. "He is generally," he says, "the laughing-stock of the school. Every trick is played upon him; the oddity of his manner, his dress, or his language is a source of eternal ridicule; the master himself now and then cannot avoid joining in the laugh; and the poor wretch, eternally resenting this ill-usage, lives in a state of war with all the family." But dreary and bitter as may have been the months spent by Goldsmith as an usher, they can scarcely have been more barren of comfort and peace of mind than those he spent as a hack-writer for the booksellers. Through Dr. Milner he became acquainted with one Griffiths, the proprietor of the *Monthly Review*, a man of coarse mind and of bullying disposition. In 1757, Goldsmith, at a small fixed salary, with board and lodging, became a contributor to the *Review*, and enriched its pages with many pieces of criticism full of delicate insight and just appreciation of merit. But Griffiths was not aware that he had in his employ perhaps the best all-round literary craftsman that ever lived; he and his wife mangled poor Goldsmith's articles, to the author's intense disgust, and reproached him for idleness, and for assuming a tone and manner above his situation. Mutual recriminations ensued, which ended in the engagement being broken off at the end of five months. Goldsmith then began writing for other periodicals, and doing such literary jobs as came in his way, endeavouring at the same time to eke out his scanty pittance by practising medicine. In 1758 he made his final attempt to escape from the poverty, the vexation, and the contempt which he found to attend a literary career, by presenting himself for examination as a hospital mate. He was rejected, and thus again driven back on literature as a profession.

"Goldsmith," Johnson truly said, "was a plant that flowered late." Such of his juvenile letters as have been preserved show that he possessed at an early age that charm of style and felicity of humorous description that afterwards delighted the world; but it was necessity, not choice, that led him to adopt a literary life; and if he had been moderately successful as a physician, it is probable that the "Vicar of Wakefield" and the "Deserted Village" would never have been written. He was in his thirty-first year ere he published his first independent work, "An Inquiry into the State of Polite Learning in Europe." It was published anonymously, but was generally known to be by Goldsmith. The main object of the work was to show that as critics increase, men of original power decrease. It is an interesting and ingenious essay, written with very imperfect knowledge, but with Goldsmith's usual grace of composition, and containing, amidst many absurdities, not a few observations that are still worthy of attention. In 1759, also, he began a weekly series of essays under the title of the "Bee." It was not a success, reaching only eight numbers. In the following year he contributed to Newbery's *Public Ledger* the "Chinese Letters," afterwards republished under the title of "The Citizen of the World," a series of essays of great though unequal merit. They purport to be letters written by a Chinese newly arrived in England to his friends, but the mask is not well kept up, nor, indeed, does Goldsmith seem to have intended that it should be kept up. The weakest parts of the work are those which treat of moral subjects after the fashion of the *Rambler*. Goldsmith had no great powers of reasoning; and he seems, judging from the air of constraint and artificiality which pervades them, to have known that he was going beyond his true sphere when writing essays on such subjects as the "Difference between Love and Gratitude," &c. But nothing can be finer than his sketches of character and pictures of life, or than his criticisms on the reigning modes of the time, which show wonderful powers of humour and gentle satire. The account of Beau Tibbs, for example, is equal to anything in Addison, and would alone be sufficient to stamp Goldsmith as a writer of a very high order of genius.

From the time of the publication of the "Inquiry into the State of Polite Learning," Goldsmith was a singularly prolific author. Whenever any literary job came in his way by which he might earn some money, he was ready to execute it, whether he had any previous acquaintance with the subject or not. Much of what he wrote has doubtless passed into oblivion, but enough remains to show the truth of Johnson's assertion in his epitaph, that "he left almost no kind of writing untouched, and touched nothing that he did not adorn." For John Newbery, the famous publisher of children's books, he did a great deal of work, including (if an old tradition, which Mr. Charles Welsh has supported by many strong arguments, may be credited) the tale of "Little Goody Twoshoes," which has earned the heartfelt approbation of so many juvenile readers. Among his pieces of honest journey-work, executed not for fame, but to meet his incessant calls on his purse, may be mentioned the "History of England, in a Series of Letters from a Nobleman to his Son," which was published anonymously, and by many attributed to Lord Lyttleton (1762); "History of Rome" (1769); "History of England," in four volumes (1771); "History of Animated Nature" (1774). Neither in his historical nor in his scientific productions did Goldsmith make any profession of original research; what he aimed to do, and what he succeeded in doing, was to give a clear, concise, and readable account of his subject. Johnson excited the astonishment of Boswell by preferring Goldsmith as an historian to Robertson; but there is more to be said for Johnson's opinion than may at first sight appear possible.

We turn to the writings to which Goldsmith owes his immortality. In 1764 appeared the "Traveller," the first work to which he prefixed his name. He lived, as he himself often pointed out, both in writing and in conversation, in an age singularly deficient in poetry of any high order of merit. Versifiers there were in abundance, men destitute alike of imagination, spirit, and sensibility, but Goldsmith himself was the only writer who deserved to be called a poet in any high sense of the word. It may be granted at once that he does not reach to very lofty heights, and that his range was somewhat limited; but our literature does not afford an instance of a poet to whose writings we constantly return with greater pleasure, or who (with the possible exception of Mr. Tennyson) has written fewer imperfect lines. The powers displayed in the "Traveller" astonished all Goldsmith's friends, and raised him at once from the position of a scribbler to the booksellers into that of a literary lion of some magnitude. Its success led to the publication in 1766 of the "Vicar of Wakefield," which had been written two years previously. One day Johnson received a message from Goldsmith that he was in great distress, and begging him to come to him as soon as possible. Johnson sent him a guinea, and promised to call on him directly. When he arrived, he found the unfortunate author in a violent passion, because he had been arrested by his landlady for his rent. "I perceived," relates Johnson, "that he had already changed my guinea, and had a bottle or madeira and a glass before him. I put the cork into the bottle, desired he would be calm, and began to talk to him ot the means by which he might be extricated. He then told me he had a novel ready for the press, which he produced to me. I looked into it, and saw its merit; told the landlady I should soon return; and having gone to a bookseller, sold it for sixty guineas. I brought Goldsmith the money, and he discharged his rent, not without rating his landlady in a high tone for having used him so ill." This novel was the "Vicar of Wakefield," which the purchaser did not venture to publish till after the assured success of the "Traveller." Its reception soon made him ashamed of his over-cautiousness. Within a year it went through three editions, and has always since remained popular. Samuel Rogers, the length of whose literary experience is illustrated by the fact that he contrived to pay a call on Samuel Johnson, and lived to prophesy the future greatness of Algernon Charles Swinburne, declared that of all the books which, during the fitful changes of three generations, he had seen rise and fall, the charm of the "Vicar of Wakefield" had alone continued as at first; and that could he revisit the world after an interval of many more generations, he should as surely look to find it undiminished. The plot contains many incongruities and absurdities, but these are forgotten or unnoticed amidst the delight afforded by its sly humour, its inimitable sketches of character, its geniality, and its perfect purity of tone, affording so pleasing a contrast to most of the works of fiction that had preceded it. It is a book which has charmed young and old, rich and poor, the learned and the ignorant. A child of twelve years old may read it with pleasure; such a man as Goethe did not scruple to declare how much he owed to it. The characteristics that distinguish the "Vicar of Wakefield" are conspicuous also in Goldsmith's two comedies, the "Good-Natured Man" (1768), and "She Stoops to Conquer" (1773). The second is considerably the superior, both in the construction of the plot and in humorous effect; but they alike display a great power of good-humoured satire, a healthy and genial tone of mind, and (as indeed is the case with all Goldsmith's writings) a disposition to make literary capital out of his own early scrapes and peccadilloes. The mistaking of a private house for an inn, the incident upon which the plot of "She Stoops to Conquer" turns, was suggested by Goldsmith's having actually made the same mistake himself when a raw youth of sixteen.

In 1770 appeared Goldsmith's finest poem, the "Deserted Village," full of tender recollections of his beloved native country, which he was never again to behold. In 1774 he wrote that admirable series of poetical characters called "Retaliation," of which posterity has endorsed almost every word. The poem was, alas! never finished. That hand, which had never lost its cunning, was not destined to write more. On 4th April 1774 poor Goldsmith expired. "He died of a fever," wrote Johnson to Boswell, "made, I am afraid, more violent by uneasiness of mind. His debts began to be heavy, and all his resources were exhausted. Sir Joshua [Reynolds] is of opinion that he owed no less than two thousand pounds. Was ever poet so trusted before?" Though, during the latter part of his life, Goldsmith was making an income sufficient to maintain him in comfort if not in affluence, his affairs were greatly embarrassed, owing to his boundless charity and never-failing goodness of heart, which made him treat his friends to sumptuous banquets, and, from his incapacity to turn a deaf ear to a touching tale, rendered him the dupe of many designing rogues.

Though undoubtedly the greatest poet, and, with only one or two exceptions, the greatest prose writer of his time, Goldsmith was generally spoken of by his contemporaries with a kind of supercilious condescension, which, though in the highest degree unjust, is not difficult to account for. Impulsive, reckless, and generous, his character was of the kind which commands affection rather than respect; he lacked that worldly wisdom which is often so much more serviceable to its possessor than higher and better qualities; and though his biographers have gallantly attempted to prove that his contemporaries were mistaken in supposing him to be a poor talker, it is impossible not to credit the practically unanimous testimony of the latter, summed up by Johnson's remark, "Sir, no man was ever so foolish when he had not a pen in his hand, or so wise when he had one." The homeliness of his appearance no doubt contributed not a little to diminish the esteem felt for his conversation. "In person," writes Judge Day, "he was short, about five feet five or six inches; strong but not heavy in make; rather fair in complexion, with brown hair—such at least as could be distinguished from his wig. His features were plain but not repulsive—certainly not so when lighted up by conversation. His manners were simple, natural, and perhaps on the whole we may say not polished, at least without the refinement and good-breeding which the exquisite polish of his language would lead us to expect."

A very different man from Goldsmith was another distinguished member of the Literary Club, his countryman Edmund Burke, the greatest writer on political philosophy in our language, and, if Mr. Matthew Arnold's judgment be accepted, the greatest master of English prose style that ever lived. Unlike Johnson and Goldsmith, he had not to pass his youth in a bitter apprenticeship to want and "the spurns which patient merit of the unworthy takes," for his parents were, if not wealthy, at least well-to-do people. He was born in Dublin in 1729, received most of his elementary education at a school in Kildare kept by Abraham Shackleton, a Quaker, and in 1743 entered Trinity College, Dublin, where he remained for five years. His University career, if not brilliant, was far from an idle one; though he did not apply himself very closely to the studies of the place, he read largely and acquired a fund of miscellaneous knowledge. In 1750 he came to London to study law at the Middle Temple; but he soon found that legal studies were irksome to one of his discursive temper, and began to cast longing eyes upon the more pleasant field of general literature. He used to boast that "he had none of that master-vice sloth in his composition," and with perfect justice, for, while neglecting the study of the law, his time, instead of being spent in idleness or dissipation, was employed in amassing those vast stores of knowledge which called forth the admiration of his contemporaries, and fitted him for the great career on which he was soon to embark. During this period no doubt he scribbled much, but he did not formally appear before the public as an author till 1756, when he published two works, "A Vindication of Natural Society," and "A Philosophical Inquiry into the Origin of our Ideas on the Sublime and Beautiful." The first of these productions is a short tract, designed as a parody on the style and mode of thinking of Lord Bolingbroke, whose works were then considerably in vogue. Bolingbroke in his writings had attempted to render religion ridiculous by an exaggerated view of its abuses. Adopting the same course of argument, Burke endeavours to show that as civil society carried in its train a number of evils, it would be well to return to a state of savage nature. The pamphlet received the highest praise it could possibly have gained in being taken by many for a genuine production of Lord Bolingbroke. The essay on the sublime and beautiful is an interesting contribution to a subject on which many able and subtle writers have discoursed; but though it contains several striking passages, it cannot be said to show much philosophic depth or precision. Burke himself is said to have thought little of it in his latter years. In 1758 he was engaged by Dodsley to edit the "Annual Register." He is said to have written the whole of the volumes for 1758 and 1759; he contributed largely to it for a good many years afterwards.

These occupations soon introduced him into literary society, where his width of knowledge and powers of conversation eminently qualified him to excel. In that year he became acquainted with Johnson, an intimacy to which we owe some of the best of the conversations recorded by Boswell. Though very unlike in many respects, there were several points of resemblance between Burke and Johnson. Both were high-minded, honourable men, both were prone to place rather too much confidence in the rectitude of their own opinions, both were exceedingly benevolent; and, above all, both were copious and excellent talkers. "That fellow calls forth all my powers," exclaimed Johnson, who was never tired of praising the extraordinary readiness and affluence of Burke's conversation.

The leading incidents in Burke's life belong rather to political than to literary history, but they may be briefly mentioned here. In 1759 he became private secretary to "Single-speech" Hamilton, with whom he went to Ireland in 1761. Their intimacy, owing to no fault on Burke's part, ended in an open rupture in 1765. In the same year he was appointed private secretary to the Marquis of Rockingham, then Prime Minister and the leader of the Whig party. In the following year he was returned member for the pocket borough of Wendover. From this time he took an active part both by tongue and pen in all the leading political struggles of the era. He supported a conciliatory policy towards the American colonies, advocated the abolition of certain restrictions which hampered the trade of Ireland, brought forward (in 1780) a great scheme of political reform, and was the leading spirit in the impeachment of Warren Hastings. Though his abilities were universally known and acknowledged, he never obtained very high parliamentary office. For this various reasons may be given. In the first place, he was not high born, and the great offices of state were then, so far as possible, parcelled out among patricians. In the second place, although his orations when read appear far superior to those of any other speaker of his time, and may indeed be placed in the same rank as those of Cicero and Demosthenes, he was, partly from his tendency to lengthiness, partly from his faults of manner, so unpopular a speaker, that his rising was looked on as a signal for members to leave the House. In the third place, and this perhaps was the most powerful reason, his temperament was excitable, and when carried away by passion he was apt to speak out what he felt, regardless of prudential considerations. To what heights of vehemence and invective his impassioned genius could carry him was not fully known till the time of the French Revolution, when he broke from his party, quarrelled with his oldest friends because he could not bring them to think on the subject as he did, and became the principal advocate of a crusade against France. Alike in the House of Commons and in private society, he never ceased dwelling on the abhorrence he felt for the terrible Revolution, and the hatred with which he regarded its leaders. It would have done his old friend, Samuel Johnson, good could he have lived to see Burke, whose Whiggish opinions were, of course, disliked by him, adopt language regarding the French Revolution which would have satisfied even his strongest prejudices.

In 1794 Burke retired from Parliament, his son being returned member in his stead. Shortly afterwards his son (who, in spite of his father's fondness for him, appears to have been a silly and priggish young man) died, leaving Burke, as he wrote to William Elliot, "desolate at home, stripped of my boast, my hope, my consolation, my counsellor, and my guide." In 1794 he received a pension from Government, which was assailed by the Duke of Bedford as in contradiction to the whole scheme of economic reform. To this attack Burke replied in his famous "Letter to a Noble Lord" (1795), which is a fine example of spirited invective. He died at Beaconsfield on July 8, 1797.

In private life Burke was a man of unbounded benevolence, great affability of manners, and spotless morality. In public life he sometimes allowed the passion of the moment to get the better of him, and said things which would have been better left unsaid. But no one ever doubted his thorough honesty and integrity of purpose; he was, indeed, as Goldsmith said, "too fond of the right to pursue the expedient;"

and if he had been less scrupulous might have attained greater success as a practical politician.

Burke's principal works, besides those already mentioned, are "Thoughts on Present Discontents" (1770), one of the most wise, sober, and weighty of his productions; "Reflections on the French Revolution," probably his most generally known work (1790); "An Appeal from the New to the Old Whigs" (1791), and his four "Letters on a Regicide Peace," two of which were published posthumously. His leading speeches are those on conciliation with America (1755), on economical reform (1780), on Fox's East India Bill (1783), on the Nabob of Arcot's debts (1785), and on the impeachment of Warren Hastings (1786). His speeches and writings display the same qualities — a contempt for merely theoretical politicians, a boundless wealth of imagination, which enabled him to set forth the driest facts surrounded by a panoply of splendid eloquence, a style frequently filled with similes and metaphors, and (especially in his speeches) an occasional absence of good taste and self-restraint. Every production of his is, as Mr. Matthew Arnold says, "saturated with ideas;" hence his speeches, which, owing to his amplifications and deviations from the subject in hand, were often found tedious by his hearers, attract and reward the attention of the reader, while those of such men as Fox and Sheridan are of interest only to the historian, and have little merit considered merely as literature. "He can seldom," writes Mr. Henry Rogers, speaking of Burke as an orator, "confine himself to a simple, business-like view of the subject under discussion, or to close, rapid, compressed argumentation on it. On the contrary, he makes boundless excursions into all the regions of moral and political philosophy; is perpetually tracing up particular instances and subordinate principles to profound and comprehensive maxims; amplifying and expanding the most meagre materials into brief but comprehensive dissertations on political science, and encrusting (so to speak) the nucleus of the most insignificant fact with the most exquisite crystallisations of truth, while the whole composition glitters and sparkles again with a rich profusion of moral reflections equally beautiful and just."

Now that the heat of the political controversies of his time has died away, Burke's writings, so far from having become obsolete, as referring to questions which do not at this period engage our attention, have become more valuable. In particular points he was, no doubt, wrong and misleading, as every party writer must necessarily be; but his mastery of general principles, his large views, and his constant flow of original and striking ideas, lift him far above the level of the political writer who addresses himself merely to the question at issue, and whose work consequently loses its interest when that question has been settled. "Burke had the style of his subjects, the amplitude, the weightiness, the laboriousness, the sense, the high flight, the grandeur, proper to a man dealing with imperial themes, the freedom of nations, the justice of rulers, the fortunes of great societies, the weightiness of law. Burke will always be read with delight and edification, because in the midst of discussions on the local and the accidental he scatters apophthegms that take us into the regions of lasting wisdom. In the midst of the torrent of his most strenuous and passionate deliverances, he suddenly rises aloof from his immediate subject, and in all tranquillity reminds us of some permanent relation of things, some enduring truth of human life or society. We do not hear the organ tones of Milton, for faith and freedom had other notes in the seventeenth century. There is none of the complacent and wise-browed sagacity of Bacon, for Burke's were days of eager personal strife and party fire and civil division. We are not exhilarated by the cheerfulness, the polish, the fine manners of Bolingbroke, for Burke had an anxious conscience, and was earnest and intent that the good should triumph. And yet Burke is among the greatest of those who have wrought marvels in the prose of our English tongue."[1]

During Burke's lifetime he was frequently credited with the authorship of the famous letters of "Junius," which created an

[1] "Burke," by John Morley (English Men of Letters), p. 213.

excitement such as perhaps has never been called forth by any other political writings, and which still, owing to their great contemporary fame, and to the mastery they display over keen, vigorous invective, retain a place in literature. The main reason for attributing their authorship to Burke was because of certain real or fancied resemblances between their style and that of Burke's acknowledged works; but Burke positively declared to Dr. Johnson that he was not the writer of them, and his claim is now, we believe, abandoned by all competent authorities. The letters, of which the first appeared in January 1769, were published in Woodfall's *Public Advertiser*, one of the leading newspapers of the time, and attracted great and universal attention, not only on account of their fierce invectives against the leading contemporary politicians, but because they showed a minute acquaintance with the inner life of politics, and a knowledge of state secrets which could not have been possessed by an outsider. Among the many claimants who have been put forward as their probable author are Colonel Barré, Thomas Lord Lyttleton, Lord Temple, and Lauchlin MacLeane; but there is an overwhelming consensus of authorities that their real writer was Sir Philip Francis, who was a clerk in the War Office at the time of the appearance of the letters. His claims have been warmly supported by such great names as Macaulay, Earl Stanhope, Brougham, Lord Campbell, and De Quincey, who declares that the proofs of Francis's authorship rush in upon us more plentiful than blackberries, and that the case ultimately becomes fatiguing from the very plethora and riotous excess of evidence. It is not unlikely that the controversy as to their authorship has done more than their intrinsic merits to keep the "Letters" alive; for it must be confessed that they now present little attraction save to students of political history. Many will sympathise in this matter with Mr. Carlyle, who once bitterly complained of having been wofully bored about the matter at a dinner-party —"as if it could matter the value of a brass farthing to any human being who was the author of 'Junius.'"

A greater contrast can scarcely be imagined than that

afforded by the impetuous, brilliant, imaginative Burke and the "douce," tranquil, sober-minded Scotchman of whom we are now to speak. Both were great writers and original thinkers, but Burke was fitted for a life of action and ambition, and was in his element while engaged in the bustle of political controversy, and in taking part in the great conflicts waged in Parliament, while Hume, had the Fates so willed it, would have been quite content to pass the life of the ideal philosopher, devoting himself to the society of his books and his friends, and letting the turmoil of the outside world pass unheeded. He was born, the younger son of a good Scotch family, at Edinburgh in April 1711. According to his own account, which is corroborated by what we know otherwise, he passed through the ordinary course of education with success, and was seized very early with a passion for literature, "which has been the ruling passion of my life, and the great source of my enjoyment." With all his love of study and desire for literary distinction, Hume was by no means what would be called a brilliant youth: he seemed more likely to pass his time in reading and in vague day-dreaming than to rise in the world. "Oor Davie's a fine good-humoured crater," his mother is reported to have said of him, "but uncommon wake-minded." As, however, his fortune was very small, it was necessary that he should exert himself in some way or other to provide for his support. Accordingly, to use his own words, "My studious disposition, my sobriety, and my industry gave my family a notion that the law was a proper profession for me; but I found an unsurmountable aversion to everything but the pursuits of philosophy and general learning; and while they fancied I was poring upon Voet and Vinnius, Cicero and Virgil were the authors which I was secretly devouring." Law having failed, commerce was next tried, but it proved a still more unsuitable occupation for the young philosopher, who in 1734, "letting fortune and the world go by," retired to France, there to prosecute his studies, resolving to make a very rigid frugality supply his deficiency of fortune. In France he resided for three years, first at Rheims, and afterwards at La Fleche, in

Anjou, and there he composed his first work, his "Treatise of Human Nature." It was published in 1738, and, greatly to the author's vexation, fell "still-born from the press." This work was followed in 1742 by a volume of essays which had more success; then came in 1748 the "Inquiry Concerning Human Understanding," a revised and much altered edition of the "Treatise of Human Nature;" then, in 1752, his "Political Discourses," and his "Inquiry Concerning the Principles of Morals," which he himself considered incomparably the best of all his works. Lastly, to conclude the list of his philosophical writings, there appeared in 1779, three years after his death, his "Dialogues on Natural Religion." We have here to do with Hume as a man of letters, not as a philosopher, and may therefore pass over his philosophical writings, the sceptical views of which are so well known, with the remark that they are written in a style always perspicuous, and often rising into elegance.

While engaged on the above philosophical works, Hume improved his slender fortune by engaging in more remunerative pursuits. He passed a most wretched but not unprofitable year as guardian to the Marquis of Annandale, a partially idiotic, partially insane young nobleman, and he was for two years secretary to General St. Clair, whom he accompanied on an expedition, "which was at first meant for Canada, but ended in an incursion on the coast of France," and with whom, in 1747, he went on an embassy to the courts of Venice and Turin. "These two years," he writes, "were almost the only interruptions which my studies have received during the course of my life. I passed them agreeably and in good company; and my appointments, with my frugality, had made me reach a fortune which I called independent, though most of my friends were inclined to smile when I said so; in short, I was now master of near a thousand pounds."

In 1752 Hume was appointed to succeed Ruddiman, the illustrious Latin scholar, as librarian of the Advocates' Library, Edinburgh. The salary attached to the post was small, but his duties were not onerous, and he had full command of a large and excellent collection of books. The opportunities for literary research thus afforded him caused him again to think of a scheme he had formerly projected of writing a History of England. Till this time England had been singularly destitute of historians of any high order of merit. Clarendon's "History of the Rebellion," indeed, is, from its grave and weighty style, a work of great literary value; but it scarcely even pretends to impartiality, and may be more fitly designated "Political Memoirs" than a history; while the Rymers, the Echards, and the Cartes, who had aspired to relate the history of their country, were destitute alike of genius, of discrimination, and of accurate research. Frightened at the notion of continuing a narrative through a period of seventeen hundred years, Hume commenced with the accession of the House of Stuart, an epoch when he thought the misrepresentations of faction began chiefly to take place. "I was," he goes on to say, "I own, sanguine in my expectations of the success of this work. I thought that I was the only historian who had at once neglected present power, interest, and authority, and the cry of popular prejudices; and as the subject was suited to every capacity, I expected proportional applause. But miserable was my disappointment: I was assailed by one cry of reproach, disapprobation, and even detestation; English, Scotch, and Irish, Whig and Tory, churchman and sectary, freethinker and religionist, patriot and courtier, united in their rage against the man who had presumed to shed a generous tear for the fate of Charles I. and the Earl of Strafford." Dr. Johnson used sometimes to regret that his works were not enough attacked, as controversy about them attracted public attention and promoted their sale; but Hume had not even this consolation to compensate for the storm of detraction with which his work was assailed, for within a year after its publication only forty-five copies of it were sold. With his usual calm stoicism, he was not daunted by the want of popular appreciation, but quietly went on with his task. In 1756 appeared the second volume; three years after the "History of the Tudors" followed; and in 1761 the work was completed by the publication of two volumes containing an inadequate, and, even for the time, an unscholarly account of the early period of English history. The work gradually stole into popularity, and several years before the author's death had come to be reckoned the standard History of England, a position which it maintained till within comparatively late years. Nor was its proud position undeserved. As an historian, Hume possessed some highly estimable qualities. His style is lucid and excellent, his narrative flows on in a calm, equable course, his reflections are generally judicious and sometimes profound, and his sense of proportion is admirable. Few writers have excelled him in the art of giving to each event its fit place and its proper degree of length. But these excellences are counterbalanced by grave faults. In common with all the historians of the eighteenth century, with the exception of Gibbon, he forgot that truth was the first requisite in an historian, and aimed rather to lay before his readers a polished and philosophic narrative than the results of patient accuracy and original research,—in this respect affording a notable contrast to the latest school of historians, who sometimes in their anxious care to avoid the Charybdis of inaccuracy appear to make shipwreck on the Scylla of pedantry. Moreover, his spirit of political partisanship was unworthy of so great a philosopher. Like Dr. Johnson, he always took care "that the Whig dogs should not have the best of it." Still, with all its defects, his History is a great work; and if later writers have superseded it as an historical authority, it is yet worth reading as in many respects a model of style. We should not omit to mention that Hume was the first to mix with his account of public affairs chapters on the condition of the people and on the state of literature.

From his tranquil, studious life in Edinburgh, Hume was, in 1763, drawn by an invitation from Lord Hertford to attend him on his embassy to Paris. He was soon appointed secretary to the embassy, and passed three years very pleasantly in the glittering capital, where his fame had preceded him. "Le bon David," as he was fondly called, found himself surrounded by an admiring crowd of male and female adorers, who were never tired of admiring the stout old philosopher. On his return from Paris, he was appointed, in 1767, Under Secretary of State for the Northern department, a position which he retained for two years. In 1769 he returned to Edinburgh, having amassed a fortune sufficient to yield him an annual revenue of over £1000. There he passed the remaining six years of his life, engaged in his favourite studies, and exercising a bounteous hospitality to his large circle of friends. On August 25, 1776, he died as he had lived, with tranquillity and cheerfulness.

Hume's personal appearance was not prepossessing. Lord Charlemont, describing him during his residence at Turin, says: "The powers of physiognomy were baffled by his countenance; neither could the most skilful pretend to discover the smallest traces of the faculties of his mind in the unmeaning features of his visage. His face was broad and fat, his mouth wide, and without any other expression than that of imbecility, his eyes vacant and spiritless, and the corpulence of his whole person was far better fitted to communicate the idea of a turtle-eating alderman than of a refined philosopher." Of his character he has himself, in the brief narrative which he calls "My Own Life," given a sufficiently correct description. He was, he says, "a man of mild disposition, of command of temper, of an open, social, and cheerful humour, capable of attachment, but little susceptible of enmity, and of great moderation in all my passions. Even my love of fame, my ruling passion, never soured my temper, notwithstanding my frequent disappointments."

There can be no better evidence of Hume's amiability of disposition and freedom from petty jealousy than the friendly terms on which he lived with a large circle of literary acquaintances, and the heartfelt applause which he bestowed upon Robertson and Gibbon, his rivals in the field of historical composition. When Robertson's "History of Scotland" appeared, he was one of the loudest in its commendation, declaring to Robertson (with, as his whole conduct showed, perfect truth) that he had not for a long time had a more sensible pleasure than the good reception of Robertson's History had given him. Robertson is one of the few instances of an author's being raised from obscurity to great and wide-spread fame by the publication of his first work. He was born in 1721, the son of an Edinburgh clergyman, and after passing through the usual course in Arts and Divinity, was appointed in 1743 minister of Gladsmuir, a small parish in East Lothian. There his duties were light and his natural love of study found full scope, but, unlike most of those who are fond of reading, he was in no hurry to appear as an author. His "History of Scotland" which was begun in 1752, did not appear till 1759, and previous to that time his only publications were a sermon, and one or two insignificant articles which appeared in the "Edinburgh Review," a short-lived periodical supported by the leading Northern literati of the time, such as Adam Smith, Blair, Jardine, Wedderburn, &c. His History, unlike Hume's, was received immediately on its publication with loud and general applause, and the whole edition was exhausted in less than a month. One reason why it was so much more successful than Hume's doubtless was because it did not to such a degree run counter to popular prejudices. Robertson is compelled to admit Mary's guilt, but he does it with reluctance, and endeavours to excite in the breast of the reader so strong a feeling of pity for her that none but the most fanatical Jacobite could take great offence at anything he says.

A few months before the publication of his "History," Robertson removed to Edinburgh, having been appointed minister of Old Greyfriars'. Honours were soon thickly bestowed on him. In 1759 he was appointed one of the chaplains-royal, and in 1762 he was elevated to the dignity of Principal of the University. Despite the studious solitude in which the early part of his life had been spent, Robertson was a man eminently adapted for public life; an excellent speaker, and a cool and cautious debater. He soon became one of the leaders of the General Assembly, advocating the claims of the "moderate" or anti-evangelical party, and made his tact and ability so widely felt, that it was a common saying that he would have been better employed in acting history than in writing it. Although his first work had been so successful, he was in no hurry to appear again as an author. It was not till 1769, ten years after his "History of Scotland," that his "History of Charles V.," which is generally regarded as his finest work, was published. How much his fame had advanced within these ten years is clearly shown by the fact that while for his "History of Scotland," by which the booksellers made about £6000, he received only £600, he sold the copyright of "Charles V." for £4500.[1] In 1777 appeared his "History of America." Robertson's last work was a "Disquisition on Ancient India," which was published in 1791, about two years before his death, which occurred in 1793. On the whole, it can scarcely be said that the great contemporary fame of Robertson has been justified by the verdict of posterity. His writings, it is true, belong to the category of standard works, but they are now pretty generally consigned to the dreary limbo of "books which no gentleman's library can be complete without"—books of which everybody is supposed to know something, but which, in reality, very few ever read. Robertson was one of the writers who steadfastly kept up the so-called dignity of history, thinking it beneath him ever to descend from his stilts, and edify the reader with any of those little anecdotes of fashion and character, or details of domestic life, which are so often much more instructive than pages of pompous dissertation. Of his style, which was elaborated with scrupulous care, Johnson once truly observed that it had the same fault as his own, "too big words and too many of them." It is, however, always sonorous and dignified, and sometimes, as in the account of Mary's execution, rises into very impressive eloquence.

We now come to the last and by far the greatest of the

[1] Hume appears to have received £700 a volume for his History—that is, £4200 for the entire work. Gibbon got £8000 for the "Decline and Fa l."

famous trio of historians who adorned the eighteenth century, Edward Gibbon, whose "Decline and Fall of the Roman Empire" towers above all the other historical compositions of the period, like a great cathedral dominating a city. Alone of the histories of that time, it has sustained uninjured the fierce light of modern research, and it is very unlikely that it will ever now be dislodged from the lofty pedestal which it occupies by any later production. In his "Autobiography"—to any one with a taste for literature one of the most fascinating and stimulating compositions in the language—Gibbon has recorded the principal events of his life with something of the same pomp and swell of style as he employed in describing the decline and fall of the Roman Empire. He was born at Putney in 1737, the son of a wealthy gentleman, who had estates in Surrey and Hampshire. His mother, who died while he was young, was, from various causes, incapacitated from paying much attention to him, but the maternal office was discharged with the most tender assiduity by his aunt, Mrs. Catherine Porten, to whom he felt a lifelong gratitude. So frail and sickly was he in his early years, that it was scarcely anticipated that he would ever reach maturity, and he may be described as almost entirely self-educated, for his ill-health incapacitated him from learning much at the various schools to which he was sent; and if his desire for knowledge had not been unusually strong, it is probable that he would have become one of those ignorant, illiterate squires then so common. To the kind lessons of his aunt he ascribed his early and invincible love of reading, "which I would not exchange for the treasures of India." He read variously and widely, studying all the historical books that fell in his way, and acquiring a knowledge, wonderful for one so young, of ancient geography and chronology. "In my childish balance," he says, "I presumed to weigh the systems of Scaliger and Petavius, of Marsham and Newton, which I could seldom study in the originals; and my sleep has been disturbed by the difficulty of reconciling the Septuagint with the Hebrew computation." When, ere he had reached the fifteenth year of his age, he was entered at

Magdalen College, Oxford, he possessed "a stock of erudition which might have puzzled a doctor, and a degree of ignorance of which a schoolboy would have been ashamed." In other words, his miscellaneous and historical knowledge was great: his acquaintance with Latin more extensive than accurate; while of Greek he scarcely knew even the elements.

In one of the most eloquent and vindictive passages in the "Autobiography," he has told us how small was his debt to Oxford, the presiding spirits of which, "steeped in port and prejudices," seem then to have very slenderly recognised their duty to the young men committed to their charge. "To the University of Oxford," he says, "*I* acknowledge no obligation, and she will as cheerfully renounce me for a son as I am willing to disclaim her for a mother. I spent fourteen months at Magdalen College: they proved the fourteen months the most idle and unprofitable of my whole life, the reader will pronounce between the school and the scholar; but I cannot affect to believe that nature had disqualified me for all literary pursuits." The cause of his quitting Oxford so soon forms one of the few romantic episodes of Gibbon's life. In the course of his omnivorous reading he came across two treatises of Bossuet, and was by them converted to the Roman Catholic faith. The young heretic, who for a time clung to the opinions he had embraced with the tenacity of a martyr, was compelled to withdraw from Oxford, and soon after was placed by his indignant father under the care of M. Pavilliard, a worthy and learned Protestant clergyman, who lived at Lausanne, in Switzerland. There he remained for nearly five years, and was induced, after many arguments with his tutor, to renounce the Catholic faith. These five years were for the most part spent in a course of study so wide and so severe as to be almost without parallel. In them Gibbon read all the Latin authors of importance, not slightly and hastily, but critically and with elaborate commentaries; he acquired such a knowledge of French, that it became more familiar to him than his mother tongue; and he laid a solid foundation wherewith to prosecute the study of Greek literature.

In 1758, Gibbon, long since reconciled to his father, returned to England, where he resided principally at his father's house at Buriton, Hampshire, carrying on, though not perhaps in so thoroughgoing a fashion, the studies he had begun in Switzerland. In 1761 he published his first work, an essay on "The Study of Literature," written in French. It is a series of very loosely connected observations, often true and ingenious enough; and it attracted considerable attention abroad, although it was almost entirely neglected at home. Shortly before its publication, Gibbon joined the Hampshire Militia, where he served for two years and a half, thus acquiring, at the cost of much inconvenience and interruption to his studies, a knowledge of military tactics which stood him in good stead when he came to write his History. In 1764, having qualified himself for his tour by a most laborious course of study of Roman antiquities and ancient geography, he visited Italy, perhaps, it has been justly remarked, better furnished for his expedition than any traveller ever was. It was during this visit that he formed the project of writing the history of the decline and fall of the Roman Empire. Previous to this time he had meditated various historical compositions, but for one reason or another they were all abandoned. "It was at Rome," he tells us, "on the 15th of October 1764, as I sat musing amidst the ruins of the Capitol, while the bare-footed friars were singing vespers in the Temple of Jupiter, that the idea of writing the decline and fall of the city first started to my mind." The actual composition of the work, however, was not begun till 1772, two years after his father's death, which left him in possession of a moderate fortune—about £800 a year, it would seem. When he began to write the History, he found it very difficult to "hit the middle tone between a dull chronicle and a rhetorical declamation," but with practice facility soon came, and the vast proportion of the work was printed from the first draft. The first volume appeared in 1776, a year memorable in the history of literature. In it Hume died; and Campbell's "Philosophy of Rhetoric," still one of the best treatises on the subject, and

Adam Smith's "Wealth of Nations," which first placed the study of political economy on a firm basis, were published. However high Gibbon's hopes may have been, the success of the first volume must have surpassed them. It created a *furore* comparable to that which attended the publication of Macaulay's "History of England;" three editions were speedily exhausted, and the book was to be found not only on the table of students, but in the hands of ladies and of men of fashion. It was warmly welcomed by Hume and Robertson, and met with the common penalty of success by being vigorously attacked by a host of adversaries. In 1781 the second and third volumes were published, and in 1787 the work was completed. "I have presumed," he writes in his "Autobiography," "to mark the moment of conception: I shall now commemorate the hour of my final deliverance. It was on the day, or rather night of the 27th of June 1787, between the hours of eleven and twelve, that I wrote the last lines of the last page, in a summer-house at my garden [at Lausanne]. After laying down my pen, I took several turns in a berceau, or covered walk of acacias, which commands a prospect of the country, the lake, and the mountains. The air was temperate, the sky was serene, and the silver orb of the moon was reflected from the waters, and all nature was silent. I will not dissemble the first emotions of joy on the recovery of my freedom, and, perhaps, the establishment of my fame. But my pride was soon humbled, and a sober melancholy spread over my mind, by the idea that I had taken an everlasting leave of an old and agreeable companion, and that whatsoever might be the future fate of my History, the life of the historian must be short and precarious." The publication of the last three volumes of the "History" was deferred till April 27, 1788, so as to coincide with his fifty-first birthday.

Like Macaulay, to whose character Gibbon's in several respects bore a considerable resemblance, Gibbon found the composition of his "History" less of a toil than of a pleasure. He was a thorough scholar, finding in study its own exceeding great reward, and never happier than when at his desk or engaged in laborious researches. In 1774 he was, by the interest of Lord Eliot, returned to Parliament, where he sat for eight sessions, steadily supporting the ministry of Lord North; for, like many who have held advanced opinions upon other subjects, Gibbon was strongly conservative in politics. When the French Revolution broke out he was panic-stricken by it to an extent altogether unworthy of his philosophical mind. Gibbon never made any attempt to win oratorical laurels. The great speakers, he said, filled him with despair; the bad ones with terror; and he therefore preferred the safe though inglorious position of a silent member to risking the consequences of a failure.

His early residence abroad gave Gibbon a fondness for Continental life; and after 1783 most of his time was passed at Lausanne, where the "Hotel Gibbon" still keeps his memory alive. There he had many friends; and as his fortune was superior to that of most of those around him, he occupied a higher relative social position than he could have done in England. In 1793 he was recalled to his native country by the death of the wife of his dear friend, Lord Sheffield. His own death followed on 16th January 1794. Gibbon was a man of small stature, very corpulent in his latter years, and always very neatly dressed. He had a disproportionately large head, and "his mouth," writes Colman, "melifluous as Plato's, was a round hole nearly in the centre of his visage." His moral character seems to have been stainless. He was a dutiful son, and a tender and generous friend. "His honourable and amiable disposition," writes Brougham, "his kind and even temper, was praised by all."

Carlyle, in a conversation with Emerson, once described the "Decline and Fall" as "the splendid bridge from the old world to the new." It comprises the history of the world for nearly thirteen centuries, from the reign of the Antonines to the taking of Constantinople by the Turks. When we consider the vastness and complexity of the subject, Gibbon's learning and power of arrangement alike inspire us with wonder. Mistakes there are, doubtless, but they are wonderfully few and insignificant. The general accuracy is such, that Niebuhr, the great German historian, declared that the more a man knew, the more he would hesitate to contradict Gibbon. The style is ornate and sarcastic; often too allusive and artificial, yet always having a certain harmony with the lofty theme. The great fault of the work arises from Gibbon's bias against Christianity. It appears clear that when he renounced Catholicism, he at the same time abandoned all religious belief; and when he refers to Christianity, it is generally with a covert sneer. The 15th and 16th chapters of his "History," giving an account of the early progress and extension of Christianity, have been particularly objected to, and called forth a crowd of antagonists, who were, however, quite incapable of coping with so great an adversary. Gibbon maintained a disdainful silence till his veracity was attacked by the charge of false quotations, when he published his "Vindication" of the 15th and 16th chapters of his "History." "This single discharge," writes Dean Milman, "from the ponderous artillery of learning and sarcasm, laid prostrate the whole disorderly squadrons of rash and feeble volunteers who filled the ranks of his enemies, while the more distinguished theological writers of the country stood aloof." It is not specific statements, but the general character and temper of the references to Christianity that are liable to attack.*

* "I picked up Whitaker's criticism on Gibbon," writes Macaulay in his Diary (9th October 1858). "Pointless spite, with here and there a just remark. It would be strange if in so large a work as Gibbon's there were nothing open to just remark. How utterly all the attacks on his 'History' are forgotten! this of Whitaker, Randolph's, Chelsum's, Davies's, that stupid beast Joseph Milner's, even Watson's. And still the book, with all its great faults of substance and style, retains, and will retain, its place in our literature; and this though it is offensive to the religious feeling of the country, and really most unfair where religion is concerned."

VIII.

THE NEW ERA IN POETRY.

Percy's "Reliques;" Warton's "History of English Poetry;" Ossian, Chatterton, Shenstone, Beattie; Blake; Cowper; Burns; Crabbe; Wordsworth, Coleridge, Southey; Byron, Shelley, Keats; Rogers, Hogg, Campbell, Moore.

THE influence of Pope over the poets of his own age and those who came after him was far-reaching and prolonged, but it must not be supposed that it was universal. Even during his lifetime poets arose who were not animated by the same spirit, to whom "the town" and its intellectual and moral atmosphere presented few attractions, and whose verse, even while hampered by artificial shackles and disfigured by poetic commonplaces and pseudo-classicalism, deals with an altogether different range of subjects from his, and has an altogether different inner meaning and substance. This is true of the poetry of Thomson, of Collins, of Gray, who have been mentioned in a previous chapter, and it is also true of the poetry of Allan Ramsay, not so great as any of these three, but still a very remarkable poetic phenomenon, considering the age in which he lived. A Scotchman, like Thomson, he stood alone, or almost alone, among the poets who flourished from 1680 to 1730, in having a genuine love for and pleasure in natural scenery. His pastoral drama, "The Gentle Shepherd," published in 1725, is, with its freshness and simplicity of style, and its picturesque and charming delineations of country life, an almost startling contrast to the frigid and unnatural pastoral poetry of Pope and his followers. But what perhaps tended as much as any single cause to overthrow Pope's influence, and to bring the couplet metre of which he was such a master into disgrace and almost total desuetude, was the crowd of imitators who arose during his lifetime and after his death. As Cowper says in his "Table Talk," Pope had—

> "Made poetry a mere mechanic art,
> And every warbler had his tune by heart."

When smoothly turned and deftly rhymed couplets were used by every poetaster to give utterance to empty nothings, people began to get tired of that form of verse. But it lingered long and died hard. It was employed by Johnson, by Goldsmith, by Cowper, by Campbell, not to mention others; and its vitality clearly shows how popular it was at one time, and how well adapted it is for dealing with a certain class of subjects.

The decay of Pope's favourite metre, however, is but a secondary matter: much more important is the reaction which, during the last thirty or forty years of the eighteenth century, set in against the whole tone and character of the artificial school of poetry. Men began to turn with eager eyes to our older poets, too long neglected; ballads, which in Queen Anne's time would have incurred almost universal ridicule, were sought out and fondly pondered over; the great book of nature was studied with impassioned zeal; and poets, tired of conventionality, begun to aspire to portray the deeper emotions and feelings of men. As time went on, the movement became more and more powerful; one great poet after another arose, different in many ways, it may be, from his brother bards, but alike them in singing from a natural impulse, and alike them in having little or nothing in common with the preceding generation of poets. Never, save in the Elizabethan era, was there such a gorgeous outburst of song as during the first thirty years of the nineteenth century. The causes of the new movement were various; but in great measure it must be attributed to the vast upheaval of men's minds, which took place not in this country only, but in France and Germany, about the time of the French Revolution. During that stirring epoch, when old creeds and old modes of government were worn loosely for want of a better covering, a revolutionary spirit was abroad, not in poetry only, but in politics, in philosophy, in science, and in all forms of literary art. No doubt Mr. Palgrave is right in thinking that the French Revolution was only one result, and in itself by no means the most important, of that far wider and far greater spirit which, through inquiry and doubt, through pain and triumph, sweeps mankind round the circles of its greater development.[1] But the French Revolution itself, attracting the profound attention, and, in its earlier stages, the fond sympathy, of all those aspiring young souls who, tired of effete and outworn formulas, were looking eagerly forward to the dawn of a better day, was unquestionably an important factor in the new literary renascence which produced such great results.

Of the general characteristics of the brilliant band of poets whom we shall have to deal with in this chapter, no better summary could be furnished than that given by Mr. Palgrave. They "carried to further perfection the later tendencies of the century preceding in simplicity of narrative, reverence for human passion and character in every sphere, and impassioned love of nature: whilst maintaining, on the whole, the advances in art made since the Restoration, they renewed the half-forgotten melody and depth of tone which marked the best Elizabethan writers; lastly, to what was thus inherited they added a richness in language and a variety in metre, a force and fire in narrative, a tenderness and bloom in feeling, an insight into the finer passages of the soul, and the inner meanings of the landscape, a larger and wiser humanity, hitherto hardly attained, and perhaps unattainable even by predecessors of not inferior individual genius." But before proceeding to the discussion of Wordsworth, Coleridge, and their compeers, we must go back to the more prominent sources of the magnificent stream of poetry whose course it is so pleasant

[1] "Golden Treasury," p. 320.

and inspiring to trace. Only a few of the more significant can be mentioned here. Bishop Percy, by the publication in 1765 of his "Reliques of Ancient English Poetry," revealed to many, to whom they had hitherto been unknown, the wealth of true poetry, of free, wild, natural feeling, which lay in our old ballads. The semi-apologetic tone of his preface shows how such things were generally regarded by the cultured society of his day. "In a polished age like the present," he says, "I am sensible that many of these reliques of antiquity will require great allowances to be made for them. . . . The editor hopes he need not be ashamed of having bestowed some of his idle hours on the ancient literature of our own country, or in regaining from oblivion some pieces (though but the amusements of our ancestors) which tend to place in a striking light their taste, genius, sentiments, or manners." Thomas Warton's "History of English Poetry" (1774–1778), which is still, despite its many inaccuracies, a useful and entertaining work, did good service by attracting the attention of cultured people to our old poets, which then, in most cases, if known at all, were only known at second hand. The same author's elaborate essay on the "Faerie Queen" answered a similar purpose. More important, however, than prose works, though these were largely efficacious in educating the public taste, were the poems which heralded the coming era. Of these, "Ossian," published in 1762, is one of the most remarkable. Whether the work of James Macpherson, or whether translated from ancient Gaelic manuscripts—a question which has led to discussions as eager, as interminable, and nearly as profitless, as those about the authorship of the letters of "Junius," "Ossian" may almost be called an epoch-making poem. It attracted profound attention both in this country and abroad, and the work, which has been admired by critics so keen-sighted and able as Goethe and Mr. Matthew Arnold, deserved better treatment at the hands of Macaulay than to be spoken of with ill-judging and unintelligent contempt. Descriptions of Nature in her wildest and stormiest aspects, as seen beneath a lowering and tempest-tossed sky, in the most barren and desolate mountain solitudes, afforded quite a new sensation to readers of the Georgian era. Goethe, in the thirteenth book of his "Dichtung und Wahrheit," while recording the state of mind which led him to the composition of "Werther," and which, being generally prevalent, brought about the great enthusiasm with which that book was received, says, speaking of the fondness for gloomy literature and the feeling of melancholy dissatisfaction which then pervaded many youthful minds: "And that to all this melancholy a perfectly suitable locality might not be wanting, Ossian had charmed us even to the *Ultima Thule*, where on a grey, boundless heath, wandering among prominent moss-covered gravestones, we saw the grass around us moved by an awful wind, and a heavily clouded sky above us. It was not till moonlight that the Caledonian night became day; departed heroes, faded maidens, floated around us, until at last we really thought we saw the spirit of Lodo in his fearful form." Something of the spirit of "Ossian" animates the pseudo-antique "Mediæval Romances" (1768) of Thomas Chatterton—

> "The marvellous boy,
> The sleepless soul that perished in his pride,"—

the story of whose stormy and ill-regulated life and tragic death by suicide, at the age of seventeen, is one of the most touching and melancholy pages of literary history. How powerfully the tide was turning in the direction of our older literature is clearly proved by the fact that in no age has the imitation of Spenser been more common than during the eighteenth century.[1] The "Schoolmistress" (1742), incomparably the finest poem of William Shenstone, and the "Minstrel" (1774) of James Beattie, at one time Professor of Moral Philosophy at Aberdeen, are both written in the Spenserian stanza. Beattie was a genuine poet, though not a very great one, and his descriptions of natural scenery and of the more delicate human emotions are drawn with loving sympathy and

[1] This fact is pointed out in an able and instructive article on "English Poetry from Dryden to Cowper" in the *Quarterly Review* for July 1862.

insight. In his own time he was more celebrated as the author of the "Essay on Truth" (a reply to the philosophical speculations of Hume regarding miracles) than as the writer of the "Minstrel"—a curious instance of how incorrect contemporary judgments may be. The "Essay on Truth," though extravagantly praised by Dr. Johnson and many other celebrated men of the time, and read with great admiration by that worthy monarch, George III., who bestowed a pension on its orthodox author, has long since taken its due place as a weak and insufficient handling of an important and difficult theme; while the "Minstrel" still retains its far from unimportant place in the history of English poetry.

Another poet, of a much more unique genius than Beattie, was William Blake (1757-1828), who occupies a place by himself among the forerunners of the new era. Charles Lamb rightly regarded him as "one of the most extraordinary personages of the age," for both as poet and painter his work was altogether original. His "Poetical Sketches," published in 1777, bear trace of the reviving influence of the Elizabethan poets; and the union of simplicity of language with truly poetical thoughts upon ordinary subjects in them and in his "Songs of Innocence and of Experience, Shewing the Two Contrary States of the Human Soul," anticipate Wordsworth. Blake's reputation stands much higher now than it did during his life, or for some time after his death. Of late years, the enthusiasm of many writers of high culture, who have found in him a vein of power marking him off from his contemporaries, have done much to bring into vogue the drawings and the poetry of this strange child of genius.[1]

[1] The "Poetical Sketches" are all the more remarkable when we remember that they were written between the twelfth and the twentieth year of his age. "Blake, in truth, when in his teens," says Mr. W. M. Rossetti (Prefatory Memoir to the Aldine Edition of Blake, p. cxv.), "was a wholly unique poet; far ahead of his contemporaries, and of his predecessors of three or four generations, equally in what he himself could do, and in his sympathy for olden sources of inspiration. In his fragmentary drama of 'Edward the Third' we recognise one who has loved and studied Shakespeare to good purpose; and several of the shorter lyrics in the

Such is a brief outline of the more prominent minor poets of the latter part of the eighteenth century. We now come to William Cowper, whose character, alike as a man and a poet, is a singularly interesting and attractive one. A man of genius, but not of very powerful or original genius; full of good taste, and grace, and tenderness, but almost altogether destitute of fire and passion; fond of the country and of country things, yet far from being imbued with Wordsworth's passionate love of Nature, he was not at all the sort of writer whom we should expect to be one of the leaders in a literary revolution. Yet this position Cowper unconsciously occupied, partly by natural genius, partly by the accidents of his career. The story of his life, darkened as it was by frequent thunderclouds of insanity, through which the blue sky of hope was unable to pierce, is a very touching one. Born in 1731, a descendant of an ancient family, which ranked not a few distinguished names among its members, the shrinking, sensitive boy had early experience of those hardships of life which he was so ill fitted to struggle against. At an elementary school to which he was sent, he was brutally tormented by one of the boys, whom he held in such dread that he did not dare to lift his eyes to his face, and knew him best by his shoe-buckle. Removed from this school, Cowper's spirits recovered their tone, and at the age of ten he was sent to Westminster, where he seems to have led a happy life enough, not studying very hard, but acquiring a competent knowledge of Greek and Latin, and distinguishing himself as a cricketer and football-player. After leaving Westminster, he was entered of the Inner Temple, and passed three very pleasant and very idle years as a law-clerk, making love to his cousin Theodora, and associating much with Edward Thurlow,

'Poetical Sketches' have the same sort of pungent perfume—undefinable but not evanescent—that belongs to the choicest Elizabethan songs; the like play of emotion,—or play of colour, as it might be termed; the like ripeness and roundness, poetic, and intolerant of translation into prose. At the time when Blake wrote these songs, and for a long while before, no one was doing anything at all of the same kind. Not but that, even in Blake, lines and words occur here and there betraying the *fadeur* of the eighteenth century."

who, though insubordinate and fond of amusement and dissipation, already gave signs of that strength of character and power of strenuous exertion which afterwards made him Lord Chancellor. When, in 1752, Cowper, his clerkship over, went into residence at the Temple, the seclusion of his abode so weighed on him as to bring on the first of those fits of deep melancholy which afterwards darkened into madness. A prolonged residence in the country cured him; and on his return to London in 1754, he was called to the Bar. But his illness put an end to his hopes of marrying Theodora Cowper. Her father refused to sanction the engagement, and Theodora and Cowper never saw each other again. But in both of them the old love remained deeply rooted till the close of their lives: Theodora, who never married, fondly treasured up the letters and poems she had received from Cowper, and always took the warmest interest in his welfare.

During the years he spent in the character of a briefless barrister, Cowper made his first attempts at literature by contributing a few papers to the *Connoisseur* and the *St. James's Chronicle*, then under the management of certain of his friends. But his contributions put no money into his pocket, and as his father's death in 1756 had left him poor, he was obliged to look to the more influential members of his family for aid. In 1763 the offices of Clerk of the Journals, Reading Clerk, and Clerk of Committees of the House of Lords became vacant; and Major Cowper, in whose disposal they were, offered the two latter to his cousin. The offer was accepted—unfortunately, as it proved. Their duties required that Cowper should frequently appear before the House of Lords, and the thought of doing so was so abhorrent to his retiring, nervous nature, that he almost immediately resigned them, accepting instead the office of Clerk of Journals. But in this case the Major's right to nominate was questioned, and Cowper was called upon to submit to the ordeal of an examination at the bar of the House before being allowed to take office. "To require from me," he says in his Autobiography, "my attendance at the bar of the House, that I might there publicly entitle myself to the office, was in effect to exclude me from it. In the meantime, the interest of my friend, the honour of his choice, my own reputation and circumstances, all pressed me to undertake that which I saw was impracticable." A fearful mental struggle, during which he several times attempted suicide, ensued, and ended in his becoming quite insane. He was placed in an asylum, where, under kindly and judicious treatment, he gradually recovered, after a residence of about a year and a half.

It was now, of course, painfully obvious to all Cowper's friends that he was totally unfit for an active life. They accordingly subscribed together to make him an annual allowance, and a quiet lodging was procured for him in the town of Huntingdon, where he went to reside in 1765. After a few months' experience of housekeeping, he found that he would live much more economically and comfortably if he became a boarder in some suitable family; and towards the end of the year became a lodger in the family of the Rev. John Unwin, the clergyman of the place. He soon became very much attached to the Unwins, who were excellent and cultivated people, and his attachment was reciprocated. In 1767 Mr. Unwin was killed by a fall from his horse, and the household was broken up. Mrs. Unwin had to remove, and Cowper, to whom her behaviour had "always been that of a mother to a son," determined to accompany her. Shortly after Unwin's death, the Rev. John Newton, Rector of Olney, in Buckinghamshire, had called on Mrs. Unwin, and promised to look out a house for her at Olney. To Olney, accordingly, in September 1767, she and Cowper removed.

Now began Cowper's connection with Newton, which exercised a powerful, and, upon the whole, an unfortunate influence on his life. No two men could well be imagined more different than the shrinking, nervous, desponding poet, and the strong-minded, strong-willed, energetic Rector of Olney. Newton had in his youth been a sailor, of wild and dissipated habits, but a narrow escape from death changed his character, and he became a highly religious man, of strong Calvinistic opinions. For some time he was master of a vessel engaged in the slave-trade, but ill-health brought his life as a sailor to an end; and, after many difficulties, he was in 1764 ordained to the curacy of Olney. Cowper and he soon became fast friends, and in 1771 Newton proposed that they should write together a volume of hymns. But ere it was completed, Cowper, harassed by religious doubts and difficulties, again became insane. For four years his mental derangement continued, but at length, largely owing to the assiduous attention of Mrs Unwin, light dawned upon his troubled faculties. The "Olney Hymns" were published in 1779, Cowper's poems being distinguished by the letter C. Many of them are beautiful, and have passed into universal use, but the despairing tone of some shows the mental anguish which Cowper went through at the time of their composition. In 1779, also, Newton left Olney, an event which probably may be regarded as conducive to Cowper's happiness; as Newton's austere Calvinism was ill adapted to deal with the terrible religious doubts which often beset the clouded mind of the poet.

In 1780 Mrs. Unwin suggested to Cowper that he should employ his mind by engaging in the composition of some work of greater importance than he had yet attempted. He consented, and in a few months the "Progress of Error," "Truth," "Table-Talk," and "Expostulation," were completed. These, together with some shorter poems, of which "Hope" and "Charity" are the most important, were published in 1782. They attracted little attention among readers in general, but had the good fortune to win the favourable opinion of Benjamin Franklin, one of the most sagacious men of his time. Soon after, at the suggestion of Lady Austen, a widow, who had come to reside near Olney, and who soon became a great friend of the poet, Cowper began his greatest work, "The Task." It was published in 1785, along with some other poems, including the famous "John Gilpin," which also owed its origin to a suggestion of Lady Austen. It met with a most enthusiastic reception, putting Cowper at once at the head of the poets of the age.

About a year before the publication of "The Task," Cowper began the last great work of his life, his translation of Homer. It was interrupted in 1787 by an attack of insanity, during which he attempted to commit suicide; but at length, in 1791, it was completed and published. Much truer to the original than Pope's version, it wants the interest and animation which characterise the latter translation; and while it always has been and always will be a favourite with scholars who can appreciate its fidelity, it will never be popular among the large class of unlearned readers, for whose sake mainly translations are issued. In 1796 Cowper's best friend, Mrs. Unwin, died. He had attended her with loving devotion during a long illness, and when the end came, his grief was terrible. He sank into a state of hopeless despondency, which continued till the end of his life. His last poem, "The Castaway," in which we hear "no throb of sorrow, only the cry of despair," was written on March 20, 1800. On the 25th April of the same year his troubled spirit found peace in death.

A man of gentle, loving nature, endowed in his better moments with much sound sense and genial humour, surrounded by friends who liked and respected him, fond of simple pleasures and of cheerful company, Cowper, had it not been for the mysterious malady which wasted his life, might have lived very happily. His spotless moral character and deep religious feelings, his childlike playfulness, his simplicity and naturalness, have combined to make him one of the most lovable figures in the history of English poetry. It is rather a puzzling question to decide how far his attractive personality and his attitude towards Christianity have influenced his literary position. "Any one," says Mr. Goldwin Smith in his monograph on Cowper, "whose lot it is to write upon the life and works of Cowper must feel that there is an immense difference between the interest which attaches to him and that which attaches to any one among the far greater poets of the succeeding age. Still there is something about him so attractive, his voice has such a silver tone, he retains, even in his ashes, such a faculty of winning friends, that his biographer and critic may be easily beguiled into giving him too high a place. He belongs to a particular religious movement, with the vitality of which the interest of a great part of his works has departed, or is departing. Still more emphatically, and in a still more important sense, does he belong to Christianity. In no natural struggle for existence would he have been the survivor; by no natural process of selection would he ever have been picked out as a vessel of honour. If the shield which for eighteen centuries Christ by His teaching and His death has spread over the weak things of this world should fail, and might should again become the title to existence and the measure of worth, Cowper will be cast aside as a specimen of despicable inferiority, and all who have said anything in his praise will be treated with the same scorn." In this there is a good deal of truth mixed up with a large amount of exaggeration. No doubt some portion of Cowper's popularity has been brought about by the fact that he is a distinctively *Christian* poet. Until comparatively late years he was almost the only poet who found any considerable favour among Evangelical circles; and even yet many people read his poetry, and recommend it to others, not owing to its excellence as poetry, but because of its religious and moral tone. No doubt, also, it is true that Cowper not unfrequently wrote verses which would have come with better grace from the pen of his friend Hayley, that type of poetical mediocrity. But, nevertheless, Cowper owes his high position in literature not to any adventitious cause, but on account of his intrinsic merits. In an age steeped in conventionality, he was natural and unconventional. His powers of simple pathos, as exemplified in his "Lines to Mary Unwin" and to his "Mother's Picture," are almost unsurpassed; and in his humorous and didactic poems he shows a shrewdness, a knowledge of human nature, a command of genial sarcasm, which prove that, secluded as his life for the most part was, he was a keen and accurate observer of men and things. He, first of the English poets, brought men back from the town to the country. "His landscape, no doubt, was the tame one of the English Midland Counties; there was in it nothing of the stern wild joy of the mountains. His sentiments moved among the household sympathies, not the stormy passions. But in Cowper's power of simple narrative and truthful descriptions, in his natural pathos and religious feeling, more truly than elsewhere may be discovered the dawn of that new poetic era with which this century began." Nor, in appraising Cowper's literary merits, should we forget his exquisite letters, the finest specimens of epistolary composition the English language affords. Their beauty and vivacity, their ease and humour, their purity and tenderness, combine to render them inapproachable in their own sphere.

Even Cowper's warmest admirers are obliged to confess that he was deficient in force and passion. His vein of poetical genius was a real one, but it was rather a tranquil stream, unruffled save when a cry of emotion broke from his overburdened heart, than an overflowing and irresistible current. He rarely or never seems to have felt that divine and unrestrainable impulse to sing which has possessed many poets. Very different was the case with Robert Burns, undoubtedly the most richly dowered by nature of all the poets of the eighteenth century. Born in 1759, in Alloway, Ayrshire, the son of a small farmer, his youth was spent in toil and poverty. Such slender educational facilities, however, as were afforded him he availed himself of to the fullest extent; and he fostered his genius by the perusal of such poems as fell in his way—old ballads, the works of Allan Ramsay, of Robert Fergusson, another Scotch poet, &c. Another equally important part of his poetical education must not be passed over. "In my infant and boyish days," he says, "I owed much to an old woman who resided in the family, remarkable for her ignorance, credulity, and superstition. She had, I suppose, the largest collection in the country of tales and songs concerning devils, ghosts, fairies, brownies, witches, warlocks, spunkies, kelpies, elf-candles, dead-lights, wraiths, apparitions, cantrips, giants, enchanted towers, dragons, and other trumpery. This cultivated the latent seeds of poetry; but had so strong an effect upon my imagination, that to this hour, in my nocturnal rambles, I sometimes keep a sharp look-out in suspicious places; and though nobody can be more sceptical than I am in such matters, yet it often takes an effort of philosophy to shake off these idle terrors." Strong evidence this of both the precocity and the strength of Burns's imaginative genius.

As from his poetic temperament may easily be supposed, Burns early began to write verses. His first composition was the lines commencing, "Oh, once I loved a bonnie lassie," written in his fifteenth year, and addressed to a girl whom he had worked alongside of in the harvest-field. Few and fleeting were the pleasures that visited him while as a youth he toiled on his father's farm, leading a life combining, as he afterwards bitterly said, "the cheerless gloom of a hermit with the unceasing moil of a galley-slave." As he grew up, he felt the degradations and hardships incident to his lot more and more galling. Conscious, no doubt, as he could not but be conscious, of his great natural endowments, finding no fit scope for their exercise, with no bright prospect before him to encourage him to bear cheerfully the ills which at last he would triumphantly vanquish, it is no wonder though Burns, with his effervescing passions, his naturally high animal spirits, and his love of society, should, as he approached manhood, have sought to drown the sense of his troubles by indulging pretty freely in conviviality in jovial social gatherings. The life and soul of every company into which he went, his society was much sought after, and by degrees he began to acquire that fatal love of dissipation from which he never got free.

Meanwhile all attempts he made to better his condition proved unfortunate. Thinking to commence business as a flax-dresser, he took a share of a shop in Irvine, but the enterprise did not succeed, and was soon put a final end to, the shop catching fire and being burned to the ground. After the father's death in 1784, the Burns family removed to Mossgiel, and stocked a farm with their individual savings; but bad seed and bad harvests played havoc with their hopes, and Robert, who had worked very assiduously for a time at the new farm, became more discontented with his lot than ever. His unfortunate connection with Jean Armour, and her father's refusal to allow her to marry him, was the crowning ingredient in his cup of sorrows. Carlyle in his fine essay has well described the condition of Burns at this time. "He loses his feeling of innocence; his mind is at variance with itself; the old divinity no longer presides there; but wild desires and repentance alternately oppress him. Ere long, too, he has committed himself before the world; his character for sobriety, dear to a Scottish peasant as few corrupted worldlings can even conceive, is destroyed in the eyes of men, and his only refuge consists in trying to disbelieve his guiltiness, and is but a refuge of lies. The blackest desperation now gathers over him, broken only by red lightnings of remorse." He determined to go abroad, and in order to defray the expenses of his passage to the West Indies, where he had accepted a situation as book-keeper, was advised to publish his poems. He agreed to do so, and in 1786 an impression of six hundred copies was struck off at Kilmarnock.

The sensation produced by the volume was immense. Among the class to which Burns himself belonged it was received with rapturous enthusiasm. They recognised in the author a poet, one of themselves in his feelings and sympathies and aspirations, but lifted far above them by his genius, and able to give fit utterance to sentiments and opinions which lay concealed in their own breasts, but to which they were powerless to give expression. The demand for copies was eager; many peasants denied themselves other luxuries in order to procure the cherished volume; and Burns had the satisfaction of clearing about twenty pounds by his venture. But the admiration excited by the poems was not confined to his own circle. Copies found their way to the "Modern Athens," as Edinburgh proudly called itself, with perhaps a better title to the name then than it has now; and just as Burns was on the eve of setting out to a distant land, his plans were suddenly altered by a letter a friend of his received from Dr. Blacklock (a blind poet, of powers slightly superior to mediocrity), giving it as his opinion that Burns should go to Edinburgh and issue a second edition of his poems. To Edinburgh accordingly he went, and the admiration of his powers, which had been excited in the breasts of many there by the perusal of his poems, suffered no abatement when their author appeared on the scene. He comported himself like a man conscious of his own talents; in no way overawed by the crowd of scholars and professors with whom he was brought into contact. "He manifested," as Lockhart says, "in the whole strain of his bearing and conversation a most thorough conviction that in the society of the most eminent men of his nation he was exactly where he was entitled to be; hardly deigned to flatter them by exhibiting even an occasional symptom of being flattered by their notice; by turns calmly measured himself against the most cultivated understandings of his time in discussion, overpowered the *bon-mots* of the most celebrated convivialists by broad floods of merriment, impregnated with all the burning life of genius; astounded bosoms habitually enveloped in the thrice-piled folds of social reserve by compelling them to tremble—nay, to tremble visibly—beneath the fearless touch of natural pathos." Subscriptions to the second edition of the poems poured in liberally, and by its publication in 1787 the poet realised a sum which to him must have appeared an almost inexhaustible treasury of wealth.

Out of the money thus earned, Burns generously advanced £200 to help his brother Gilbert, then struggling to maintain himself and other members of the family at Mossgiel. With the remainder he stocked a farm for himself at Ellisland, about six miles from Dumfries; and being now in a more prosperous worldly condition, was able, in 1788, to marry his old sweetheart, Jean Armour. Soon after he obtained, through the kindness of a friend, a position in the Excise, with a salary of £50 a year at first, but afterwards increased to £70. The duties of his office led him into many temptations to indulge in those convivial pleasures to which by nature he was only too prone to yield. He neglected his farm, and in 1792 was obliged to give it up altogether and remove to Dumfries. His hopes of promotion in the Excise were blasted by his habit of freely speaking his mind regarding dignities, and by his ardent sympathy with the French Revolution and advanced liberal opinions generally; for, like most of his class then and now, Burns was a thorough Radical in politics. His last important work in literature was a hundred songs, which he contributed gratuitously to his friend Thompson's "Melodies of Scotland," published in 1792. The closing years of Burns's life were clouded with sorrow and suffering, partly the results of his own misconduct, partly of causes over which he had no control. His brief and troubled career came to a close in 1796.

Burns may be best contemplated under two aspects. First, there is Robert Burns the Scotch ploughman, with the faults and the virtues belonging to his class; honest, manly, vigorous, but lacking in self-restraint; an easy prey to his passions; not altogether superior to that sort of cant which consists in endeavouring to compensate for one's most serious and often-repeated errors by loud declarations of the goodness of one's heart however faulty one's life may be; and fond to excess of every kind of rough fun, practical jokes, and conviviality. Next, there is Robert Burns the poet, with a heart full of love and reverence for all created beings; tender towards the "ourie cattle" and the "silly sheep;" so full of charity that he can breathe an expression of hope even for "Auld Nickie Ben" himself; so full of sympathy with all sides of human nature, that he is equally at home in depicting the decent "Cottar's Saturday Night" and the wild revelry of the vagabond "Jolly Beggars;" skilled alike to cause his readers to laugh and to weep—now producing merriment, not unmingled with a sort of astonishment and awe, by the strange adventure of "Tam o' Shanter," now irresistibly touching our more tender feelings by the simple and affecting pathos of such verses as those "To Mary in Heaven." Not that Burns kept his poems altogether pure from the defilements with which, from his character as a man and from his position in society, we should expect to find them occasionally stained; with sorrow it must be said he did not always refrain from touching with the orient gold of his genius the bestial side of man. But when all the circumstances of his birth and career are considered, he would be a foolish and purblind critic who should condemn Burns too severely for his occasional transgressions against decorum and good taste. His work is fragmentary—as a rule, mere snatches of song thrown off at idle moments when the impulse seized him; but how full of variety it is, how rich is the evidence it affords of great intellectual resource and versatility! Many other poets have excelled Burns in depicting particular emotions, but how few there are who like him have attained equal mastery in the expression of various states of feeling! Whether writing songs of love or lyrics of war, whether serious or humorous, he is equally at home, and uniformly displays that almost infallible mark of a good poet, the power of so choosing the rhythm and words of his verse as to be an echo to the sense. He never attempted a large continuous work, and we can form but little conception how he would have succeeded in the enterprise if he had attempted it. The probability is that he did wisely in confining himself to lyrics and occasional pieces. Taking quantity and quality both into account, he may be unhesitatingly pronounced the greatest song-writer in the language.

A less important figure in the history of poetry than Cowper or Burns, yet neither an unimportant nor an insignificant one, is George Crabbe, "Nature's sternest painter, yet the best," as Byron with considerable truth described him. During his long life, extending from 1754 to 1832, he witnessed many fluctuations of literary taste, and was acquainted with great writers belonging to two widely different eras. Befriended in his youth by Burke and Lord Chancellor Thurlow, he lived to win the applause of Jeffrey, and Christopher North, and Sir Walter Scott; and he whose early works had the honour of being read, and admired, and corrected by Johnson and Fox, found his fame so far undimmed, even amidst the bright constellation of poetic stars which shone in the beginning of the present century, as to receive in 1819 the sum of £3000 for his "Tales of the Hall" and the copyright of his other poems. Crabbe's chief works besides the "Tales of the Hall" are the "Village" (1783), the "Parish Register" (1807), the "Borough" (1810), and "Tales in Verse" (1812). Of a matter-of-fact imagination, with a passion for details, closely adhering to facts, and never throwing any poetical glamour over his tales and descriptions of vice, and poverty, and misery, Crabbe in his main features is thoroughly original. He "handles life so as to take the bloom off it," describing "with a hard, resolute pen, idealising nothing; but, on the contrary, often omitting all that casts a veil over meanness and deformity." It is this firm adherence to relentless truth that constitutes at once his weakness and his strength. He never shuts his eyes to plain facts; and although in his youth he had had bitter experience of poverty, and might therefore have been more disposed to sympathise with poor people than with the wealthier classes, he perceived quite clearly that vice, and meanness, and evil passions might have their abode as well in the breast of Hodge the labourer, toiling hard to earn a scanty pittance, as in the breast of Squire Hazeldean, brought up in the lap of wealth and luxury. But his range of vision was narrow; he had little sympathy with the idyllic aspects of life; he lacked humour and genial sympathy; and in his pathos often by too forcible expression overstepped the limits of literary art. The main characteristics of his writings are well indicated by Mr. W. C. Roscoe.[1] "The common feature throughout all his works which gives this author his hold upon his readers is his singular insight into the minute working of character, his wondrous familiarity with so vast a number of various dispositions, and the unerring fidelity with which he traces their operations and discerns their attitudes under every sort of circumstance. It would be difficult in the whole range of literature to point to more than two or three who have rivalled him in this respect. Chaucer is one; and a curious and not uninteresting comparison might be instituted between the two, though the old poet far surpasses the modern one in love of beauty, liveliness of fancy, and breadth of genius. . . . One

[1] "Poems and Essays," vol. ii. p. 220.

great source of his strength is, that he dared to be true to himself, and to work with unhesitating confidence in his own peculiar vein. This originality is not only great, but always genuine. A never-failing charm lies in the clear simplicity and truthfulness of nature which shines through all his writings. Nothing false or meretricious ever came from his pen; and if his works want order and beauty, neither they nor his life are destitute of the higher harmony which springs from a character naturally single and undeteriorated by false aims and broken purposes."

Modern as Cowper, Burns, and Crabbe are in their poetic tendencies, they do not affect us in the same way as the poets who occupy the rest of this chapter. It cannot be said of them, as of Wordsworth, Keats, Byron, and the others, that they are still active factors in our literature, influencing profoundly the poets of the age we live in. We may begin our survey with the group called the Lake School, of which the most prominent members were Wordsworth, Coleridge, and Southey. The nickname "Lake School," given them because Wordsworth and Southey most of their lives, and Coleridge for a time, lived in the Lake district, is not an appropriate one, for Wordsworth's best poems are different in character from Coleridge's, and Southey, either as regards genius or in mode of literary treatment, cannot be ranked with the two others. But they were intimate friends, endeared by family relationships and by mutual sympathy and admiration, and it is therefore convenient in many respects to treat of them together. Of this group, the first, both in point of time and in point of genius, was William Wordsworth. He was born at Cockermouth in 1770, the son of an attorney who superintended part of the Lowther estate in Cumberland. Exposed from his youth to the influence of sublime and ennobling scenery, Wordsworth spent a happy childhood, not manifesting any extraordinary precocity of genius, but even from his earliest years imbued with that deep love of Nature which was afterwards to bear such magnificent fruit. In 1783 his father died, leaving £5000 in the hands of Sir James

Lowther, afterwards Earl of Londsdale, from whom it was found impossible to obtain it. By his successor it was in 1801 repaid with interest; but in the meantime the Wordsworth family was left poor, and William owed his university education to the liberality of his uncles. He entered St. John's College, Cambridge, in his eighteenth year. To the ordinary studies of the place he paid little more attention than enabled him, in 1791, to take his degree of B.A.; but he studied Italian and the works of the greatest English poets, and acquired a rich store of new ideas by a pedestrian tour with a friend Jones, in 1790, through France, Switzerland, and the North of Italy. After leaving the University, he spent some time in London, living on an allowance from his friends, and without any definite aim. He then, in 1791, went over to Paris, at that time in the heat of the Revolution frenzy. Like Southey and Coleridge, Wordsworth in his youth shared the golden hopes of universal emancipation then current among many men, and at one time even had serious intentions of becoming naturalised as a Frenchman in order to take part in the great struggle. His friends, it appears, had more sense of the dangers to which he was thinking of exposing himself than he had, and in 1792 prudently recalled him to England by stopping the supplies. Of the many enthusiasts whose hearts were chilled and whose hopes of a new era for humanity were rudely shattered by the bloody massacres and cruelty of the French Revolution in its latter stages, none was more deeply affected than Wordsworth, and it took a considerable time to heal the wound thus caused.

In 1792 Wordsworth began his literary career by the publication of two poems, "The Evening Walk" and "Descriptive Sketches." They did not attract much attention, but Coleridge had the sagacity to see in them the promise of better things, and that they announced "the emergence of an original poetic genius above the literary horizon." But the poet had as yet earned nothing, and was now obliged to bestir himself to obtain some field of labour. He thought of joining the newspaper press, and had actually written to a friend asking him to find him a situation of this nature, when he was rendered comparatively easy as to money matters by a legacy of £900 left him in 1795 by his friend and adviser, Raisley Calvert. Upon this sum Wordsworth and his gifted and devoted sister, Dorothy, set up housekeeping. They first settled at Racedown in Dorsetshire, where Wordsworth wrote some of his early poems, and where he became acquainted with Coleridge. Soon after, in the autumn of 1797, the Wordsworths removed to Alfoxden, near the village of Nether Stowey in Somersetshire, where Coleridge was then staying. Here Coleridge and Wordsworth saw much of each other, and spent many pleasant and profitable hours in discussing the principles of poetry and in planning the pieces composing the volume of "Lyrical Ballads," published in 1798. Most of the little book was Wordsworth's; but Coleridge contributed to it that priceless gem, the "Ancient Mariner." Wordsworth's share comprised some poems which were justly liable to ridicule, such as "Goody Blake" and the "Idiot Boy," but it also comprised such fine pieces as "Expostulation and Reply," and the immortal "Lines Written above Tintern Abbey," dear to the hearts of all who reverence his memory. After the publication of the "Ballads," Wordsworth and his sister spent a winter in Germany, where he began the "Prelude," and wrote some of the best of his shorter poems. Soon after his return to England, the poet took a cottage at Grasmere, and there entered upon his life in the Lake country, almost every notable spot of which he has celebrated in his poems. In the beginning of the century he received his share of his father's money, which had been honourably paid by the new Marquis of Lonsdale, and was thus, in 1802, enabled to marry, the object of his choice being Mary Hutchison, whom he describes in the often-quoted lines—

> "A creature not too bright or good
> For human nature's daily food;
> A perfect woman, nobly planned,
> To warn, to comfort, and command;
> And yet a spirit still, and bright
> With something of an angel light."

Such is a hurried outline of the principal events in Wordsworth's early life. The main features of the rest of his career can be only briefly alluded to. Of external events of general interest his life does not afford many. His is pre-eminently the history of a mind. No poet ever lived who cherished a more intense and thoroughgoing devotion to his art; under all circumstances of his life it was the uppermost thing in his thoughts, and to it everything else was made subservient. In 1802 he published another volume of "Lyrical Ballads," containing, with two volumes of "Poems" published in 1807, the cream of his poetry; for, as Mr. Matthew Arnold has pointed out, almost all Wordsworth's really first-rate work was produced between 1798 and 1808. Jeffrey, a shrewd enough critic within a certain range, but apt to make terrible blunders when dealing with high-class works of the imagination, attacked the "Ballads" in the *Edinburgh Review;* and so powerful were then the critical dicta of that organ, that his criticism almost entirely stopped the sale. But Wordsworth's serene self-confidence enabled him to bear up manfully against criticism from whatever quarter, however unjust or injurious. He knew well that all writers of commanding originality have to labour on till they educate the public sufficiently to appreciate their work, and was quite content to write what he was fully assured would be both unpopular and immortal.

In 1813 Wordsworth removed to Rydal Mount, his residence for the remainder of his life. About the same time he was, through the influence of Lord Lonsdale, appointed to the almost sinecure office of Distributor of Stamps for the county of Westmoreland, with a yearly salary of £500. In 1814 he published his largest, but by no means his greatest work, the "Excursion." Long though the "Excursion" is, it is only part of a greater design thus described in its preface: "Several years ago, when the author retired to his native mountains with the hope of being enabled to construct a literary work that might live, it was a reasonable thing that he should take a review of his own mind, and examine how far nature and education had qualified him for such an employment. As subsidiary to this preparation, he undertook to record in verse the origin and progress of his own powers, so far as he was acquainted with them. That work, addressed to a dear friend most distinguished for his knowledge and genius, and to whom the author's intellect is deeply indebted [Coleridge], has been long finished, and the result of the investigation which gave rise to it was a determination to compose a philosophical poem, containing views of man, nature, and society, and to be entitled the 'Recluse.'" Of the "Recluse," which was to consist of three books, the "Excursion" was to form the second, but the design was never completed. The biographical poem referred to above, which "conducts the history of the author's mind to the point where he was emboldened to hope that his faculties were sufficiently matured for entering upon the arduous labour which he proposed to himself," was completed in 1806, but not published till 1850, when it appeared under the title of the "Recluse."

Many other poems, among which "The White Doe of Rylstone" (1815), and the "Ecclesiastical Sonnets," are not of great poetical value, but interesting as showing how thorough a Churchman and Conservative the quondam ardent sympathiser with the French Revolution had become, may be specially mentioned, were published by Wordsworth during the remaining years of his life. Gradually the taste for his poetry began to spread; he lived to witness the rise and fall of the overwhelming popularity of Scott and Byron; and the storm of applause which greeted him when, in 1839, he appeared in the Sheldonian Theatre at Oxford to receive the degree of Doctor of Laws, showed he was the favourite poet of, at all events, the rising generation. In 1842 he received a pension of £300 a year, and in the following year succeeded Southey as Poet-Laureate—rewards righteously earned, and bestowed with well-nigh universal approval. He died in 1850.

Wordsworth did not consider poetry a mere instrument of pleasure, a thing to be read or written in hours of relaxation. To him it was an art—the highest of all arts—to which life might be profitably devoted, and in the exercise of which no pains were to be grudged by the singer gifted with the divine faculty of imagination. To his principles regarding this matter his practice fully corresponded. He was constantly meditating on his art, and gathering together materials for its exercise. For books he cared little, and most of his literary judgments were narrow and prejudiced. Of contemporary poets, the only one whom he at all cordially appreciated was Coleridge; Scott and Southey he did not think highly of; Shelley and Byron he knew only slightly; Keats not at all. His study was in the open air; his sources of inspiration caught from wandering to and fro amid the beautiful scenery of the Lake district. "Nine-tenths of my verses," said the poet in 1843, "have been murmured out in the open air. One day a stranger, having walked round the garden and grounds of Rydal Mount, asked of one of the female servants who happened to be at the door permission to see her master's study. 'This,' said she, leading him forward, 'is my master's library, where he keeps his books, but his study is out of doors.' After a long absence from home, it has more than once happened that some one of my cottage neighbours has said, 'Well, there he is! We are glad to hear him *booing* about again.'" It was a natural result of his self-contained and independent mode of life acting upon a mind constitutionally self-confident that Wordsworth should have a very high opinion of his own works. No false delicacy restrained him from praising them himself when occasion offered. For example, when Harriet Martineau told him that his "Happy Warrior" was a favourite poem of Dr. Channing's: "Ay," replied Wordsworth, "that was not on account of the *poetical conditions* being best fulfilled in that poem, but because it is" (solemnly) "a chain of extremely valooable thoughts; you see it does not best fulfil the conditions of poetry, but it is" (solemnly) "a chain of extremely valooable thoughts." Considering the high estimate Wordsworth had of his own powers and the fixity with which he clung to his own opinions, it is not surprising that he should have had a strong tendency to think everything he wrote equally good. Unlike many great poets, he was quite unconscious when his flow of inspiration ceased; and hence it is that, especially in his longer poems, there are so many tedious passages. It is this probably more than any other single cause that has tended to retard Wordsworth's popularity. He is an unequal poet—capable of rising to great heights, capable, also, it must be said, of sinking to great depths of prosiness and dulness. No one can read the "Excursion" without being painfully impressed by the contrast between the sublimity and beauty of certain passages and the flatness and insipidity of others.

None the less is Wordsworth indisputably a poet of the first rank. With him originated an altogether new way of looking at Nature. To him Nature was not a dead machine; it was alive. He felt that behind the colours and forms and sounds of the material universe there was something more than meets the external senses, "something which defies analysis, undefined and ineffable, which must be felt and perceived by the soul." "I have learned," he says in the "Lines on Tintern Abbey"—

> "To look on Nature, not as in the hour
> Of thoughtless youth; but hearing oftentimes
> The still, sad music of humanity,
> Nor harsh, nor grating, though of ample power
> To chasten and subdue. And I have felt
> A presence that disturbs me with the joy
> Of elevated thoughts; a sense sublime
> Of something far more deeply interfused,
> Whose dwelling is the light of setting suns,
> And the round ocean, and the living air,
> And the blue sky, and in the mind of man;
> A motion, and a spirit, that impels
> All thinking objects, all objects of all thought,
> And rolls through all things."

There is nothing like this in the poetry of Cowper, or Burns, or Crabbe; and it is no wonder that this doctrine, deeply as it has influenced literature and thought since, should have proved a stumbling-block to many critics when it was first promulgated. Regarding Nature as no mere collection of isolated phenomena, but as a living and mysterious whole, constantly acting on humanity, Wordsworth found the contemplation even of the "common things that round us lie" full of lessons of instruction and wisdom. To him no natural object was common or unclean; from all spiritual truth was to be extracted. With such a high reverence for Nature, Wordsworth united an equally high reverence for man; the visible universe and its inhabitants were to him alike full of wonder and awe and mystery.

Disgusted at the outset of his life as a poet by the stilted poetical commonplaces which the feeble herd of Pope's imitators had made so nauseous, Wordsworth adopted a theory, fully expounded in various of his prefaces to his poems, that there neither is, nor can be, any essential difference between the language of prose and metrical composition. "I have proposed to myself," he said, "to imitate and, as far as is possible, to adopt the very language of men. . . . I have taken as much pains to avoid what is usually called poetic diction as others ordinarily take to produce it." Except in a few poems which are failures, Wordsworth, however, never acted up to his theory of poetical diction, which, indeed, though correct in so far as it was a protest against the practice, common in his youth, and by no means yet gone into desuetude, of prostituting the name of poetry by bestowing it upon phrases and metaphors hackneyed by a thousand versifiers, was one that could not, and ought not, to have been acted up to.[1] How little he himself, at his best, was affected by it is conclusively shown by his Sonnets, of which, in point of thought and dignity and power, he has written a larger number that are excellent than any other English author. Of the whole collection very few, and these the least excellent, are written in the language of prose.

From Wordsworth, with his blameless life, his sustained

[1] The whole subject is excellently discussed by Coleridge in his "Biographia Literaria."

devotion to poetry, his single aims, his resolute self-confidence, it is in many ways a strange contrast to pass to his friend Samuel Taylor Coleridge, weak and erring, many-sided and fond of trying various fields of literature, changeable and hesitating, fonder of beginning new projects than of finishing old ones. Born in 1772, the son of a clergyman more eccentric even than he himself afterwards proved to be, and educated at Christ's Hospital, where he was the companion of Charles Lamb, and where he showed his life-long addiction to deep meditation and the reading of all sorts of books, Coleridge entered Jesus College, Cambridge, in 1791, a little after Wordsworth quitted the university. Like Wordsworth, Coleridge, while at Cambridge, neglected the studies of the place for those to which he felt himself attracted; he read poetry and philosophy, and ardently perused and discussed all the many pamphlets which came out about the French Revolution, with which, it need scarcely be said, he sympathised greatly. The calm tenor of his college life was interrupted by an extraordinary incident. Depressed by the thought of a debt of £100, which he was unable to pay, he went to London, and enlisted under the name—a very appropriate one—of Private Comberbach. After four months spent in the disagreeable situation of a private soldier, he was recognised by an acquaintance, who informed his friends of his whereabouts. He was then bought off, and returned to Cambridge, which he left in 1794, without taking a degree.

Coleridge's life was a shifty and rather eventful one. We are not going to enter into detail regarding his adventures as Unitarian preacher; his domestic infelicity—mainly caused by himself, it may be said; his slavery for many of the best years of his life to opium; his innumerable magnificent projects, which, alas! generally remained projects. Like that of De Quincey—like, probably, that of most opium-eaters—his true moral character is somewhat of a puzzle. No doubt he did many things which would be considered mean and dishonest if done by ordinary people; but at heart he seems to have been a good man, always ready to acknowledge and repent of his errors, constantly striving after better things, and having his good aims constantly thwarted by his fatal weakness of will. Throughout life he was fortunate in finding friends who loved and aided him, and who were one and all impressed by a deep sense of his wonderful powers. Few men, indeed, have ever lived who have been so much admired by their greatest contemporaries as Coleridge was. "He is the only person I ever knew," said Hazlitt, "who answered to the idea of a man of genius." "I have known many men who have done wonderful things," said Wordsworth, "but the most wonderful man I ever knew was Coleridge." De Quincey called him "the largest and most spacious intellect, the subtlest and most comprehensive, that has yet existed among men." "I am grieved that you never met Coleridge," wrote Southey to Taylor of Norwich; "all other men whom I have ever known are mere children compared to him." Charles Lamb's admiration of his school companion is well known; and Shelley's fine lines—

> "He was a mighty poet and
> A subtle-souled psychologist;
> All things he seemed to understand
> Of old or new, of sea or land,
> But his own mind, which was a mist,"—

are a strong and true testimony to his astonishing powers, which were admired even by those who on many matters of opinion had little sympathy with him. During the last eighteen years of his troubled life-journey he found a safe and comfortable harbour of refuge in the house of Mr. Gilman, a surgeon at Highgate. There he was visited by many admirers, chiefly young men, who listened with wonder and admiration to the oracles which the sage poured forth in an unceasing flow. Among others came Carlyle; but to him the utterances which to not a few seemed almost inspired appeared little better than "transcendental moonshine." Perhaps he, impatient of words which led to nothing clear and definite, judged the old man too harshly; but his incomparably graphic and vivid account of Coleridge's appearance and talk in the

"Life of Sterling" remains by far the most lifelike description we have of the philosopher in his old age.[1]

Coleridge died in 1834, leaving nearly all his most brilliant projects unexecuted, but not without having left conclusive evidence that he was possessed of a genius so profound, so subtle, and so versatile, that if only strength of will had been added to it, he might have been ranked among our very greatest writers. As a poet his total work is not large, and what of it is really excellent might be comprised in a very tiny volume. It is a curious fact that nearly all his best poems, "Genevieve," "Kubla Khan," the "Ancient Mariner," and the first part of "Christabel," were written in a single year, 1797. On the peculiar and universal charm of works so familiar as these it is unnecessary to dwell. Most of his prose works were written after he, in 1816, took up his abode with Mr. Gilman. Among these are two "Lay Sermons," published in 1816 and 1817; the "Biographia Literaria" (1817), perhaps the most generally interesting of his prose works, containing as it does, amidst much irrelevant matter, a great store of valuable criticism and many original and profound observations; a revised and greatly enlarged edition of "The Friend" (1818), "a periodical of weekly essays, intended to help to the formation of opinions on moral, political, and artistic subjects, grounded upon true and permanent principles," carried on by Coleridge, at considerable pecuniary loss, between June 1809 and March 1810; and "Aids to Reflection" (1825). After his death appeared four volumes of "Literary Remains," of which the most valuable portions are the criticisms, often singularly just and subtle, on Shakespeare. By J. S. Mill, Coleridge was ranked with Jeremy Bentham, the Utilitarian thinker, as the great seminal

[1] It is a wonder that in these days of innumerable biographies no one has written a good Life of Coleridge. None such exists; and many particulars regarding his life and character are still shrouded in partial darkness. So many reminiscences, &c., of Coleridge are to be found, that, with the necessary research, a very instructive and entertaining book might be written on the subject.

mind of his generation. No man, Mill declared some forty years ago, did so much to shape the opinions among younger men, who could be said to have any opinions at all. Coleridge may be said to have been the founder of the "Broad Church" School, many of whose earlier representatives could scarcely find words to express their admiration of him as a thinker. "Arnold . . . called him the greatest intellect that England had produced within his memory. . . . Julius Hare spoke of him as 'the great religious philosopher, to whom the mind of our generation in England owes more than to any other man.' . . . Mr. Maurice has everywhere spoken with deeper reverence of him than of any other teacher of these latter times."[1] To Coleridge belonged one of those rare intellects whose products are valuable not so much, it may be, for what they actually express, as because they open up new vistas of thought and speculation which the student may pursue for himself. To this a great part of the extraordinary influence which he at one time exerted is due. His vogue as a thinker has now in great measure gone by; what he did in that way was more adapted to the wants of his own age than to all time; and his style is, like his conversation, apt to be dreamy and long-winded.

Coleridge's eldest son, Hartley (so called after the celebrated philosopher), (1796–1849), deserves a word of mention here, as having inherited a considerable portion of his father's literary genius. Unfortunately, also, he inherited a more than considerable share of his weakness of will. While at the University he became a slave to intemperate habits, and never was able to free himself from the bondage. Of amiable, childlike nature, considerable scholarship, and fine poetic taste, he won the regard and pity of many friends, notably of Wordsworth. Many of his sonnets, especially those relating to himself, are singularly beautiful. His most important prose work is his "Worthies of Yorkshire and Lancashire," containing some excellent biographies. Coleridge's daughter Sara (1802–1852)

[1] Principal Shairp's "Essay on Coleridge," originally published in *North British Review* for December 1865.

had no small share of her father's poetical and philosophical genius, added to scholarship almost unique in a woman.

Robert Southey, the last of the Lake trio, did not approach either of the other two in poetical genius. Indeed, we do not risk much by saying that his poems, with the exception of a few short pieces, which hold their ground in books of extracts, are now almost forgotten. But he has many other claims to remembrance. Master of a prose style clear, simple, and elegant, he takes much higher rank as a prose writer than as a poet, while his pure and blameless life, his large-hearted charity, his unswerving industry, and his intense devotion to literature should keep his memory alive in the hearts of all who can appreciate a true, honest, and courageous life, Southey was born at Bristol in 1774, educated at Westminster and Cambridge, and, like Wordsworth and Coleridge, was in his youth an ardent partisan of the French Revolution and of Radical opinions generally. As he grew older, however, he resembled his friends in veering to the other extreme of the scale; indeed, no more unbending Tory, no more strenuous advocate of "the established constitution in Church and State," could have been found than was in his later years the man who had begun his literary career by the writing in 1794 of a revolutionary poem, "Wat Tyler," published many years later by an unscrupulous bookseller, who wished to annoy the author by taunting him with the opinions he had advocated in his hot youth. While at college Southey also wrote an epic poem, "Joan of Arc," published in 1796. Previous to this date he had become acquainted with Coleridge, and the young men, along with one or two others, had spent much time unprofitably, but no doubt pleasantly, in discussing socialistic schemes, including a "Pantisocracy" on the banks of the Susquehanna, where they could live a pure and innocent life according to Nature, untrammelled by the iron tyranny and conventionalism of the Old World. Want of money put an end to the enterprise, and its only important result was that in 1795 Southey, unknown to his relatives, married Edith Fricker, sister of the wife of one of the "Pantisocrats." Her sister Sarah married

Coleridge. Immediately after the marriage ceremony was over, Southey reluctantly bade his wife farewell, being obliged by dire pecuniary necessity to start for the Continent with his uncle, Mr. Hill. He spent six months in Portugal, thus acquiring that knowledge of the language and literature of Spain and Portugal which was afterwards so serviceable to him. On his return to England, Southey, aided by the generous assistance of a friend, commenced the study of the law. But he soon found that it was utterly uncongenial to him, and gave it up after a year's trial. In 1801 he became private secretary to the Chancellor of the Exchequer for Ireland. This office too he abandoned after six months' trial. Literature was the avocation for which nature had designed him, and to literature he was attracted by an irresistible impulse. In 1803 he fixed his residence at Greta Hall, Keswick, and fairly began his earnest career of literary labour, almost unparalleled in its constant assiduity. There, too, he gave shelter to the family of Coleridge, and to Mrs. Lovell, a widowed sister of his wife's, never complaining of the burden, though his means were far from abundant, but accepting it cheerfully and bravely.

To enumerate all Southey's writings would be tedious and unnecessary. His most ambitious poetical works were "Thalaba" (1801), "Madoc" (1805), "The Curse of Kehama" (1810), "Roderick, the Last of the Goths" (1814). None of them was very successful in point of sale or otherwise; but the always sanguine author consoled himself by thinking that their copyright would eventually prove a mine of wealth—a hope never fulfilled. In 1807 he obtained from Government a pension of about £160 net. In 1813 he accepted the laureateship, which had been declined by Scott; and in 1835 Sir Robert Peel conferred on him a pension of £300 a year. Until he received the last-named amount Southey had to live from hand to mouth. With so many claims upon him as he had, duty and inclination alike called upon him to exert himself to the utmost. His most profitable literary connection was that with the *Quarterly Review*, to which he contributed largely, receiving sometimes as much as £100 for an article. But his writings in it were only a small portion of his labours. He wrote a "History of Brazil," a "History of the Peninsular War," "Colloquies on Society" (the theme of Macaulay's famous article on Southey), "Lives of the British Admirals," Lives of Wesley, of Kirke White, of Chatterton, of Cowper, of Nelson, of Bunyan, &c., &c. His most popular prose work is his admirable sketch of Nelson (1813). The secret of how Southey managed to get through such an immense amount of work, and the secret also, it must be added, of the inferiority of a great deal of it, was that he laboured continually, day by day, hour by hour, not waiting for moments of inspiration, but performing each day his allotted task. No wonder that he broke down under the burden, and that the three years previous to his death in 1843 were passed in a state of mental decay. "This [" work, continually work "], for thirty or forty years, he had punctually and impetuously done. No man so habitual, we were told; gave up his poetry at a given hour, on stroke of the clock, and took to prose, &c., &c.; and as to diligence and velocity, employed his very walking hours—walked with a book in his hand; and by these methods of his had got through perhaps a greater amount of work, counting quantity and quality, than any other man whatever in those years of his, till all suddenly ended. I likened him to one of those huge sandstone grinding cylinders which I had seen at Manchester, turning with inconceivable velocity (in the condemned room of the iron factory, where 'men die of lung disease at forty,' but are permitted to smoke in their damp cellar, and think that a rich recompense!)—screaming harshly, and shooting out each of them its sheet of fire (yellow, starlight, &c., according as it is brass or any other kind of metal that you grind or polish there) —beautiful sheets of fire, pouring out each as if from the paper cap of its low-stooping-backed grinder, when you look from rearward. For many years these stones grind so, at such a rate, till at last (in some cases) comes a moment when the stone's cohesion is quite worn out, overcome by the stupendous velocity long continued; and while grinding its fastest it flies off altogether, and settles some yards from you, a grinding-stone no longer, but a heap of quiet sand."[1]

Surrounded by women who looked up to him—as well they might—as the greatest and best of men, Southey formed the most extravagant estimate of the importance and value of his own writings. He was indeed, as Macaulay remarks in his Diary, arrogant beyond any man in literary history [Carlyle, it may be said in passing, was at least equally arrogant, though with better grounds for so being], for his self-conceit was proof against even the severest admonitions; and the utter failure of one of his books only confirmed him in his opinion of its excellence. But we should not bear too hardly on Southey for the self-complacency with which he regarded his productions. If he had not thought highly of them he could never have had courage to labour as he did, and his lofty opinions regarding them did no injury to any one, and probably did himself more good than harm.

While the genius of Wordsworth was unknown to readers in general, or known only to be ridiculed, a much younger man had attained a vogue as a poet probably unexampled in England, and was also regarded on the Continent as the brightest of Britain's intellectual stars. Not only his writings, but the rumours—often absurd and false enough—regarding his life and character, which circulated plentifully, were received with the keenest interest. If we placed authors according to the time when their popularity was at its height, Lord Byron would have been noticed before Wordsworth, for he undoubtedly was by far the best known and most admired poet of the early part of this century. Not only the fact that he was a great genius, but the fact that he was a lord who led a wild life and defied social conventions contributed to this result. George Noel Gordon Byron was born in London in 1788. He was the son of a Scotch heiress, who had married an extravagant and worthless Captain Byron, who consumed her fortune, and from whom she separated, to live upon £150 a

[1] Carlyle's "Reminiscences," vol. ii. p. 329.

year, all that remained of her wealth. Byron's early years were spent in Aberdeen, where the house in which his mother lived is still pointed out to visitors. He was unfortunate in both his parents. His father was a reckless blackguard; his mother a foolish, proud, violent-tempered woman, who at one time spoiled her son by over-indulgence, at another time provoked his sensitive and irritable nature almost to madness by her taunts about his lameness (a sore point with him throughout life). These facts should be taken into account in estimating Byron's character. A man of such antecedents who had turned out blameless and beneficent would have been a singular phenomenon.

While studying at the Aberdeen Grammar School, Byron was recalled to England, having, when little more than ten, succeeded to his grand-uncle's estate and title. After studying for some time at Nottingham and Dulwich, he was sent to Harrow, where he remained for two years. While there, his character was that of a clever, idle, impetuous, generous boy; one whom, as the head-master declared, it was easier to lead by a silken string than by a cable. In 1805 he entered Trinity College, Cambridge, where he led the frivolous, unprofitable, half-dissipated, half-foolish sort of life common to many young patricians during their university career. But already his poetical genius was beginning to dawn, and in 1807 he published his first volume, "Hours of Idleness," a collection of verses from which it would have required a very shrewd critic indeed to infer that a new star had arisen on the poetic horizon. A severe and contemptuous critique, by, it is said, Lord Brougham, of "Hours of Idleness" in the *Edinburgh Review*, had the effect of putting the young poet on his mettle, and of showing that he possessed powers which none of the readers of his first volume could have supposed to belong to him. He replied to his critic in the stinging and vindictive satire "English Bards and Scotch Reviewers" (1809), in which, in his blind indignation, he ran amuck not only of those who had given him real cause for offence, but of all the writers who happened to be popular favourites. Spirited and well adapted for its purpose though "English Bards" be, it is not a poem of a high order. The depths of passion and feeling which lay in Byron's nature were first shown by the publication, in 1812, of the two first cantoes of "Childe Harold," written during a two years' tour through Portugal, Spain, Greece, and Turkey. The poem was received with intense enthusiasm. In the author's own words, "he awoke one morning and found himself famous." "At twenty-four," writes Macaulay, "he found himself on the highest pinnacle of literary fame, with Scott, Wordsworth, Southey, and a crowd of other distinguished writers beneath his feet. There is scarcely an instance in literary history of so sudden a rise to so dizzy an eminence. Everything that could stimulate and everything that could gratify the strongest propensities of our nature, the gaze of a hundred drawing-rooms, the acclamations of the whole nation, the applause of applauded men, the love of lovely women, all this world and all the glory of it were at once offered to a youth to whom Nature had given violent passions, and whom education had never taught to control them. He lived as many men live who have no similar excuse to plead for their faults. But his countrymen and his countrywomen would love him and admire him. They were resolved to see in his excesses only the flash and outbreak of that same fiery mind which glowed in his poetry. He attacked religion, yet in religious circles his name was mentioned with fondness, and in many religious publications his works were censured with singular tenderness. He lampooned the Prince Regent, yet he could not alienate the Tories. Everything it seemed was to be forgiven to youth, rank, and genius."

While still a London literary lion, admired and sought after by all, Byron maintained his fame by producing in 1813 the "Giaour" and the "Bride of Abydos;" and in 1814 the "Corsair" and "Lara." In 1814 occurred his unfortunate union to Miss Millbanke. The ill-assorted pair lived together only twelve months; in 1815 Lady Byron left him for ever, for what exact causes has never been clearly explained. About this time a loud cry of indignation against Byron began to arise; he was lampooned in newspapers; fabulous stories of his debauchery were whispered from ear to ear; society frowned on him; with a genius almost divine, it was said and thought, he united a character diabolic in its wickedness. Burdened by debt, full of that ennui which a long course of dissipation never fails to bring at last, feeling that his life was sick and an error, indignant at the world and at himself, Byron determined to bid farewell to England. The "Siege of Corinth" and "Parisina," written about this time, bear testimony to the bitter feelings which were gnawing at his heart. In 1816 he left England, never to return alive.

After visiting Paris and Brussels, Byron went to Geneva, where the third canto of "Childe Harold" and the "Prisoner of Chillon" were written in six months. Visiting Italy, he wrote "Manfred" and the "Lament of Tasso" in 1817. At Venice, and afterwards at Ravenna, he resided till 1821, writing many of his most important works—the first five cantos of "Don Juan," "Mazeppa," and the dramas "Marino Faliero," "Sardanapalus," the "Two Foscari," "Werner," "Cain," &c. The last mentioned is, from a psychological point of view, one of the most remarkable of Byron's works, showing his attitude towards theological dogmas. In it "we see," said Goethe to Eckermann in 1824, "how the inadequate dogmas of the Church work upon a free mind like Byron's, and how he struggled to get rid of a doctrine which has been forced upon him. The English clergy will not thank him; but I shall be surprised if he does not go on treating biblical subjects of similar import, and if he lets slip a subject like Sodom and Gomorrah." "Don Juan," which, cynical and unpleasant in tone as much of it is, most judicious critics will agree in thinking Byron's most *genuine* poem, ultimately extended to sixteen cantos. It was preceded by "Beppo," written in 1817, a poem conceived in a similar bantering vein.

When, in 1822, the Greeks began their struggle for liberty, Byron threw his whole heart into their cause, and made a noble effort to redeem by his energy in its behalf the errors of his wild and wasted life. In June 1823 he set sail for Greece, and, on his arrival at Missolonghi in December, did much by his vigour and good sense to organise and discipline the army, and to check the abuses which everywhere prevailed. Had life been granted him, there is every reason to believe that he might have risen to eminence as a soldier and politician. But the end was near. A fever, brought on by exertion and exposure, proved fatal in April 1824, and thus, "at thirty-six, the most celebrated Englishman of the nineteenth century closed his brilliant and miserable career."

"In my mind," wrote Carlyle to Macvey Napier in 1832, "Byron has been sinking at an accelerated rate for the last ten years, and has now reached a very low level; I should say *too* low, were there not an *Hibernicism* involved in the expression. His fame has been very great, but I see not how it is to endure, neither does that make *him* great. No genuine productive thought was ever revealed by him to mankind; indeed, no clear undistorted vision into anything, or picture of anything, but all had a certain falsehood, a brawling theatrical insincere character. The man's moral nature, too, was bad; his demeanour as a man was bad. What was he, in short, but a large *sulky dandy*; of giant dimensions, to be sure, yet still a dandy, who sulked, as poor Mrs. Hunt expressed it, 'like a schoolboy that had got a plain bun given him instead of a plum one'? His bun was nevertheless God's universe, with what tasks are there, and it had served better men than he. I love him not; I owe him nothing; only pity and forgiveness; he taught me nothing that I had not again to forget." So far as Byron's personal character is concerned, this seems to us thoroughly sound and good. What he might have become, had he lived, it is vain to conjecture; possibly time and strenuous action might have ameliorated his character; but it is only too plain that he was sensual, cynical, vindictive, unamiable, and disposed to disbelieve in the existence of virtue because he himself was not virtuous. The best proof of the radically bad character of his temperament is that he inspired none of his friends with a sincere love for him; many admired him and liked his company in his agreeable moods, but we doubt very much if any regarded him with deep affection. Byron was a man of great genius, but his many serious faults and vices ought not on that account to be glossed over—

> "'Tis too absurd, 'tis weakness shame,
> This low prostration before fame,
> This casting down beneath the car
> Of idols, whatsoe'er they are,
> Life's purest, holiest decencies,
> To be careered o'er as they please." [1]

Byron's work as a poet is intensely personal; he loved to portray his own dark and stormy feelings in those of his characters. Hence it is not singular that many of his writings should belong to what Goethe called the "literature of despair;" echoes of the old lament, "Vanity of vanities, all is vanity!" Much of the gloom and bitterness of heart, and wearied satiety of life and its pleasures, which we find in "Childe Harold," was mere affectation. Byron liked to pose before the world as a defiant, cynical, melancholy man, who had tasted all the world's joys and found them to bring nothing but vexation of spirit, and whom the world's censure or applause was powerless to affect. All the while, however, he was childishly sensitive to opinion, and writhed as much beneath the lash of some petty critic as the smallest poetaster could have done. As he grew older, he became more sincere; if there is something of affectation even in the mocking laughter of "Don Juan," it is at all events a welcome contrast to the gloomy misanthropy of "Childe Harold." But Byron's faults as a writer and a man should not blind us to his transcendent merits. The fire and passion, the lofty imagination, the power and strength, the impetuous rush and glow which characterise his verse, give him quite a distinctive position among the poets of his age. Adhering in theory to the school of Pope, he was in reality thoroughly under the influence of the new era, and all his best work breathes its spirit. During his lifetime the vast majority of people considered him the greatest

[1] Moore.

poet of the day, and even now not a few critics hold the same opinion. But poets cannot be ranked in definite order like schoolboys in a class; and no good result comes of the discussion of such subjects as whether Byron was a greater poet than the profound and lofty-minded Wordsworth or the ethereal Shelley. It is sufficient to say that in his own line of poetical expression he was superior to them; whether that line was higher or lower than theirs is a subject on which opinions will differ to the end of time. It should not be forgotten that, with the exception of Scott, Byron was the only author of his time who attained Continental celebrity—a good omen for the permanence of his fame, if it be true (which may be doubted) that the judgment of foreigners generally anticipates the judgment of posterity. Mr. Matthew Arnold has done his best to minimise Goethe's praises of Byron; but it nevertheless remains clear that Goethe thought Byron the greatest poet of the day. "When he will create," he said to Eckermann, "he always succeeds; and we may truly say that with him inspiration supplies the place of reflection. He was always obliged to go on poetising, and then everything that came from the man, especially from his heart, was excellent. He produced his best things, as women do pretty children, without thinking about it or knowing how it was done. He is a great talent, a born talent, and I never saw the true poetical power greater in any man than in him."[1]

Resembling Byron in his defiance of control and his contempt for social restrictions, like him also in that during his lifetime the wildest and falsest stories of his private life were circulated and credited, Percy Bysshe Shelley differed from his noble friend in having a sweet, lovable disposition; a heart full of charity, full of hope and eager aspiration, constantly longing for the dawn of a better day to humanity. "He was," said Byron, "without exception, the best and least selfish man I ever knew." His friend Trelawny pronounced him "a man absolutely without selfishness." Leigh Hunt,

[1] Eckermann's "Conversations of Goethe" (Oxenford's translation), p. 116.

who knew him well, declared that "he was pious towards nature, towards his friends, towards the whole human race, towards the meanest insect of the forest." Bearing these testimonies in mind, it is strange to reflect that by many of his contemporaries Shelley should have been spoken of as if he had been a monster of iniquity, a poisonous reptile, whom every good man should do his best to crush underfoot. But there were circumstances in his life and character which tend to explain such utterances, extravagantly erroneous though they were. Shelley was the eldest son of Sir Timothy Shelley, Bart., and was born at Field Place, near Horsham, Sussex, in 1792. Sent to Eton about the age of thirteen, he early showed his habitual abhorrence of tyranny by his refusal to fag. Leaving Eton in 1808, he passed some months at home, employing himself in the composition of worthless tales. He then in 1810 entered University College, Oxford, where he studied hard by fits and starts, and spent much time in chemical experiments, for which he had always a fondness. The circulation of a two-page pamphlet, "A Defence of Atheism," led to the expulsion of the youthful freethinker from Oxford in March 1811; and his father's natural irritation on this account was deepened by Shelley's rash marriage, in August of the same year, to Harriet Westbrook, the daughter of a retired innkeeper. Henceforth Sir Timothy refused to have any intercourse with his son, to whom, however, he granted a liberal annual allowance. Shelley's hasty marriage was tragical in its issue: he soon became tired of his young wife, who could have no intellectual sympathy with him. In 1814 they were separated, and about two years later Mrs. Shelley committed suicide by drowning herself in the Serpentine. With sorrow it must be said that in his relations with her Shelley behaved badly; after making all allowances for his strange and erratic disposition, his conduct in this matter must be condemned as selfish and cruel. Before his separation from her he became acquainted with a woman of much more congenial disposition, Mary Godwin, daughter of William Godwin, the author of "Caleb Williams." With her, in 1814, he travelled through France, Switzerland, and Germany, and in 1816, on the death of Harriet Westbrook, she became his second wife. In 1813 Shelley printed (for private circulation only) his first important poem, "Queen Mab," expressing his aspirations after a future golden age for humanity, and giving violent expression to his atheistic opinions. When, in 1816, after the death of his first wife, he laid claim to the custody of his children, the claim was successfully resisted at law by their grandfather, on the ground of his atheism, as exhibited in "Queen Mab," despite the fact that the poem had not been published, only privately printed. In 1816 appeared "Alastor," one of his most finished productions, describing the life of a solitary poet. Then came, in 1817, the "Revolt of Islam," composed during his residence at Marlow. In 1818 he left England—never to return, as it proved—and went to Italy, where in the following year he produced his magnificent lyrical drama "Prometheus Unbound" and the tragedy of "The Cenci," undoubtedly the most powerful drama written since the Elizabethan era. His other chief works are "Julian and Maddalo" (1818), the "Witch of Atlas" (1820), "Epipsychidion" (1821), "Adonais" (1821)—a lament for the death of Keats, fit to be ranked with the Lycidas of Milton, and "Hellas" (1821), in which he celebrated the outbreak of the Greek war of liberty. On July 8, 1822, while he was out boating (a sport which he always loved) in the Bay of Spezzia with a friend, a sudden squall arose; the boat was upset, and all on board perished. Some days later Shelley's body was cast ashore. It was burnt, as the quarantine law of the country required, and the ashes were deposited in the Protestant burial-ground at Rome, near the grave of Keats.

Shelley never has been, and never will be, a popular poet. A few of his shorter pieces, such as "The Cloud" and "To the Skylark" (both written in 1820), are, it is true, universally known; but to the multitude most of his poems are a sealed book. For this several reasons might be given. For one thing, he is a difficult poet; to follow his meaning with ease and security requires a nimble and poetic intelligence, which comparatively few readers are possessed of. But the main reason why his poems are not popular is because they want human interest: when we look for something real and tangible which may awaken our sympathies, we are often put off with cloudy metaphysics, clothed, indeed, in magnificent words, but vague and impalpable. A good deal of Shelley's poetry might almost have been written by a denizen of another world, so remote it seems from all earthly interests. To many, as to Carlyle, "poor Shelley always was, and is, a kind of ghastly object, colourless, pallid, without health, or warmth, or vigour; the sound of him shrieky, frosty, as if a ghost were trying to 'sing to us.'" It must not be supposed from this that Shelley is always deficient in human interest or feeling. Frequently he is not so: he was filled with the enthusiasm of humanity, and often employed his verse to give utterance to his hopes of that golden age which always lies in the future. But even where he does so, his conceptions are not, to quote the words of an admirer, "embodied in personages derived from history or his own observation of life," and hence, to readers in general, have a misty and far-away aspect. It ought to be mentioned that Shelley wrote excellent prose: indeed, Mr. Matthew Arnold considers that his letters and essays bid fair to have a more enduring life than his poems. Few will agree with this judgment; but all who care to read the thoughts of a great poet upon many points of high literary and philosophical interest will find a rich treat in the alas! too scanty prose remains of Percy Bysshe Shelley.

Near the grave of Shelley in the Protestant cemetery at Rome lies another great poet, cut off in the pride of his youth and genius, but not before, in spite of the deplorable brevity of his career, he had done such work as to place him in the first rank of English poets, far above other "inheritors of unfulfilled renown," who have died at an early age. The few events in the life of John Keats may be very briefly related. He was born in London in 1795, and leaving school in 1810, was apprenticed for five years to a surgeon at Edmonston. The reading of Spenser in 1812 fired his poetical genius, and he began to write verses. After his apprenticeship was over, he came to London to walk the hospitals; but he soon found that surgery was unsuited to one of his sensitive nature, and gave up the study. In 1817 was published his first volume of poems, miscellaneous products of his youth, not sufficiently noticeable to excite either much praise or much censure. In 1818 appeared "Endymion." Nothing could better show how worthless contemporary criticism often is than the fact that this poem was received with a well-nigh universal shout of derision. Gifford, the editor of the *Quarterly Review*, in a coarse and virulent article denounced Keats as the "copyist of Leigh Hunt," "more unintelligible, almost as rugged, twice as diffuse, and ten times as tiresome." *Blackwood* followed suit; and even more lenient critics showed their want of discernment by "damning with faint praise." Yet it would be difficult to give an example of a poem written at so early an age as "Endymion" so rich in the loftier attributes of poetry; its faults are those of an undisciplined but luxurious imagination, from which great things might have been looked for in the future. The extraordinary rapidity of Keats's poetical growth is shown by the finish and maturity of the poems composed within the two years after "Endymion" was written—the noble fragment of "Hyperion," "Lamia," the "Eve of St. Agnes," and the immortal odes, one or two of which are of almost peerless beauty. Meanwhile it was becoming only too evident to all his friends that the poet's life was to be a brief one. Consumption had laid its fatal hand upon him, and he was gradually wasting away. In 1820 he embarked for Naples, accompanied by his artist friend Severn. From Naples they proceeded to Rome, and in the Eternal City, in February 1821, Keats breathed his last. To him, indeed, as his biographer, Lord Houghton, himself a poet of no mean talent, remarks, the gods were kind, and granted great genius and early death. Whether the verse he left behind him was but as a prelude to the music never played; whether he would have gone on increasing in poetic stature as the years went on, cannot be said with certainty. When we remember within how short a period the best poetry of Wordsworth and Southey was written, it would be unwise to determine too confidently that, had life been spared, his growth in the poetic art would have been continuous. Brief though his career was, it sufficed him to write poems which can only perish with the language. His passionate love of beauty, his strong and swift imagination, his luxurious flow of language, and his felicity of phrase, rank him among the great masters of English song. How powerful and wide-spread has been his influence is clearly proved by the many echoes of his verse which are found in succeeding writers.

We have now gone over the greatest names in the poetical literature of the nineteenth century. But a few writers have yet to be mentioned, one or two of whom were in their lifetime far more widely read than Wordsworth or Keats. Samuel Rogers (1763–1855) is remarkable as having, alone among the poets of his time, remained altogether untouched by the influence of the new era. He was a disciple of Pope, born out of due time, and sedulously followed the footsteps of his master. His poems, of which the principal are the "Pleasures of Memory" (1792), "Human Life" (1819), and "Italy" (1822), are now almost forgotten; they have not sufficient fire or strength to stand the ordeal of time. Their contemporary fame, which was considerable, owed a good deal to the social repute of their author, a rich banker, who was for many years a prominent figure in London society. Many amusing stories of his cynicism and biting and sarcastic remarks are on record, and tend to keep his memory alive. James Hogg (1770–1835), the "Ettrick Shepherd," was a genuine poet, with great but very ill-cultivated and undisciplined abilities. Much of his prose and a good deal of his poetry are worthless, but some of his songs, and the exquisite "Kilmeny," in the "Queen's Wake" (1813), reach a very high level of excellence. His rough and boisterous manners, and his unique and colossal self-conceit, rendered the "Shepherd" a favourite butt among the Edinburgh wits. Another Scotsman, Thomas Campbell (1777–1844), like Rogers, began his poetic career with the publication of a didactic poem, the "Pleasures of Hope" (1799), which in a short time went through many editions. His next long poem, "Gertrude of Wyoming" (1809), breathed more of the modern spirit. Campbell's longer poems have now ceased to be much read or quoted, except in single lines; but his ringing war-ballads, such as the "Battle of the Baltic" and the "Mariners of England," are about the best things of the kind in the language, full of spirit and fire, and written in metre admirably adapted to the subject. Besides his poetry, Campbell wrote a good deal of prose, mostly done as hack-work, and of little permanent value. His "Specimens of the British Poets" is, however, a very good book; and if he had husbanded his energies better, he might have done excellent work as a prose writer, for his style is correct and elegant, and his literary judgments are in general accurate and judicious. Thomas Moore (1779–1852), whose "Life of Byron" (1830) is, considering all the many difficulties of the task, a very creditable performance, was one of the most popular poets of his time. An amiable, good-hearted, cheerful Irishman, possessed of many excellent qualities, he was content to fritter away his life dangling on the skirts of the great, and was never so happy as when in titled company. His "Irish Melodies" are thin and artificial when compared with the songs of Burns, but they are light and graceful enough in their way, and well adapted to be linked to music. His most elaborate performance, "Lalla Rookh" (1817), an Eastern tale, is overloaded with gaudy ornament; but while containing little to satisfy the earnest student of poetry, is spirited and interesting. Some of his other writings show a marked talent for lively satire, which he was not slow to exercise against his political opponents.

IX.

SIR WALTER SCOTT, AND THE PROSE LITERATURE OF THE EARLY PART OF THE NINETEENTH CENTURY.

Sir Walter Scott; Mackintosh, Hallam, Alison; Jeffrey, Sydney Smith; Wilson, Lockhart, De Quincey; Lamb, Hazlitt, Hunt; Landor; Chalmers.

IN our survey of the poets of the new era in the last chapter, one great name was omitted,—the name of one who, till his less intense and dazzling light paled before the brilliant and captivating radiance of Byron, was far and away the most popular poet of his time. It is scarcely necessary to say that we refer to Sir Walter Scott. But Scott's poetry, excellent though in some respects it be, is by no means his most enduring title to remembrance. If he had written nothing else, he would not now have ranked among the first writers of his time, far less would he have occupied among British authors a place in the opinion of many second only to that of Shakespeare. It is as the writer of a long series of fictions which, when we consider their excellence, their interest, their variety, their width of range, their accurate delineations of nature, of life, and of character, may be safely pronounced matchless, that Scott's name is, and in all probability will continue to be, cherished with fond and admiring reverence by millions of readers. But not only did Scott reign supreme as a novelist, and occupy an elevated position in the kindred realm of poetry; it may be said of him, as of Goldsmith, that there was almost no kind of writing that he did not touch, and none which he touched that he did not adorn. The fertility, the affluence, the readiness of Scott's intellectual resources were indeed such that to contemplate them almost strikes one dumb with amazement. He was a manly and judicious critic, an accomplished antiquary, no contemptible historian, and a careful and painstaking editor. The amount of literary work of various kinds he managed to get through, while living, not the life of a recluse, but that of an active and bustling man of the world, attending carefully to his ordinary business, and always observant of the rites of hospitality, is something portentous and unexampled. To record with any fulness the life of a man of such various occupations and talents, of such boundless energy, would require a volume, not a few pages. Only the leading features, therefore, can be noted here.

Walter Scott was born at Edinburgh on August 15, 1771. His father was a "douce," careful, precise Writer to the Signet, whose chief features have been portrayed in indelible characters by his son in the portrait of Mr. Saunders Fairford in "Redgauntlet." Like many able men,—like, for example, his great contemporary, Goethe,—Scott owed the more rare and distinguished features of his intellectual character to his mother, a woman of taste and imagination. A lameness—never cured—in his infancy, and weak health, caused Scott in his third year to be sent to the house of his grandfather at Sandyknowe, near Kelso, in order to try the efficacy of country air and diet. The period of his residence there was a very happy one. He passed his days in the open fields, "with no other fellowship than that of the sheep and lambs;" and in the long winter evenings his early passion for the romantic past was nurtured by the traditionary legends of Border heroism and adventure repeated by an aged female relative. In his eighth year he was sent to the High School of Edinburgh, of which the then headmaster was Dr. Adam, almost as celebrated a figure in Scottish educational history as Dr. Arnold of Rugby is in that of England. During his school career he did not attend very sedulously to the ordinary studies there followed, but he read omnivórously, and delighted his companions with frequent examples of his talent as a narrator of fictions, plentifully seasoned with the marvellous, and often relating to knight-errantry. "Slink over beside me, Jamie," he would whisper to his schoolfellow Ballantyne, afterwards, alas! inseparably connected with the darkest pages of his history, "and I'll tell you a story." When about thirteen, he first, during six months he passed with his aunt at Kelso, became acquainted with Percy's "Reliques." "I remember well," he says, "the spot where I read these volumes for the first time. It was beneath a huge plantanus tree, in the ruins of what had been intended for an old-fashioned arbour in the garden I have mentioned. The summer day sped onward so fast that, notwithstanding the sharp appetite of thirteen, I forgot the hour of dinner, was sought for with anxiety, and was still found entranced in my intellectual banquet." Truly the child is father of the man. From his earliest years Scott showed that love of old-world stories, of the days of chivalry and romance, and of all "auld nick-nackets" tending to make the past more real to him, which he afterwards displayed to its full extent in the gathering of ancient armour and miscellaneous articles of antiquity which he collected around him at Abbotsford, and which, more than anything else, was the source of his originality as a novelist and poet.

After leaving the High School, Scott entered the University of Edinburgh, where he studied in the same irregular and miscellaneous fashion as before and afterwards. Every great man is for the most part self-educated; what he acquires from schoolmasters and professors is trifling both in quantity and in value compared to what, following the bent of his genius, he acquires for himself. Scott was not a scholar; he was too careless of minute accuracy ever to trouble himself about those trifling facts and verbal subtleties a thorough acquaintance with which is the glory of University magnates. But he acquired in rough-and-ready fashion such a knowledge of various languages as to enable him to assimilate the literature best suited to his needs contained in them. The small store of Greek, it is true, which he was taught at the University, he, in the lapse of years, managed to forget so utterly that he did not even know the letters; but he read Latin with fluency, and could peruse without difficulty any book written in French, German, Italian, or Spanish. Entering his father's office as apprentice in his fifteenth year, he managed so far to curb his restless energies as to go through with credit a fair amount of legal drudgery, acquiring, besides some knowledge of the technicalities of the law, those habits of method, punctuality, and laborious industry which afterwards were such a powerful auxiliary to him. His somewhat dry and mechanical duties as legal apprentice and budding advocate he diversified not only by reading, but by frequent excursions into the Highland and Lowland districts, acquiring there a rich store of traditions, and becoming acquainted with all those types of Scottish character which he was afterwards to delineate in imperishable colours. "He was makin' himsel a' the time," says one of his companions, speaking about those raids, "but he didna ken, maybe, what he was about till years had passed. At first he thought o' little, I daresay, but the queerness and fun."

In 1792 Scott was admitted to the Scottish bar. Through the influence of his father he received enough employment to keep him from being entirely idle, but not nearly enough to occupy all the hours of so quick and energetic a worker. It is a wonder that Scott, with his great fondness for reading and his wonderful abilities, did not sooner make an entry into the fair realm of literature, which has afforded kindly aid to so many young subjects of Themis. It was not, however, till 1796 that he first appeared before the public as translator of Bürger's ballads "Lenore" and the "Wild Huntsman." These attracted considerable attention, and led to his contributing a few pieces to "Monk" Lewis's "Tales of Wonder," and to his translating in 1799 Goethe's "Götz von Berlichingen." Previous to the publication of the last-mentioned productions, Scott had married Miss Carpenter, the daughter of a French refugee, who brought with her a small fortune. She was not his first love: before he met with her he had been deeply in love with a lady who afterwards became wife of Sir William Forbes of Pitsligo. His attachment was returned, but circumstances opposed their union, and their intercourse was broken off, leaving a wound in Scott's heart which the lapse of time was powerless altogether to heal. Whenever in any of his works he has occasion to mention an early and unfortunate "first love," he does so with peculiar tenderness and feeling.

In 1802 Scott published the first two volumes of the "Border Minstrelsy," printed by his old schoolfellow Ballantyne, who had set up in business in the pretty little town of Kelso, and the first important specimen of an afterwards famous press. There was no work of Scott's after-life which showed the result of so much preliminary labour. Before he was ten years old he had collected several volumes of ballads and traditions, and we have seen how diligently he pursued the same task in later years. The collection was admitted to be far more faithful, as well as more skilfully edited, than its prototype, the "Reliques" of Bishop Percy, while the notes contained a mass of information relative to Border life, conveyed in a style of beauty unprecedented in matters of this kind, and enlivened with a higher interest than that of fiction. Percy's "Reliques" had prepared the way for the kind reception of the "Minstrelsy" by the general relish which—notwithstanding Dr. Johnson's protest—it had created for the simple pictures of a pastoral and heroic time. Burns had since familiarised the English ear with the Doric melodies of his native land; and now a greater than Burns appeared, whose first production, by a singular chance, had come into the world in the very year in which the Ayrshire minstrel was withdrawn from it, as if nature had intended that the chain of poetic inspiration should not be broken. The delight of the public was further augmented by the appearance of the third volume of the "Minstrelsy" (1803), containing various imitations of the old ballads, which contained "all the rich fashion of the antique, purified from the mould and rust by which the beauties of such weather-beaten trophies are defaced." The first edition was disposed of in less than a year; and on the publication of a second, the copyright was sold to Longman for £500—a very fortunate bargain for the publisher, as it proved.

Passing over minor writings, we come to the next important event in Scott's literary life,—the publication of the "Lay of the Last Minstrel" in 1805. It met with a colossal and unprecedented success; edition after edition was called for; with a single bound Scott leaped to the position of the most popular poet of the day. There are several causes which combine to account for this extraordinary popularity. In the first place, the poem was original in subject and mode of treatment; the description of the old romantic past, in free and flowing verse, was felt as refreshing to those tired of poetical commonplace and conventionality as is the fresh air of the mountains to those long detained in stifling London drawing-rooms. Again, Scott's poems have what many greater poems want—an interesting story, which, apart from their poetical beauties, keeps the reader's attention fixed. In the third place, they do not require any thought or elaborate culture to understand them; their beauties are easily perceptible by all, as their popularity among schoolboys sufficiently attests. General intelligibility is one of the prime requisites of immediate popularity as a poet, though not of permanent fame; a fact of which the immense sale of Longfellow's writings in our day is a convincing illustration. The "Lay" was followed in 1808 by "Marmion," and in 1810 by the "Lady of the Lake," to which poem, with its fine descriptions of scenery, is mainly due the great influx of tourists every season to the Trossachs. With the "Lady of the Lake" Scott's popularity as a poet reached its zenith. His subsequent poems, the "Vision of Don Roderick," "Rokeby," the "Lord of the Isles," &c., were not so well received. "Well, James," said Scott to Ballantyne a few days after the publication of the "Lord of the Isles" in 1815, "I have given you a week; what are people saying about the 'Lord of the Isles'?" Ballantyne hesitated a little, but Scott speedily brought the matter to a point. "Come," he said, "speak out, my good fellow; what has put it into your head to be on so much ceremony *with me* all of a sudden? But I see how it is; the result is given in one word,—*disappointment*." Ballantyne's silence admitted the inference to its fullest extent. As Scott had been wholly unprepared for the event, his countenance looked rather blank for a few seconds. At length he said, with perfect cheerfulness, "Well, well, James, so be it; but you know we must not droop, for we can't afford to give over. Since one line has failed, we must stick to something else." Thus, almost by chance, was Scott's genius driven into the line in which its highest triumphs were achieved. He had already, with characteristic caution, made his first essay in it.

But before beginning the history of the wonderful Waverley series, we may glance a little at Scott's occupations and circumstances at this time. In many ways he had much cause to felicitate himself on his lot. In 1799 he was appointed Sheriff of Selkirkshire, with an annual salary of £300. Some years later he procured an appointment as one of the principal clerks of the Court of Session, worth about £1500 a year. Altogether, counting the interest of his small fortune, he had an income of about £2000, independent of his literary exertions, which brought him in large sums. Yet Scott was not a rich man; and though his income had been tenfold what it was, would not have been a rich man. His ambition was not to write great works (he always regarded his literary faculty merely as a convenient means of filling his purse), not to acquire great fame as an author, but to be a large landed proprietor, the founder of a race of Scottish lairds. With this end in view he toiled late and early; he went through labours which in a short time would have brought a man of less vigorous constitution to the grave; he plunged himself in debt, and engaged in commercial transactions which finally proved his ruin. In 1812 he removed to Abbotsford, where he built and fitted up the fine mansion so closely associated with his name, and drained and planted the bleak moorland around at the cost of many thousands. Cautious and judicious in everything else, he had a sort of craze for the purchase of land, and could no more resist the purchase of any plot of ground in tempting proximity to his estate of Abbotsford that was offered to him, than an opium-eater can withstand the fascinations of his favourite drug. The burning ambition to be a territorial magnate was a sad and pitiful one for a man of Scott's powers, but it carried with it a terrible revenge.

On a certain day in June 1814, while a party of young law students were chatting gaily in the library of a house in George Street, Edinburgh, a shade was observed to come over the countenance of their host. One of them having intimated a fear of his being unwell: "No," said he; "I shall be well enough presently, if you will only let me sit where you are and take my chair, for there is a confounded hand in sight of me here which has often bothered me before, and now it won't let me fill my glass with good-will." His companion rose to change places with him, and had pointed out to him this hand, which, like the writing on Belshazzar's wall, disturbed his host's hour of hilarity. "Since we sat down," he said, "I have been watching it; it fascinates my eye; it never stops; page after page is finished and thrown on that heap of manuscript, and still it goes on unwearied, and so it will be till candles are brought in, and God knows how long after that. It is the same every night; I can't stand a sight of it when I am not at my books." "Some stupid, dogged, engrossing clerk probably," exclaimed one of the youths. "No, boys," replied the host, "I know well what hand it is—'tis Walter Scott's." It *was* the hand of Walter Scott, busily engaged in his Castle Street lodging in writing the last two volumes of "Waverley"—a task which occupied him only three weeks. "Waverley" had been begun nine years before, in 1805 (hence the second title, "'Tis Sixty Years Since"), but the friend to whom Scott submitted what of it was then written did not speak of it in sufficiently high terms to encourage him to run the risk of somewhat dimming his poetic laurels by its publication.

When, however, his popularity as a poet began to decrease, and he was desirous of hitting upon a new vein wherewith to satisfy the capricious taste of the public, his thoughts reverted to the almost forgotten manuscript of "Waverley," and he determined to complete it. It was published anonymously in July 1814, the authorship being kept a strict secret lest the novel should prove a failure. Any such apprehension, however, was soon dispelled. With extraordinary rapidity it rose into an unprecedented degree of favour; everywhere it was talked about, and everywhere eager discussions were carried on as to who the unknown author could be. Scott, however, jealously preserved his incognito, and the rapidly succeeding series of great fictions by him—"Guy Mannering," "The Antiquary," "Old Mortality," "Rob Roy," &c., &c.—bore on their title-pages simply "By the Author of 'Waverley.'" Many supposed, on the appearance of the early volumes of the series, that Scott was the writer, and as time went on supposition gradually deepened into certainty; but he never publicly acknowledged his authorship till the state of his affairs compelled him to do it in 1827. It would be impossible to exaggerate the enthusiasm with which "Waverley" and its successors were welcomed. Carlyle, who lived through all the *furore* which they excited, shall describe it: "In the spring[1] of 1814," he says, "appeared 'Waverley,' an event memorable in the annals of British literature; in the annals of British bookselling thrice and four times memorable. Byron sang, but Scott narrated; and when the song had sung itself out through all variations onwards to the 'Don Juan' one, Scott was still found narrating and carrying the whole world along with him. All bygone popularity of chivalry lays was swallowed up in a far greater. What 'series' followed out of 'Waverley,' and how and with what result, is known to all men—was witnessed and watched with a kind of rapt astonishment by all. Hardly any literary reputation ever rose so high in our island; no reputation at all ever spread so wide. Walter Scott became Sir Walter Scott, Baronet, of

[1] Incorrect. See above.

Abbotsford, on whom fortune seemed to pour her whole cornucopia of wealth, honour, and worldly good, the favourite of princes and of peasants and all intermediate men. His 'Waverley' series, swift following one on the other apparently without end, was the universal reading; looked for like an annual harvest, by all ranks, in all European countries."

The vast sums Scott received for the novels which he produced with such extraordinary rapidity and with so little apparent exertion, naturally led him to regard his literary powers as a boundless mine of wealth, which it was scarcely possible for him to exhaust. Hence he went on "adding field to field," buying, often at extravagant prices, any tempting piece of land which he found in the market, and fitting up Abbotsford in a style of the most luxurious splendour. To the money thus spent must be added that expended in the exercise of a boundless hospitality. Scott and Abbotsford became sights which no Scottish tourist of any pretensions to rank or fame could omit; it was not unusual, we are told, for a dozen or more coach-loads to find their way into the grounds of the "Great Unknown" in the course of the day, most of whom found or forced an entrance into his mansion. There could be no better proof of Scott's thorough healthiness of character and freedom from all those petty vices which are commonly supposed to belong to the literary profession, than the manner in which he conducted himself while "lionised" above any one before or since. He took the praises copiously bestowed on him for what they were worth, pleased with them, no doubt, but nowise unduly elated; was gratified when among the crowd of his visitors he found any of talent and good sense with whom it was a pleasure to converse; and regarded the numerous specimens of folly and presumption whom he was compelled to put up with, not with indignation or bitterness, but with a humorous appreciation of their character which left little room for anger or contempt. For many of the honours bestowed on literature Scott cared little. He on several occasions declined the degree of D.C.L., offered him by the Universities of Oxford and Cambridge; and the higher distinction of a baronetcy, conferred on him in 1820, was chiefly gratifying to him, not because he cared for the title himself, but because it pleased his family pride to think that Abbotsford would henceforth be occupied by a race of baronets.

One of the most striking features of Scott's character was the indomitable tenacity with which he went on with whatever literary task he had in hand. Few and far between were the occasions when, however busily engaged otherwise, his daily literary task was left uncompleted. As a rule, he rose betimes in the morning, and had his little parcel of "copy" ready before the other members of the house were astir. But as to time and place of composition he was nearly indifferent; and though, like many great authors, he preferred to write in the morning hours, it cost him no great effort to carry on the work in which he was engaged at almost any time or under almost any circumstances. "When once I set my pen to the paper," he wrote to his friend Morritt, "it will walk fast enough. I am sometimes tempted to leave it alone and see whether it will not write as well without the assistance of my hand as with it. A hopeful prospect for the reader." When a friend asked him how, amidst such a constant whirl of various occupations as occupied him, he managed to write so much, he replied, "Oh, I lie *simmering* over things for an hour or so before I get up, and there's the time I am dressing to overhaul my half-sleeping, half-waking *projet de chapitre*, and when I get the paper before me, it commonly runs off pretty easily. Besides, I often take a doze in the plantations, and, while Tom [Purdie, his faithful attendant] marks out a dyke or drain, one's fancy may be running its ain rigs in some other world." Well was it for Scott that in the days of his prosperity he accustomed himself to perform his daily task cheerfully under difficulties which would have utterly discomfited a less strenuous worker. The time came too soon when his fair prospects of wealth and prosperity were to prove to be mere castles of cards, destined to tumble into the dust at the first stroke of adversity. The commercial whirlwind of 1825–26, which shook down so many apparently prosperous commercial fabrics, proved fatal to Scott's prosperity as to that of many thousands of lesser men. Unknown to his friends, he had become a partner in the printing firm established in Edinburgh by his old friends the Ballantynes. The great Scottish publisher Constable, who, both by the magnitude and boldness of his plans and the brilliance of his publishing exploits, deserved the title Scott laughingly applied to him of "the great Napoleon of the realms of print," was compelled, after a brief but brave struggle, to succumb to the tide of ruin which could not but overwhelm him. He became bankrupt, and the Ballantyne firm soon followed suit. In February 1826 he found himself bankrupt—a debtor to the extent of over £120,000.[1]

The catastrophe was heavy; to most men it would have been a crushing one. Nothing in his life better shows his courage and his honesty than his behaviour under this great calamity. He determined that if his creditors would but grant him time they should be paid to the very uttermost farthing. "I am always ready," he said, "to make any sacrifice to do justice to my engagements, and would rather sell anything or everything than be less than a true man of my word." The estate of Abbotsford had, shortly before the crash, been secured to his son on the occasion of his marriage, so it was beyond the creditors' reach; but Scott's house and furniture in Edinburgh were sold by auction, and his personal effects at Abbotsford,—books, pictures, &c.,—were delivered over to be held in trust for his creditors. Having bound himself to limit the cost of his living to his official income, and to employ what he earned by his pen in liquidating his debts, Scott took second-rate lodgings in Edinburgh and began his Herculean task. "For many years," he said to a friend, "I have been accustomed to hard work, because I found it a pleasure; now, with all due respect for Falstaff's

[1] For a statement of the business relations between Sir Walter Scott and the Ballantynes, see a "Refutation of the Misstatements and Calumnies contained in Mr. Lockhart's Life of Sir Walter Scott, Bart., respecting the Messrs. Ballantyne. By the Trustees and Son of the late Mr. James Ballantyne." London: Longman & Co., 1838.

principle, 'nothing on compulsion,' I certainly will not shrink from work because it has become necessary." Misfortunes, it is said, never come singly, and the death of his wife, which followed soon after the ruin of his fortunes, intensified Scott's woes. Still he did not yield to despair. Day after day, despite his mental and bodily troubles, he diligently toiled on. The following entry in his diary for June 8, 1826, may be taken as typical of the rest :

"Bilious and headache this morning. A dog howled all night, and left me little sleep. Poor cur! I daresay he had his distresses, as I have mine. I was obliged to make Dalgleish shut the windows when he appeared at half-past six as usual, and did not rise till nine. I have often deserved a headache in my younger days without having one, and nature is, I suppose, paying off old scores. Ay! but then the want of the affectionate care that used to be ready, with lowered voice and stealthy pace, to smooth the pillow and offer assistance,—gone—gone—for ever—ever—ever. Well, there is another world, and we'll meet free from the mortal sorrows and frail ties which beset us here. Amen! so be it. Let me change this topic with hand and head, and the heart must follow. I finished four pages to-day, headache, laziness, and all."

Scott's first published work after the catastrophe which overwhelmed his fortunes was "Woodstock" (1826), which realised for his creditors over £8000. Then in the following year came his long "Life of Napoleon," written with almost incredible speed, of which the first and second editions brought £18,000. It is inaccurate and one-sided, interesting as having been written by Scott, but not of great value otherwise :—

> "When the harness galls sore and the spurs his side goad,
> The high-mettled racer's a hack on the road."

In two years, by incessant industry, Scott paid off £40,000 of his debts, and in the course of four years nearly £70,000. No wonder though under the strain of constant exertion added to sorrow and anxiety his health gave way. His last novels, "Count Robert of Paris" and "Castle Dangerous," gave painful evidence that the wand of the Great Magician, which had charmed so long, had at length lost its power. The last important work of his closing years was the excellent notes and introductions which he furnished for a new edition of the Waverley novels. His "Tales of a Grandfather," "History of Scotland," &c., &c., are not of a quality to add anything to the lustre of his fame.

In 1831 he was induced to abandon literary labour for a time, and to undertake a voyage to the Continent. After a residence of five months in Italy, he returned to London in June 1832. It was now painfully evident that his health was irretrievably ruined, and after a few weeks he was conveyed to Abbotsford, where, writes his biographer, "about half-past one P.M. on the 21st of September, Sir Walter breathed his last, in the presence of all his children. It was a beautiful day, so warm that every window was wide open, and so perfectly still that the sound of all others most delicious to his ears—the gentle ripple of the Tweed over its pebbles—was distinctly audible as we knelt around the bed, and his eldest son kissed and closed his eyes." He was buried by the side of his wife in Dryburgh Abbey. It is pleasing to be able to relate that the collected editions of his works were after his death found sufficient to remove the mountain of debt which he struggled so manfully to discharge. His hopes of founding a family proved as fallacious as many of his other ambitions. All his children died within fifteen years of his own death, and only one or two very remote descendants of the Great Enchanter now survive. "It is written," he said, with melancholy truth, a year or two before his death, "that nothing shall flourish under my shadow; the Ballantynes, Terry, Nelson, Weber, all came to distress. Nature has written on my brow, 'Your shade shall be broad, but there shall be no protection from it to aught you favour.'"

Scott's personal character is a wide subject, on which much might be said. It is rather remarkable that it seems to have affected two great writers of our time, of very different tendencies, in much the same way. Carlyle and Macaulay, to whom one scarcely looks for agreement on such points, alike take a severe view of it. Carlyle's famous estimate of Scott as author and man, in which he figured so conspicuously in the character of a "hanging judge," is well known, and should be carefully read by all who wish to form an intelligent estimate of the Wizard of the North. Macaulay, writing in June 1838 to Macvey Napier, who had asked an article for the *Edinburgh Review* on Scott's life, says, "I have not, from the little that I do know of him, formed so high an opinion of his character as most people seem to entertain, and as it would be expedient for the *Edinburgh Review* to express. He seems to me to have been most carefully and successfully on his guard against the sins which most easily beset literary men. On that side he multiplied his precautions and set double watch. Hardly any writer of note has been so free from the petty jealousies and morbid irritabilities of our caste. But I do not think that he kept himself equally pure from faults of a very different kind—from the faults of a man of the world. In politics a bitter and unscrupulous partisan; profuse and ostentatious in expense; agitated by the hopes and fears of a gambler; perpetually sacrificing the perfection of his compositions and the durability of his fame to his eagerness for making money; writing with the slovenly haste of Dryden, in order to satisfy wants which were not, like those of Dryden, caused by circumstances beyond his control, but which were produced by his extravagant waste or rapacious speculation. This is the way in which he appears to me. I am sorry for it, for I sincerely admire the greater part of his works, but I cannot think him a high-minded man or a man of very strict principle." There is considerable truth in this estimate. Scott was not a man of high, heroic spirit. He looked upon life precisely as we may imagine some industrious merchant doing, anxious to get the best price he could for his wares, and caring more for their saleable qualities than for any other features in them. His letters afford fine examples of the worldly wisdom of his disposition. It is amusing and curious to notice how carefully he adapted their tone to suit the particular temperament of whatever correspondent he happened to be addressing. Those to his son Walter may be described as resembling Lord Chesterfield's letters to his son *minus* the immorality. There is no trace in them of any high or ennobling principle. "Don't do rash and foolish things; take care of yourself; be sure to get on in the world," is the gospel they proclaim. But if Scott's character lacked somewhat of the loftier virtues, it was full of those endearing qualities which men of higher aspirations have, alas! too often been without. He was totally free from any taint of vanity, envy, or malice. Like his great contemporary Goethe, he liked much better to praise the good than to condemn the evil. No critic was ever more lenient in his judgments; indeed he carried literary tolerance so far that praise from him became almost a brevet of mediocrity. In his relations with his family and his dependants he acquitted himself in a manner deserving of the highest praise. Never was there a better master than he, never a more loving and devoted parent.

To do full justice to Scott's writings would require large space; it is so various in kind and so large in quantity. He cannot be ranked amongst our greatest poets, nevertheless his stirring lays have great merit of their kind. The tendency nowadays is to underrate them as much as they were overrated at the time of their appearance. Their generous, healthy, open-air tone, their ringing vivacity, their rush and vigour, have very rarely been successfully imitated. Scott's miscellaneous prose works, if not brilliant, furnish extraordinary proofs of the soundness of his judgment and the width of his knowledge. His "Lives of the Novelists" are models of sensible and manly criticism; and the lives and notes added to his editions of Dryden (1808) and of Swift (1814) show an extraordinary knowledge of the byways of English literary history, and evince a capacity for patient research with which one would scarcely be prepared to credit a man of Scott's rapid-working habits. Of the great Waverley series the worst that criticism can say was said long ago by Carlyle. All cultivated readers of Scott are, we suppose, prepared to admit that his psychological insight was not very deep; that his style lacks force and concentration; that his representations of the life of the past in such novels as "Ivanhoe" and "Kenilworth" are often "stagey" and unreal; that in his novels no new view of life, no fresh inspiring idea, was given to mankind. But Scott had in almost unequalled abundance qualities possessed by few writers, but without which a great novelist is impossible—breadth and healthiness of mind. In tolerance and catholicity of feeling he resembled Shakespeare. Bating a slight infusion of Tory and cavalier prejudice, which appears to some extent in two or three of his novels, his representations are scrupulously just. As he always felt himself at his ease, and could talk unceasingly to any companion he happened to meet with, however lowly his rank, so he could portray the feelings and talk of all classes of men with equal accuracy and sympathy. Contemporary verdicts on his novels have been a good deal reversed by subsequent criticism. Few, for example, would now consider "Ivanhoe" his best novel, as was pretty generally the opinion at the time of its publication (1819). Undoubtedly his best novels are those dealing with the subjects which he knew and loved best—Scottish life and Scottish scenery. In his historical novels dealing with foreign countries and remote times, the colours are sometimes coarsely laid on, and the whole treatment strikes one as artificial and wanting in vraisemblance. But when his foot touches his native heath, Scott is always himself again—always clear, vivid, and accurately pictorial. Carlyle's estimate of Scott (which, just as in some ways it is, does not give anything like full praise to the great qualities of his novels) has so powerfully influenced succeeding criticisms on them, that it may be well to quote, as weighing heavily in the opposite scale, the estimate formed of them by his illustrious contemporary, Goethe, whose opinion Carlyle himself would have been the first to pronounce to be of the greatest value. "I have just begun 'Rob Roy,'" said Goethe on one occasion to Eckermann, "and will read his best novels in succession. All is great—material, import, characters, execution; and then what infinite diligence in the preparatory studies! what truth of detail in the execution!" Again, speaking of the "Fair Maid of Perth," certainly not one of the best of Scott's novels, he said, "You find everywhere in Walter Scott a remarkable security and thoroughness in his delineation, which proceed from his comprehensive knowledge of the real world, obtained by lifelong studies and observations and a daily discussion of the most important relations. Then come his great talent and his comprehensive nature. You remember the English critic who compares the poets to the voices of male singers, of which some can command only a few fine tones, while others have the whole compass, from the highest to the lowest, completely in their power. Walter Scott is one of this last sort. In the 'Fair Maid of Perth' you will not find a single weak passage to make you feel as if his knowledge and talent were insufficient. He is equal to his subject in every direction in which it takes him; the king, the royal brother, the prince, the head of the clergy, the nobles, the magistracy, the citizens and mechanics, the Highlanders, are all drawn with the same sure hand and hit off with equal truth." Such utterances of the first poet and critic of modern times deserve to be deeply pondered.

With the exception of Scott, few prose writers who flourished in the early part of the eighteenth century were possessed of so striking and commanding a genius as belonged to some of their poetical contemporaries. But there were many prose writers of gifts considerably superior to the average—so many, indeed, that our limits compel us to adopt a pretty severe principle of selection, and to exclude not a few who won literary laurels not yet altogether effaced by the lapse of time. The leading prose writers of this period fall easily into well-marked groups, and it will be convenient thus to consider them instead of adopting strict chronological order. Historians may come first. Sir James Mackintosh (1765–1832) is now remembered more for his contemporary reputation as a talker and for the frequent allusions to him in memoirs of celebrities of his time, than for what he actually accomplished. His life was one of much promise but of little performance. He himself relates that a French lady once said to him, "What have you done that people should think you so superior?" In reply, he says, "I was obliged as usual to refer to my projects." Mackintosh was born in Inverness-shire, and educated at King's College, Aberdeen, and at Edinburgh, where he studied medicine. Coming to London in 1788, he attracted great attention by his "Vindiciæ Gallicæ," a pungent and vigorous reply to Burke's "Reflections on the French Revolution," which brought him at once into notice in literary society, and had the honour of being praised by Fox in Parliament. Abandoning medicine for the study of law, he was called to the bar; and his fine speech in defence of Peltier in 1803 brought him a great deal of practice and the prospect of earning a large income by his forensic ability. However, in the words of Lord Dalling, "three months had not elapsed when, with the plaudits of the public and the praise of Erskine still ringing in his ear, he accepted the Recordership of Bombay from Mr. Addington, and retired with satisfaction to the well-paid and knighted indolence of India. His objects in doing so were, he said, of two kinds: to make a fortune and to write a work. The whole man is before us when we discover how far either of these objects was attained by him. He did not make a fortune; he did not write a work." After a residence of seven years in India, he returned to England and entered Parliament, where, although he distinguished himself in carrying on the Criminal Code reform begun by Romilly, his reputation scarcely answered to the high hopes of him formed by his friends. He also wrote a good deal, contributing miscellaneous articles to the *Edinburgh Review;* an interesting and able, if occasionally inaccurate, "Dissertation on the Progress of Ethical Philosophy" to the "Encyclopædia Britannica;" and a short "History of England," carried down to the Reformation, and a "Life of Sir Thomas More" to "Lardner's

Encyclopædia." His *magnum opus* was meant to be a history of England, for which he collected copious and valuable materials, but only a fragment on the "Causes of the Revolution of 1688" was ever completed. Mackintosh did not possess a creative mind, but he was unwearied in the acquisition of knowledge, and if he had had more tenacity of purpose might have left a permanent mark on literary history. His style is elegant and carefully wrought, but somewhat languid and wanting in pith and power. His conversational powers by all accounts must have been extraordinary. "Till subdued by age and illness," said Sydney Smith, who knew well all the celebrated talkers of the day, "his conversation was more brilliant and instructive than that of any human being I ever had the good fortune to be acquainted with."

Henry Hallam (1777–1859) was an historian of powers, perhaps, not originally superior to those of Mackintosh, but put to infinitely better account. He was educated at Oxford, and studied for the bar, but never depended on his profession for a livelihood, as, in addition to possessing a private fortune of a considerable amount, he was the lucky holder of a Government sinecure. His works are on subjects requiring such research and labour that they scarcely could have been written by any one less happily circumstanced. A staunch Whig, he began his literary career by writing articles in the early volumes of the *Edinburgh Review*, of which one on Dryden, *apropos* of Scott's edition, is the most notable. In 1818 he took his place as the first historian of his time by the publication of his "View of the State of Europe during the Middle Ages," a work rather pompous and Latinised in style, but showing extremely wide knowledge and great judicial acumen. His second great work, the "Constitutional History of England," appeared in 1827. The labours of Dr. Stubbs have superseded Hallam's "Constitutional History" in its early portions; but for the rest it is still the standard authority, not likely to be soon superseded. Its carefulness and accuracy, its impartial summing up of facts and candid estimate of men and opinions, can scarcely be too highly commended. In 1838–39 his last important publication, "An Introduction to the Literature of Europe during the Fifteenth, Sixteenth, and Seventeenth Centuries," was issued. From the nature of the subject, as well as for other reasons, this work is not of equal value to the "Constitutional History." No man, however wide his learning and accomplishments (and Hallam's were very wide), could discuss with equal certainty and firmness of touch the literature of all the European countries during three centuries. To enable any one to do that in a perfectly satisfactory manner, he would require to have his life prolonged to patriarchal limits. Hence Hallam's treatise is in parts a compilation, and compilations, however well done, are always inferior to first-hand works. As a critic he is generally sound and judicious; never, however, showing much depth of penetration or delicacy of touch. The following remarks in a letter of John Sterling's, written after reading the three concluding volumes of the "Literature of Europe," may be accepted as a substantially correct criticism of the work. "It is one of the few classical books which have appeared in English in our day. Sense, acuteness, thoughtfuiness, care, elegance, information, mark it throughout. There is more of cold candour than of enthusiastic warmth, with a decided tendency to moderation and caution, verging sometimes towards indifference. The criticism on works of imagination is always excellent, though one may sometimes see grounds to differ from him. The comments on the physical sciences are more a compilation, but, I suppose, very well done. It is on philosophy and the higher theology that I see most room to dissent, though even here there are a multitude of good remarks, and some extremely neat and concise accounts of the systems of great men. I cannot feel that he is at home in this highest region of thought, or is always just to those who are."[1] All Hallam's works are dignified—perhaps too dignified—in style. He never condescends to descend from his stilts and adopt a conversational manner, as the custom of some recent writers is. He took great pains with

[1] Hare's "Life of Sterling," p. 181.

his writings, never being in a hurry to complete them, and revising and re-revising them with the utmost care. In private life he was an unceasing and eager talker, very prone to argumentation and discussion. To his inferiors he is said to have adopted a rather haughty manner. Charles Knight, who, as publisher for the Society for the Diffusion of Useful Knowledge, in which Hallam took a warm interest, came a good deal into contact with him, gives no very favourable account of the learned historian in his entertaining volumes, "Passages of a Working Life."

The works of Sir Archibald Alison (1792–1867) have not stood the test of time so well as Hallam's. Though he wrote many other works, his fame, such as it is, rests almost wholly upon his "History of Europe from 1789 to the Restoration of the Bourbons in 1815," which appeared between 1833–42. It was afterwards, between 1852–56, continued to the accession of Louis Napoleon in 1852. The contemporary success of Alison's History was prodigious: it went through edition after edition and was translated into all European languages. Nevertheless it has many great faults. The author was a rigid and uncompromising Tory, regarding the Reform Bill and Free Trade with absolute abhorrence; indeed, as has been said, going so far as to date the fall of the British constitution from the fatal year 1832. Holding his political principles so firmly as he did, he did not even attempt to exclude their influence from his History, but wrote, as Disraeli wittily said, "to prove that Providence was always on the side of the Tories." His style is very tautological and diffuse; it may be said, without much exaggeration, that by striking out superfluous words and phrases the History could be abridged almost a third without any loss. But its great popularity shows that it possesses the prime merit of being interesting, and perhaps a certain amount of verbosity is not an error in a work intended for popular perusal. All critics of Alison agree in praising his industry and research.

The establishment of the *Edinburgh Review* in 1802 brought to the front two writers who have left a deep impress on the literary history of the nineteenth century. One of these was Francis Jeffrey (1773–1850), to whose energy and talents the great success of the *Review* is chiefly to be attributed. Jeffrey was the son of a depute-clerk of the Court of Session, and received his early education at the High School of Edinburgh. He was then sent to the University of Glasgow, where he attended various classes with some distinction. In 1791 he went to Queen's College, Oxford, but his stay there only lasted nine months. He never entered at all into the spirit of English university life; the studies pursued were uncongenial to him; he was full of home-sickness; and altogether the period of his residence at Oxford seems to have been about the most miserable of his very happy and bustling life. One thing he did acquire at Oxford—an affected, mincing, Anglo-Scotch accent, which never left him. It is said that when Judge Braxfield (the subject of many amusing anecdotes) heard him speak after his Oxford sojourn, he exclaimed, "The laddie has clean tint (lost) his Scotch and found nae English." His mode of speaking, combined with his airy levity, proved at first a considerable obstacle to Jeffrey's progress at the Scotch bar, to which he was called in 1794, but success in his profession soon followed his irresistible energy and vivacity, and he came to have a large practice. From his youth Jeffrey trained himself for his literary career by constantly writing essays, poems, &c., on all sorts of subjects—admirable preparation for his future work in the *Edinburgh Review*, of his connection with which he gives the following account in the preface to his "Collected Contributions:"—"I wrote the first article in the first number of the *Review* in October 1802, and sent my last contribution to it in October 1840. It is a long period to have persevered in well or in ill doing; but I was by no means equally alert in the service during all the intermediate time. I was sole editor from 1803 till late in 1829, and during that period was no doubt a large and regular contributor. In that last year, however, I received the great honour of being elected by my brethren of the bar to the office of Dean of the Faculty of Advocates, when it immediately occurred to me that it was not quite fitting that the official head of a great law corporation should continue to be the conductor of what might be fairly enough represented as in many respects a party journal, and I consequently withdrew at once and altogether from the management, which has ever since been in such hands as can have left those who take an interest in its success no cause to regret my retirement. But I should not have acted up to the spirit of this resignation, nor felt that I had redeemed the pledge of neutrality I meant to give by it, if I had not at the same time ceased to contribute to, or to concern myself in any way with the conduct or future fortunes of the *Review.* I wrote nothing for it, accordingly, for a considerable time subsequent to 1829, and during the fourteen years that have since elapsed have sent in all but four papers to that work, none of them on political subjects. I ceased, in reality, to be a contributor in 1829." Jeffrey's rise to the highest honours of his profession was rapid. In 1829 he was appointed, as mentioned above, Dean of the Faculty of Advocates; in 1831 he received from the Whig Ministry the office of Lord Advocate; and in 1834 he was made one of the Judges of the Court of Session. His parliamentary career as Lord Advocate scarcely corresponded to the high expectations of him that had been cherished; but he is allowed on all sides to have been an admirable Judge.

Few men who have taken such an active part in political and literary controversies as Jeffrey did have less exposed themselves to hatred or attack. His private character was in all respects admirable. He was beloved by his relations and by a very wide circle of friends—with reason, for no more generous and kind-hearted man ever lived. He was not one of the numerous class of men who allow their goodness of heart to evaporate in empty words, and who endeavour to succour the distressed by a copious supply of that cheap commodity—advice. When Moore was involved in pecuniary difficulties, Jeffrey at once placed his purse at his disposal; when Hazlitt, from his deathbed, wrote asking him for a loan of £10, Jeffrey at once sent him £50; and all readers have of late been made familiar with his unwearied kindness to Carlyle. Such published instances, however, are only a small part of what Jeffrey did in this way; all his kind acts were done by stealth, and most of them therefore are unrecorded. Even Harriet Martineau, who, in her splenetic "Autobiography," has rarely a good word to say for any one, speaks in warm terms of Jeffrey's boundless generosity. Acuteness, vivacity, and brilliance are his most prominent intellectual qualities. He had little depth, and as a critic could never bring himself to do justice to men of intellectual type opposed to his own. Few better examples of "Philistine" criticism could be pointed out than his review of Carlyle's translation of "Wilhelm Meister;" and his articles on Wordsworth's poetry prove conclusively how narrow was his range and how imperfect was his discernment. Within his own limited range, however, he was often exceedingly acute and brilliant; nothing could excel the skill and severity with which he broke literary butterflies on the wheel. Unfortunately for his fame, his most incisive satirical articles are not reprinted in his "Collected Contributions;" hence only a very imperfect idea of his powers can be formed by one who does not put himself to the trouble of looking up, in the old volumes of the *Edinburgh Review*, his unreprinted articles. Jeffrey's writings are now little read; and had it not been for his connection with the *Review*, his chance of obtaining permanent record in literary histories would have been small. Very likely it would have been otherwise had he ever concentrated his talents and accomplishments on the composition of some independent work, instead of constantly frittering them away in the composition of periodical articles, the fame of which is apt to be shortlived But his other occupations prevented this; and perhaps, after all, he judged rightly in employing his powers as he did. As an editor, Jeffrey magnified his office. He conceived it to be an editor's duty not only to select articles for publication, but to go over them carefully, adding a little here and erasing a little there—a process by no means agreeable to some contributors, and of which Carlyle complained bitterly. Something may be said both for and against this practice. By adopting it a judicious editor may no doubt greatly improve the articles offered to him, pruning away their extravagances, and freeing them from those little eccentricities of style and diction from which few writers are exempt. It also tends to give the various articles a certain unity of tone desirable in a periodical work conducted on fixed principles. But there is always a danger of carrying the practice too far, and infusing too much of the editor's own personality into articles "touched up" by him. Charles Dickens, who took even greater liberties than Jeffrey with the contributions to his periodical, by additions and emendations, often made them so "Dickensesque" as to impart to them a disagreeable mannerism.

Scarcely less prominently connected than Jeffrey with the origin and early career of the *Edinburgh Review* was the Rev. Sydney Smith (1771–1845), whose unique vein of wit and almost unequalled power of sarcasm gave to his contributions on temporary subjects an enduring literary value. The son of a clever but odd English gentleman, he was educated at Winchester, of which school he in due course rose to be captain. Referring to this period of his life, he used to say, "I believe, whilst a boy at school, I made above ten thousand Latin verses, and no man in his senses would dream in after-life of ever making another. So much for life and time wasted." From Winchester, Sydney went to Oxford, where, at the close of his undergraduate career, he obtained a fellowship worth about £100 a year. From this period his father left him to shift for himself, and, wanting the means necessary to gratify his desire to study for the Bar, he was compelled to enter the Church. After acting for three years as curate in a small village in Salisbury Plain, the squire of the parish engaged him as tutor to his eldest son. "It was arranged," writes Sydney, "that I and his son should proceed to the University of Weimar, in Saxony. We set out, but before reaching our destination Germany was disturbed by war, and in stress of politics we put into Edinburgh, where I remained for five years." He arrived at Edinburgh in 1797, and soon found many congenial friends among the numerous clever young men then staying there. In 1804 we find him in London, and during that and the two following years he lectured on Moral Philosophy at the Royal Institution. His lectures, which were attended by crowded and fashionable audiences, were published after his death under the title of "Elementary Sketches of Moral Philosophy." They make no pretension to philosophic depth, but, like everything that came from his pen, they are amusing and instructive. In 1806 he obtained, through the influence of the Whig Government, a presentation to the small living of Foston-le-Clay, in Yorkshire. In 1828 Lord Lyndhurst presented him with the Canonry of Bristol Cathedral; and it was through the influence of the same nobleman, though differing from him in politics, that he was enabled to exchange Foston-le-Clay for the living of Combe Florey, near Taunton. His pen had been such a powerful auxiliary in aiding the Whig party, that from them he might reasonably have expected high ecclesiastical promotion, but such never came. All they did for him was to make him a prebend of St. Paul's in 1831. This neglect of his reasonable claims Sydney felt bitterly. It is not easy to say exactly from what cause it arose. Perhaps it may have been because some of his writings were considered to be inconsistent with clerical decorum, but there were probably other and more cogent reasons. At any rate, his great Whig friends were always full of specious promises of promotion to him, which they were either unable or unwilling to translate into acts.

Sydney Smith's contributions to the *Edinburgh Review* began with its first number, and were continued till 1828, when, owing to his ecclesiastical promotion, he ceased to write in it. They embrace a very wide range of topics—Education, Methodism, Indian Missions, the Game-Laws, the Poor-Laws, Prisons and Prison Discipline, Irish Grievances, &c., &c., all handled with great acuteness and incisiveness, an abundance of sparkling wit, and in general much good feeling and sound sense. They contributed much—as well they might—to the success of the *Edinburgh*, though some people complained of their light style of treating grave topics. Even Jeffrey, it would seem, sometimes joined in this charge, which Smith successfully combated in an admirable and spirited letter written in 1819. "You must consider," he wrote to Jeffrey, "that Edinburgh is a very grave place, and that you live with philosophers who are very intolerant of nonsense. I write for the London, not for the Scotch market, and perhaps more people read my nonsense than your sense. The complaint was loud and universal against the extreme dulness and lengthiness of the *Edinburgh Review*. Too much, I admit, would not do of my style; but the proportion in which it exists enlivens the *Review*, if you appeal to the whole public, and not to the eight or ten grave Scotchmen with whom you live. I am a very ignorant, frivolous, half-inch person; but such as I am, I am sure I have done your *Review* good, and contributed to bring it into notice. Such as I am, I shall be, and cannot promise to alter. Such is my opinion of the effect of my articles. . . . Almost any of the sensible men who write for the *Review* would have written a much wiser and more profound article than I have done upon the game-laws. I am quite certain that nobody would obtain more readers for his essay upon such a subject; and I am equally certain that the principles are right, and that there is no lack of sense in it." There was never a lack either of sense or wit in anything he wrote. Ridicule was invariably employed in his writings to aid the cause and opinions which he considered to be true, and just, and honourable. A hard hitter, with a keen eye for the weak points in an opponent's armour, he delighted in combat, not content with only acting on the defensive, but sallying into the enemy's country and vigorously attacking him. He would have made an admirable writer of leading articles—his clearness, point, and vigorous way of stating facts and arguments would have made his services invaluable to newspaper editors. The only recent writer we can think of whose political articles have something of the flavour of Smith's, and, like them, bear reading after the interest of the questions which caused them has passed away, is Charles Lever, whose "O'Dowd Papers," different though they are from Smith's articles in many ways, resemble them in their emphatic, epigrammatic way of putting things, and in their skill in hitting the right nail on the head. Besides his *Review* articles, Sydney Smith wrote two volumes of sermons, not of very great merit, and an admirable and trenchant discussion of the Catholic Question, under the title of "Letters on the Subject of the Catholics, by Peter Plymley" (1808), in addition to a few smaller performances. Mr. Hayward complains that Smith's humorous writings are often deficient in ease, smoothness, grace, rhythm, and purity, because he constantly aimed at effect by startling contrasts, by the juxtaposition of incongruous images or epithets, or by the use of odd-sounding words and strange compounds of Greek and Latin derivation—speaking of a preacher as wiping his face with his "cambric *sudarium;*" of a schoolmaster as a "mastigophorous superior;" of a weak and foolish man as "anserous and asinine," &c. There does not seem much force in this criticism. Sydney Smith's mode of producing humorous effects was always original, and always well adapted to the subject in hand; and if his writings were weeded of the kind of expressions Mr. Hayward objects to, we should lose some of their wittiest and most telling strokes.

Robust in constitution, constantly cheerful, and one of the most entertaining talkers ever listened to, Sydney Smith was a "diner-out of the first water," much sought after in London society. Many of his good sayings have been preserved, and amply prove (what the recorded sayings of many other London wits certainly do not prove) that his great contemporary fame as wit and conversationist was amply deserved. Though he gave free scope to his exuberant humour, and did not scruple to ridicule the little eccentricities and angularities of his friends, he had the gift, granted to but few, of expressing his witticisms so good-humouredly that the subject of them laughed as heartily as any one. There could be no better testimony to the want of the venom in his jokes than Lord Dudley's remark, that Sydney Smith had been laughing at him for many years, and yet had never said a word to hurt him. In addition to his gifts as a talker and writer, Smith possessed the higher qualities of courage, honesty, and independence. A somewhat too great fondness for the good things of this life, which he always candidly avowed; an over-eager love of London society and the things which it prizes, were almost the only weaknesses which could be laid to his charge. He was better fitted for the Bar than the Church; and though he performed his duties as clergyman conscientiously according to his lights, his heart was never really in the work.

The establishment of *Blackwood's Magazine* in 1817 brought into notice another group of writers not less distinguished than the early contributors to the *Edinburgh*. Of this group the most prominent members were Wilson and Lockhart, to whose labours *Blackwood* owed as much of its early success as the *Edinburgh* did to Jeffrey and Sydney Smith. John Wilson (1785–1854) was born at Paisley, the son of a wealthy manufacturer there. When twelve years of age he became a student at Glasgow University, where he carried off the first prize in the Logic class, besides distinguishing himself, as at all subsequent periods of his life, by his personal prowess and athletic feats. From Glasgow, in 1803, he proceeded to Oxford, where he became a gentleman commoner of Magdalen College. There he lived a very wild and energetic life, which would probably have soon broken down any one of inferior constitution. He managed to be at the same time a hard student, a jolly companion who never flinched at his cups, and a daring and indefatigable athlete. In 1807 he quitted Oxford, having obtained his degree with singular distinction, and leaving behind him many anecdotes of his eccentric life and his great physical and intellectual capacities. His father's death had left him possessed of an ample fortune, and soon after leaving the University he purchased the small estate of Elleray, a charming property on the banks of Windermere. During his residence there he married, and for some years lived a life of unclouded prosperity, indulging in long solitary rambles on the mountains, and keeping a fleet of boats on the lake. In 1812 he published his first poem, the "The Isle of Palms," which met with praise fully commensurate to its merit, though by no means answering to the author's sanguine expectations. In 1815 his affairs suffered a sudden and severe reverse. The money bequeathed him by his father had been allowed to remain in the hands of an uncle who carried on the business, and his failure left Wilson almost penniless. From indulging in all sorts of sports and amusements, and from using his pen merely as an amusement when it suited him, he was called upon to work hard for the support of himself and his family. He accepted his altered conditions of life cheerfully and bravely. The establishment at Elleray was broken up, and he betook himself to Edinburgh, where in due course he was called to the Bar. Literature, however, and not law, was to be his profession, and he scarcely attempted to secure a practice. In 1816 he published his second volume, "The City of the Plague," containing some remarkably powerful descriptive passages. It was not, however, till the establishment of *Blackwood's Magazine* that he found a fit field for the exercise of his erratic and impulsive genius. To that periodical he was a constant contributor from its commencement to within eight or ten months of his death. So close, indeed, was his connection with it, that he was popularly supposed to be its editor—a mistake, that office being in the hands of its able and sagacious publisher. But popular opinion was not so very far wrong after all; for though not actual editor, Wilson's advice regarding contributions was very frequently asked. He himself in a letter thus accurately states the facts of the case:—"Of *Blackwood* I am not the editor, although I believe I very generally get both the credit and discredit of being Christopher North. I am one of the chief writers, perhaps the chief writer, but never received one shilling from the proprietor except for my own compositions. Being generally on the spot, I am always willing to give him my advice, and to supply such articles as are most wanted, when I have leisure." In 1820 Wilson, after a hard contest, was appointed Professor of Moral Philosophy in Edinburgh University. The rival candidate was Sir William Hamilton (1788–1856), a man of great erudition and profound philosophical genius, who was afterwards appointed Professor of Logic in Edinburgh University, and attained by his writings a European reputation. In all the qualifications for the chair Wilson was infinitely Hamilton's inferior; but Hamilton was a Whig, while Wilson was a Tory, and as most of the Town Councillors, in whose hands the appointment lay, were Tories also, he was the fortunate candidate. Few professors have entered on their duties more slenderly equipped for their task, and fewer still have succeeded as Wilson did in rapidly overcoming their defects. He never became a great philosopher, but he managed to inspire his pupils with admiration for his enthusiastic genius, and not many professors have been so much respected and loved by their pupils as he was. In 1851 he retired from his chair upon a pension of £300.

Wilson's magnificent physique; the countless anecdotes told of his wonderful feats of strength; his great brilliance in conversation; the admiration felt by many for his intellectual powers; even his numerous extravagances of conduct, all of which were set down to the eccentricity of genius, made him beyond all doubt the most popular Scotsman of his time. By many he was regarded as one of our very greatest writers. Even a critic usually so cautious as De Quincey declared that from Wilson's contributions to *Blackwood*, and more especially from his meditative examinations of great poets ancient and modern, a florilegium might be compiled of thoughts more profound and more gorgeously illustrated than exist elsewhere in human composition. Yet the truth is that people are already beginning to wonder on what rested Wilson's great fame as a man of genius. As a poet he does not occupy very high rank. No doubt beautiful passages may be pointed out in his verse, but no one probably would maintain that it bids fair to have a long life. His tales, "Lights and Shadows of Scottish Life," "The Trials of Margaret Lindsay," &c., are faulty in construction, and are already almost forgotten. Of his criticisms, many are excellent, but they are often extravagant both in praise and blame. His impulsive temperament was constantly hurrying him into extremes; he could commend and condemn with great dash and vigour, but he was constitutionally incapable of forming judicious and well-balanced estimates. Of his most famous work, the "Noctes Ambrosianæ," what shall we say? Here is the opinion of an admirer of Wilson, Professor Ferrier, on the principal figure in the "Noctes," "the Ettrick Shepherd:"—"The Ettrick Shepherd of the 'Noctes Ambrosianæ' is one of the finest and most finished creations which dramatic genius ever called into existence. Out of very slender materials, an ideal infinitely greater, more real, and more original than the prototype from which it was drawn has been bodied forth. Bearing in mind that these dialogues are conversations on men and manners, life and literature, we may confidently affirm that nowhere within the compass of that species of composition is there to be found a character at all comparable to this one in richness and readiness of resource. In wisdom the Shepherd equals the Socrates of Plato; in humour he surpasses the Falstaff of Shakespeare. Clear and prompt, he might have stood up against Dr. Johnson in close and peremptory argument; fertile and copious, he might have rivalled Burke in amplitude of declamation; while his opulent imagination and powers of comical description invest all that he utters either with a picturesque vividness or a graphic quaintness peculiarly his own," &c., &c. The character of the Shepherd has certainly considerable merit, but to say that he surpasses Falstaff in humour is as absurd as it would be to pronounce Wilson a greater man than Shakespeare. The fact of the matter is, that the "Noctes" are now for the most part unreadable. They breathe an atmosphere of whisky-toddy, of rough fun, and of practical jokes, with which the society of to-day has no sympathy. Who now cares a straw for the vast powers of eating and drinking which the heroes possess? A few fine descriptions of scenery, a few profound observations, a few just and eloquent criticisms, are buried beneath mountains of rhapsodical magniloquence and of wit which has lost its savour. Much the same remarks apply to Wilson's other writings resembling the "Noctes," such as his "Recreations of Christopher North," his "Dies Boreales," &c., &c. All his articles were written *currente calamo*, dashed off at a white heat, without much previous thought or preparation ; and they all bear traces of their hasty composition. Some admirer of Wilson ought to carry out De Quincey's notion and collect an anthology from his various writings. A moderately-sized volume of great interest and value might be thus compiled, and only in some such condensation can Wilson's works hope to escape the ravages of time. Wilson's influence upon the style of the minor writers of his day was bad, inspiring them with a passion for gorgeous colouring and picturesque epithets which led to such strange excesses as we find in many of his imitators.

John Gibson Lockhart, Wilson's friend and fellow-contributor to *Blackwood*, while lacking Christopher North's luxuriance and fertility of genius, had a much more clear-cut and well-balanced mind. He was born in 1794, the son of a Lanarkshire minister. Even while a mere child he showed the qualities which distinguished him throughout life, reserved manners, power of concentration, a keen sense of the ludicrous, which found vent in the many admirable caricatures that fell from his pen, and remarkable quickness of perception. "His reading, like that of clever children in general, was, to be sure, miscellaneous enough, for whatever came in his way he devoured. But whatever he had once devoured he never forgot. This was an advantage over other boys, which he owed in part at least to nature. His memory was retentive in the extreme, and continued so through life. Like Lord Macaulay and Sir George Cornewall Lewis, Lockhart, in the maturity of his days, seldom thought it necessary to verify a quotation of which he desired to make use."[1] After leaving the Glasgow High School, where he always managed to keep his place as dux, Lockhart entered the University of Glasgow,

[1] From an article in the *Quarterly Review* for October 1864, containing the fullest account of Lockhart which, so far as we know, has ever been published.

where, although apparently very idle and employing himself in drawing caricatures of the professors instead of attending to their lectures, he contrived to acquit himself with distinction. At the close of his Glasgow curriculum he was presented to one of the Snell Exhibitions to Oxford, and became a commoner of Balliol College ere he had completed his fifteenth year. He left Oxford in 1813, having obtained a first-class in classics, "notwithstanding that he, with unparalleled audacity, devoted part of his time to caricaturing the examining masters." After a visit to Germany, where he saw Goethe, whom through life he regarded with a reverence second only to Carlyle's, he executed his first avowed piece of literary work, a translation of Schlegel's "Lectures on the History of Literature." In 1816 he was called to the Scottish bar, but he never attained, nor indeed attempted to attain, any success in his profession. In 1817 he began to contribute to *Blackwood*, to which his pungent and graphic pen lent powerful aid, writing articles on all sorts of subjects, besides many excellent rollicking ballads, conceived in a style of which he alone possessed the secret. In 1819 he published "Peter's Letters to his Kinsfolk," clever and witty sketches of the more prominent Edinburgh celebrities of the day, which created no small stir, and were bitterly reviled by many on account of their personalities. In 1820 he married the eldest daughter of Sir Walter Scott, who fitted up for the young couple the cottage of Chiefswood on his own estate. During the following five or six years Lockhart produced his "Metrical Translations of Spanish Ballads," which Macaulay thought decidedly superior to the originals; "Valerius, a Roman Story," the first of those novels which endeavour to portray ancient life; and three other fictions, "Adam Blair," "Reginald Dalton," and "Matthew Wald." In 1826 he removed to London, having been appointed editor of the *Quarterly Review*, at a salary of £1200 a year, and, if he wrote a certain number of articles, £1500.[1] While contributing largely to the *Quarterly*—he wrote altogether over a hun-

[1] So stated in Moore's Diary (Russell's "Memoirs of Moore," vol. iv. p. 334).

dred articles for it—Lockhart found time to write besides a "Life of Burns" for "Constable's Miscellany," and a "Life of Napoleon" (mainly an abridgment of Scott) for "Murray's Family Library." In 1838 he published the last volume of his greatest and most enduring work, the "Life of Scott," the profits of which he generously handed over to Scott's creditors. He died in 1854, worn out, like Wilson, in body and in mind.

Lockhart's cold, sarcastic manners to people in general, and his power of trenchant ridicule, which he never hesitated to exercise, brought him more ill-will than falls to the lot of men in general. "Some," it is said in the article above referred to, "even felt themselves repelled from him altogether by terror of a sarcasm, for tokens of which they were constantly on the look-out; and as his manly figure was eminently stiff, those who were afraid of him saw little more than an unbending back. But this was a great mistake. In mixed companies, especially if composed of persons for whom he had little regard, Lockhart was apt enough to maintain a somewhat stately reserve. Whenever he felt that he was among men and women between whom and himself no such barrier was interposed, he became the most agreeable of companions." Certainly, however, though Lockhart may have made himself very pleasant in the society of a few eminent men, he was far from amiable, and to his unfortunate propensity to snub and quiz people he disliked must be attributed many of the disparaging stories relative to his private life which have been freely circulated, but which probably had little or no foundation in fact. In the famous "Chaldee Manuscript," the appearance of which in the first number of *Blackwood* caused such a sensation, and in the authorship of which Lockhart himself had a considerable share, he is described as "the scorpion which delighteth to sting the faces of men;" and Wilson's daughter, in her Life of her father, says of him, "Cold, haughty, supercilious in manner, he seldom won love, and not unfrequently caused his friends to distrust it in him, for they sometimes found the warmth of their own feelings thrown back upon them in presence of this cold indifference."

Lockhart is one of the select class of writers, the perusal of whose works impresses one with the idea that they might have done greater things than they actually accomplished. He possessed an intellect of great acuteness and refinement; his style is polished, terse, and vigorous; and his learning and accomplishments were far beyond the common. His novels are not of much value except for the singular elegance of their style: his most ambitious attempt in this direction, the classical tale "Valerius," must be pronounced tedious, as, indeed, novels written on the same plan generally are. He was not well qualified to be a novelist; he lacked the breadth and generosity of nature, the sympathy with different types of humanity, without which it is impossible to write a really good work of fiction. Biography was the province in which his best work was done. His "Life of Burns" is a really admirable sketch, by far the most charmingly written of all the many biographies of the great Scottish peasant. In his most ambitious performance, the "Life of Scott," faults may no doubt be pointed out. It is too long; the extracts from Scott's correspondence might have been pruned down with great advantage; he might have indulged less copiously in quoting reminiscences of Scott by other writers; and he is unjust to Constable and the Ballantynes. Yet it is an excellent biography, inferior only to Boswell's "Johnson." Lockhart faithfully carried out the biographer's first duty, to extenuate nothing and to set down naught in malice. We have in it a genuine picture of Scott as he really was, in his greatness and his littleness, his weakness and his strength. The portions of the work which come from Lockhart himself are written with such force and incisiveness as to make us wish that he had less frequently resorted to paste-and-scissors work. It is greatly to be regretted that a selection from his contributions to the *Quarterly Review* has not been published. It would give a better idea than anything else of the copiousness and energy of his style, of his keen discernment of character, and of his rare talent for biography. He was an excellent editor, accurate and punctual in money matters, and exercising wisely and well his editorial privileges over the articles submitted to him. "Every one," we are told, "who had an opportunity of knowing how Lockhart treated the essays which it was his function to introduce to the public, will remember the exquisite skill with which he could, by a few touches, add grace and point to the best-written paper—how he could throw off superfluous matter, develop a half-expressed thought, disentangle a complicated sentence, and give life and spirit to the solid sense of a heavy article, as the sculptor animates a shapeless stone."

Among the early contributors to *Blackwood* was a friend of Wilson, Thomas De Quincey, the greatest prose writer of his time, and one of the greatest writers of English prose of all times. De Quincey, who came of an ancient Norwegian family which came over with the Conqueror, was born in Manchester in 1785. His father was a wealthy merchant, who died when his son was in his seventh year, leaving his widow a fortune of £1600 a year. About 1791 the family removed to a country-house, Greenhay, about a mile from Manchester, and there they remained till 1796, when they removed to Bath. At the grammar school of that town De Quincey distinguished himself by remarkable precocity, earning fame, in particular, by the excellence of his Latin verses. He was always a thoughtful, observant child; much more introspective than children generally are, and fond of reading and solitary meditation. After having been for about two years at the Bath Grammar School, he was sent to a private school in Wiltshire, "of which the chief recommendation lay in the religious character of the master." He remained there but a year, after which he was indulged in the pleasure of a tour through Ireland, along with a young friend, Lord Westport. On his return he spent three months at Laxton, the seat of Lord Carbery, where he talked about theology to Lady Carbery, a friend of his mother's, and taught her Greek. He was then, in 1800, sent, much against his will, to Manchester Grammar School, where his guardians had decided that he should remain for three years. Though young in years he was old in mind; he felt something of degradation in the idea of associating with schoolboys; and after a year and a half's experience of the school, he found his condition so intolerable that he resolved to run away. This he accordingly did, walking all the way to Chester, where his mother was then residing. He was not sent back to school; on the contrary, at the suggestion of a kindly relative, it was arranged that he should have a guinea a week allowed him for a while, and have liberty to make a short excursion. Then ensued the most romantic episode of his erratic life. He set out for Wales, and, after wandering for some time among the mountains, it struck him that he would break off all connection with his relatives, set out for London, and borrow £200 on the strength of his expectations. Having borrowed £12 from two friends in Oswestry, he arrived in London in November 1802. Of his strange experience there, of his negotiations with the money-lenders, of how he was often on the brink of starvation, of how he was succoured by the poor outcast Anne, he has given a full and touching account in his "Confessions of an Opium-Eater." At length he was discovered and taken home, after going through experiences unique in their character, and leaving an indelible impress on the rest of his life. He remained with his mother for some time, after which, in 1803, he entered Worcester College, Oxford. His guardian could be prevailed upon to grant him only the shabby annual allowance of £100; but as he had recourse to his old friends the money-lenders, he was able to make himself tolerably comfortable. His University career was spent in as eccentric a manner as the rest of his life. Though he was an excellent classical scholar, he never attempted to make any figure in the studies of the place; following the bent of his own mind, he read what pleased him, and put academical routine at defiance. "Oxford, ancient mother!" he exclaimed, "heavy with ancestral honours, time-honoured, and, haply it may be, time-shattered power, I owe thee nothing! Of thy vast riches I took not a shilling, though living among multitudes who owed to thee their daily bread." He speaks of the "tremendous hold taken at this time of his entire sensibilities by our own literature;" and he appears also to have bestowed attention on the study of German literature and philosophy. He continued in nominal residence at the university till 1808, but never made any attempt to obtain a degree.

While at Oxford, De Quincey made frequent visits to London, and became acquainted with some literary celebrities. In 1809 he took up his residence in the Lake district, occupying the cottage at Grasmere which had been quitted by Wordsworth, with whom and Coleridge he had previously become acquainted. This cottage remained in his tenancy for twenty-seven years, and during twenty of these it was his principal place of abode. "From this era," he writes, "during a period of about twenty years in succession, I may describe my domicile as being amongst the Lakes and mountains of Westmoreland. It is true, I have often made excursions to London, Bath, and its neighbourhood, or northwards to Edinburgh; and perhaps, on an average, passed one-fourth part of each year at a distance from this district; but here only it was that henceforwards I had a house and small establishment." At Grasmere, De Quincey first became a confirmed opium-eater. He began to use the pernicious drug in 1804, but till 1812 he only took it occasionally, "fixing beforehand how often in a given time, and when, I would commit a debauch of opium." In 1813 "I was attacked," he says, "by a most appalling irritation of the stomach, in all respects the same as that which had caused me so much suffering in youth, and accompanied by a revival of the old dreams. Now then it was, viz., in the year 1813, that I became a regular and confirmed (no longer an intermitting) opium-eater." His appetite for the fatal narcotic grew by what it fed on, till in 1816 he was taking the enormous quantity of 8000 drops of laudanum per day. About the end of that year he married, and by vigorous efforts succeeded in reducing his daily allowance to 1000 drops. About a year after, however, he again succumbed to the tempter, and for three or four years took sometimes even so much as 12,000 drops per day. His affairs having become embarrassed, he made a second attempt to free himself; and so far succeeded, that, though he remained an opium-eater till the end of his life, he did not again carry the practice to such an extent as to incapacitate him for literary exertion.

De Quincey's first published literary efforts appeared in the *Westmoreland Gazette*, which he edited for about a year, between 1819–20, for the slender remuneration of a guinea a week. In the *London Magazine* for 1821 appeared his most popular work, the "Confessions of an English Opium-Eater." They created, naturally enough, a great sensation, and at once gave the author widespread celebrity. In the following year they were reprinted in a separate volume. To the *London Magazine* De Quincey continued a frequent contributor to 1824. His other principal literary engagements may be briefly summed up. In 1826 began his contributions to *Blackwood's Magazine*, for which he wrote about fifty papers. In 1834 he became a writer in *Tait's Magazine*, to which he contributed many of his most characteristic autobiographical papers, some of which have never been reprinted, although they are well worth reprinting. In 1849 he began his connection with *Hogg's Instructor*, to the publisher of which, Mr. James Hogg, we are indebted for the English edition of his collected works. He also wrote certain articles in the *North British Review* and in the "Encyclopædia Britannica," and published in 1844 a volume on the "Logic of Political Economy." From 1843 he lived at Lasswade, a small village near Edinburgh, in which city he died in 1859.

De Quincey's eccentric appearance and habits have made him the theme of many anecdotes and reminiscences. He was a very little, slender figure, not more than five feet high, with a finely intellectual head, and square, lofty brow. He took pleasure in alluding to his feeble constitution and slender frame. "A more worthless body than his own, the author is free to confess, cannot be. It is his pride to believe that it is the very ideal of a base, crazy, despicable, human system, that hardly ever could have been meant to be seaworthy for two days under the ordinary storms and wear and tear of life; and, indeed, if that were the creditable way of disposing of human bodies, he must own he should almost be ashamed to bequeath his wretched structure to any respectable dog." Nevertheless his frame must have possessed considerable powers of endurance, for he often accompanied Wilson in his walks about the Lake district; and the man who was capable of doing that must have been no contemptible pedestrian. As a conversationist his talents were great; he would go on for hours talking in the most fascinating manner in silvery, gentle accents. His manners were extremely graceful and polished; but to many of the ordinary rules of society he paid no heed, being in these matters a law unto himself. Calling at Wilson's house in Edinburgh on one occasion to avoid a shower, he remained there for the greater part of a year, spending the earlier part of the day prostrated under the influence of opium, but recovering towards night, and delighting all by his brilliant conversation. "The time," writes Mrs. Gordon, Wilson's daughter, "when he was most brilliant was generally towards the early morning hours; and then, more than once, my father arranged his supper parties so that, sitting till three or four in the morning, he brought Mr. De Quincey to that point at which in charm and power of conversation he was so truly wonderful." About money matters he was exceedingly negligent; those who knew him closely, it is said, laughed at the idea of coupling any notion of pecuniary or other like responsibility with his nature. Perhaps the tendency among those who have written on De Quincey has been to underrate his worldly wisdom and "knowingness." At any rate, while reading certain reminiscences of him, one cannot help thinking that the Opium-eater sometimes laughed in his sleeve at those who were admiring his simple-mindedness.

The Opium-eater was a man of genius, if ever there was one. Most of his faults, even his wire-drawing, his over-elaboration, his occasionally too profuse display of his knowledge, could scarcely have been committed by one less richly endowed. The crowning glory of his writings is their style, so full of involved melody, so exact and careful, so rich in magnificent apostrophes, so markedly original, so polished and elaborate. He never forgot that the prose writer, if he wishes to attain excellence, must be as much of an artist as the poet, and fashion his periods and paragraphs with as much care as the poet elaborates his rhymes and cadences. Many passages might be quoted from De Quincey of which the melody is so striking as to irresistibly attract attention, and make us linger lovingly over them apart altogether from the matter they contain. He cannot be altogether acquitted from the charge of egotism and pedantic quibbling; and it must be admitted that his humour is sometimes ponderous and far fetched. As a critic, he is in general remarkable for the breadth and fulness of his judgments; his mind had ranged over the whole world of literature, and he was singularly free from those limitations of taste which mar the work of many critics. He could read with equal pleasure Pope and Wordsworth, Coleridge and Goldsmith, Shakespeare and Milton. To say that he sometimes blundered as a critic is only to say that he was mortal—he never fully realised Goethe's genius, and he was unjust to Keats and Shelley. Some of the papers where he airs his scholarship most profusely are built up of materials obtained at second-hand, but his classical erudition was certainly extraordinary for one not a scholar by profession. Altogether, this century has produced no more remarkable literary phenomenon, certainly none who has more fully developed the resources of the English language as the vehicle of harmonious prose.

The mantle of Addison and Steele fell upon three essayists who adorned the beginning of the present century, Lamb, Hazlitt, and Leigh Hunt, men of very different talents and idiosyncrasies, but alike in having a genius for that most difficult species of composition, essay-writing. Of these, the greatest was Charles Lamb (1775–1834), one of the most captivating and graceful writers of the century. His work is small in quantity, but how rare and delicate is it in quality! The son of a London lawyer's clerk, he was educated at Christ's Hospital, where he became acquainted with Coleridge, and, had not unkindly fate prevented, would have pursued his studies at Oxford or Cambridge. To one of his simple, studious tastes, a college life would have been excellently suited; no man would have more cheerfully and gracefully accepted the position of a Fellow of a college, with no particular duties to attend to beyond the daily routine of ordinary tasks. But he never had the chance of obtaining a fellowship, becoming, when he left Christ's Hospital, a clerk in the Old South Sea House, which he has so inimitably described in one of his essays. From it, at the age of seventeen, he was transferred to the service of the East India Company, in whose employ he remained till 1825, when he retired on a handsome pension. Lamb's life was uneventful, except for one great tragedy. There was a taint of insanity in his family; and one day in 1796, his sister Mary, in a paroxysm of madness, stabbed her mother to the heart. From this time Charles became the guardian of his sister, unselfishly sacrificing for her sake a passion he had conceived for a young lady mentioned in the Essays as "Alice W.," and devoting himself to her care with that noble love which refuses to regard its efforts as anything praiseworthy or out of the way. It has been well remarked that the history of the long association between brother and sister, broken from time to time by a fresh accession of the fatal malady, is one of the most touching things in fact or fiction. Carlyle, whose remarks on Lamb in his "Reminiscences" are positively cruel, would have done well to ask himself before penning them whether he, superior to the gentle Elia as he thought himself, would have been capable of such continuous self-devotion. Lamb's first publications were some verses contributed to a volume of poems by Coleridge and Lloyd, published in 1797. His prose tale "Rosamond Gray" followed in 1798, and in 1801 his drama, "John Woodvil," based on Elizabethan models, which was unmercifully criticised in the *Edinburgh Review*—not altogether undeservedly, though it contains some fine passages. In 1807 he published his "Tales from Shakespeare," written in conjunction with his sister. They form one of the best books for intelligent youthful readers with which we are acquainted. The "Essays of Elia," those charming papers which will keep his memory alive for many generations, appeared from time to time in the *London Magazine*, from which they were reprinted in a collected form in 1823.

Lamb was a slight, nervous, excitable man, full of odd whims and fancies, and greatly given to the utterance of paradoxical remarks, made all the more strange by his stammering mode of speaking. Two or three glasses of wine were sufficient to intoxicate, or at least to elevate him; and hence those convivial excesses, in which there is reason to fear that he indulged too freely during the latter years of his life, were apt to be exaggerated. Before condemning him too severely for his habits of intoxication, we ought to consider how heavy and trying was the burden which he had to bear. Lamb's style, quaint, full of ingenious turns, having little affinity with that of any writer of his day, but full of resemblances to his favourite authors of bygone eras, was a reflex of himself. He disliked new books, new friends, and new fashions. For the literature of his own time, with the exception of the limited portion of it written by his own friends, he cared little; but with what delight did he hang "for the thousandth time over some passage in old Burton or one of his strange contemporaries;" and with what enthusiasm would he point out the beauties in a play written by some forgotten Elizabethan dramatist; with what eager zest would he peruse one of the comedies of intrigue of which Charles II.'s time produced so many examples! He was an admirable critic of what really pleased him; no one has handled some of our older authors with finer discrimination. The brief notices of the Elizabethan dramatists in his "Specimens" are perfect masterpieces in their way, full of that swift insight, that delicate appreciation of merit, which only long and loving study can give. As a humorist, Lamb is quite *sui generis:* he resembled no one, and has found no successful imitator. His humour had a fine literary flavour about it; no one who does not love reading is ever likely to be a thoroughgoing admirer of Lamb's. It is also intensely personal; Lamb's likes and dislikes, his whims, caprices, and fancies, figure on every page. Few great humorists have been less dramatic than Lamb; whatever the topic on which he was writing, he could never get rid of his own idiosyncrasy. In his various essays he has left a faithful and true portrait of himself, with all his out-of-the-way humour and opinions; and irresistibly attractive the portrait is. How delightful it is, after having experienced the glitter and glare of much of our modern literature, to converse with the tranquil and gentle Elia, with his calm retrospective glance, and his love of communing with invisible things! "He would," said Leigh Hunt, "beard a superstition and shudder at the odd phantasm while he did it. One would have imagined him cracking a joke in the teeth of a ghost, and then melting into thin air himself out of sympathy with the awful." Not many authors are held in more kindly remembrance than Lamb by those who have really learned to love his frolic and gentle spirit. "Lamb's memory," said Southey—and hundreds of readers will re-echo the words—"will retain its fragrance as long as the best spice that ever was expended upon the Pharaohs."

From the placid and sweet-tempered Elia we pass to the vindictive and irascible William Hazlitt (1778–1830), a writer of very remarkable but ill-regulated powers. The son of a dissenting minister, he was educated with a view to adopting his father's profession. When seventeen years of age, however, he determined to become a painter, and spent some years in artistic labour, till he finally turned aside to literature. His first publication was a tiny volume on the "Principles of Human Action." This work, which found few to admire it except its author, who regarded it with a parent's love, was followed by many pieces of literary journey-work—abridgments, translations, compilations, and the like. The first performance of his which attracted attention was his lectures at the Surrey Institution on the "English Poets" (1818), after which came his lectures on "English Comic Writers," on the "Dramatic Literature of the Age of Elizabeth," and on the "Characters of Shakespeare's Plays"—volumes containing much sound and striking criticism, but often misleading as containing judgments based on imperfect acquaintance with the works of the writer criticised. Hazlitt, it must be owned, was by no means sufficiently impressed with the truth of the great fact that before writing about an author it is desirable to read his works. For example, he did not begin to write his lectures on the Elizabethan dramatists till within six weeks of the time when they had to be delivered, and his judgments on their qualities were based on his hasty study of their works within that very limited period. His other chief works are his "Table-Talk" (1821–22), a series of miscellaneous essays; his "Spirit of the Age" (1825), containing criticisms on contemporary authors; the "Plain Speaker" (1826), another collection of miscellaneous essays, and his "Life of Napoleon" (1828–30), which is his most ambitious performance. It is a characteristic and not altogether useless production, in which he takes the side of the Emperor as strongly as a French writer could have done, and has nothing but contempt and hatred for his opponents. It did not sell, and poor Hazlitt died in poverty after a struggling, restless, unhappy life. Most of his mischances were more or less due to himself; his disposition was such that it is impossible to imagine him happy and contented, however prosperous had been his fortunes.

Hazlitt had a genuine gift for style; he was no mere mechanical stringer together of phrases. His chief characteristics as a writer are well pointed out by Mr. Leslie Stephen. "Readers," he says, "who do not insist upon measuring all prose by the same standard will probably agree that if Hazlitt is not a great rhetorician, if he aims at no gorgeous effects of complex harmony, he has yet an eloquence of his own. It is indeed an eloquence which does not imply quick sympathy with many modes of feeling, or an intellectual vision at once penetrating and comprehensive. It is the eloquence characteristic of a proud and sensitive nature, which expresses a very keen if narrow range of feeling, and implies a powerful grasp of one, if only one side of the truth. Hazlitt harps a good deal upon one string, but that string vibrates forcibly. His best passages are generally an accumulation of short, pithy sentences, shaped in strong feeling and coloured by picturesque associations, but repeating rather than corroborating each other. Each blow goes home, but falls on the same place. He varies the phrase more than the thought; and sometimes he becomes obscure, because he is so absorbed in his own feelings that he forgets the very existence of strangers who require explanation. Read through Hazlitt, and the monotony becomes a little tiresome; but dip into them at intervals, and you will often be astonished that so vigorous a writer has not left some more enduring monument of his remarkable powers." As a critic, Hazlitt's judgments, whether on contemporary or on former writers, must be accepted with reserve. He could always clothe his opinions in fitting words, but he was not always equally careful to see that his estimates were not marred by personal prejudice or by the desire of saying a striking thing, whether applicable to the subject in hand or not. His accounts of the eminent writers of his day, much abused though they were at the time of their publication, are perhaps the most interesting and valuable portions of his works. Often vindictive and splenetic, they are always graphic and incisive, and rarely fail to call our attention to traits in the character of those under notice which might otherwise have escaped us.

The essays of Leigh Hunt cannot be pronounced equal in value to those of Hazlitt and Lamb. But besides being an essayist, he was a poet of powers considerably superior to mediocrity. James Henry Leigh Hunt was born in 1784, the son of a lawyer, and, like Lamb, was educated at Christ's Hospital. His genius was precocious, and in 1802 his father published a collection of his verses under the title of "Juvenilia." In 1808 he became connected with his brother in conducting the *Examiner*, in which he resolved to speak out his mind upon men and measures without fear and without favour. This resolution he carried out so vigorously as to expose himself to several prosecutions for libel; for the Government of that day looked with a jealous eye on the press, and free discussion and ventilation of public grievances were frowned on as much as possible. In 1813 for a certainly rather trenchant but perfectly just comment on the Prince

Regent in the *Examiner*, he was sentenced to imprisonment for two years. Hunt's works were many and various. We need only enumerate a few. A poem, the "Story of Rimini," appeared in 1816; in 1819–21 he published the "Indicator," a series of essays on the plan of the *Spectator*, followed by one or two similar periodicals; in 1832, "Sir Ralph Esher," a fictitious biography dealing with the times of Charles II.; in 1839 a poem of considerable merit, "Captain Sword and Captain Pen;" and in 1850 his most interesting work, his "Autobiography." In 1847 he received a pension of £200 per annum from Government, which he lived to enjoy till 1859. The works above mentioned are only a small portion of Hunt's contributions to literature. He wrote lives of the chief Restoration dramatists, two volumes, "Imagination and Fancy" and "Wit and Humour," excellent companions for those beginning the study of English literature, and many other works. In 1828 he published a book, "Recollections of Lord Byron and his Contemporaries," which made a great noise at the time. It was the record of a brief and disappointing companionship with his Lordship in Italy, and was written in a strain far from pleasing to his Lordship's friends, to whom it gave great offence. There does not appear to have been anything in it but what was strictly true, but as it was written when Hunt was smarting under the feeling that he had been ill-used by the noble bard, its tone and its revelations of Byron's character were such that Hunt afterwards regretted its publication.

Hunt's personal appearance is graphically described in Carlyle's "Reminiscences:" "Dark complexion (a trace of the African, I believe), copious, clean, strong black hair, beautifully-shaped head, fine beaming serious hazel eyes; seriousness and intellect the main expression of the face (to our surprise at first); . . . fine clean elastic figure too he had, five feet ten or more." His manner was particularly winning and attractive; it is said that no one, however strongly opposed to his opinions, could become personally acquainted with him without liking him. His character was one very ill adapted to practical hard-working

England. He was the child of sentiment, careless about business matters to an extent that sorely tried the patience of his best friends, and taking no more thought than lilies about the pressing demands of active life. His careless and sanguine temperament led him to have no proper self-respect about pecuniary obligations; though earning by literature what ought to have decently supplied his wants, he was constantly in debt, and relied to a considerable extent upon the benefactions of the many friends whom his amiability of character brought him. No one can have the notions about money matters which Hunt had without incurring a good deal of contempt—good-humoured contempt it may be, but nevertheless contempt of a kind which a high-spirited man would rather die than expose himself to. The sneering way in which Hunt was regarded by some of the friends who aided him may be learnt from the remarks on him in Macaulay's diary and letters, and from the use Dickens made of various traits of his character in delineating Harold Skimpole in "Bleak House." Hunt's essays and other writings are pleasant and graceful. He had an unusually delicate and catholic literary taste, and considerable powers of good-humoured sarcasm occasionally reminding us of Addison. His "Story of Rimini" has been called the finest narrative poem since Dryden; and though this is rather exaggerated praise, Hunt's poems are of such merit which ought to have saved them from the oblivion into which they have fallen of late years.

In "Bleak House" another character besides Harold Skimpole is copied from an eminent literary celebrity. Walter Savage Landor, whose works are regarded by a select public with an admiration which they are never likely to obtain from the world at large, sat for the portrait of Laurence Boythorn in that novel. Landor was born in 1775, and was educated at Rugby and Oxford. Very early he gave evidence of his haughty, insubordinate spirit, and of his ungovernable temper ("the worst," he himself very justly said, "that ever man was cursed with"). He was obliged to quit both Rugby and Oxford in consequence of his defiance of the constituted authorities. At the same time he did not neglect scholarship, showing in his Rugby days, as afterwards, a wonderful taste and power for making Latin verses, and imbuing himself deeply in the spirit of the classical writers. After his rustication from Oxford he was put upon a yearly allowance, with liberty to travel where he pleased. His first important work was a poem, "Gebir" (1797), much admired by Shelley (who, it is related, "would read it aloud to others or to himself with a tiresome pertinacity"), and by the author himself, but which, like the rest of Landor's works, proved "caviare to the general." Left wealthy by the death of his father in 1805, Landor lived a rather "fast" and very extravagant life at Bath and Clifton for two or three years, after which in 1808 he made a rash but generous raid into Spain to assist in the war of liberation, which deeply engaged his sympathies, he being then, as always, a zealous republican. Having quarrelled with some of his associates, he soon came home again, "heartily disgusted with the whole affair, having wasted time and money to no good whatsoever." In 1812 he published his tragedy of "Count Julian," which was written at Llanthony, a small estate, his purchase of which must be reckoned one of the most unfortunate events of his stormy career. Nothing prospered with him there. He got into endless disputes with his tenantry and his neighbours, and in 1814 he came to the resolution to quit it and England, never to return. Arriving in Italy, he spent twenty years there, writing his "Imaginary Conversations" (1824–29), and his "Pericles and Aspasia" (1836), and living more peacefully than at any other period of his life. In 1835 he was driven from Italy by a furious quarrel with his wife, and returning to England, a second time took up his residence at Bath. In 1847 he published his "Hellenics," and in 1853 "Last Fruit off an Old Tree," containing some imaginary conversations and other miscellanies. The story of his remaining years has been thus tersely summed up:—"He fell into bad hands, got mixed up in a disgraceful scandal, published a libel for which he was cast in damages, and, to avoid payment of the fine, left England for Florence in 1858, where he died miserably, September 17, 1864, æt. 89."

Landor was a man of fine physique and distinguished bearing, with a wide and full but retreating forehead, massive head, and large grey eyes—in every respect a very noticeable man. His vehement, reckless, passionate temper and his absence of self-control and moderation embittered his life; but he had in many respects a noble and generous nature, and succeeded in endearing to himself not a few distinguished friends who patiently put up with his many eccentricities and freaks of temper. It may be doubted whether he ranks highest as a poet or as a prose writer. Some of his poems are of such classic finish and grace as to be perfect gems of song, unique and unapproachable; and De Quincey ranked his character of Count Julian with the Satan of Milton and the Prometheus of Æschylus. His "Imaginary Conversations" are full of fine thoughts, expressed in a style so finished, so eloquent, so clearly bearing the impress of genius and cultivated taste, so felicitous in imagery and in diction, that one wonders why they are in general so little read. The reason probably is that their subjects have little interest to people in general, and that their tone of sentiment does not for the most part appeal to the ordinary sympathies and emotions of humanity. "No man," says an admirer, with pardonable exaggeration, "since Shakespeare's time, has written so much wisdom or so much beauty; in no other man's work is there such exquisite tenderness, so much subtlety of thought, such wealth of imagery, yet all chaste and nothing glaring, so much suggestiveness, yet such ample fulness. Not a page but contains the most deathless beauty."

By far the most eminent divine and preacher of the time with which we are dealing was Dr. Thomas Chalmers (1780–1847), a name still never pronounced without reverence by many in Scotland, on the ecclesiastical history of which country he exercised great influence. Chalmers was born at Anstruther in Fifeshire, educated at St. Andrews, and licensed to preach in 1799. The more notable dates in his life are the following:—From 1802 to 1815 he was minister of Kilmany in Fifeshire. In the latter year he was called to the Tron Church in Glasgow, and from this period dates his great vogue as a preacher. In 1823 he was appointed Professor of Moral Philosophy in St. Andrews, and in 1828 Professor of Divinity in Edinburgh. Always a prominent figure in church courts, he was one of the prime movers in the conflict which terminated in the disruption of the Scottish Church in 1843, and from that time till his death was the presiding spirit of the new Free Church, being appointed moderator of its first Assembly, and principal of its college in Edinburgh. The description of Chalmers in Carlyle's questionable "Reminiscences" is a very admirable piece of character-painting: "He was a man of much natural dignity, ingenuity, honesty, and kind affection, as well as sound intellect and imagination. A very eminent vivacity lay in him, which could rise to complete impetuosity (growing conviction, passionate eloquence, fiery play of heart and head), all in a kind of *rustic* type, one might say, though wonderfully true and tender. He had a burst of genuine fun too, I have heard, of the same honest, but most plebeian, broadly natural character; his laugh was a hearty loud guffaw; and his tones in preaching would rise to the piercingly pathetic. No preacher ever went so into one's heart. He was a man essentially of little culture, of narrow sphere all his life; such an intellect professing to be educated and yet so *ill-read*, so ignorant in all that lay beyond the horizon in place or in time, I have almost nowhere met with. A man capable of much soaking indolence, lazy brooding, and do-nothingism, as the first stage of his life well indicated; a man thought to be timid almost to the verge of cowardice, yet capable of impetuous activity and blazing audacity, as his latter years showed. I suppose there will never again be such a preacher in any Christian church." If Chalmers was constitutionally indolent, he certainly managed to overcome his indolence to an unprecedented extent, for few have passed more active lives than he. A man of much force of character, he was formed by nature to take a leading part in all public movements in which he took an interest. Few have excelled him in his genius for organisation, and his skill in the management of men. He was an earnest social reformer, took a keen interest in political economy and kindred subjects, and was indefatigable in forming plans for the relief of the poor. A born orator, wherever he preached he was attended by admiring crowds, who hung eagerly upon every word that fell from his lips. In spite of his constant exertions in other fields, he found time to write a great deal, his works extending to over thirty volumes, of which a considerable proportion consists of lectures, sermons, &c. His literary aptitude was unquestionably great, though he was not free from the common vice of preachers—a tendency to diffuseness and repetition. He has few superiors as a master of luminous exposition, and not unfrequently we find in his writings bursts of splendid eloquence which enable us to comprehend the wonderful influence which he exerted over his hearers. His "Astronomical Discourses" may be mentioned as a favourable specimen of his style. Altogether he was the most notable Scotchman of his time (Scott, who died before his fame was at its height, alone excepted), a wonderful example of the union of literary genius, oratorical powers, and practical ability.

X.

OUR OWN TIMES.

Dickens, Thackeray, Lytton, Charlotte Brontë; George Eliot, Lever, Charles Kingsley, Lord Beaconsfield, Charles Reade, Anthony Trollope, Blackmore, Hardy, Black; Tennyson, Browning, Mrs. Browning, Rossetti, Morris, Swinburne; Macaulay, Carlyle, Grote, Froude, Freeman, Lecky; Ruskin, Matthew Arnold, Sir Arthur Helps, John Morley, W. H. Pater; Theology, Philosophy, Science.

MANY difficulties beset any one attempting to deal, however briefly, with the literature of one's own time. As distance is required to judge properly of the comparative height of mountains, which, when we are beside them, seem of about the same size, so before an author can be justly estimated, sufficient time must have elapsed to allow the din of contemporary applause or censure to subside, and to enable us to clear our eyes from the mists of prejudice and personal predilection which always more or less prevent us from forming perfectly impartial judgments on the men of our own era. It requires no very extensive acquaintance with literary history to know that many reputations which once blazed high have in a few short years sunk into nothing and been heard of no more; that writers of the greatest popularity with their own generation have been pronounced worthless and unreadable in the generations that came after. How, then, we may ask ourselves, as we call to mind some great literary celebrity of the present day, can we be sure that the case will prove otherwise with him? have we any solid ground for thinking that his fame too, great as it now appears, is not founded upon some shifting rock of popular caprice or bad taste which the remorseless tide of time will wash away?

Moreover, when one begins to reflect upon the literature of one's own time, so many eminent names crowd in upon one's recollection, that the task of selecting the greatest of them appears full of almost insuperable difficulties. It is a case of not being able to see the wood for trees; we need, but cannot find, some vantage-ground from which we may survey the surrounding landscape. The limits of this book require that only a few of many names deserving notice shall be mentioned here; but we shall endeavour to make the selection as representative as possible.

As the drama was the favourite vehicle of Elizabethan genius, so the novel has been the most richly cultivated field of literature during the reign of Queen Victoria. More pens have been employed in this department, and greater successes have been gained, than in any other. We may therefore fitly begin our survey with fiction, being farther induced to do so by the consideration that by far the most popular author of recent times was a novelist. It is scarcely necessary to say that we refer to Charles Dickens, whose literary career began earlier, continued longer, and was more brilliant than that of any preceding English writer of fiction. He was born at Landport, Portsea, in 1812. His father, John Dickens, a clerk in the Navy Pay Office, was the good-hearted, shiftless, sanguine, and unfortunate individual afterwards portrayed in immortal colours as Mr. Micawber. In the silken sail of Dickens's infancy the wind of a by no means particularly joyful dawn blew free. His youth was a hard one, and the dark reflection of what he then endured coloured more or less distinctly the whole of his subsequent life. While he was yet little more than an infant his father was brought up by his duties from London to Portsmouth; soon after he was placed upon duty at Chatham Dockyard; and at Chatham Charles lived from his fourth or fifth year till he was nine. There he received the elements of education, first from his mother, and afterwards at two schools. He was a small sickly boy, unfitted to join in the rough sports of his companions, and he read incessantly, devouring with intense eagerness such glorious books as the

"Arabian Nights," the "Vicar of Wakefield," "Roderick Random," "Robinson Crusoe," "Gil Blas," &c., &c. But his love of reading was not the only token of his precocity. He wrote a tragedy called "Misnar, the Sultan of India;" was an excellent storyteller; and sang comic songs so well that admiring friends used to hoist him on a chair in order that he might delight their guests with an exhibition of his powers. When the boy was nine years old, his father was removed from Chatham to Somerset House, and it was now that Dickens began to have experience of those wretched shifts and petty trials brought on by poverty, with which he has filled many pages of his novels. His father fell into the clutches of his creditors, and was lodged in the Marshalsea; and Dickens, never a particularly well-taken-care-of boy, was now employed in such vile offices as running errands and taking messages to the prisoner, and pledging one by one nearly all the household goods at the pawnbroker's shop. The worst, however, was yet to come. A relative, James Lamert, who had started a blacking business, knowing the depressed circumstances of the Dickens family, offered Charles employment in his warehouse at a salary of six or seven shillings a week. The offer was at once thankfully accepted. In the description of the life which David Copperfield led at Murdstone and Grimby's, Dickens has revealed to all the world how infinitely bitter and agonising to him was the time he passed at Lamert's blacking warehouse. A proud, sensitive boy, he shrank both from entering into close companionship with his rough fellow-drudges, and from taking any one into his confidence and revealing the secret misery which was gnawing at his heart. Unconsciously, all through the troubled years of his boyhood, he was receiving a better training for his future work in life than any school or University could have given him. He employed his faculty of observation, which appears from his earliest years to have been almost morbidly keen, in noting in his mind in indelible characters all the odd scenes, and things, and persons that he met with in his diversified existence. What is perhaps even more remarkable than the extraordinary faculty of observation which he possessed while yet a mere child, is the fact that, in spite of all his bitterness of spirit at this time, he seems to have seen quite clearly the humorous side of his father's misfortunes. At last a fortunate mischance released him from the slavery of the blacking business. His father and James Lamert quarrelled, and although his mother set herself to accommodate the quarrel, his father decided that he should go back no more, but should be sent to school. Fortunately for Dickens and for the world this determination was acted on. "I do not write regretfully or angrily," he wrote many years afterwards in words whose apparent harshness it is impossible not to condone, "for I know how all these things have worked together to make me what I am; but I never afterwards forgot, I never shall forget, I never can forget, that my mother was warm for my being sent back."

Dickens was now sent to a school called "Wellington House Academy," where he remained for nearly two years, quitting it when a little over fourteen years of age. While here he, according to his own account, "distinguished himself like a brick;" according to the more credible narratives of his school companions, he was remarkable rather for his fondness for fun and practical jokes than for learning. Nevertheless he somehow managed to pick up a good deal of information, including a smattering of Latin. Soon after he left school he became a clerk in a lawyer's office, at the modest salary of ten shillings and sixpence a week. Encouraged by the example of his father, who had become a reporter for the *Morning Herald*, Dickens determined to follow in his footsteps, and set himself resolutely to the study of shorthand, in order that he too might obtain employment in that fairly remunerated and not unattractive profession, which has afforded a stepping-stone to higher positions to so many young men of literary capacity. After much arduous labour Dickens succeeded in obtaining a mastery of the crooked cipher; and there being at that time no opening in the Gallery, he became a reporter for one of the offices in Doctor's Commons. The work there was uninteresting and precarious, and he made an attempt to escape from it by going upon the stage. Had this attempt succeeded, there can be no doubt he would have distinguished himself; and instead of a great comic author, we should have had a great comic actor. Fortunately, however, it came to nothing; and, advancing in his career as reporter, he was employed on various newspapers, including, last and most important, the *Morning Chronicle*, one of the leading daily journals of the time. He was an excellent reporter—not particularly neat indeed, but almost unprecedentedly rapid in his execution.

From reporting, the transition to original writing is not difficult. One day in 1834 Dickens dropped "Mrs. Joseph Porter over the Way," the first of the afterwards well-known "Sketches by Boz," into the letter-box of the *Old Monthly Magazine*. It was, to the author's great pride and joy, accepted, and was followed by eight more in the same periodical, the remainder of the series appearing in the *Evening Chronicle*, the afternoon edition of the newspaper with which Dickens was connected. In 1836 the "Sketches by Boz" were reprinted in book form. They were very successful for a first publication; and Messrs. Chapman & Hall were induced by their originality, and the promise of future power which they exhibited, to ask Dickens to write the text of a humorous work to be illustrated by Seymour, and to be published in monthly numbers. He consented, and the result was the "Pickwick Papers." The original plan of the work was considerably modified, owing to the suicide of Mr. Seymour before the second number was completed. As number after number appeared, its circulation grew greater and greater, until by the time half of it had been issued Dickens had taken the position, which he maintained till his death, of the most popular novelist of the day. During the publication of "Pickwick," "Oliver Twist," another work of great power, of a different kind, however, from "Pickwick," was appearing in *Bentley's Miscellany*, a monthly periodical of which Dickens had become editor. No better proof of the extraordinary rapidity with which his fame had increased could be given than the fact that when, after the publication of "Pickwick," he tried to buy back the copyright of the "Sketches," which he had sold for £150, the publisher refused to sell it for less than £2000. After "Oliver Twist" came "Nicholas Nickleby," which was completed in October 1839. Then followed the collection of stories published under the name of "Master Humphrey's Clock:" "The Clock," "The Old Curiosity Shop" (containing what is perhaps the finest specimen of Dickens's pathos—the death of Little Nell), and "Barnaby Rudge." A tour in America in 1842 led to the writing of "American Notes for General Circulation," and "Martin Chuzzlewit" (1844), the latter of which, in some portions of it, must stand for his greatest success. In 1843, while "Chuzzlewit" was appearing in monthly parts, he began that series of Christmas books which charmed so many hearts, by writing the "Christmas Carol." "Dombey and Son" came out in 1847–48; "David Copperfield," a semi-autobiographical story, which was the favourite child of the author, and of perhaps the majority of his readers, in 1849–50; "Bleak House" (which marks the beginning of the decadence of his genius), in 1853; and thereafter "Hard Times," "Little Dorrit," "A Tale of Two Cities," "Great Expectations," and "Our Mutual Friend." In 1870 began the publication of "Edwin Drood," never, alas! completed, death staying the progress of his magic pen on June 9, 1870. The above is not by any means a full list of his publications. He wrote besides "A Child's History of England," excellent in plan but not in execution, which was published originally in *Household Words*, a weekly periodical begun by him, and carried on till 1859, when, owing to a quarrel with his publishers, it was incorporated with *All the Year Round*, and went on with unflagging success until the editor's death; "Pictures from Italy," &c., &c. Among his more notable contributions to his magazine were the Christmas numbers, which he wrote in whole or in part for some years. He left behind him a fortune of £95,000, amassed partly by the success of his works, partly by the enormous sums he received for his public readings, begun in 1858 in this country and in America, to which he paid an extremely lucrative and successful visit in 1867–68.

Dickens's character was not a very complex or puzzling one. A man of great "push" and energy, casting aside any obstacle which came across his path with a sort of fiery vehemence, always sure of his ground, and equally sure that he was putting his best foot foremost, he would have made his mark in any calling. Much of his confidence in himself, his thorough conviction that he could fight through any struggle, must be attributed to the extraordinary rapidity with which he attained fame and fortune. His remarkable self-complacency, however natural, was not a pleasing trait in his character; his letters frequently weary us by their persistent egotism; their constant ringing of the changes on the same theme, "the inimitable Boz." It never seems to have occurred to him that anything he did could be faulty; everything that proceeded from his pen was in his eyes perfect of its kind. A natural result of his intense conviction of the greatness of his own genius was that he sometimes thought that he had a right to be a law unto himself, and to disregard those rules which are binding on lesser men. His separation from his wife in 1858, brought about, so far as appears, by no other cause than an alleged incompatibility of temper, and the circumstances attending that unfortunate occurrence, were not at all to his credit. Yet he was a man of very affectionate nature, singularly fond of his children, and so charitable that he met many of the countless applications to him for aid with a generosity that could hardly be surpassed. His love of the poor was not of that specious sort which evaporates in sentimental writing and gushing after-dinner oratory. In contrast to many of his literary brethren, Dickens, like Scott, was of remarkably methodical business habits, always carrying out his favourite maxim that whatever is worth doing at all, is worth doing well. Among his other characteristics, we should not omit to mention his remarkable liking and talent for acting, which he displayed whenever a good opportunity offered, his favourite character being Bobadil in Ben Jonson's "Every Man in his Humour." The enormous success of his readings from his own works was partly owing to his remarkable elocutionary powers, and to the same cause was partly due his many triumphs as an after-dinner speaker.

To the question, what is the quality in Dickens's writings which stands out most prominent, and which will in all probability secure for them a permanent place in English literature? most readers will return the same answer. Undoubtedly it is their humour. The man is not be envied who can read the "Pickwick Papers"—which, despite its faulty construction, will stand as long and as sure as anything that Dickens has written—without frequent and hearty bursts of unrestrainable laughter; and in all his novels the humorous portions are as a rule infinitely the most attractive. There are few cultured readers of "Martin Chuzzlewit," for example, who, on a second or third perusal, do not sagaciously skip the chapters devoted to Tom Pinch and his sister, while lingering fondly over the exquisite portions which deal with Mr. Pecksniff and with Martin's adventures in America. All critics and the vast majority of readers are now agreed in regarding Dickens's pathos as immeasurably inferior to his humour, looking upon the former as coarse and unrefined, and ridiculously sentimental. Yet at one time not only did thousands of ordinary readers cry over his pages, but such men as Jeffrey and Macready followed suit. It is difficult to account for this change of popular taste; unless we admit it to be the case that the fashion of pathos changes much more quickly than that of humour, so that what was considered pathos in one generation is often pronounced bathos by the succeeding one. In Dickens's latter books, the humorous element grew more and more scanty and thin. After "David Copperfield," he wrote no story containing in it a large portion of the fresh hearty laughter that we find in every page of "Pickwick." Yet there was no falling off in his popularity; the public stood by him to the last. "Little Dorrit," for example, which has always seemed to us to resemble a story written by a man of genius in a nightmare, sold as largely as any of its predecessors, in spite of the denunciations of the critics. It is not at all unlikely that one of Dickens's defects helped in securing his extraordinary popularity, viz., his ignorance. Perhaps no modern author of equal eminence ever cared so little for literature: indeed, there is not much exaggeration in saying that his works might have been written equally well though he had never read a book. Thus he appealed to two publics, while other novelists of wider culture have appealed to only one. His genius was such that people of refinement could not but read him, even though they found in him much that was repellent to them; while his ignorance prevented him from flying over the heads of the multitude by learned allusions, and kept him close to a style of narrative which, whatever may be its artistic faults, is always such as to command popular sympathy.

While Dickens was at the height of his popularity, his great rival, William Makepeace Thackeray, was slowly climbing up the ladder of fame, attaining each additional step with difficulty. Thackeray was born at Calcutta on July 18, 1811, the son of a gentleman employed in the East India Company's Service. His father died while he was yet a child, and he was brought to England and sent early to the Charterhouse, of which his recollections were by no means pleasant. In 1829 he entered Trinity College, Cambridge, where, however, his residence was very short. There he gave the first indication of his literary powers by taking part in editing a little paper called the *Snob*, to which he contributed some burlesque verses in the peculiar vein in which he afterwards distinguished himself. On leaving Cambridge he went to Weimar, and for some years alternated between it and Paris, studying drawing, as he at that time intended to become an artist. Possessed of a very considerable fortune, young Thackeray, with his quick sense of humour, his enjoyment of life, and his propensity to indolence, which he was at this time easily able to gratify, doubtless led a very jovial existence. But in two or three years his fortune had utterly disappeared. Part of it was lost at card-playing, part by unlucky speculation, part by two disastrous newspaper enterprises in which he had been induced to embark. Then, finding that art was not likely to afford him means of subsistence, he was induced to become a writer by profession. Toilsome and trying was his upward path in that most alluring yet often most deceptive profession. His first important engagement was on the staff of *Fraser's Magazine.* In it he wrote among other things the "Yellowplush Correspondence," of which the first instalment appeared in 1837; the "History of Mr. Samuel Titmarsh and the Great Hoggarty Diamond;" and "Barry Lyndon," a story of the "Jonathan Wild" stamp, and, though unpleasant in subject, in some respects one of the most powerful productions of his pen. About 1840 he began his connection with *Punch*, to which some of his best work, including the inimitable "Snob Papers," was contributed. In 1840 appeared his "Paris Sketch Book;" in 1843 his "Irish Sketch Book," and in 1844 his "Journey from Cornhill to Grand Cairo," all appearing under the pseudonym of Michael Angelo Titmarsh, though the dedication to the "Irish Sketch Book" was signed with his own name. In addition to the above, he performed a variety of other work during his literary "journey-years," contributing to the *Times*, the *New Monthly Magazine*, &c.

Up to 1846 Thackeray's name, though no doubt familiar enough to literary people, was almost unknown to the world at large. Some clear-sighted critics, such as John Sterling, had indeed recognised the originality and genius of his work; but he had not yet made what is called a "hit," and had still to make his voice heard above the hundreds of clever writers whose work perishes with their lives. In the above-mentioned year, however, began the publication of "Vanity Fair," in the monthly parts which Dickens had made popular. Its progress in popular estimation was slow at first; but gradually it began to be talked about, and on its completion in 1848 it had raised Thackeray to such a position that, in the opinion of all competent to judge, he now divided with Dickens the throne of the realm of fiction. Its success was aided by a friendly and appreciative notice in the *Edinburgh Review* for January

1848, which introduced Thackeray to many to whom he had scarcely been known previously. This notice was written by a friend of his, Mr. Abraham Hayward, whose anecdotal and entertaining pen is still busy, he having written an article in nearly every number of the *Quarterly Review* for the last twelve years. Following "Vanity Fair," appeared in 1850 "Pendennis;" in 1852, "Esmond," and in 1855, the "Newcomes." Meanwhile Thackeray had begun his very profitable career as a lecturer. The course on the "English Humorists of the Eighteenth Century" was first delivered in London in 1851, afterwards repeated in many provincial towns, and in the winter of 1852–53 delivered with great success in America. In 1853 he prepared an equally successful and equally able course on the "Four Georges." In 1857–59 appeared the "Virginians," a sequel to "Esmond." In January 1860 the *Cornhill Magazine* was begun with Thackeray as editor. Issued under the auspices of so great a name, its circulation was extraordinary, the sale of its early numbers exceeding one hundred thousand, and it proved a mine of wealth for both editor and publishers. But Thackeray was ill-fitted to conduct a periodical; his habits of procrastination, the difficulty of selecting suitable contributions, and the vexation which he felt in returning rejected ones, made the editorial chair to him a bed of thorns, and he was glad to abandon it in April 1862, continuing however to write for the magazine to the last. In it appeared his delightful "Roundabout Papers," "Lovel the Widower," the "Adventures of Philip," besides the fragment of a novel, "Denis Duval," published in 1864, after his death, which occurred on Christmas Eve, 1863.

Thackeray, as compared with Dickens, occupies in some respects the same position among the public as Macaulay does compared with Carlyle. It has been said by certain critics, particularly in the so-called "Society" journals, that Carlyle's chief admirers were found among the less cultured classes—intelligent artisans, clerks, shopmen, and the like. This is not true, for some of the greatest and most original minds of this generation have held the Seer of Chelsea in the highest reverence; but it is true that among the classes indicated a far larger number make, as it were, companions and friends of Carlyle's writings than of Macaulay's. The reason is not far to seek. Macaulay's works are profitable for information, for the excellence of the style, for their unflagging interest, but scarcely for instruction in righteousness. His was a singularly happy life; he never had any perplexities about the mysteries of existence; doubts and fears as to points of conduct never troubled him; and nothing will be found in his writings for those who, harassed by daily trials and toils, look in the books they read for some spiritual nourishment, for something to help them in the steep and thorny way which they have to tread. Precisely the reverse is the case with Carlyle; and hence it is that he finds so many readers among those who care little for literature in itself, but who value his works, not on account of their great genius and picturesque style, but because they are useful to them from a moral and spiritual point of view. All this, of course, does not apply to Thackeray as compared with Dickens, but it does so partially. The people to whom Macaulay and Thackeray pre-eminently addressed themselves, whom consciously or unconsciously they had in their mind's eye as they wrote, were those who are clothed in purple and fine linen, and who fare sumptuously every day. Thackeray's works are full of moral instruction of a kind, but it is of a kind which scarcely applies except to the higher orders; of the lower sections of society he had very little knowledge. With them his writings never have been and never will be popular; the pleasures of life and character with which he loves to deal, and his mode of dealing with them, alike prevent that. Dickens sprung from the people himself, and early made acquainted with poverty, had, with all his theatrical pathos and tendency to gushing sentiment, a deep and genuine sympathy with the poor and their trials; and to this sympathy is, we believe, in no small measure due the fact that he enjoyed a wider and deeper popularity than has ever been attained by any other novelist.

Thackeray had none of Dickens's sanguine temperament and

resolute confidence in himself. He was always inclined to look rather on the dark than on the sunny side of things; doubtful about the success of his works, and feeling acutely adverse criticism upon them. In his latter years, at any rate, he was a slow and careful writer, satisfied if he accomplished in a month as much as Scott did in a few days; and always disposed to postpone till to-morrow what ought to be done to-day. Unlike Dickens, he was a bookish man, perfectly at home in some fields of English literature, especially in the eighteenth century, whose writers he knew and loved so well. His inimitably graceful style, in which he has been excelled by no novelist, may be in part due to his familiarity with Addison, Steele, Swift, and their contemporaries, especially if it be true, as certain critics aver, that in the eighteenth century English prose reached its high-water mark.

Of Thackeray's works certainly the most remarkable and perhaps the best is "Esmond." Many novelists following in the wake of Scott have attempted to reproduce for us past manners, scenes, and characters; but in "Esmond" Thackeray not only does this—he reproduces for us the style in which men wrote and talked in the days of Queen Anne. To reproduce the forgotten phraseology, to remember always not how his age would express an idea, but how Steele, or Swift, or Addison would have expressed it, might have been pronounced impossible of accomplishment. Yet in "Esmond" Thackeray did accomplish it, and with perfect success. The colouring throughout is exquisite and harmonious, never by a single false note is the melody broken. Of his writings in general perhaps the most noticeable characteristic is the hatred they express for all sorts of false pretences, sham sentiment, and unreal professions. He is never wearied of directing his scathing satire against whited sepulchres of all descriptions. "Call things by their right names; do not gloss over the villany of Lord Steyne because he is a lord; do not condone George Osborne's selfishness because he is handsome; don't pretend to be what you are not, and do not let false shame make you conceal what you are," is the burden of his message. To his scorn and hatred of vice and meanness he added sincere love and admiration of all that is true, and good, and honourable. A large-hearted, thoughtful man, the temptations and trials and sorrows of humanity affected him deeply. His pathos is as touching and sincere as his humour is subtle and delicate. His numerous "asides" to the reader are full of "that sad wisdom which experience brings," in striking contrast to those of Dickens, who, when he leaves his story to indulge in moralising, is generally trite and feeble. In a characteristic passage Thackeray apologises for the frequency of his casual reflections. "Perhaps of all novel-spinners now extant," he says, "the present writer is the most addicted to preaching. Does he not stop perpetually in his story and begin to preach to you? . . . I say *peccavi* loudly and heartily," he adds, but there was no need of this expression of repentance, whether sincere or not, for none ever wished Thackeray's "asides" fewer or shorter. Thackeray's fame as a novelist has caused his poems, of which he wrote a good many, generally in a half-serious, half-comic vein, to be frequently less noticed than they deserve. His admirable mock-heroic ballads and society verses attain a degree of excellence very rarely reached by such performances.

Was Thackeray a cynic? The question has been often asked and variously answered. If we use "cynic" in the proper sense of the word as defined by Johnson, "a philosopher of the snarling or currish sort; a follower of Diogenes; a rude man; a snarler; a misanthrope," most assuredly it cannot with any propriety be applied to him. But in ordinary *parlance* we use "cynic" in a sense different from any of these, meaning by it a man who is apt to look on life with a glance half sad, half humorous, who is prone to be distrustful of fine appearances and professions, who sees keenly the grains of dust mingled in the gold of the finest character, and who is fully aware of the latent meanness and selfish ambition which often lurk under actions professing to be noble and generous. In this sense of the word, Thackeray was a cynic. *Vanitas vanitatum:* all is vanity, is his often-repeated cry; none knew better than he with what richly gilded coverings we are apt to clothe the evil passions and desires of our nature.

One of the most industrious literary craftsmen of the Victorian era was Lord Lytton—Edward George Earle Lytton Bulwer Lytton, to give him his full name. Born in 1805 of an ancient family, he was, after a brilliant literary and political career, elevated to the peerage in 1866. During his busy life, there were few departments of literature which he did not attempt. Not only did he write novels, but also history, poetry, essays, and plays. The bare enumeration of his writings would alone occupy more space than can here be afforded. One of his first writings, "Falkland," a tale full of that sham Byronic sentiment with which many young writers were infected at the time of its publication, proved a failure, but with "Pelham," which appeared in 1828, began that career of popularity which was closed only by the author's death. It is a novel of fashionable life, full of those errors of taste into which a young writer is apt to fall, but undeniably clever, and containing some brilliant sketches of society. After it came in quick succession "The Disowned," "Devereux," and "Paul Clifford," the last one of those attempts to "make a hero out of a scoundrel" against which Thackeray during his early career directed some of his most pungent satire. In 1831 Bulwer (his name till he became a peer) entered Parliament. In the following year appeared "Eugene Aram," a tale of the "Paul Clifford" species. Within a few years came his first historical novels, "The Last Days of Pompeii" and "Rienzi," followed in 1843 and 1848 by two others of a similar class on subjects taken from English history—"The Last of the Barons" and "Harold." All these are distinguished by the accuracy of their archæological and historical colouring, though in picturesqueness and ease they are far inferior to the wonderful series in which Scott made bygone times and men real to us. In 1849 appeared "The Caxtons," in which the versatile author took a new departure. It is a novel of domestic life, more natural and pleasing than any of his previous productions. Its success was followed up by two other novels of the same series, "My Novel" and

"What will He Do with It?" the former of which is generally considered his masterpiece. In 1862 appeared "A Strange Story," one of those tales of mystery of which he wrote several, "Zanoni" (1842) being perhaps the most striking. It was a great favourite with the author, to whom the study of magic and kindred arts always presented a great attraction. He remained ardent in his devotion to literature to the end. A novel from his pen, "The Parisians," was appearing in *Blackwood* at the time of his death, which occurred in 1872; and the final proofs of another novel, "Kenelm Chillingly," were corrected by him only a few days before the sad event.

Lytton cannot be called a novelist of the first class. There is an air of artificiality about everything he says, a "stagey" sentiment, a love of concealing feeble or inaccurate thought beneath a sort of philosophical jargon, which, added to other faults, place him below the really great masters of the art of fiction, the Fieldings, the Scotts, and the Thackerays. But he was a man of very remarkable endowments, ardent ambition, and indomitable perseverance. In 1856, addressing the boys of a school, he said, "Boys, when I look at your young faces I could fancy myself a boy once more. I go back to the days when I too tried for prizes, sometimes succeeding, sometimes failing. I was once as fond of play as any of you, and in this summer weather I fear my head might have been more full of cricket than of Terence or even Homer. But still I can remember that, whether at work or at play, I had always a deep though quiet determination, that sooner or later I would be a somebody or do a something. That determination continues with me to this hour." Hence his desire to excel in various fields. His first play was a comparative failure, but he had set his heart upon winning dramatic laurels, and to a certain extent he succeeded. "The Lady of Lyons," "Richelieu," and the brilliant comedy of "Money" are always welcome on the stage. To the fame of the writer of works of the imagination he aspired to add that of the scholar, and an unfinished "History of Athens" and a translation of the "Odes of Horace" with notes, show at all events that he kept up his acquaintance with the classics to an extent very rare among men so multifariously occupied as he was. In one ambition only he altogether failed; but unfortunately that ambition was his most burning and unquenchable one. There was something almost pitiable about the way in which he went on publishing poem after poem without ever attaining such success as would place him high even in the second rank of writers of verse. Nature, bountiful to him in many respects, had denied him the poetical faculty; even his highest performances of this kind would have been better had they been written in prose. His son, the present Lord Lytton (born 1831), better known as a writer under his pseudonym of "Owen Meredith," has been more fortunate in his poetical attempts. All his poems, if occasionally marred by faults of diction and sentiment, have about them that indescribable something which distinguishes the work of a genuine poet from that of the mere verse-writer.

Few novels have made a greater sensation at their first appearance than "Jane Eyre," published in 1847. All competent critics, however much they might differ about certain features in the work, were agreed in acknowledging its original power and its thrilling interest, and conjectures were rife as to who could be the unknown "Currer Bell" whose name appeared on its title-page. Most of these conjectures were very wide of the mark. "Currer Bell" was the name adopted by Charlotte Brontë, a poor girl, brought up in a homely parsonage amid the bleak wilds of Yorkshire, without any literary friends to aid her in her struggle for fame. There are few more interesting and pathetic stories than that of her and her gifted sisters Emily and Anne. Charlotte, the eldest of the three, was born at Thornton, in Bradford parish, in 1816. Four years later her father, who was a clergyman, removed to Haworth, and there she was brought up and wrote her wonderful novels. Her life was a sad one enough, chequered by poverty, by poor health, by family trials, and by the yearnings of an ambition which was late in finding any fit field for its exercise. All the family were remarkably gifted, and many were the manuscripts which proceeded from their pens, but it was not till 1846 that Charlotte appeared before the public as an author. In that year was published (at the expense of the writers) a small volume of poems "by Currer, Ellis, and Acton Bell," the two last names being the pseudonyms of her sisters Emily and Anne. It attracted very little attention. "The book was printed," wrote Charlotte, in the biographical notice of her sisters; "it is scarcely known, and all of it that merits to be known are the poems of Ellis Bell." During the same year a tale of Charlotte Brontë's, "The Professor," was plodding a weary round among the London publishers. "Currer Bell's book," she says, "found acceptance nowhere, nor any acknowledgment of merit, so that something like the chill of despair began to invade his heart." Two other novels, "Wuthering Heights," by Emily Brontë, a tale of great, though morbid and undisciplined power, and "Agnes Grey," by Anne Brontë, had found publishers, though on such terms as could afford no gratification to the authors; but Charlotte found no gleam of encouragement till the MS. of "The Professor" was returned to her by Messrs. Smith, Elder, & Co., to whom it had been submitted, along with a courteous letter, declining the tale, but adding that a novel in three volumes would meet with careful consideration. "Jane Eyre," on which she had been for some time engaged, was accordingly sent to them, and at once accepted. Its publication soon after gave her at once a fame and popularity which suffered no diminution from her two succeeding novels, "Shirley" (1849), in which she availed herself of her experience of Yorkshire character, and "Villette" (1852), in which she made use of some of the material of "The Professor," containing faithful transcripts from her experiences as teacher and pupil in Belgium. In 1854 she married Mr. Nicholls, who had been for eight years her father's curate. The union was a very happy one; but her health, always delicate, gave way, and she died in March 1855. Her two sisters had preceded her to the still country. Charlotte Brontë's life was written with admirable literary skill and good taste by her friend Mrs. Gaskell (1810–1865), herself a novelist of high merit. Among her best-known works are

"Mary Barton," a story of factory life, "Ruth," and "Crauford."

Charlotte Brontë had high notions of her calling. In signal contrast to the many lady-novelists, who nowadays pour forth novel after novel with such unceasing rapidity that the panting critic toils after them in vain, she published nothing till it was as good as she could make it, and never wrote except when she felt that she was really in the vein for doing so. Like all who labour conscientiously, she has had her reward. Her works have not, like many other fictions, been sought eagerly at circulating libraries for a season or two and then forgotten; on the other hand, they have taken a secure place in the list of English classics. Her style is intense, vivid, and glowing; and in the descriptions of certain aspects of nature—for example, of a stormy, cloudy sky—it would be hard to mention a writer who is her superior. There are no dull places in her narratives. Everywhere we find that vigour and animation which are a sure sign of a writer having fully matured his conceptions. Harriet Martineau complained that in her novels she always wrote as if love was woman's chief, almost woman's only, interest in life. There is a good deal of force in this remark, but no writer had ever a more pure and high-souled idea of what passionate love really is than Charlotte Brontë had. Her want of knowledge of the usages of society, and her limited experience of life and manners, led her into some mistakes, but they are so comparatively insignificant as in no way to detract from the nobleness of her work. We entirely agree with Mr. W. C. Roscoe[1] in utterly repudiating the cry of "coarseness" with which "Jane Eyre," in particular, was assailed. "Coarse materials, indeed," he says, "she too much deals with, and her own style has something rude and uncompromising in it not always in accordance with customary ideas of what is becoming in a female writer; but it would be scarcely possible to name a writer who, in handling such difficult subject-matter, carries the reader so safely through by the

[1] Essays, vol. ii. p. 351.

serene guardianship and unconsciously exercised influence of her stainless purity and unblemished rectitude."

It has been well said that if, after the university method, we arranged our dead authors in order of merit, the only novelists since Scott who would by general consent be placed in the first class would be Thackeray, Dickens, and George Eliot; other names, indeed, would be added by many, but hardly any other would receive a unanimous suffrage. As everybody knows, George Eliot was the pseudonym under which a female writer, Mary Anne Evans, chose to veil her identity. She was born in 1820 at Griff House, near Nuneaton, in Warwickshire, the daughter of Robert Evans, a land agent there. She received an exceptionally good education, and in 1846 began her literary career by a translation of Strauss's "Leben Jesu," for which she received the beggarly pittance of £20. In 1851 she removed to London to assist Mr. John Chapman in editing the *Westminster Review*, to which, between the years 1852 and 1859, she contributed several articles. Her connection with the *Review* brought her into contact with George Henry Lewes (1817–1878), himself a writer and philosopher of some mark, to whom she linked her fate. In 1857 her first work of fiction, the "Scenes of Clerical Life," appeared in *Blackwood's Magazine*. They did not attract much notice at first, though Dickens, to his honour be it said, recognised their rare merit as successive instalments came out. In 1859 appeared "Adam Bede," which at once elevated her to the front rank among the imaginative writers of her time. Then followed the "Mill on the Floss" (1860); "Silas Marner" (1861); "Romola" (1863); "Felix Holt" (1866); a poem, "The Spanish Gipsy" (1868); "Middlemarch" (1872); "Daniel Deronda" (1877); and "Impressions of Theophrastus Such" (1879), which, for want of a better name, may be described as a volume of essays. In May 1880 she married Mr. J. W. Cross. The union was a happy but brief one, lasting only seven months. On December 22, 1880, the great novelist expired.

George Eliot's personal characteristics are thus described

by one who knew her well:[1]—"Everything in her aspect and presence was in keeping with the bent of her soul. The deeply lined face, the too marked and massive features, were united with an air of delicate refinement, which in one way was the more impressive, because it seemed to proceed so entirely from within. Nay, the inward beauty would sometimes quite transform the outward harshness; there would be moments when the thin hands that entwined themselves in their eagerness, the earnest figure that bowed forward to speak and hear, the deep gaze moving from one face to another with a grave appeal—all these seemed the transparent symbols that showed the presence of a wise benignant soul. But it was the voice which best revealed her, a voice whose subdued intensity and tremulous richness seemed to environ her uttered words with the mystery of a world of feeling that must remain untold. . . . And then, again, when, in moments of more intimate converse, some current of emotion would set strongly through her soul, when she would raise her head in unconscious absorption and look out into the unseen, her expression was one not to be forgotten."

Like Charlotte Brontë, George Eliot was a most painstaking and conscientious writer. No ill-considered or slipshod sentence ever fell from her pen. Her rich culture and large knowledge of life in all its manifestations, give a breadth and accuracy to her delineations of character which are lacking in the products of Charlotte Brontë's more fiery and impetuous genius. Her sympathy with all classes of society was wide, and proceeded from the general source of all such sympathy—thorough insight into their several modes of thought and life. Herself an unbeliever, she could do full justice to those of intense religious convictions, analysing and describing them in a way which showed that she thoroughly understood them. Her humour cannot be said to be of equal excellence and spontaneity to that of Dickens or Thackeray, but it is excellent of its kind, quiet and unobtrusive, and full of that kindly yet

[1] Mr. F. W. H. Myers in the *Century Magazine* for November 1881.

accurate appreciation of the oddities and follies of men which is so rare. It has been truly said that, omitting the very highest and the very lowest sections of modern society, her novels present photographic pictures of English life which will give to the future reader the same sort of truthful information of the early Victorian time that Shakespeare's plays do of Elizabeth's England. Not only are George Eliot's novels excellent as works of art; their moral tendency is in the highest degree beneficial. No novelist has dwelt more strongly upon the necessity of the ready performance of duty if we are to lead noble lives; none has painted in more vivid colours how a character, naturally amiable perhaps, sinks deeper and deeper in sin from weakness of will and the inability to practise self-renunciation. In her poems, as well as in her novels, these are themes she often recurs to. She loves also to impress on her readers the sacredness of work, and the value of true performance, in however humble a sphere. In her two last novels she erred by over-elaboration, making them the vehicle for many observations, good enough in themselves, but altogether out of place in a novel, which ought to be a delineation of life, with just so much subsidiary matter as may be necessary for the intelligent comprehension of the narrative. "Daniel Deronda," in particular, contains a great deal of matter which would have found its fit abode in a philosophical treatise. Her poems are full of deep thought and noble ideas, but she lacked the accomplishment of verse, and was out of her true element when writing it.

The few other novelists who can be mentioned here must be disposed of very briefly. There never lived a more manly and true-hearted writer of fiction than Charles Lever (1806–1872), a lively and mirth-loving Irishman, whose stirring life furnished him with not a few traits wherewith to embellish the portraits of his heroes. His novels may be divided into three classes, answering to corresponding features in the author's life. First, we have the youthful series, filled with practical jokes and merriment, and peopled with those dashing dragoons who rode, and fought, and made love with such incredible vivacity in his earlier novels. As time wore on, the fun became less boisterous, though far from being altogether excluded; and Lever's works, if perhaps less pleasing to youthful readers who delight in the accounts of extraordinary exploits, showed a much wider and deeper knowledge of life. But in our opinion his best work was done in his latter years, when in a series of novels, wanting, indeed, the fire and dash of his early performances, but infinitely more accurate as delineations of life and character, he gave to the world the mellowed experience of an acute observer who had seen many phases of existence, and could comment on them with shrewdness and accuracy. Among his best works may be mentioned "Harry Lorrequer," "Jack Hinton," "The Dodd Family Abroad," "Sir Brook Fosbrooke," and "Lord Kilgobbin." The last mentioned is an excellent specimen of his matured style, well worth reading for its shrewd common sense and its many acute observations on the state of Ireland. The "O'Dowd Papers," with which for some years he delighted the readers of *Blackwood*, discoursing month by month on such topics as happened to strike his fancy, were, of course, of mainly temporary interest, but their lively style and numerous well-told anecdotes make them still interesting reading.

Charles Kingsley (1819–1875), who, after holding various ecclesiastical appointments, became Canon of Westminster in 1873, was very justly styled by J. S. Mill "one of the good influences of the age." His earnest advocacy of courage, purity, and love, healthy manhood and firm adherence to duty, added to his vivid and kindling personality, caused him to be looked up to by many young men as a master in whose steps they were proud to follow. In 1847 he published a dramatic poem, "The Saint's Tragedy," founded on the story of St. Elizabeth of Hungary, which at once made his genius known. The Chartist movement in England called forth from him two novels, "Alton Locke" (1850) and "Yeast" (1851), which, amidst much that is crude and chaotic, are full of eloquent writing and breathe a spirit of earnest sympathy with the sufferings of the poor.

Other novels, "Westward Ho!" "Hereward the Wake," &c., followed, along with poems, sermons, historical sketches, and writings on natural history, to which his keen delight in all the influences of sea and sky gave singular force and attractiveness. No more thoroughly healthy-souled man has adorned this generation, and few have been more potent for good.

Benjamin Disraeli, Earl of Beaconsfield (1804–1881), son of Isaac D'Israeli, whose gossiping volumes, "Curiosities of Literature," &c., still retain their popularity, is one of the most remarkable of English novelists, entirely original, and never echoing any other writer. Doubtless part of the great sale which his fictions enjoyed is to be attributed to his renown as a politician, but they possess intrinsic merit sufficient to justify their popularity. His first novel, "Vivian Grey," was published in 1826, and, despite its affectations and errors in point of taste, is certainly an amazing production for a youth of two-and-twenty. During the next ten years appeared "The Young Duke;" "Venetia," a tale founded on the lives of Shelley and Byron; "Contarini Fleming," and "Henrietta Temple," the last entirely a love story. "Coningsby" and "Sybil," two political novels, remarkable for their keen and incisive portraits drawn from actual life, followed in 1844-1845; then, in 1847, came "Tancred," in which the author gave vent to his peculiar notions about the Hebrew race, and in 1870 "Lothair," and in 1880 his last novel, "Endymion." All display a remarkable mastery of style, and that luminous epigrammatic power which was the glory of Lord Beaconsfield's speeches. One of the most notable characteristics of the whole series, a characteristic which has scarcely received from critics the attention which so striking a feature deserves, has been thus dealt with by Mr. J. H. Bryce[1]:—"They [the novels] are as far as possible from being immoral; that is to say, there is nothing in them unbecoming or corrupting. Honour, friendship, love, are all recognised as powerful motives of human conduct. That which is wanting is the sense of right and wrong. Very

[1] In the *Century Magazine* for March 1882.

rarely does any one of his personages ask himself whether such and such a course is right. They move in a world which is polished, agreeable, dignified, but in which conscience and religion do not seem to exist—a world more like that of Augustus or Lorenzo de' Medici than like modern England. Though the men live for pleasure or fame, the women for pleasure or love, both are capable of making sacrifices at the altar of affection; but the idea of duty does not cross their minds."

Our living novelists are such a countless host, and many of them are so equal in ability, that it is an invidious task to select two or three for special mention. Far at the head of the "sensational" novelists of the day stands Charles Reade (born 1814), whose plots we follow, if not always with pleasure—the colour is often too thickly laid on, and horror too rapidly piled upon horror for that—at any rate with constant excitement and never-failing interest. It is perhaps unfair to place a writer of crisp, nervous style, and extraordinary power of graphic description, in the same category with a crowd of authors who hope to gain popularity by no higher artifice than an improbable and sensational plot; yet "sensational" is the only epithet we can think of which describes Mr. Reade's best work with any degree of exactness. He does not excel in the depth and accuracy of his delineations of character; he does not hold the mirror up to nature and give us a faithful picture of life as it actually is; his reflections on character and manners are neither very trustworthy nor very profound. His strength lies in the elaborate ingenuity with which his plots are worked out, in the number of striking incidents with which a prolific fancy enables him to embellish his tales, and in the great mastery he has attained over the difficult but very necessary art of keeping the reader's attention enchained to the end. "Hard Cash" (1863) and "Griffith Gaunt" (1866) may be mentioned as favourable specimens of his genius.

One of the most popular and one of the most industrious novelists of the age is Anthony Trollope (born 1815). How he has found time to go through the amount of work he has accomplished is a perfect marvel. He has written above eighty novels and novelettes; has written about almost all English-speaking peoples; besides a "Life of Cicero," memoirs of Cæsar, Thackeray, and Palmerston, and a large amount of anonymous journalistic work. In addition to his literary exertions he has been twice round the world, and for thirty-five years held an appointment in the post-office. Mr. Trollope's works, if occasionally rather spun out, are all characterised by sound judgment and a wonderful acquaintance with the higher phases of English society. He especially excels in his description of the life of the English clergy. Among his best writings may be mentioned "Framley Parsonage," "Orley Farm," and the "Last Chronicle of Barset." Richard Doddridge Blackmore (born 1825) has, after writing for some time in comparative obscurity, at length obtained the recognition due to his great merits as a describer of bygone life in country districts of England and Wales. He excels in the description of scenery, and in painting the wilder aspects of the life of our ancestors some generations ago. "Lorna Doone, a Romance of Exmoor," and "Alice Lorraine," are perhaps his best productions. Of Thomas Hardy (born 1840) the chief excellence consists in his peculiar power of painting rural life, especially in its idyllic aspects. Of his best and greatest work, "Far from the Madding Crowd" (1874), the great attraction is the way in which, by the studied quietness of the style, the delicate shading of the characters, and the descriptions of scenery, the reader is led, as it were, gradually to breathe the slumbrous atmosphere of a sequestered rural district, where the bustle and turmoil of city life are scarcely apprehended even in imagination, and where the annual sheep-shearing and the harvest-home dinner are the most important events of the year. The quiet humour and sympathy with which the conversations of the farm-labourers are related, and the technical accuracy with which various pastoral operations are described, show that Mr. Hardy's accounts of country life are drawn from careful personal observation and not from books. William Black, who was born in Glasgow in 1841, attained his first great success by the publication, in 1871, of "A Daughter of Heth," one of the most pleasing and healthy novels of this generation. In 1872 followed the "Strange Adventures of a Phaeton," founded on a driving excursion made by the author from London to Edinburgh, a book full of high spirits, genial humour, and showing an excellent eye for scenery. "A Princess of Thule," which has been translated into many foreign tongues, and is perhaps the most popular of Mr. Black's novels, appeared in 1873. It has been succeeded by many other excellent novels, all written in a healthy genial spirit, displaying a wide knowledge of character, and never wearying the reader with needless digressions and moralisings. Mr. Black's power of painting scenery is such as is possessed by few writers. The word-painting of most novelists is mere padding, and is generally skipped by the reader—wisely, because it is impossible that the description given could convey to the mind any real idea of the scene portrayed. With Mr. Black the case is different; his descriptions always stand forth vivid and lifelike. Other eminent novelists of the day, such as James Payn, George Meredith, George MacDonald, Wilkie Collins, Mrs. Oliphant, Mrs. E. Lynn Linton, our limits forbid us to deal with.[1]

We now turn to the poetry of our own time. There can be no doubt as to who is the most popular poet of the Victorian era. It is long since Mr. Tennyson took that proud

[1] As illustrating the rich rewards which await a successful writer of fiction in these days, it may be worth while to mention some facts which came out during an action for damages by Charles Reade against the proprietors of the *Glasgow Herald* in 1876. From Mr. Reade's evidence it appeared that Dickens gave him £5 per page for the publication of "Hard Cash" in *All the Year Round*, Mr. Reade retaining the copyright. Mr. Andrew Chatto (of Messrs. Chatto & Windus) stated that for a series of stories which Mr. Reade was then contributing to *Belgravia* they paid him £5 a page, or rather more than twopence-halfpenny a word, if the stories did not exceed four pages, and £4 a page if the stories were over that limit, Mr. Reade's copyright being reserved. He also corroborated what Mr. Reade had mentioned, that Mr. Chatto had offered him £2000 for a three-volume story, to be published in *Belgravia* and separately, Mr. Reade retaining the copyright.

position, and though since then many rivals have appeared, none has ever come near to dislodge him from it. Alfred Tennyson was born on August 5, 1809, at Somersby, a hamlet in Lincolnshire, about six miles from Horncastle. Of Somersby and a neighbouring parish his father was Rector. After having received the elements of education from his father and at the village school, Tennyson was sent to the grammar-school at Louth. While there he prepared, along with his brother Charles, his first volume of poems, which was published in 1827 under the title of "Poems by Two Brothers." It is scarcely necessary to say that none of the pieces contained in the little book have been reprinted. About 1828 the poet went to Cambridge, and in the same year he wrote a poem of greater promise than his previous attempts, "A Lover's Tale," not printed till 1833, and not published till 1879, when the author was compelled to resuscitate it to prevent its being pirated. At Cambridge, which he left without taking a degree, Tennyson gained in 1828 the Chancellor's prize for a poem on "Timbuctoo," and there began that friendship for Arthur Henry Hallam, son of Hallam the historian, which he has rendered immortal by "In Memoriam." In 1830 appeared "Poems, chiefly Lyrical, by Alfred Tennyson," a volume containing 154 pages, of which about sixty have been thought worthy of preservation. Another little volume, containing amongst other poems such gems of song as "The May Queen," "The Miller's Daughter," "Œnone," followed in the winter of 1832. Both were on the whole favourably received, but as yet Tennyson had not caught the public ear.

In 1842 appeared "Poems by Alfred Tennyson," in two volumes, consisting partly of selections from the 1830 and 1832 volumes, partly of poems published for the first time. The reception of these volumes was most enthusiastic; all the critics were loud in their praise, and such men as Wordsworth, J. S. Mill, and John Sterling joined to swell the popular applause. In 1847 appeared "The Princess," suggested apparently by a passage in Johnson's "Rasselas:"—"The Princess thought that of all sublunary things, knowledge was the best. She desired first to learn of sciences, and then proposed to found a college to teach women, in which she would preside." In 1850 was published "In Memoriam," a record of the poet's love for Arthur Hallam, a young man full of promise, who died abroad in 1833, at the early age of twenty-two. In the same year, on the death of Wordsworth, Tennyson received—

> "The laurel, greene from the brows
> Of him that uttered nothing base.'

"Maud" appeared in 1855; the "Idylls of the King" in 1859; "Enoch Arden" in 1864; "The Holy Grail and other Poems," containing four new idylls, in 1870; two dramas, "Queen Mary" and "Harold," in 1875 and 1877 respectively. The volume, "Ballads and other Poems," published in 1881, shows that the Laureate's genius has suffered no diminution by age; and the fervent prayer of all who love poetry is that he may long be spared to enrich our literature with many more masterpieces of art.

Mr. Tennyson's great fame has not been attained without much patient labour. The research of commentators on him has shown that his poems bear many marks of careful revision, the textual variations in different editions of some of them being considerable. Refined taste and exquisite workmanship are the characteristics of all he has written. Fully alive to all the influences of his time, there are few phases of modern thought which are not touched on in his writings; while his rich gift of imagination, his pure and elevated diction, and his freedom from faults of taste and manner, give his writings a place among those which the world will not willingly let die. His range of poetic power is wide. As a describer of natural scenery he is so accurate that it has been said that a painter might perfectly rely on his statements of facts.

> "Perhaps, compared with the great old masters,
> His range of landscape may not be much;
> But who, out of all their starry number,
> Can beat our Alfred in truth of touch?"

Exquisite lyrics of love, and stirring war-ballads of equal excellence, have come from his pen. He is as much at home in giving dramatic utterance to the reflections of the "Northern Farmer" as in picturing the feelings of St. Simeon Stylites. Among the least successful of his works must be placed his dramas, full as they are of passages of noble poetic eloquence. Why the writer who has shown such admirable dramatic skill in the monologues put in the mouth of Ulysses, the Northern Farmer, and others, should have comparatively failed when he came to write a complete play, is a question which must have puzzled many readers. The answer to it may perhaps be found in the following extract from Mr. W. C. Roscoe, who has written one of the best of the many estimates of the Laureate's genius. "He is," says Mr. Roscoe, "at once the most *creative* and the *least dramatic* of poets; the nearest to Shakespeare, and the furthest from him. He has in the highest degree the fundamental poetic impulse. He fuses all things, and golden shapes spring from his mould, with only the material in common with his ore; rather, ideas are sown in his brain, and spring up in concrete organic forms. The passion to reproduce in concrete wholes constitutes, indeed, that fundamental poetic impulse which we have ascribed to him. He may be didactic, philosophical, oratorical, sentimental, but all these things he encloses in a golden ball of poesy. He may have, and often has, an ultimate moral object. This is by no means inconsistent with the highest effort of artistic production, as has been sometimes too easily assumed. It is true, you cannot comply with the conditions of art, you cannot have the feelings of the artist, if you drive directly by the medium of verse at a moral result or an intellectual conclusion; but you may have these for your ultimate object, and you may embody them in true poetical forms. . . . To say that Tennyson's genius is not dramatic, is certainly to contradict some of his critics. Something depends on what is meant by the term. He certainly has the power of penetrating the mood of another mind; but it will generally be found that this is another mind *in a special situation;* and this is a very different thing from exhibiting character *through the medium of situations and the self-expression elicited by these situations;* and in this, we take it, consists the essence of the drama." The essay from which these words are taken was written in 1855, long before Mr. Tennyson formally appeared as a dramatist. They certainly afford a very remarkable instance of acute critical insight.

While Tennyson's works are read and admired by all who make any pretensions to literary taste, it is only to a limited circle that the genius of Robert Browning is known except by hearsay. The frequent harshness of his phraseology; his obscurity, his love of dealing with subjects which have little interest for the majority of people, have combined to confine him to an audience fit, perhaps, but certainly very few. Yet by those who really appreciate him, no poet is prized more highly; and his originality and genius have long since been acknowledged by the general consent of all competent judges. No poet since Dryden has equalled him in the power of reasoning in verse; and his masculine vigour of thought and remarkable faculty of setting dramatically before us different types of character, give him a place by himself in the roll of English poets. He was born at Camberwell on May 7, 1812. From his earliest years he was fond of writing verse, and by the time he was twelve years of age had collected poems enough to form a volume, for which he tried to get a publisher—fortunately in vain, he was afterwards doubtless glad to think. His first publication, "Pauline," a little volume of seventy pages, appeared in 1833. In 1835 followed "Paracelsus," a drama of a shapeless kind, which found not a few imitators. "Paracelsus" is a very stiff morsel for the student of poetry, and it is not wonderful that its sale was small and the criticisms of it for the most part unfavourable. In 1837 Mr. Browning's tragedy of "Strafford" was brought out on the boards of Drury Lane Theatre. In 1840 appeared one of his most characteristic works, the epic "Sordello." In 1841 he began the publication of the series of "Bells and Pomegranates," which extended to eight numbers, concluding in 1846. In it was published much of Browning's finest poetry, including his tragedy of the "Blot on the Scutcheon," and the graceful dramatic poem of "Pippa Passes." In 1846 he was married to Miss Elizabeth Barrett, on the whole perhaps the greatest poetess England has produced. Our history now requires us to retrace our steps a little.

Mrs. Barrett Browning (to give her at once the name by which she is best known to literature) was born in 1809, at Hope End, near Ledbury. Like Mr. Browning, she very early gave evidence of her taste for poetical composition. "I wrote verses," she says, "as I daresay many have done who never wrote any poems, very early: at eight years old and earlier. But what is less common, the *early fancy* turned into a *will* and remained with me; and from that day to this poetry has been a distinct object with me—an object to read, think, and live for. And I could make you laugh, although you could not make the public laugh, by the narrative of nascent odes, epics, and didactics crying aloud on obsolete muses from childish lips." Her first publication was an "Essay on Mind," "a didactic poem," she writes, "written when I was seventeen or eighteen, and long repented of as worthy of all repentance." Several years after its publication were spent in the assiduous study of Greek literature, of which one result was a translation of the "Prometheus" of Æschylus. Other writings followed, and in 1850 her collected works, together with several new poems, were published. "Casa Guidi Windows," a poem commemorating the struggle of the Tuscans for liberty in 1849, appeared in 1851. "Aurora Leigh," a novel in verse, full of power, but occasionally exaggerated and spasmodic, was published in 1856. Mrs. Browning died at Florence in 1861. Apparently poured off hastily, without any attempt at correction or curtailment, her poems contain many flaws—faults of language, and faults of thought, but they also show genuine lyric impetuosity, true pathos, and unfailing freshness and force. Her so-called "Sonnets from the Portuguese," commemorating the progress of her wooing, are among the most enchanting love poems in the language.

Mr. Browning is a very voluminous poet. His writings since the publication of those mentioned above have been many, including "Men and Women," "The Inn Album," "The Ring and the Book," "Fifine at the Fair," &c. The progress of time cannot be said to have done anything to abate his faults; indeed, his most recently published works are even more full than their predecessors of crabbed phraseology and almost studied obscurity. This is greatly to be regretted, especially as Mr. Browning has proved in many of his poems that eccentricity of diction is not a necessary concomitant of his genius. What, for example, could be more exquisite than the following picture :—

> "Nobly, nobly, Cape St. Vincent to the north-west died away;
> Sunset ran, one glorious blood-red, reeking into Cadiz Bay;
> Bluish 'mid the burning water, full in face Trafalgar lay;
> In the dimmest north-east distance, dawned Gibraltar grand and grey;
> Here and here did England help me: how can I help England?—say,
> While Jove's planet rises yonder silent, over Africa."

From a poet who can write lines like these, the lover of poetry is content to put up with occasional fantasticality and with a sometimes even exasperating portion of obscurity. When the dust and refuse of his writings shall have been purged away in the furnace of time, enough of pure gold will still remain to justify the placing of Robert Browning among the great masters of song.

We come now to a group of poets whose fame has been won within the last twenty years. Their work had its origin in a literary movement corresponding to the pre-Raphaelite movement in art. About all they have done is a flavour of "æstheticism," and of none of them can it be said that, like Tennyson or Browning, he appeals to the general hopes and fears of humanity. Around all, or almost all, their writings there is a certain artificial atmosphere; their poems rather resemble hot-house plants than bright, fresh, hardy flowers reared in the open air. One of the chief members of the school was Dante Gabriel Rossetti, the most gifted of a very gifted family. He was born in 1828, the son of an Italian refugee, well known as a commentator on Dante, and for many years Professor of Italian Literature in King's College, London. Art was Rossetti's profession; and as one of the leading members of the pre-Raphaelite brotherhood he early attained great fame as a painter by his originality of design and vividness of colouring. From an early age he also wrote verse, and in 1861 published a series of admirable translations, under the title of "Early Italian Poets from Ciullio d'Alcanno to Dante Alighieri." In 1870 he was, rather reluctantly, induced to publish a collection of his poems, some of them written many years previously. Another volume followed in the year preceding his death. Rossetti has been well described by a eulogistic critic as "distinctively, though not exclusively, the poet of the romance and mastery of personal passion—passion uttered sometimes in narrative and sometimes in lyric form—his favourite type of narrative being the archaic ballad, in which a story is told and its scenery realised at a sustained, unflagging pitch of detailed vividness and intensity; and his favourite type of lyric, the sonnet, in which he is accustomed to embody a mood or phase of feeling in a pageant of descriptive images and symbols rather than in direct terms, although in directness, too, he can be a master when he chooses." His sonnets, admirable in their refined construction, are among the best of the kind in the language; and it would be difficult to find a parallel to the strain of weird pathos which vibrates through "Sister Helen" and some other of his ballads. Mr. Rossetti died in April 1882, having shortened his life by the use of chloral, which he took as a cure for insomnia. His brother, William Michael Rossetti (born 1829), is well known as a critic and writer on art; and his sister, Christina Georgina Rossetti (born 1830), is one of the greatest of living poetesses.

William Morris (born 1834), the leading partner in the well-known firm of Morris, Marshall, & Faulkner, which has done so much for decorative art, as a storyteller has no rival among living poets; indeed, there are very few since Chaucer who have approached him in this difficult art. Among his chief works are the "Defence of Guenevere" (1858), the "Life and Death of Jason" (1867), and the "Earthly Paradise" (1868–

70). He has also written a verse translation of the Æneid, which, in the opinion of many, conveys to the unlearned reader a truer idea of the charm of the original than any other. The grace and melody of Mr. Morris's versification, the delightful ease and delicacy with which he tells his stories, the air of culture and refinement which surrounds everything he writes, give his works an irresistible attractiveness to every reader who can feel the charms of beautiful tales beautifully related.

The youngest of the leading members of the school of poetry to which Mr. Rossetti and Mr. Morris belong, and perhaps the greatest, is Algernon Charles Swinburne (born 1839), whose great genius has long since made itself heard above the storm of adverse criticism which certain features in his early works evoked. In 1861 he published two plays, "The Queen Mother" and "Rosamund," juvenile productions which attracted but little attention, and that little not of a favourable kind. The two works following these, "Atlanta in Calydon," a tragedy on the Greek model, and "Chastelard," the first of three plays he has written founded on the story of Mary Stuart, gained more admirers, but as yet his circle of readers was narrow and his fame limited. It was not till the publication of "Poems and Ballads," in 1866, that he obtained any general or widespread popularity. Few who take an interest in literary history can have forgotten the mingled storm of detraction and praise which that volume called forth; how by some organs of opinion it was hailed with such laudations as would have required modification if applied to Shakespeare or Milton; and how by other journals it was treated with affected contempt as the frenzied and meretricious production of a naughty schoolboy. Part of the praise and part of the censure were merited. The volume, no doubt, contained many objectionable features, but it also showed a luxuriant imagination, great command of language, and consummate mastery of metre. As his other works appeared in rapid succession, it became universally recognised that in Mr. Swinburne we possess a writer who, in spite of some grave defects, can with justice be ranked among our great poets. He has not Mr. Tennyson's depth and tenderness of feeling; he lacks Mr. Browning's masculine intensity and great faculty for reasoning in verse; it is often painfully obvious, especially in his shorter pieces, that his command of metre and language greatly surpasses the worth of what he has to say. Nevertheless his works constantly possess that indefinable aroma which is always found in the poetry of genius, and which is always absent from the poetry of mere talent, however high that talent may be. The list of Mr. Swinburne's works is a long one, when we consider that he may yet look for many years of productiveness. Excellent specimens of his style may be found in "Mary Stuart, a Tragedy" (1881), the last portion of the triology of which "Chastelard" and "Bothwell" form parts; and in "Tristram of Lyonesse, and Other Poems" (1882). He has also written extensively in prose,—among other works, a volume of essays, containing much eloquent and subtle, if occasionally one-sided and exaggerated criticism; a critical study of William Blake; a "Note on Charlotte Brontë," and various contributions to the edition of the "Encyclopædia Britannica" now publishing. His prose style has many of the qualities of his poetry; it is so highly coloured, so gorgeous and glaring, as to be sometimes positively repugnant to those who think compression and sobriety of language among the lamps of style. Both praise and blame are apt to be dealt out in excess by him. Mr. Swinburne is not among those who consider a middle course the safest and best.

We would willingly be detained by many other poets of the Victorian age, such as Arthur Clough, Sydney Dobell, Alexander Smith, Gerald Massey, Lewis Morris, Bell Scott, but we must pass on. In the department of history, two great writers, second to none in power and popularity, have adorned our time —Lord Macaulay and Thomas Carlyle. Thomas Babington Macaulay was born on October 25, 1800, at Rothley Temple, in Leicestershire. His father was Zachary Macaulay, a most conscientious, laborious, and highly respected man, who devoted himself with unwearied assiduity and persistence to the cause of slave-trade abolition. Never was the adage that the child is father of the man better exemplified than in Macaulay's case. Even when little more than a baby his unquenchable love of reading showed itself; and what he read was firmly retained in a memory of such iron tenacity that anything fixed in it was scarcely ever forgotten. He was a remarkably precocious child, writing when about twelve verse and prose which would have done credit to much maturer years. It is curious to find in his letters to his parents, written when he was a mere boy, that literary way of putting things which never deserted him either in his conversation or in his most familiar correspondence. In his nineteenth year he entered Trinity College, Cambridge. Nothing could be imagined more to the taste of a youth of Macaulay's temperament than a university life, with its abundant means of access to books, and the facilities it affords for becoming acquainted with persons of similar character to oneself. The years of his residence at Cambridge were among the happiest of his very happy life, though he detested mathematics, then as now the favourite study of the place, and devoted as little time to them as possible. But in classics he acquired such facility as in 1821 to gain the proud distinction of the Craven Scholarship; and he twice gained the Chancellor's Medal for English verse. He also acquired great renown among his companions as one of the best orators of the Cambridge Union, and became noted among his friends for his perpetual flow of talk and his propensity to indulge in argument. In 1822 he took his degree of B.A., and in 1824 was elected a Fellow of Trinity College.

Macaulay's literary life began by some contributions to *Knight's Quarterly Magazine* in 1823–24. Most of these have been reprinted in his miscellaneous works, and prove that he was already master of that singularly readable, clear, incisive style to which he owes so much of his popularity. His abilities soon made him known, and in 1825 overtures were made to him to become a contributor to the *Edinburgh Review*, Jeffrey being anxious to introduce a little fresh blood into the organ of the Whigs. The result of these overtures was the famous article on Milton, published in the *Review* for August 1825. Though containing many assertions that will not stand the test of sober and rational criticism, and, as the author afterwards acknowledged, too glaring and redundant in style, the article, with its enthusiastic fervour, its sonorous rhetoric, and its bursts of splendid, if occasionally misleading eloquence, was one eminently calculated to attract attention. It did so to an extent almost without parallel in the history of periodical literature. "The effect on the author's reputation was instantaneous. Like Lord Byron, he awoke one morning and found himself famous." Invitations to dinner-parties came in crowds, and Macaulay soon became a great figure at Holland House, where the *élite* of Whig society gathered together, and began to associate on equal terms with Rogers, Sydney Smith, Luttrel, Allen, and other famous talkers who made that edifice famous in social annals. In 1826 he was called to the Bar and went the Northern Circuit, but he never looked seriously to law as a profession. It was to distinction in literature and in politics that his aspirations were turned. He was, and he felt himself to be, equally qualified to succeed in both. His literary fame steadily rose as article after article from his brilliant pen appeared in the *Edinburgh Review*. In 1828 Lord Lyndhurst made him a Commissioner of Bankruptcy, an office which, with the sums he derived from his Trinity Fellowship and from his contributions to the *Edinburgh Review*, made up his annual income to about £900. In 1830 he was, through the influence of Lord Lansdowne, who had been much struck by his articles on Mill, and wished to be the means of first introducing their author to public life, returned member of Parliament for the borough of Calne.

Macaulay soon made his mark in Parliament. He was one of the chief speakers in favour of the Reform Bill, and many were the eulogiums with which his orations were greeted by those whose praise was all the more valuable because they were themselves distinguished speakers. In 1832 he was appointed one of the Commissioners of the Board of Control, and in the same year was returned member for Leeds. During the first session of the reformed Parliament he spoke frequently, and always with success. In 1834 he was made president of a new Law Commission for India, and one of the members of the Supreme Council, with a salary of £10,000 a year. The motives which induced him to exchange the comforts, the books, and the lettered society of England for the heat and isolation of Calcutta are well explained in a letter of his to Lord Lansdowne. "I feel," he says, "that the sacrifice which I am about to make is great, but the motives which urge me to make it are quite irresistible. Every day that I live I become less and less desirous of great wealth, but every day makes me more sensible of the importance of a competence. Without a competence it is not very easy for a public man to be honest; it is almost impossible for him to be thought so. I am so situated that I can subsist only in two ways: by being in office, and by my pen. Hitherto, literature has been merely my relaxation—the amusement of perhaps a month in the year. I have never considered it as the means of support. I have chosen my own topics, taken my own time, and dictated my own terms. The thought of becoming a bookseller's hack; of writing to relieve, not the fulness of the mind, but the emptiness of the pocket; of spurring a jaded fancy to reluctant exertion; of filling sheets with trash merely that sheets may be filled; of bearing from publishers and editors what Dryden bore from Tonson, and what, to my own knowledge, Mackintosh bore from Lardner, is horrible to me. Yet thus it must be if I should quit office. Yet to hold office merely for the sake of emolument would be more horrible still." During his outward voyage to India, Macaulay passed his time in reading, with, to use his own words, "keen and increasing enjoyment. I devoured Greek, Latin, Spanish, Italian, French, and English; folios, quartos, octavos, duodecimos." He arrived at Madras in June 1834, and returned to England in 1838. The most important piece of official work done by Macaulay during his residence in India was the Indian Penal Code. He always regarded this piece of work with very considerable pride and satisfaction. During his residence in India his contributions to the *Edinburgh Review* continued as before, and his insatiable love of reading suffered no abatement. Among other articles, that on Bacon (one of the most elaborate and ambitious, if also one of the most misleading of his performances) was written there; and there also he went through a course of classical reading almost incredible in its extent and variety. He used to define a scholar as "one who could read Plato with his feet on the fender." To this definition he himself exactly answered. While reading the works of the great Greek writers, he did not pause to trouble himself about verbal subtleties or grammatical minutiæ; he read them, as he would have read Shakespeare, or Milton, or Burke—for the sake of their literary charm. It should not be forgotten that to Macaulay's exile in the East we owe the local colouring of two brilliant essays from which most people have drawn their slender store of Indian history —those on Lord Clive and Warren Hastings.

After a tour on the Continent, Macaulay was, in 1839, elected member for Edinburgh, and was appointed Secretary at War, with a seat in the Cabinet. On the fall of the Melbourne Ministry, of which the country had got heartily tired, he was re-elected for Edinburgh. In 1842 he published his "Lays of Ancient Rome," stirring ballads, not containing many intrinsically poetical qualities, but full of fire and spirit. In the following year he was prevailed on to republish his *Edinburgh Review* essays, of which, as in the case of the similar productions of De Quincey and Carlyle, a collected edition had already appeared in America. The most prominent event of his political career during the time his party was in opposition was the part he took in bringing about the present state of the law of copyright. In 1846, on the return of the Whigs to power, he obtained, in Lord Russell's administration, the office of Paymaster-General, with a seat in the Cabinet. At the general election which followed the dissolution of Parliament in 1847, Macaulay, who, principally by his attitude with regard to certain religious questions which then excited much attention, had contrived to make himself exceedingly unpopular in Edinburgh, lost his seat for that city. With his rejection his political life may be said to have closed. Edinburgh, indeed, atoned for its error in discarding one of the most honest and manly politicians that ever lived by returning him, unasked and free of expense, in 1852; but by that time all his thoughts and time were occupied in the composition of his History, and he took very little part in public business.

Macaulay's last article for the *Edinburgh Review*—the sketch of Chatham's later years—was written in 1844. After that all his literary energy was devoted to his History, of which the first two volumes appeared at the close of 1848. A few days after their publication he wrote in his diary, "I have felt to-day somewhat anxious about the fate of my book. . . . All that I hear is laudatory. But who can trust praise which is poured into his own ear? At all events, I have aimed high; I have tried to do something that may be remembered; I have had the year 2000, and even the year 3000, often in my mind; I have sacrificed nothing to temporary fashions of thought and style; and if I fail, my failure will be more honourable than nine-tenths of the successes which I have witnessed." His apprehensions were groundless. The History obtained enormous and universal success. In 1855 appeared the second two volumes, which were received with at least equal avidity. In 1857 he received a well-merited acknowledgment of his fame by being raised to the peerage as Baron Macaulay of Rothley. Induced by personal regard to the publisher, Mr Adam Black, he was induced to furnish, between 1853–1859, for the eighth edition of the "Encyclopædia Britannica," masterly sketches of Atterbury, Bunyan, Goldsmith, Johnson, and Pitt. The biography of Pitt, which is one of the finest specimens of style, was the last work that he lived to publish. He died on December 28, 1859, leaving behind him the rough draft of what was afterwards published as the fifth volume of his History by his sister, Lady Trevelyan.

Macaulay's outward man, his nephew tells us, was never better described than in two sentences of Praed's Introduction to *Knight's Quarterly Magazine*. "There came up a short manly figure, marvellously upright, with a bad neckcloth, and one hand in his waistcoat pocket. Of regular beauty he had little to boast, but in faces where there is an expression of great power, or of great good-humour, or both, you do not regret its absence." In everything that requires manual dexterity he was singularly awkward, and he was utterly destitute of all bodily accomplishments. When, during his attendance at Windsor as a Cabinet Minister, he was informed that there was a horse at his disposal, he replied, "If Her Majesty wishes to see me ride, she must order out an elephant." Much might be said in praise of the dignity, honesty, and manliness of his private character. No language could be too strong to describe the deep affection which he felt for some of his relatives, especially his sisters and a few cherished friends. For them he considered no sacrifice too great. Yet he was not exactly what is known as a good-hearted man. He was, it is true, generous in supplying the pecuniary wants of the many applicants for his bounty; but the money so bestowed was often given with a grudge and a sneer.

As an author, Macaulay's conscientious industry and never-ceasing carefulness deserve the highest commendation. It is, indeed, as Mr. Gladstone, in his most candid and judicious essay on Macaulay, has observed, delightful to find that the most successful prose-writer of the day was also the most painstaking. Though, after the establishment of his fame, he could have commanded whatever price he chose for anything that came from his pen, his vigilance never for a moment relaxed. He "unshrinkingly went through an immense mass of inquiry, which even he felt sometimes to be irksome, and which to most men would have been intolerable. He was perpetually picking the grain of corn out of the bushel of chaff. He freely chose to undergo the dust, and heat, and strain of battle before he would challenge from the public the crown of victory." His method in composing his History was first to write rapidly out a rough draft, and then begin to fill it in at the rate of six pages of foolscap every morning, written in so large a hand and containing so many erasures as to make on an average not more than two pages of print.

Now that the heat of contemporary feeling has subsided, Macaulay's merits can be appraised with some degree of accuracy. Narrative was his peculiar forte. As a critic his work is not of great value. He could point out the inaccuracies of a Croker or the absurdities of a Robert Montgomery with inimitable vigour and power of rough raillery, but that "slashing" kind of criticism has had its day, and no writer of equal eminence would now think of engaging in such work. The higher kind of criticism, which consists in trying to get at the inner meaning and substance of great literary works, he had, as he himself was aware, little talent for and rarely attempted. His poetry, with the exception of a few lines, may be described as brilliant rhymed rhetoric. But his biographical papers, in which in terse and striking fashion are set forth the main features of the lives of such men as the Earl of Chatham, Warren Hastings, Addison, are matchless in their own department. They are not, like the similar essays of Carlyle, a series of original reflections suggested by the subjects under discussion, with the leading details about whom the reader is supposed to be familiar, but vigorous *résumés* in which are comprised all the leading features in the life and character of the men who are handled. His "History of England from the Accession of James II.," to give the full title, is but a fragment of a much larger design which death prevented him from accomplishing. He prepared, as he tells us in the first words of the opening chapter, "to write the history of England from the accession of King James II. down to a time which is within the memory of men still living;" but he lived to bring it down only to the death of William. His reading in all sorts of the contemporary literature, pamphlets, squibs, songs, &c., joined to his extraordinary strength of memory, enabled him to give his History a picturesqueness and freshness of colour after which every historian ought to aspire, but to which very few have attained in anything like the same degree. No writer ever possessed in a higher measure the art of rendering whatever he dealt with interesting and attractive. To say that he is not an impartial historian is only to say what must to some extent be said of every writer who treats of subjects regarding which party prejudice has not altogether subsided. His History has been described as "an epic poem, of which King William is the hero," and certainly he sometimes allows his Whig propensities to get the better of strict justice. Many assaults have been made upon his accuracy, but they have had little effect upon his fame. It would be strange indeed if in so large a work as the History, containing innumerable petty facts, no errors could be pointed out; but of direct errors there are not many. The real and weighty objection to Macaulay's accuracy is his habit of making broad, sweeping statements, which have indeed some foundation, but not enough to support the assertion based on them. The same fault occurs in all his writings. For example, in his "Encyclopædia Britannica" sketch of Johnson, he says that Johnson was "repeatedly provoked into striking those who had taken liberties with him." The "repeatedly" is a gross exaggeration. The opinion of some of the best recent critics has been strongly adverse to Macaulay's style. It is said to be rhetorical, to want repose, to have about it a hard metallic ring, and to be disfigured by too frequently employed and obvious artifices. In these censures there is a good deal of truth; nevertheless, there was never a better style for purposes of popular effect. It is always lucid and vigorous and telling. Its influence upon the style of contemporary writers has been very wide, and upon the whole beneficial. Force and clearness are qualities to which many other less important qualities of writing may well be sacrificed.

There are almost no points of comparison between Macaulay and Thomas Carlyle. In their ways of life, their characters, their mental habits, their way of writing, they were well-nigh totally dissimilar. Macaulay found Carlyle's literary heterodoxy so obnoxious to him that he would not read his works; and it is easy to imagine that Carlyle found certain features in Macaulay's writings which rendered them almost equally repugnant to him. Carlyle was born at Ecclefechan, Dumfriesshire, on December 4, 1795. His father, originally a stonemason, afterwards a small farmer, was an excellent specimen of the best type of Scottish peasant, a man of great force of character, rigid morals, deep religious feelings of the Calvinistic kind, and of abilities which, if cultivated, would have made their mark in any sphere. His mother, whom throughout life he loved as he never loved any one else, was a woman of gentle nature and much practical good sense. After acquiring the elements of knowledge at the parish school of Ecclefechan, Carlyle was sent to the academy at Annan, where he remained till, in 1809, he entered the University of Edinburgh. There he went through the ordinary course, distinguishing himself in mathematics, but quitting it in 1804 without taking a degree. His parents had indulged the hope, common to Scottish people of their class, that they might yet see their son "wag his head in a pulpit." But it was not destined so to be. After leaving the University, Carlyle, to use his own words, "got (by competition at Dumfries, summer 1814) to be 'mathematical master' in Annan Academy, with some potential outlook on divinity as ultimatum (a rural divinity student visiting Edinburgh for a few days each year, and 'delivering' certain 'discourses'). Six years of that would bring you to the church gate, as four years of continuous 'divinity hall' would; unluckily only that in my case I never had the least enthusiasm for the business, and there were even grave prohibitive doubts more and more rising ahead." His theological studies were pretty much confined to the writing and delivering in the Divinity Hall of two discourses—one in English, the other in Latin. In 1816 he was appointed "classical and mathematical" master at Kirkcaldy, in room of the old parish schoolmaster, who had been bought off as incapable. Edward Irving, whose death he commemorated in words of burning eloquence, was then master of an "academy" there, and Carlyle and he, who were previously acquainted with each other, spent much time together. From the books in Irving's library Carlyle derived great benefit. The destinies of the two friends were very different. Irving, after a career of blazing popularity as a London preacher, is now a name and nothing besides; Carlyle, long unnoticed and unknown, has left an abiding impress on the literature of the nineteenth century.

Carlyle was ill fitted to be a teacher, and his impatience of folly and stupidity made him a harsh and stern preceptor. "In 1818," he writes, "I had come to the grim conclusion that schoolmastering must end, whatever pleased to follow; that 'it were better to perish,' as I exaggeratively said to myself, than continue schoolmastering." He accordingly went to Edinburgh, "intending, darkly, towards potential 'literature.'" His first publications were sixteen articles, mostly biographical, contributed to Brewster's "Edinburgh Encyclopædia" in 1820–23. These articles, which have never been reprinted, cannot be said to show any extraordinary promise. To the *New Edinburgh Review*, a short-lived periodical, he contributed in 1821 a paper on Joanna Baillie's "Metrical Legends," and in 1822 another on Goethe's "Faust," interesting as being his earliest reference to the great German whom he did so much to make known in this country. In 1822 he became tutor to Charles Buller, whose premature death in 1848 cut short the course of a politician of whom great things were expected. This connection was profitable to Carlyle in many ways. He received £200 a year as salary; and the Bullers, who recognised the great genius that lay beneath his rough and occasionally harsh exterior, were instrumental in introducing him to a better order of society than he had previously been accustomed to. Meanwhile his pen was not idle. In 1823–24 his "Life of Schiller" appeared by instalments in the *London Magazine*. In 1824 were published his translation of "Legendre's Geometry," with an able essay on Proportion by Carlyle himself; and his first important work, the admirable translation of Goethe's "Wilhelm Meister." In the same year he paid his first visit to London, and in 1824, also, his engagement with the Bullers was brought to an end at his own desire. In 1825 his "Life of Schiller" was republished in book form. In the following year occurred his marriage to Miss Jane Welsh, only daughter of Dr. John Welsh, a Haddington physician, who, as Carlyle liked to think, was believed to be a lineal descendant of John Knox. Along with his wife, Carlyle settled at Comely Bank, Edinburgh, where his first two articles for the *Edinburgh Review*,—those on "Richter" and on the "State of German Literature,"—were written. They were published in 1827, in which year also appeared, in four volumes, "German Romance," a series of translations, which formed Carlyle's last piece of literary journey-work.

In 1828 he removed to Craigenputtoch, in Dumfriesshire, a small estate belonging to his wife, where, for about six years, he lived amid the bleak mountain solitudes, "in those quiet ways where alone it is well with us," perfecting his self-culture. There he wrote many articles for the *Edinburgh Review*, the *Foreign Quarterly Review*, and *Fraser's Magazine*; and, in 1830, "Sartor Resartus," which may be described as a spiritual biography of himself, containing the leading features of all his subsequent teaching. In 1834 he removed to London, fixing his residence at 5 Cheyne Row, Chelsea, where he remained for the rest of his life. In the same year he began the writing of his "French Revolution," published in 1837. "Sartor Resartus," for which he failed to find a publisher, had appeared by instalments in *Fraser's Magazine* in 1833–34. In 1838 it was published in book form, after having been reprinted in America with a preface by Emerson. In the following year his essays were collected and published. In 1837 he delivered in London a course of lectures on German Literature; in 1838 a course on the History of Literature; in 1839 a course on the Revolutions of Modern Europe, and in 1840 a course on Hero-Worship. Of these only the last series was published, appearing in 1841. "Chartism," in which he broke ground upon the "Condition of England" question, appeared in 1839; "Past and Present" in 1843; "Oliver Cromwell's Letters and Speeches" in 1845; "Latter-

Day Pamphlets," a series of fiery diatribes on social and political problems, in 1850; and the "Life of John Sterling" in 1851. In 1858 the first two volumes of his "Life of Frederick the Great" were published, the third in 1862, the fourth in 1864, and in 1865 the work was completed. In 1865 he was appointed Lord Rector of Edinburgh University, and in April of the following year delivered his installation address to a crowded and enthusiastic audience. All the pleasure of his triumph on this occasion was drowned in his sorrow at the sudden death of his wife, which occurred during his absence in Edinburgh. The only important publication of the solitary years of his old age was his "Early Kings of Norway" and "Essay on the Portraits of John Knox," reprinted in 1875 from *Fraser's Magazine*. He died on February 5, 1881.

Such is a brief summary of the more important events in Carlyle's life. It was the lot of the present writer to read nearly all the obituary notices of him which appeared in the leading journals after his death. With not an exception they were extremely eulogistic, praising his works and applauding in the highest terms the dignity and stern conscientiousness of his life. But when, about three weeks later, the "Reminiscences" were published by Mr. Froude, the tide took a turn. They were found to be full of harsh, and, as in the case of Charles Lamb, even cruel and heartless judgments; and Carlyle's faults of temper, his malice, and his uncharitableness began to be sharply commented on. A few of the more sturdy admirers of the Seer of Chelsea protested that the "Reminiscences" did not give any idea of the real Carlyle at all; that nothing could be more unjust than to form an estimate of his character from angry passages written in his old age, when weak health and agonising sorrow had rendered him scarcely responsible for his utterances. This defence proved to be but a refuge of lies. In 1882 Mr. Froude published his memoir of the first forty years of Carlyle's life, and it was found that the most sharp and biting passages of the "Reminiscences" might be easily paralleled from the letters he wrote when in the prime of manhood. The truth is, that Carlyle was very far indeed from being a faultless character. The higher duties of morality he acted up to as few have done. No praise can be deemed too high for the resolute devotion with which, through evil report and good report, through poverty and riches, through obscurity and fame, he remained constantly honest to his convictions; resolved to write on no subject which he had not studied to the bottom, and determined to speak out what he believed to be the truth, however unpalatable it might be to the world. Nor are we soon tired of admiring his inflexible integrity, his lofty spirit of independence, his unwearied affection for all the members of his family, and the stern dignity which prevented him from ever, even on a single occasion, treading the miry ways of falsehood or chicanery. But it must be confessed that in him virtue was often clothed in a very unattractive guise. He was arrogant and contemptuous beyond any man recorded in literary history. Whatever was foolish and vicious in a character was sure to be carefully noted by him, while geniality, kind-heartedness, and self-sacrifice often passed with no recognition at all, or at best a very slight and grudging one. He was constantly intolerant of those who differed from him; never by any chance imagining the possibility that they might be right and he wrong. Always proclaiming in his books the infinite virtues of silence and patience, he made no attempt whatever to practise as he preached. The least illness, the least personal inconvenience, such as getting his tea too weak or his coffee too cold, made him complain as if all the world had been going headlong to ruin, and he himself were the only righteous man left alive. His temper, which he was at no particular pains to curb, was harsh and violent. Altogether he was, as his mother well observed, "gey ill to live wi'." There is something very pathetic in the story of the relations of himself and his gifted wife, as retold by Mr. Froude. The bond which linked them together was one of duty rather than of love. Both were persons of strong character, sharp temper, and a rather cynical way of looking at things. They admired each other cordially; but they never knew that mutual confidence and domestic felicity which has thrown a halo over thousands of humble hearths.

Carlyle's works fall naturally into three divisions. First we have his writings on literary subjects, including his Lives of Schiller and Sterling, and most of his essays. Then there are his lucubrations on political subjects, comprising "Chartism," the "Latter-Day Pamphlets," and, in part, "Past and Present." Lastly come his historical works, "The French Revolution," "Oliver Cromwell," and the "History of Frederick." "Sartor Resartus" belongs to none of these classes, but contains the great principles which underlie the works contained in all of them. "To blench at no paradox, to accept no convention, to pierce below the surface at whatever cost apparently of safe and comfortable foothold, to get rid of belief in believing and assumption of knowing—these are the lessons taught in this earliest book, as it may perhaps be allowably taken to be, of the master, and no others will be learned from the most attentive student of his latter lucubrations." Carlyle's essays are among the most valuable of his writings. He was the first to make the great writers of Germany known in this country; and his writings on the more illustrious figures of the epoch of the French Revolution—Voltaire, Diderot, Mirabeau—are models of insight into character, profound and discriminating estimates of men who had hitherto proved stumbling-blocks to British critics. The essays on Burns and Johnson may be said to have struck the keynote of all succeeding writings on these men; while his criticism of Scott, which has provoked a good deal of hostility, is more and more coming to be generally recognised as substantially correct in its main features. The "Life of Schiller," though warmly praised by Goethe, who added a preface to the German translation of it, is not a first-rate performance. But the "Life of Sterling" is a perfect triumph of literary art, far and away the best biography of its size in the language. Those who wish to see how differently the same subject may be handled by a second-rate man and by a man of genius should compare Archdeacon Hare's memoir of Sterling with Carlyle's. From the poor and priggish book of the worthy Archdeacon we get no picture of the man Sterling at all; no bright, vivid portrait of his life and environment, such as remains permanently fixed on the memory of every one who reads Carlyle's matchless memoir. The "Life of Sterling" is valuable, also, in that, more than any other of his books, it throws light on Carlyle's personal character—his half-contemptuous, half-pitying estimate of most of those with whom he came into contact—and on his religious belief, which may be described as Catholicism *minus* Christianity. Carlyle's political writings display, in very marked fashion, both the strength and limitations of his mind. They are full of that protest, which it is the glory of literature to uphold, against selfish utilitarianism and Iago's gospel, "put money in your purse." Not in the worship of the "almighty dollar," not by making "getting on in the world" one's purpose in life, can we hope to find rest and peace. Our social shams, the weak and faulty points in our political organisation, are exposed with remorseless sarcasm, and, as men of all parties will admit, with only too much truth. But Carlyle was never careful to bear in mind that "'Tis better to fight for the good than to rail at the ill." He is barren of practical suggestion to remedy the evils of which he so eloquently declaims, except what may be summed up in the too vague words, education and emigration. Of his historical works, the most wonderful, as regards literary effect, is the "French Revolution," that extraordinary series of historical paintings, sketched in colours so vivid and gorgeous as to rivet themselves upon the memory of the reader for ever. As scene after scene of the terrible drama passes before our eyes, we almost seem to view the dreadful deeds done and the men who did them. Through all the book we breathe the same sultry atmosphere, full of thunder and lightning, which hung over the Paris of the Revolution. Yet accuracy is never sacrificed to pictorial effect. It has been said by a very competent authority that "to most Englishmen, even if they have taken the trouble to ascertain the facts by careful reference to authorities the most indisputable and the most diverse, the mysterious and almost incredible events of the French Revolution range themselves into a possible and intelligible whole in Mr. Carlyle's account, and in that account almost alone." But Carlyle's most important service to historical truth was his "Letters and Speeches of Oliver Cromwell," a work of enormous research and labour, which none but himself could have done so well. It put an end at once and for ever to the extraordinary amount of misrepresentation and absurdity with which the memory of the great Protector had been assailed since his death. In the "Life of Frederick," the most laborious and the most irksome task of his life, Carlyle had the disadvantage of dealing with a man who was, and who will probably always remain, hateful to the majority of English readers. Moreover, even his genius for graphic representation cannot make uniformly interesting to us the tangled maze of eighteenth century politics; and throughout the work the endless eccentricities of his style reach a height which sometimes becomes positively wearisome. Yet some episodes in the book—for example, the account of the relations of Frederick and Voltaire—are entirely admirable; and none of his writings affords better illustrations of Carlyle's faculty of hitting off a character in two or three descriptive touches of marvellous felicity. By Carlyle's earliest critics, no feature in his works was more objected to than his style, which is certainly often of a kind to make the hair of those whose literary orthodoxy is strict stand on end. But it is now pretty generally agreed that a writer of first-rate genius has a right to choose the mode of expression best suited to him, and that all attempts to make him alter it in accordance with the dicta of critics are as vain as to expect grapes from apple-trees or roses from oaks. No competent critic would be willing to have Carlyle's power of humorous description and exquisite felicity of epithet pruned down for the sake of making his style bear a closer resemblance to conventional models.

The greatest contribution to the history of the ancient world which has appeared since Edward Gibbon laid aside his philosophic pen is the "History of Greece" by George Grote, published between 1846–1856. Like Gibbon, Grote owed nothing to University education; his vast fund of knowledge was entirely the result of his own exertions. Born in 1794, the son of a wealthy London banker, he entered upon business life at the age of sixteen; but every available leisure hour was devoted to study—not light, miscellaneous reading, but works of philosophy and classical literature. His design of writing a history of Greece was formed as early as 1823. In 1832 he entered Parliament as member for the City of London, but retired from political life in 1841, in order that he might devote himself exclusively to his great work. The most prominent feature of his parliamentary career was his advocacy of vote by ballot. The practical experience of political affairs which he gained in the House of Commons was of great service to him in dealing with the political life of ancient Greece. After his History, his most important works are his elaborate study of "Plato and other Companions of Socrates," and a fragment of a similar work on Aristotle, published after his death, which occurred in 1871. Grote's learning, sagacity, candour, and perfect mastery over his materials give his work a place among the very few great histories which England has produced. But its literary execution is by no means first-rate; he never seems to have realised that prose composition is an art. Comparing the excellent "History of Greece" by Bishop Thirlwall (originally published in 1835–41 in "Lardner's Cabinet Cyclopædia," afterwards in 1845–52 reprinted and revised) with Grote's, a recent critic[1] has observed, that "when we come to compare Thirlwall with Grote, we find . . . the full opposition of the presence of style on the one hand, and the absence of it on the other. The late Bishop of St. David's will probably never be cited among the greatest masters of English prose style, but still we can see without difficulty that he has inherited its traditions. It would be difficult, on the other hand, to persuade a careful critic that Grote ever thought of such things as the cadence of a sentence or the composition of a paragraph. That he took so much trouble as might suffice

[1] Mr. George Saintsbury, in a suggestive and interesting article on "Modern English Prose," in the *Fortnightly Review* for February 1876.

to make his meaning clear and his language energetic is obvious; that in no case did he think of looking beyond this is I think certain."

No one is likely to make any such criticism on the style of James Anthony Froude (born 1818), of which, says the critic quoted above, "it may be asserted, without any fear whatever of contradiction carrying weight, that at its best it is surpassed by no style of the present day, and by few of any other." Nevertheless no historian, perhaps, of equal eminence, indeed few who deserve to be called eminent at all, has met with so much severe and searching criticism as has fallen to the lot of Mr. Froude. He has written extensively; but his most important works are his "History of England from the Fall of Wolsey to the Death of Elizabeth," in twelve volumes (1856–70), and his "English in Ireland in the Eighteenth Century" (1871–74). With all their charm of style it may be doubted whether these works will stand the test of time. Mr. Froude is very apt to fall into the besetting sin of an historian, colouring his facts to suit preconceived theories instead of adapting his theories to suit his facts. His Histories may always be read with pleasure, but to read them with profit we must take care not to trust them implicitly, but to correct his judgments by those of less paradoxical if not so brilliant authorities. A great living historian has thus expressed his opinion of him, in words too harsh indeed, but unfortunately not without a strong basis of facts:—"Mr Froude is a man of undoubted ability, of undoubted power of writing. If there is any branch of science or learning in which accuracy of statement is a matter of indifference, in which a calm putting forth of statements which are arbitrary can be accepted in its stead, in that branch of science or learning Mr. Froude's undoubted ability, his gift of description and narrative, may stand him in good stead. But for the writing of history, while those gifts are precious, other gifts are more precious still. In that field 'before all things Truth beareth away the victory;' and among those whom Truth has enrolled in her following as her men, among those who go forth to do battle for her as their sovereign lady,

Mr. Froude has no part or lot. It may be his fault, it may be his misfortune, but the fact is clear. History is a record of things which happened; what passes for history in the hands of Mr. Froude is a writing in which the things which really happened find no place, and in which their place is taken by the airy children of Mr. Froude's imagination."[1]

The writer of these words, Mr. Freeman, is perhaps the most celebrated member of the recent critical school of historians, which numbers in its ranks such men as William Stubbs, whose "Constitutional History of England" is a work of great research and value; Professor S. R. Gardiner, who has thrown much new light on the history of the Stuart family in England, and Mr. J. R. Green, whose "Short History of England" has attained such extraordinary success. The leading principle of the school may be said to be its insistance upon the necessity of the historian always going to original sources for his facts, and stating these facts with minute, sometimes even, as scoffing critics would say, with pedantic accuracy. Edward Augustus Freeman (born 1823) has done a vast amount of very important historical work in various fields. Two cardinal points he has always insisted on with beneficent iteration: first, the unity of history, fighting against all arbitrary, ancient and modern, classical, and something else; second, the unbroken being of the English people from the beginning. He has nothing but contempt for people who still persist in talking about "Anglo-Saxon" instead of "Early English." His great work is his "History of the Norman Conquest in England" (1867–79), to which, in 1882, appeared a supplement in the shape of two volumes on the "Reign of William Rufus." The "Norman Conquest" will remain a standing monument to his learning and soundness of judgment, though partly owing to the subject, partly to his mode of treating it, it will probably always be rather a work for students than for general readers. Mr. Freeman cannot be said to be a very powerful or picturesque writer, but his love of truth and patient accuracy

[1] *Contemporary Review* for September 1878, p. 241.

is great, and he possesses the high merit of always trying to make his words fit his thoughts, and his thoughts the facts.

William Edward Hartpole Lecky, born near Dublin in 1838, after publishing two or three books which proved failures, obtained his first success by his "History of the Rise of Rationalism in Europe" (1865). It was followed in 1869 by a "History of European Morals from Augustus to Charlemagne," and in 1878 by two volumes of a "History of England in the Eighteenth Century," to which other two were added in 1882. Mr. Lecky is a brilliant and captivating writer, although his works are rather disquisitions on historical subjects than histories. There is little original research in his "England in the Eighteenth Century," nor are his views of men and events as a rule such as to modify received judgments; but some portions of it, as, for example, the account of the rise of Methodism, are so good that if published as essays they would have ranked almost as highly as Macaulay's.

Among what may, for want of a better name, be called the critics and essayists of the Victorian age, John Ruskin, who, as has been well said, has created a new literature—the literature of Art—occupies the foremost place. He was born in London in 1819, the son of a wine merchant. In many pleasing passages in the discursive pages of "Fors Clavigera" he has given us reminiscences of his childhood, of the perfect order and obedience in which he was trained up, of his reading the Bible carefully through from beginning to end with his mother—omitting nothing and slurring nothing; of his summer excursions with his father, who had, he says, a perfect natural taste in painting, and who took him to see all the good collections of paintings to which he could obtain access, directing him to the best paintings, and never permitting him to waste a look on inferior or worthless ones. His early education over, he entered Christ Church College, Oxford, where he graduated. Except the Newdigate prize, which he gained in 1839 for a poem entitled "Salsette and Elephanta," he did not obtain any University distinction. His blameless character, his religious nature, and his love of study led his parents to cherish the hope that he would enter the Church, and great was their grief when he decided otherwise. "He might have been a bishop," said his father regretfully in after years. As he was an only son, and as his father had by this time amassed a considerable fortune, it was not necessary for him to enter any profession, and he accordingly gratified his love of art by studying painting under Copley Fielding and J. D. Harding. To a present of Moxon's magnificent edition of Rogers's "Italy," which he received from his father in his youth, is to be attributed much of Ruskin's lifework. Many of the engravings in it were by Turner, and by their means his attention was attracted to the pictures of the greatest of modern landscape-painters, whom he henceforth admired with an intensity approaching to idolatry. Certain articles in a Review condemnatory of Turner's paintings offended him keenly, and he addresssd a letter to the editor of the Review "reprobating the matter and style of these critiques, and pointing out their dangerous tendency," because "he knew it to be demonstrable that Turner was right and true, and that his critics were wrong, false, and base." The letter grew into a book, and the defence of Turner into the most elaborate English treatise upon art. In 1843 appeared the first volume of "Modern Painters: their Superiority in the Art of Landscape Painting to all the Ancient Masters. By a Graduate of Oxford." The "Oxford Graduate," who in this work boldly set aside many of the articles of the orthodox art creed, succeeded at least in attracting attention, though most of the reviews of his book were condemnatory of its doctrines. In 1846 a second volume of "Modern Painters" was issued, to accompany an enlarged and amended edition of the first. By this time the value of the work had become widely recognised, and Mr. Ruskin was justly regarded as one of the first writers of the day. In 1856 two more volumes were added, and in 1860 the work was completed by the publication of a third volume. On the composition of "Modern Painters" the author bestowed the utmost pains, often rewriting a paragraph several times, till its melody was such as to suit his fastidious ear. A new and final edition of "Modern Painters" was issued in 1873, since which time the author has steadfastly refused to reprint it, so that it cannot be obtained unless one is prepared to pay a fancy price for it. Mr. Ruskin's reasons for not reprinting it are various. He has modified some of his opinions since it was written, and, in particular, he does not regard the Church of Rome with the same horror. When "Modern Painters" was composed his views were of the kind called "Evangelical;" and while still Protestant in the genuine sense of the word, his language in one of his latest productions, "The Bible of Amiens," regarding the worship of the Virgin, has evoked an indignant protest from a section of the press. A little volume of selections from "Modern Painters" was published in 1876 under the title of "Frondes Agrestes."

During the interval between the publication of the first and the last volume of "Modern Painters," many of Mr. Ruskin's most important works appeared. "The Seven Lamps of Architecture," which did for architecture what "Modern Painters" did for painting, was published in 1849. In 1851 he published a pamphlet advocating Pre-Raphaelitism, then in its infancy, and issued the first volume of his magnificent "Stones of Venice," which was completed by the publication of two more volumes in 1853. Among many by whom this great work was read with admiration, none was more enthusiastic in its praise than Charlotte Brontë, who declared that Mr. Ruskin seemed to her one of the few genuine writers, as distinguished from bookmakers, of this age. "His earnestness even amuses me in certain passages; for I cannot help laughing to think how Utilitarians will fume and fret over his deep, serious, and (as they will think) fanatical reverence for art. That pure and severe mind you ascribed to him speaks in every line. He writes like a consecrated Priest of the Abstract and Ideal."

"Modern Painters," "The Seven Lamps of Architecture," and the "Stones of Venice" are Mr. Ruskin's most important works, but he has written much besides. "Unto this Last," four essays on the principles of political economy, very much opposed to the received ones and extremely paradoxical, appeared in 1862, having been previously published in the *Cornhill Magazine.* "Sesame and Lilies," originally delivered as lectures in Manchester in 1864, gives his views "about books, and the way we read them, and could or should read them;" and also about the education of women. We need not chronicle "the legions of little books with parody-provoking titles" in which of late years Mr. Ruskin has lifted up his voice against our social evils, and told us how we should remove them. Of these, the most characteristic is "Fors Clavigera," a series of letters to the workmen and labourers of Great Britain, begun in 1871 and carried on for several years. It must not be supposed that Mr. Ruskin has altogether abandoned his art studies; precious productions of this nature still come from his pen, although it is his work as a social reformer which he now estimates most highly. However erroneous and one-sided many of his opinions on the condition of society and on modern improvements, however hopelessly unpractical many of his schemes for the regeneration of mankind may be, all must admire his noble purity of heart, his earnest aspirations after better things, and his unflinching devotion to what he believes to be the truth.

We have mentioned the care with which "Modern Painters" was written. This care has had its reward. The ease and grace of Mr. Ruskin's style, his appropriateness of expression, his splendour of imaginative effect, the harmonious roll of his sentences, and the beautiful thoughts sustained in them, make the study of his great works one of the highest intellectual pleasures. And they are works which none can study without learning much and benefiting greatly. Yet it is to be feared that to a very large number of readers Ruskin is a name and nothing besides. While the various editions of the works of Tennyson, the greatest poet of the day, are selling by hundreds of thousands, Ruskin, the greatest living prose writer, is known to most only by the paragraphs of true or false gossip regarding him that appear from time to time in the newspapers. The cause of this is not far to seek. In accordance with one of his peculiar theories, Mr. Ruskin has chosen to sell his books only through a provincial bookseller, to sell them at the same price to the trade as to the public, and, last but not least, to sell them at such a price as places them almost quite beyond the reach of people of moderate means. Moreover, some of them are out of print, and not to be procured save for a sum which would seem a small fortune to many a working man. Hence arises the fact, probably unique in literary history, of the writings of a man universally admitted to be one of the greatest geniuses of his time, being very little known to the reading public at large, and being absent from the book-shelves of many of the most assiduous collectors of modern literature.

The greatest living critic and one of the greatest living poets is Matthew Arnold, son of the famous Dr. Arnold of Rugby, who revolutionised the discipline of our great public schools, and who occupies no mean rank as an historian. Mr. Arnold, who was born in 1822, was educated at Rugby, on leaving which he was elected to a scholarship at Balliol College, Oxford. The following passage from a poem by Principal Shairp, himself a distinguished critic, describes how Mr. Arnold at Oxford—

> "Wide-welcomed for a father's fame,
> Entered with free, bold step, that seemed to claim
> Fame for himself, nor on another lean;
> So full of power, yet blithe and debonair,
> Rallying his friends with pleasant banter gay,
> Or half a-dream, chaunting with jaunty air
> Great words of Goethe, scrap of Béranger.
> We see the banter sparkle in his prose,
> But knew not then the undertone that flows,
> So calmly sad through all his stately lay."

During his undergraduate career, Mr. Arnold, like Mr. Ruskin, obtained the Newdigate prize for English verse. He graduated with second-class honours; and was, in 1845, elected to a Fellowship at Oriel. In 1847 he was appointed private secretary to the late Lord Landsowne, which office he retained till his marriage in 1851, when he became an inspector of schools, a position he still holds. His first volume, "The Strayed Reveller, and other Poems, by A.," appeared in 1849; the second, "Empedocles on Etna, and other Poems, by A.," in 1852. In 1853 he published a volume of poems under his own name, consisting of selections from the two previously published volumes, along with some new pieces. Another volume followed in 1855. In 1858, "Merope," a tragedy in the Greek manner, was published, and in 1867 "New Poems," in which "Empedocles," only scraps of which had been reprinted since 1852, was republished in entirety, at the request of Mr. Robert Browning. Mr. Arnold belongs to the classical school of poetry, regarding the Greeks, with their strength and simplicity of phrase and their perfect sense of form, as his masters. To the imaginative power of a true poet, he adds a delicacy and refinement of taste, and a purity and severity of phrase which uncultivated readers often mistake for boldness. Nowhere in his poems do we find those hackneyed commonplaces, decked out with gaudy and ungraceful ornament, which pass for poetry with many people. His fault rather is that he is too exclusively the poet of culture. Many of his verses will always seem flat and insipid to those who have not received a classical education, while, on the other hand, students of Greek literature will be disposed to praise certain of his pieces more highly than their intrinsic merit demands. Yet it may be doubted whether some of his work as a poet will not stand the ordeal of time better than that of any contemporary poet, Mr. Tennyson and Mr. Browning excepted. There are few poems which show such a refined sense of beauty, such dignity and self-restraint, such admirable adaptation of the form to the subject, as, to give one or two examples, Mr. Arnold's "Sohrab and Rustum," "Tristram and Iseult," and the "Forsaken Merman." On the last of these, Mr. Swinburne's eloquent and enthusiastic criticism may be quoted. "The song is a piece of the sea-wind, a stray breath of the air and bloom of the bays and hills. Its mixture of mortal sorrow with the strange wild sense of a life that is not after mortal law, the child-like moan after lost love mingling with the pure outer note of a song not human, the look in it as of bright, bewildered eyes with tears not theirs and alien wonder in the watch of them, the tender, marvellous, simple beauty of the poem, its charm, as of a sound or a flower of the sea, set it and save it apart from all others in a niche of the memory." These glowing words of Mr. Swinburne cause us to recollect that readers have now an excellent opportunity of comparing his style with Mr. Arnold's by reading together "Tristram of Lyonesse" and "Tristram and Iseult," in which the same legend is handled. Mr. Swinburne has many qualities as a poet which Mr. Arnold has not, yet not a few will be inclined to think that Mr. Arnold's thoughtful and touching treatment of the story is superior to Mr. Swinburne's more gorgeous but less impressive mode of dealing with it.

Mr. Arnold's first, and certainly not worst, work as a critic appeared in the form of prefaces to his poems. In 1857 he was appointed Professor of Poetry in Oxford University, which led to his publishing two series of "Lectures on Translating Homer" (1861–62), in which he advocates the use of the hexameter as the proper metre for the English translator of the author of the "Iliad." In 1865 appeared his most celebrated prose work, the "Essays in Criticism," a precious little book, to the influence of which much of the spirit of current criticism may be traced. Defining criticism as "a disinterested endeavour to learn and propagate the best that is known and thought in the world," Mr. Arnold spared no pains to make critics feel that their duty is "to see things as they are," to shun insular prejudice and self-complacency, to avoid all eccentricity and exaggeration, never to praise with blind enthusiasm or to condemn with equally blind indignation, and to keep themselves pure from the contagion of personal, or political, or national bias. In this, as in all his prose writings, he treated with an air of bantering ridicule, beneath which lay a serious purpose, the "Philistinism" of his countrymen, defining Philistinism as "on the side of beauty and taste, vulgarity; on the side of morality and feeling, coarseness; on the side of mind and spirit, unintelligence." One book, "Friendship's Garland" (1871), he has entirely devoted to an assault on the kingdom of Philistia. To religious thought Mr. Arnold has contributed largely. Among his writings in this department may be mentioned "Literature and Dogma," "St. Paul and Protestantism," and "Last Essays on Church and State." These cannot be criticised here. Their main purport has been thus tersely summarised: "His design is to retain the morality of the Old and New Testament without retaining what he thinks superstitious excrescences—the miracles, the promises of a physical life after death, and the like. In his view it was in righteousness, in "conduct," that the prophets and our Lord placed the kingdom of heaven. He, too, holds that happiness depends on morality, and that the Bible is the great teacher and inspirer of morality. On the Continent it is being rejected because of its want of conformity to physical science. In England and America, where religion is still so strong, Mr. Arnold hopes to anticipate and weaken the crude scepticism which rejects what is true and divine because it is mixed up with what is human and erroneous." Such views as these, it is hardly necessary to say, have met with much powerful opposition; and there are few of Mr. Arnold's admirers who will not join in regretting that his advocacy of them has occupied so much time that he would have better employed in the field of literary and social criticism. Other writings of Mr. Arnold's, besides those mentioned, are "Culture and Anarchy," "Mixed Essays," and "Irish Essays." He has also edited selections from Wordsworth and from Byron, with very suggestive introductory essays; and has done other similar work.

One of the most pleasing of the few writers of the Victorian era whose fame has been won by essay-writing, as distinct from critical and biographical articles, is Sir Arthur Helps (1817–1875). His "Essays Written in the Intervals of Business" (1841), "Claims of Labour" (1844), and "Friends in Council" (1847–49), are full of wise and kindly reflections on our everyday experiences, and of sagacious and high-minded advice on the conduct of life. He also won for himself a high position as an historian by his "Conquerors of the New World and their Bondsmen" (1848–51), and his "Spanish Conquest in America" (1855–61), and wrote one or two interesting novels touching on social questions. The chief attraction of his writings lies in their pure and graceful style and their elevated and healthy moral tone.

One of the ablest journalists of the day, and one of the first writers on subjects connected with political history, is John Morley (born 1838). Mr. Morley early took to journalism, and was connected as editor with several not very successful journalistic adventures. In 1867 he succeeded Mr. G. H. Lewes as editor of the *Fortnightly Review*, which he conducted with marked ability till October 1882, when he was succeeded by Mr. T. H. S. Escott. Towards the close of 1880 he became editor of the *Pall Mall Gazette*, when that post was vacated by Mr. Frederick Greenwood, owing to the political views of himself and the proprietor of that paper being found to be at variance. On his journalistic labours Mr. Morley has brought to bear a moral earnestness, a depth of conviction, and a ripeness and power of style surpassed by no living newspaper-writer. His principal works are two volumes on "Edmund Burke," an "Essay on Compromise;" studies of some of the leading characters of the period of the French Revolution,—Rousseau, Voltaire, Diderot; and a "Life of Richard Cobden," which may fairly claim to be more powerfully written and to contain more suggestive thought than any political biography in the language.

There are many other living essayists and critics who do credit to their age both by their literary skill and their patient research and wide knowledge. Among authors of the so-called "æsthetic" school, who have written with a refinement and subtlety of thought and an elaboration of form which would have been a stumbling-block to critics of the Macaulay and Jeffrey type, and which is foolishness to the Philistines, Mr. Walter H. Pater (born 1838) is especially noteworthy. His "Studies in the History of the Renaissance" (1873), while assailed by many critics on account of their *dilettanteism*, the supreme position they assign to art, and as being permeated by the tone of an inner circle of illuminati, was welcomed by cultivated and discerning readers for the finish and picturesqueness of its composition. The "History of the Renaissance in Italy," the chief work of John Addington Symonds (born 1840), which was published in 1875–81, has been accepted as the standard authority on the subject, and is written in a style which, though occasionally overloaded with ornament, is rarely deficient in grace and colour. Rev. Mark Pattison, the Rector of Lincoln College, Oxford (born 1813), has, among other scholarly productions, written a "Life of Casaubon" (1875), a type of scholar now altogether extinct, with an insight and sympathy which, added to his wide knowledge of the subject, make it one of the best biographies of its class. There is a distinction and strenuousness about Mr. Pattison's style which lift it above the ordinary level, but at the same time it is sometimes careless and even ungrammatical. A host of other writers who have done good service to the cause of literature—Dr. John Brown, Leslie Stephen, William Minto, Edward Dowden, George Saintsbury, R. L. Stevenson, and many others—occur to us as we write, but these we must refrain from particularising.

With the theologians, the philosophers, and the men of science of our own times we do not propose to deal. To enter at any length upon their characteristics would lead us greatly beyond our limits, besides being in some measure alien to the purpose of this work; and to give, on the other hand, a barren catalogue of names and dates would be profitless and tedious. There are few writers whose style deserves higher praise than that of Cardinal Newman (born 1801), the leading spirit in the "Oxford movement," which may be said to have been at its height between 1835–45, and which finally led so many distinguished members of the Church of England within the pale of the Church of Rome. The finish and urbanity of Cardinal Newman's prose have been universally commended, even by those who are most strenuously opposed to his opinions, and he is also the author of some of the finest religious verse in the language. Frederick Denison Maurice (1805–1872), the leader of the "Broad Church" school, is a great figure in the history of theological thought in England; and the same may be said of the late Dean Stanley (1815–1881), who always wrote in an easy and graceful, if not very powerful style. The sermons of Frederick William Robertson (1816–1853) show very well the favourable influence which literary taste and culture may have on pulpit oratory. But we need not go on mentioning more names. In philosophy, the names of John Stuart Mill (1806–1873), of Herbert Spencer (born 1820), and of Alexander Bain (1818), are perhaps the best known to general readers among those who have made their mark in the world of metaphysical speculation. The number and eminence of the men of science who appeared in the Victorian era will strike future historians as one of its most noticeable features. The theory of Evolution propounded by Charles Darwin (1809–1882) has had a powerful influence not only on scientific but on many other forms of thought—historic, scientific, and philosophical. The elegance and lucidity of style which is now a common characteristic of scientific men is one of the most marked features of the time. It is no longer the rule for chemists and natural historians to be incapable, when called on to address a general audience, of writing save in a jargon lacking ease, finish, and intelligibility. On the other hand, such men as Sir Charles Lyell, Michael Faraday, Professor Huxley, Professor Tyndall have shown that they can use the English language so skilfully, that had they made literature instead of science their specialty, they would assuredly have obtained scarcely less high honours in that profession than in that which they chose.

XI

PERIODICALS, REVIEWS, AND ENCYCLOPÆDIAS.

"THAT the highly-finished models of periodical composition which had been given to the world by Steele and Addison should excite a spirit of emulation and give birth to a number of competitors, was an event equally to be wished for and expected." So writes the industrious Dr. Nathan Drake at the beginning of his instructive, if rather long-winded essays on the *Rambler*, *Adventurer*, and *Idler*. At the conclusion of the same work he gives a chronological table, from which it appears that between the *Tatler* and *Rambler*, a period of forty-one years, one hundred and six periodical papers of a similar kind were issued, and between the *Rambler* and the year 1809, one hundred and thirteen, making altogether, with the two mentioned added, a grand total of two hundred and twenty-one—a surprising number truly. Of these, a vast proportion, as may be supposed, were quite worthless, and have been deservedly consigned to oblivion; others of more merit, indeed, but still of not sufficient excellence to stand the test of time, have shared the same fate; others, written with a political intent, are of value only to the historian. A very few, however, are still of interest, either because of the value of their contents or on account of the fame of those connected with them. Of these we shall give some brief account.

Of the many periodicals, political and social, started during the lifetime of Addison and Steele, and up till the beginning of Johnson's *Rambler* (1750), all or nearly all of any merit have been already mentioned in the account given of the literature of the reign of Queen Anne. The others form a very motley assemblage. "Fortunate," says Dr. Drake, "would it have been for the interests of general literature had the swarm of imitators strictly confined themselves to the plan of the *Spectator*, to a laudable attempt at reforming the morals and the manners of the age. The facility, however, with which this mode of writing might be rendered a vehicle for slander, for rancorous politics, and virulent satire, soon tempted many to deviate from the salutary example of the authors of the *Tatler* and *Spectator;* and the former of these papers had not run half its course before it was assailed by a multitude of writers who were actuated by no other motives than those of envy and ill-nature." One of them, the *Female Tatler*, begun in 1809, obtained such notoriety for its personalities that it was presented as a nuisance by the grand jury at the Old Bailey. Of the rest, the most notable are the *Lay Monastery* (1713 [1]), of which the principal writer was the poetical knight Sir Richard Blackmore, who was a constant butt of the wits of his time; the *Censor* (1715), conducted by Theobald, the original hero of the "Dunciad;" the *Craftsman* (1826), which proved a very powerful organ of the opposition to Sir Robert Walpole; and three papers of which the great novelist Henry Fielding was the presiding spirit, the *Champion* (1739), and the *True Patriot*, begun in 1745, and succeeded by the *Jacobite Journal.* Of these, the first, besides containing essays on the follies, vices, amusements, and literature of the age, had a political intent, being directed against the administration of Walpole; while the first and second were designed to throw ridicule upon the Jacobite party, and to aid the cause of the House of Hanover, of which Fielding was a very strenuous supporter. Some years later, in January 1752, Fielding started another

[1] When only one date is given, it refers to the beginning of the periodical.

periodical, the *Covent Garden Journal*, which was published twice a week for a twelvemonth. Most of the contents were of a humorous and sarcastic kind, and it had a considerable flavouring of personal satire.

The *Covent Garden Journal* properly belongs to the second division of our subject—the papers published after the *Rambler*. Some of these are of considerable importance, especially the *Adventurer*, which had a very considerable sale both during its publication and afterwards when collected into volumes. It was begun in November 1752, and continued till March 1754. It appeared twice a week, and the price of each number was twopence, the same as that of the *Rambler*. Of the hundred and forty numbers to which the periodical extended, Dr. John Hawkesworth, its editor, was the author of seventy. Hawkesworth (1715–1773) was one of the many imitators of Johnson, whose style, as Burke with great felicity of phrase observed to Boswell, on the latter remarking that the pompous "Life of Young," which Sir Herbert Croft contributed to the "Lives of the Poets," was very much in Johnson's manner, "has all the nodosities of the oak without its strength; all the contortions of the Sybil without the inspiration." A considerable proportion of Hawkesworth's contributions consist of those Oriental and allegorical tales of which the *Spectator* presents examples, and which may now be reckoned an extinct department of literature, though they were so popular during the last century. That they have ceased to be written is not matter for regret, for nothing can be imagined more jejune and wearisome than most of them were. Hawkesworth's principal assistants in the *Adventurer*, besides Dr. Johnson, who contributed a good many papers, were Richard Bathurst (whose name will live as long as that of the individual whom Johnson praised as "a man to my very heart's content; he hated a fool, and he hated a rogue, and he hated a Whig: he was a very good hater"); Dr. Joseph Warton; and Hester Chapone, one of the "literary ladies" of Johnson's time, whom it was his habit, when in a genial mood, to over-praise ridiculously. Joseph Warton, a brother of Thomas

Warton, the author of the "History of English Poetry," was a man of considerable note in his day, much beloved by a large circle of friends. His most important work is an "Essay on the Genius and Writings of Pope," much of which he afterwards incorporated in an edition of that poet's works. It may be mentioned that it appears from a letter of Johnson's to Warton that the pay of the contributors to the *Adventurer* was two guineas a number. There is a good deal of loose talking about the wretched remuneration writers received during the eighteenth century. Vast sums such as Scott, Dickens, and Macaulay got for their works would, of course, have appeared almost fabulous even to the most successful author of that time, when the reading public was so small compared to what it is now. But it may be doubted if literary "journey-work" was not paid just as well as at present.

The *World*, begun in January 1753, and carried on weekly for four years, is of interest as being the periodical in which appeared Lord Chesterfield's articles on Johnson's "Dictionary," which called forth the "great lexicographer's" celebrated letter. The proprietor of the *World* and its principal contributor was Edward Moore, whose tragedy, the "Gamester," is still occasionally acted. Horace Walpole, Lord Hailes, and Soame Jenyns, whose book on the "Origin of Evil" formed the subject of one of Johnson's most caustic criticisms, also occasionally wrote in it. Chesterfield's two papers in recommendation of Johnson's "Dictionary" appeared in November 28 and December 5, 1754. Johnson seems to have thought over his rejoinder for a considerable time, his letter bearing date February 7, 1755.

In the *Connoisseur*, a periodical begun in January 1754, and continued weekly for three years, appeared in 1756 the first publications of William Cowper. His first paper was on "Keeping a Secret," containing sketches of faithless confidantes; the second an account of the present state of country churches, their clergy, and their congregations; and the third an essay on conversation and its abuses. Two other papers have, on uncertain evidence, been attributed to him. The chief writers in the *Connoisseur* were George Colman, a lively play-writer, and Bonnel Thornton, who was well known in his day as a clever writer of satirical verses and essays. The character of this periodical is thus given by Dr. Drake: "The *Connoisseur* labours under the same defect which has been attributed to the *World*—it is too uniformly a tissue of ridicule and caricature. In this line, however, several of its papers are superior to those of the same species in the *World*, and it displays likewise more classical literature that its rival. It is, on the whole, more entertaining than the *World*, but, if we except a few papers, inferior in point of composition. To the juvenility of the two chief writers in it, and to their strong attachment to satire and burlesque, we are to attribute its occasional incorrectness of style and its poverty of matter."

With the *Mirror* and the *Lounger*, two periodicals published at Edinburgh, and conducted by Northern *literati*, the list of classical papers of the *Spectator* class closed, for though a few followed the two mentioned, none of them attained any celebrity. The *Mirror* was published pretty constantly every Tuesday and Saturday from January 23, 1779, to May 27, 1780. Its editor and principal contributor was Henry Mackenzie, the author of the "Man of Feeling," who gives the following account of its origin:—"The idea of publishing a periodical paper in Edinburgh took its rise in a company of gentlemen whom particular circumstances of connection brought frequently together. Their discourse often turned upon subjects of manners, of taste, and of literature. By one of those accidental resolutions of which the origin cannot easily be traced, it was determined to put their thoughts into writing, and to read them for the entertainment of each. The essays assumed the form, and soon after some one gave them the name, of a periodical publication; the writers of it were naturally associated, and their meetings increased the importance as well as the number of their productions." By and by the idea of publication suggested itself; and as number after number of the *Mirror* appeared, it came to be regarded by all Scotchmen with just pride. Of the hundred and ten numbers of which it consists, Mackenzie was the sole author of thirty-nine, besides assisting in the composition of others. Among the other contributors were Lord Hailes; Professor Richardson of Glasgow; William Strahan, the printer, frequently mentioned by Boswell; Beattie, the author of the "Minstrel;" and David Hume, the nephew of the historian. In interest and variety of contents the *Mirror* is superior to the *Adventurer*, with which its merits in other respects are about on a level. The most noticeable contribution to it is probably Mackenzie's "Story of La Roche," the pathos of which has been much praised. The publication of the *Lounger*, a continuation of the *Mirror*, possessing the same characteristics, and likewise conducted by members of the "Mirror Club," as it was called, begun on February 5, 1785, was continued till January 6, 1787.

We pass on to a new era in periodical literature, which dawned when, in 1802, the first number of the *Edinburgh Review* appeared. Of the origin of this epoch-making journal, Sydney Smith, one of its earliest and most brilliant contributors, has given the following account:—"Towards the end of my residence in Edinburgh, Brougham, Jeffrey, and myself happened to meet in the eighth or ninth storey, or flat, in Buccleuch Place, the then elevated residence of Mr. Jeffrey. I proposed that we should set up a Review. This was acceded to with acclamation. I was appointed editor, and remained long enough in Edinburgh to edit the first number of the *Review*. The motto I proposed for the *Review* was 'Tenui Musam meditamur avenâ'—'We cultivate literature on a little oatmeal.' But this was too near the truth to be admitted; so we took our present grave motto from Publius Syrus ["Judex damnatur cum nocens absolvitur"—"The judge is condemned when the guilty is acquitted"], of whom none of us had, I am sure, read a single line; and so began what turned out to be a very important and able journal. When I left Edinburgh, it fell into the stronger hands of Lord Jeffrey and Brougham, and reached the highest point of popularity and success." This account, bating a slight touch or two of humorous exaggeration, as, for example, "the eighth or ninth storey," is substantially correct. The effect of the first number of the *Review* was, says Jeffrey's biographer, Lord Cockburn, "electrical." To readers accustomed to the tedious, inane twaddle which formed the staple of the magazines of the day, it was a very welcome relief to find such fresh, vigorous writing as was to be found in the new periodical. Yet it cannot be said that the early volumes of the *Review* strike one who looks at them nowadays as of any extraordinary merit or interest. Many of the articles are of the kind called "padding," consisting of a sort of epitome of the work noticed, with copious extracts. In the early years of the *Review's* existence, it contained none of those brief monographs, often having only a very slight connection with the works nominally under notice, in which writers possessed of special knowledge on particular subjects tersely sum up the results of their investigations. Some account of Jeffrey's connection with the *Review* has already been given. He was succeeded by Macvey Napier, Professor of Conveyancing in Edinburgh University, who occupied the editorial chair till his death in 1847. The entertaining volume of selections from his correspondence, published in 1879, shows how difficult he found his position in having to settle the conflicting claims of various contributors, and, in particular, of having to pacify as best he could the vindictive passions of Brougham, who wished to make the *Review* a vehicle for venting his spite against his political opponents. Since Napier's death, the *Review* has been edited by Jeffrey's son-in-law, William Empson; Sir George Cornewall Lewis, distinguished as a statesman and a scholar; and Mr. Henry Reeve, its present editor, who succeeded Sir G. C. Lewis in 1855. Mr. Reeve, who is Registrar of the Privy Council, is chiefly known by his translation of De Tocqueville's "Democracy in America." A very long and brilliant list of the leading contributors to the *Edinburgh Review* under its various editors might be drawn up, including such men as Sir Walter Scott, Hallam, Macaulay, Carlyle, Henry Rogers, the author of the "Eclipse of Faith," whose really wonderful gift of style should keep his memory alive; Sir James Stephen, Lytton, Thackeray, Leigh Hunt, Froude, and others.

During the early years of the existence of the *Edinburgh Review* it did not adopt a very decided tone in politics. Social and political reforms were indeed advocated, but the advocacy was not carried on in very emphatic fashion; and the *Review* could scarcely be called a party organ till the appearance in 1808 of an article on the work of Don Pedro Cevallos on the "French Usurpation of Spain" gave undisguised expression to its Whig leanings. Great was the consternation and indignation excited by the article in the breasts of many Tories, not a few of whom had already begun to regard the *Review* with suspicion. When the number containing it appeared, Scott wrote to Constable, the publisher, in these terms:—"The *Edinburgh Review had* become such as to render it impossible for me to continue a contributor to it. *Now* it is such as I can no longer continue to receive or read it." The list of the then subscribers exhibits, in an indignant dash of Constable's pen opposite Scott's name, the word—"Stopt!!!" The eccentric Earl of Buchan took a more conspicuous way of showing his displeasure than Scott. Throwing the obnoxious number on the floor of his hall, he solemnly kicked it out into the street. Already there had been negotiations among various parties as to the starting of a Tory *Quarterly*, and the article on the "French Usurpation of Spain" had the effect of bringing these negotiations at once to a point. Canning, then Secretary for Foreign Affairs, was warmly interested in the new project; Scott exerted himself to the utmost to further it; many eminent writers of Tory politics promised their aid; and at length, in February 1809, the opening number appeared. The original editor was William Gifford, who retained the post till within about a year of his death in 1826. Gifford, "a little dumpled-up man," who, originally a shoemaker, had fought his way up to eminence and power, is now chiefly remembered for his connection with the *Quarterly*, and for the work he did in editing the old dramatists. His satires, the "Baviad" and the "Mæviad," are now as entirely forgotten as the schools of poetry they were meant to ridicule. The chief contributors to the early numbers of the *Quarterly* were Scott, Southey, George Ellis, William Rose, the translator of Ariosto, Reginald Heber, Sir John Barrow, and last, but by no means least notable, John Wilson Croker. To most readers of the present day, Croker is known only from the annihilating review by Macaulay of his edition of Boswell's "Johnson," and from the inimitably trenchant and incisive portrait of him under the name of Rigby in Disraeli's "Coningsby." Truculent brutality, combined with a sort of attorney sharpness, may be described as the leading characteristics of his many articles in the *Quarterly*, which may be easily recognised from their abundance of italics and small capitals.[1] On the whole, the early volumes of the *Quarterly* are not equal in interest and ability to the early numbers of the *Edinburgh*. Political partisanship appears in every page; no mercy is ever shown to the work of a Whig, however great its literary merit may be. When Gifford withdrew from the editorship of the *Quarterly*, it was for a short time held by Henry Nelson Coleridge, after which, in 1826, Lockhart became editor. Lockhart resigned the office in 1853, and was succeeded by the Rev. Whitwell Elwin, well known as the editor of Pope, who continued in office till 1860. His place was taken by a Mr. Macpherson, after which, in 1867, the present editor, Dr. William Smith, was appointed. Under his management the *Quarterly* has reached a perhaps higher level of excellence than it had ever previously attained, the articles on literary subjects being particularly able and scholarly.

Since the commencement of the *Edinburgh* and the *Quarterly*, many Reviews in imitation of them have been started. Among these may be mentioned the *Westminster Review*, begun in 1824 to advocate the views of advanced

[1] Croker was a man who incurred a great deal of enmity, and whose character possessed some highly objectionable features. An account of his life, and a not very forcible defence of his character, will be found in an article in the *Quarterly Review* for July 1876, written by the present editor, Dr. William Smith.

thinkers in religion and politics, and still continued after a not very prosperous career; the *British Quarterly*, begun by Dr. Vaughan to represent the cause of dissent; the *North British Review*, originally started as the organ of the Free Church Party in Scotland; the *Dublin Review*, the Catholic organ, &c., &c.

While in the early part of this century most of the higher and middle classes of Edinburgh were Conservative in their politics, the *Edinburgh Review*, the only Scottish literary journal on which they could look with any pride, was Liberal. Such a state of things was naturally galling to many staunch Northern Tories; but for some years nothing was done to remedy it. At length, in December 1816, William Blackwood, an enterprising young Edinburgh publisher, was applied to by two literary men of some slight reputation, James Cleghorn and Thomas Pringle, to become the publisher of a new monthly magazine, which they had projected. He consented, and in April 1817 the first number of the *Edinburgh Monthly Magazine* appeared. It was conducted with little spirit or ability, and after six numbers of it had been published, the editors, who resented Blackwood's interference with their functions, were obliged to abandon their office. Blackwood now took the editorship into his own hands, and in October 1817 appeared the first number of *Blackwood's Edinburgh Magazine*. "It needed," says the biographer of Christopher North, "no advertising trumpet to let the world know that a new reign (a reign of terror in its way) had begun. . . . Among a considerable variety of papers, most of them able and interesting, it contained not less than three of a kind well calculated to arouse curiosity and to give deep offence to sections more or less extensive of the reading public. The first was a most unwarrantable assault on Coleridge's 'Biographia Literaria,' which was judged to be a 'most execrable' performance, and its author a miserable compound of 'egotism and malignity.'" The second was an even more unjustifiable attack on Leigh Hunt, who was spoken of as a "profligate creature," a person without reverence either for God or man. "The third was the famous 'Chaldee Manuscript,' compared with which the sins of the others were almost pardonable in the eyes of the public. The effect of this article upon the small society of Edinburgh can hardly be realised." The numerous bitter personalities of the early volumes of *Blackwood*, if far from creditable to its writers, had the effect of attracting public attention to it and of promoting its sale. From its commencement till now it has been conducted with great ability, always securing as its contributors writers of the highest literary merit. Its advocacy of Conservative opinions has been uniformly staunch and vigorous. In 1830 *Fraser's Magazine*, conducted on the same lines as the early numbers of *Blackwood*, and even more intensely personal than they were, began to be published. During its long career, which came to a close in October 1882, *Fraser* numbered many very distinguished names among its contributors, including Coleridge, Carlyle, Thackeray, "Billy" Maginn, Allan Cunningham, Froude, Kingsley, and many others. When the effervescence of its youth had subsided, it became a very decorous and respectable journal, adding in its latter years not a little of the dulness of age to its respectability. At the close of 1859 a new departure was made in periodical literature by the almost simultaneous commencement of two new first-class monthly magazines, *Macmillan's* and the *Cornhill*, which still, though now surrounded by several rivals, pursue their career vigorously. The publication of the first number of *Macmillan* preceded the first number of the *Cornhill* by a month.

The issue of cheap periodicals for the million was inaugurated by the publication of the first number of *Chambers's Journal* on February 4, 1832. Other cheap periodicals had been started previously, but they had not been of sufficient excellence to ensure a large enough sale to render them remunerative and permanent. The *Journal*, consisting of four large folio pages of excellent and instructive matter at the low price of three-halfpence, was at once a great success, attaining immediately a sale of over 30,000 copies, which soon rose to 50,000. With the thirty-seventh number, the bulky folio size was exchanged for the more convenient quarto form. In 1845 the quarto form was exchanged for the octavo; and simultaneously the *Journal* somewhat altered its character, appealing more directly to educated readers. The original editor of the *Journal* was Dr. William Chambers. After the fourteenth number his brother, Robert, became associated with him as joint-editor. Between 1843 and 1844 Mr. W. H. Wills conducted it. He was succeeded by Leitch Ritchie, who was editor from 1845 to 1859. In the latter year Mr. James Payn became editor, and was a very large and constant contributor of sketches and novels till 1874, when he ceased to be connected with it. It has since been under the management of members of the firm.

As was natural, the great success of *Chambers's Journal* caused many imitations of it to be published. Most of these had only a short life. Two only we shall mention. The first number of the *Penny Magazine*, published by the Society for the Diffusion of Useful Knowledge, appeared in March 1832, a few weeks subsequent to *Chambers's Journal*, which it at first far outstripped in point of circulation. Among the contributors to the *Penny Magazine* were George Long, Allan Cunningham, and De Morgan; but as rivals pressed thickly around it, it had to succumb in the fierce struggle for life which all periodicals have to wage. *Hogg's Weekly Instructor* merits mention here as having had a more distinct character of its own than most of its compeers. It was started in March 1845, and continued in varying forms till December 1859, when it completed its twenty-ninth volume. At the time of its commencement, there was no cheap periodical accessible to the masses, except those conducted on strictly secular principles, and the monthly religious journals advocating the special views of the various denominations from which they emanated. A widespread opinion was entertained that a periodical was wanted which, while unsectarian, should yet be imbued with a decidedly religious spirit. Dr. Arnold well expressed the idea which animated the projectors of *Hogg's Instructor* when he said, "I never wanted articles on religious subjects half so much as articles on common subjects written in a decidedly Christian spirit." The mode in which the *Instructor* was conducted, by degrees attracted the attention of the leading ministers, clergymen, and professors of all denominations, many of whom wrote expressing their strong approval of the enterprise; and in 1849 Her Majesty the Queen was pleased to bestow her especial patronage upon the *Instructor.* During its course it numbered among its contributors many names well known in literature, such as Mrs. Crowe, Frances Browne, George Gilfillan, De Quincey, Dr. Peter Bayne, Francis Jacox, Rev. A. B. Grosart, and "Cuthbert Bede." The repeal of the paper duty in 1861 gave an immense impetus to cheap periodical literature, and hundreds of ventures have since been started, of which space will not permit us to give any account.[1]

The first English encyclopædia was the work of a London clergyman, John Harris. It is entitled "Lexicon Technicum, or an Universal English Dictionary of Arts and Sciences, explaining not only all the Terms of Art, but the Arts themselves," and was published in 1704 in one thick folio volume. In 1728 Ephraim Chambers published his "Cyclopædia, or a Universal Dictionary of Arts and Sciences," in two volumes folio. This was the first English work bearing the name of cyclopædia. It was a great success, and had many imitators. In 1778–88 Abraham Rees published a revised and enlarged edition of Chambers's work in two volumes folio. Previous to the publication of "Rees' Cyclopædia," as it is generally called, the first edition of the "Encyclopædia Britannica" had been issued at Edinburgh. It appeared in parts between 1768–71. It "professed to be 'by a society of gentlemen in Scotland,' but the 'society of gentlemen' consisted of Mr. William Smellie only, who, according to his biographer, Kerr,

[1] For a full account of the repeal of the taxes on knowledge, and the vast increase in periodical literature which followed that repeal, I may be allowed to refer to the chapter on the "Repeal of the Fiscal Restrictions on Literature and the Press" in my work, "Great Movements, and those who Achieved them."

compiled single-handed the whole of the first edition, and 'used to say jocularly that he had made a dictionary of the arts and sciences with a pair of scissors.'" The second edition of the "Britannica" was begun in 1777, and concluded in 1784. To the second edition historical and geographical articles, which had hitherto been excluded from English encyclopædias, were admitted, greatly against the wish of Smellie, who, because of their admission, refused to have anything further to do with the "Encyclopædia." His place was taken by a certain James Tytler, a man of thoroughly Bohemian habits, concerning whom many amusing stories are told. From the time of this second edition "every cyclopædia of note in England or elsewhere has been a cyclopædia not solely of the arts and sciences, but of the whole wide circle of general learning and miscellaneous information."[1] The publication of the ninth edition of the "Encyclopædia" is now in progress, having been begun in 1875. The seventh edition was edited by Macvey Napier, assisted by Dr. James Browne. The eighth, to a considerable extent a reprint of the seventh, was edited by Dr. T. S. Traill, Professor of Medical Jurisprudence in Edinburgh University. It contained many contributions from distinguished writers, but its crowning glory was the articles contributed to it by Macaulay, on account of his friendship for the publisher, Mr. Adam Black. The edition now publishing, edited by Professor T. S. Baynes along with (after vol. xiii.) Dr. Robertson Smith, bids fair to surpass all its predecessors in thoroughness and value; and is certainly a noble specimen of the excellent work in many fields of literature, science, and art which English writers of the Victorian era are able to perform.

Of the rivals which the success of the "Encyclopædia Britannica" brought into the field, the greatest was the "Penny Cyclopædia," the most valuable undertaking of the Society for the Diffusion of Useful Knowledge. It was begun in 1833 and concluded in 1846. In the list of contri-

[1] From an interesting article on the "History of Cyclopædias," in the *Quarterly Review* for April 1864.

INDEX OF AUTHORS.

of the miscellaneous department, did not receive its proper meed of reputation till disengaged and re-issued in a separate shape. A great portion of the Cyclopædia was, as it were, dug out of the ruins and re-issued in separate volumes by fresh publishers who acquired the property of the work, and thus distinctly recognised it as a mere quarry of valuable materials. The 'Metropolitana' ran to twenty-nine quarto volumes, and was finished in 1845." "Chambers's Encyclopædia," issued in ten royal octavo volumes between 1859–1868, is correctly described on the title-page as a "Dictionary of Universal Knowledge for the People." It was founded on the German "Conversations Lexicon" of Brockhaus; but, under the skilful editorship of Dr. Andrew Findlater, who gathered round him an excellent body of contributors, it turned out something much better than a mere adaptation. For profound or exhaustive information larger encyclopædias must be consulted; but even the possessors of these find "Chambers's" very convenient on account of the ease with which it may be consulted, and the terse way in which information on the subjects dealt with is summed up.

INDEX OF AUTHORS.